THE MASTER MUSICIANS

MUSORGSKY

Series edited by Stanley Sadie

THE MASTER MUSICIANS

THE MASTER MUSICIANS

MUSORGSKY

His Life and Works

David Brown

OXFORD
UNIVERSITY PRESS

2002

OXFORD
UNIVERSITY PRESS

Oxford   New York

Auckland   Bangkok   Buenos Aires   Cape Town   Chennai
Dar es Salaam   Delhi   Hong Kong   Istanbul   Karachi   Kolkata
Kuala Lumpur   Madrid   Melbourne   Mexico City   Mumbai   Nairobi
São Paulo   Singapore   Shanghai   Taipei   Tokyo   Toronto

Copyright © 2002 by David Brown

Published by Oxford University Press, Inc.
198 Madison Avenue, New York, New York 10016

www.oup.com

Oxford is a registered trademark of Oxford University Press

Library of Congress Cataloging-in-Publication Data
Brown, David, 1929–
Mussorgsky / David Brown.
p. cm. — (Master musicians)
Includes bibliographical references and index.
ISBN 0-19-816587-0
1. Musorgsky, Modest Petrovich, 1839–1881.
2. Composers—Russian—Biography.
I. Title.
II. Master musicians series.
ML410.M97 B75 2002
780'.92—dc21   [B]   2002020154

1 3 5 7 9 8 6 4 2

Printed in the United States of America
on acid-free paper

To the Women in my Life:

ELIZABETH

and our daughters

GABRIELLE and HILARY

Contents

Preface

FROM TIME TO TIME IN ALL SECTORS OF CREATIVE ACTIVITY there will appear some unique figure who invents a world of stunning novelty, yet who creates no school because, his genius being so largely instinctive, his style proves elusive and recycling it virtually impossible, except perhaps for details. Most likely he will be misunderstood, even ignored, by all except a few of his contemporaries. But subsequently the works of others may be conditioned by his ideals and aesthetics, and their worlds may be impregnated by elements from his until finally, when a whole generation arrives that can catch up with him, he may become a cult figure.

It would be exaggeration to say this has become Musorgsky's status, yet the degree to which his music is now a part of our musical life is remarkable. Though a virtually complete edition of his works was published in the Soviet Union between 1928 and 1939,[1] until some thirty or forty years ago such of his works as were performed were still known almost exclusively through the edited and sometimes recomposed versions made mostly by his friend and fellow-composer Rimsky-Korsakov. Yet no-one now, surely, would wish (or dare) to produce *Boris Godunov* except as Musorgsky wrote it, or to mount *Khovanshchina* in a form not based to the last possible note on Musorgsky's surviving materials, tolerating only the minimum supplementation necessary to produce a coherent experience and accepting that, since Musorgsky orchestrated hardly any of the opera himself, someone else must do that job for him. As for his songs, by the millennium we have at least three complete recordings. The first, a pioneering enterprise of the mid-1950s

---

[1] The Pavel Lamm edition has provided the main source for my examination of Musorgsky's music. But in the case of *Boris Godunov*, we now have David Lloyd-Jones's masterly edition of the full score (including the scenes that Musorgsky subsequently discarded), together with a comprehensive introduction to the opera and full critical commentary. This edition has now become standard for performances of *Boris*.

by Boris Christoff, is instructive in reflecting the attitudes and practices of that time, still on occasions using versions sanitized by Rimsky, or orchestrated by well-intentioned persons as though Musorgsky did not know his own mind when employing a piano as accompaniment. But no reputable singer today would risk peddling such benign bowdlerizations. And nearly everything else Musorgsky composed is now on CDs. All the piano music, the original *St John's Night on the Bare Mountain* (so different from the familiar Rimsky version), the various short choral-orchestral pieces, even the single act of *The Marriage*—that extraordinary experiment in operatic ultra-realism—as well as the *original* 1868–9 version of *Boris*: all are now available.

This seems therefore an appropriate moment to attempt a fresh life-and-works of the composer, especially since it is nearly fifty years since the last significant one (M. D. Calvocoressi's *Modest Musorgsky*, London, 1956) appeared in English. Every book has its priorities, and in a contribution to a series such as the Master Musicians, I believe most readers will expect a straightforward biographical-and-critical narrative that can serve as an introduction to a composer whom he or she may be investigating in detail for the first time. Inevitably this means that less attention will be devoted to certain areas and issues to which other authors in other situations might give emphasis and in which certain readers will have special interest; in addition, there will be some wishing to dig more deeply into matters I have covered. Accordingly, I have, in footnotes, directed attention to studies that may answer some of these needs. Of all recent writers on Musorgsky outside Russia, the most important by far has been Richard Taruskin. Professor Taruskin and I have been known not always to be in sweet accord on all matters musical, but he has a prodigious knowledge of Russian music, a brilliant intellect, remarkable powers of communication even on the most abstruse subjects, and a penchant for challenging judgements that may not find acceptance everywhere and may sometimes be thought eccentric but which almost always merit serious consideration.

It is a supreme arrogance for any author to suppose that his work, being more recent, must invalidate that of earlier writers on the same subject, and I would still commend the chapters on Musorgsky's technique and style in Calvocoressi's 1956 book (actually finished in 1938, but trapped in a Paris safe during World War II). I have chosen to treat such matters during my running investigation of the music, but Calvocoressi reserved his survey to his final chapters, where he systematically sifted out some of the main characteristics of Musorgsky's music and defined these with much precision and impressive detail. Any student beginning research into Musorgsky will find value in Calvocoressi's work, for his different perspective resulted in a different kind of investigation to mine. Calvocoressi was what we might now consider an 'amateur', as were pretty well all scholars of his generation, and his writings reflect many of the prevailing attitudes and priorities of his period (though to be reminded of some of these can be salutary—especially the importance to the scholar-critic of an alert ear as well as a perceptive intelligence). But he knew his Musorgsky very thoroughly, and in his time he was miles ahead in his understanding of the composer. He was one of the first to champion *Boris Godunov* as composed by Musorgsky himself, and one of the earliest to grasp the qualities of the original (and so different) version of that opera—for, in effect, Musorgsky wrote two operas on Boris. Calvocoressi deserves more than the covertly patronizing homage normally meted out a worthy pioneer.

And, perhaps even more unexpectedly, I would add a word for the Master Musicians volume that preceded this one over half a century ago. Since 1946 much has moved on in Musorgsky research, new material has become available, and there have been shifts, sometimes very significant, in critical judgements. But the earlier study of Musorgsky for the Master Musicians, which Calvocoressi had been preparing until his death in 1944[2] and which Gerald Abraham completed, retains value. Abraham was the finest western scholar of Russian music of his generation and though, self-effacingly, he withheld his name from the volume's title-page, rather more than half the critical investigation of Musorgsky's music is enclosed in those square brackets which were the indicators of his contributions. These are still well worth reading, especially for their critical insights, and also as a check on mine—as also, of course, are Abraham's other essays on Musorgsky listed in the bibliography.

---

[2] In fact, this would have been Calvocoressi's third book on the composer, his first having appeared in Paris in 1908; a revision of this (1911) appeared in 1919 in an English translation by A. Eaglefield Hull.

In more recent years the quantity of writing on Musorgsky in English has not been particularly great, though its range has been impressive. The three highly detailed analytical studies in the March 1990 issue of the periodical *Music Analysis* suffice to demonstrate how firmly founded and sophisticated were Musorgsky's musical processes, enough to scotch any lingering suspicion that he was something of an inspired imbecile. But while these probed deep into the music itself, many of the contributions to Malcolm Brown's centenary anthology *Musorgsky: in memoriam, 1881–1981*, demonstrate the diverse areas into which the ramifications of the composer's creative activities drew him. Folksong and, of course, literature both as poetry and drama—but also traditional Russian church music, Jewish church music, the visual arts, and contemporary social theory: I have pointedly drawn attention to where some of these areas have been examined. But so much remains to be discovered and scrutinized, and not only in regard to Musorgsky. True, the Russians themselves have done much more investigating of their own composers than we in the West are generally aware of, and the increasing signs that some first-rate anglophone scholars of the generation after mine are mastering the language and already producing often highly detailed, invaluable work are greatly heartening. But the subject is huge, the archives, until recently closed for the most part to outsiders (not only foreign nationals, but all but the most privileged of Soviet scholars), are now being opened, giving access not only to materials until recently known only in often bowdlerized forms in secondary sources, but also to those that remain unpublished, and to some of whose existence we perhaps know nothing. Thus there is abundant room for others to join the investigations, and I hope this book, as well as serving the general reader, can provide some sort of perspective on one of the greatest of Russian composers from which far more detailed—and maybe revisionist—investigations may follow.

The final typescript was read by Marina Frolova-Walker. Having been born and educated in Russia, she could set my work in a different but very crucial perspective, and she made some constructive suggestions which led me to a basic reconsideration of certain issues. In addition she gave invaluable help in some points of translation, and also spotted a number of minor errors. For all this help I am deeply indebted to Dr Frolova-Walker. Any remaining factual inaccuracies or deficiencies in translation are my responsibility alone.

As always, my wife has been my indispensable helper in checking and proof-reading. She first performed this service over thirty years ago, and it seemed right that the dedication should be given to her, and also to our two daughters. Being parented by (as also being married to) a writer can mean a degree of deprivation, for the creative process can be very absorbing of self as well as of time. Incidentally, I recall that our elder daughter timed her entry into this world at the very moment of my discovery of Musorgsky (though still mediated by Rimsky) through that epoch-making early-1950s recording of *Boris*, and that the very first musical sounds to which she was exposed were of that opera's final act with Boris Christoff's blood-curdling dying groans, an experience that she nevertheless seems to have survived unscathed. I have been fortunate in my family, and the dedication signals my gratitude in, I hope, appropriate terms.

David Brown

Braishfield, Hampshire
November 1999

Illustrations

Abbreviations

For full references see **Appendix D—Select Bibliography**

CAM	*Calvocoressi and Abraham: Mussorgsky*
CM	*Calvocoressi: Modest Mussorgsky*
KYM	*Keldïsh and Yakovlev, eds: M.P. Musorgsky*
MBG	*Modest Musorgsky and 'Boris Godunov'* (Emerson and Oldani)
MIM	*Musorgsky in memoriam* (Brown, ed.)
ML	*Music & Letters*
MLN1/2	*M.P. Musorgsky: Literaturnoye naslediye*, 2 vols. (Orlova and Pekelis, eds.)
MQ	*Musical Quarterly*
MR	*The Musorgsky Reader* (Leyda and Bertensson, eds.)
MT	*Musical Times*
MVS	*M.P. Musorgsky v vospominaniyakh sovremennikov* (Gordeyeva, ed.)
RKL	*Rimsky-Korsakov: Letopis moyei muzïkalnoy zhizni*
RKM	*Rimsky-Korsakov, ed.: M.P. Musorgsky: pisma i dokumentï*
SMPM	*Stasov: M.P. Musorgsky*
SSM3	*V.V. Stasov: Stati o muzike* (Simakova and Protopopov, eds.)
TDM	*Trudï i dni M.P. Musorgskovo* (Orlova, ed.)
TM	*Taruskin: Musorgsky*

A Note on Dates

Dates in Musorgsky's time were twelve days behind the Western calendar. All dates in the following pages have been adjusted to the latter.

CHAPTER 1

Childhood and Early Years

I T HAS BEEN OBSERVED THAT FOR A RUSSIAN TO CLAIM RYURIK
as his ancestor is akin to an Englishman boasting descent from William the Conqueror. In 862—so the twelfth-century *Russian Chronicle* records—the inhabitants of Novgorod, being weary of political turmoil, invited this Varangian prince to restore stable government. And so Ryurik took charge of the city and region, establishing a dynasty that quickly spread its domain south past Moscow to Kiev and the Black Sea. For some seven centuries it controlled much of what we still think of as Russia until, with the death in 1598 of Fyodor, the feeble-witted son of Tsar Ivan IV (the Terrible), the dynasty itself expired.

But if tradition is to be believed, the lines of descent from Ryurik were more numerous than those that bred the princes and warriors who shaped Russia's distant past. Modest Petrovich Musorgsky never pretended to Ryurikian lineage, but the claim has been entered on his behalf. By the fifteenth century one such line was said to have spawned, some fifteen generations on, Prince Yury Fyodorovich Smolensky, whose grandson, Roman Vasilyevich Monastïrev, gained the nickname 'Musorga', meaning in Church Slavonic 'musician'. Here, it seems, is the origin of the family name, even though none of its very varied spellings in the following centuries had included the consonant *g* (it was only in the 1860s that, for no reason that has been firmly established, this letter was reinstated).[1]

---

[1] Richard Taruskin has reflected on this omission (see 'Pronouncing the name', *TM*, pp. xxvii–xxxi), pointing out that the inherited form ('Musorsky') had no *g*, and that 'músor'

Karevo, the composer's birthplace, lay on the banks of Lake Zhizh-
itso near Toropets, some 150 miles south-east of Pskov and 250 south
of St Petersburg. For several generations members of Musorgsky's father's family had been soldiers. Musorgsky's grandfather had risen to be
a captain in the Preobrazhensky Guards, one of Russia's most prestigious
regiments, and his son, Pyotr (born 1798), the composer's father, might
well have continued the tradition, were it not that he had been born
out of wedlock and was thus ineligible for military service.[2] Instead he
embarked on a promising career in the civil service, but in 1822 resigned and settled onto the family estate. In 1828 he married Yuliya
Ivanovna Chirikova (born 1807), daughter of a government official
who was also a landowner. They were to have four children, all boys.
The first two, born in 1829 and 1833, died in early childhood, even
before the arrival of the third, Filaret, in 1836. Three years later, on 21
March 1839, was born their fourth and final child, Modest, the future
composer.[3]

Modest was to pass the first ten years of his life at Karevo. In 1880,

(accent on the first syllable) meant 'garbage' in Russian. Until 1862 Musorgsky retained the
g-less spelling, but from 1863 he introduced the now familiar g, which would still not have
been sounded in speech but which would have shifted the accent to the second syllable (i.e.
'Musór(g)sky'), thus mitigating any embarrassing resonance. Taruskin attributes this move to
pressure from Musorgsky's brother Filaret, who was sensitive to the play others might make
on the unflattering association within the authentic name, and who justified this change by
the nickname 'Musorga' ('musician') given to their fifteenth-century ancestor. Taruskin observes that from 1862 to 1863 Modest lived as the 'virtual ward' of his elder brother, and
this was when he began introducing the g and endeavouring to establish the revised name,
though he did not use this when signing business documents or writing to relatives outside
St Petersburg. Though there is some hearsay evidence that, after Filaret's departure from St
Petersburg in 1869, Musorgsky still continued to use the new second-syllable accent in
speech, the scansion of a poem by his close friend Arseny Golenishchev-Kutuzov, which
incorporates the name, places the accent decisively on the first syllable. The composer certainly continued to write 'Musorgsky' on his compositions and when signing his name in
full; nevertheless, when writing to members of the Stasov family with whom he was on
intimate terms he on occasion signed himself with nicknames which omitted the g ('Musoryanin'—even 'Musor'), and 'Músor(g)sky' is the pronunciation in general usage in present
day Russia.

[2] However, in 1820 Pyotr's father belatedly married the serf who was his mother, thus le-
gitimizing Pyotr's birth.

[3] The composer long thought that his birth had occurred a week later, on 28 March, and
this date was still set down by Vladimir Stasov in one of his obituaries of Musorgsky in 1881.

in preparing an entry on himself for Hugo Riemann's *Musik-Lexikon*, he recalled those years (referring to himself in the third person):[4]

> Under the direct influence of his nurse he made the close acquaintance of Russian tales. This acquaintance with the spirit of Russian folk life was the main stimulus for his musical improvisations until he began to learn the basics of piano playing. His mother gave him his first piano lessons, in which he could not bear what he had to play. Nevertheless, these proceeded so successfully that by the time he was seven he was playing short pieces by Liszt, and when he was nine he played a grand concerto by Field before a large gathering at his parents' home.

Sadly, there is no further direct documentation of these formative years. But all the peripheral evidence points to him enjoying a happy childhood in an environment where caring extended beyond the family circle to the large number of house-serfs and peasants whose very lives were the property of the Musorgskys. Soviet scholars inevitably presented the future composer as one who associated freely with these humble dependents, but there seems no reason to doubt that he and Filaret mixed quite naturally with the peasant children and that this kind of sympathetic association extended well into his adult years. 'As adolescent, youth, and when he was already of mature years, he related to everything of the people and the peasantry with special love. He considered the Russian peasant to be the true man'—though, brother Filaret added sourly—'in this he was bitterly deluded.'[5]

According to Vladimir Stasov, Musorgsky's first biographer, a German governess subsequently took charge of Musorgsky's piano lessons and general education until 1849, when the whole family set out for St Petersburg. The intention was that the boys should renew the family tradition of military service and enter the School for Guards' Cadets, and in preparation for this they were enrolled into the very efficient German-run Petropavlovsky School, then installed for a year with family friends, the Opochinins, until the parents themselves took

---

[4] *MLN1*, 267. The article appeared in 1882. Written in June 1880 when the composer was already in an advanced stage of alcoholism, it is factually unreliable though of interest for what it sometimes unwittingly reveals of Musorgsky's own self.

[5] *MVS*, 94.

an apartment in the Russian capital. Their father (so wrote Modest) worshipped the arts, and he arranged for his younger son to begin lessons with the pianist Anton Herke. Modest's progress was such that only two years later Herke arranged for him to play a rondo by Herz in a charity concert at the home of a lady-in-waiting. As Modest himself recorded for Riemann: 'The success [of the occasion] and the impression made by the playing of the young musician were such that Professor Herke, always rigorous in assessing his pupils, presented him with Beethoven's A flat Sonata'.[6] Also in 1851 Musorgsky was transferred to the Komarov preparatory school run by a former literature teacher at the School for Guards' Cadets. He remained a year, then entered the school itself.

There has been sharp disagreement about the educational attitudes that prevailed within this prestigious institution, and about the director, a General Sutgof. The geographer and statistician Pyotr Semyonov-Tyan-Shansky, who departed the school seven years before Musorgsky's entry, remembered Sutgof as an educated man, expert in French history and fluent in German and French, who ensured that his staff were first class and his pupils well taught. By contrast, the singer and composer Nikolay Kompaneisky, who attended the school ten years after Musorgsky, alleged Sutgof had no patience with academic activities pursued beyond official class hours and viewed the potential effect of Musorgsky's enthusiasms with irritation, even demanding of him 'what sort of officer, *mon cher*, will come out of you?'[7] Indeed, the picture Kompaneisky painted of the school was of a decadent leader preparing his charges for a decadent existence—a man who 'was proud when a cadet returned from leave drunk with champagne'.[8] Be that as it may, Filaret, who had entered the school a year earlier than his brother, made clear that the latter received special attention from Sutgof, whose daughter was also a pupil of Herke and whose lessons Modest was allowed to attend. Frequently on other occasions Modest himself played the piano at the director's home, sometimes in duets with the daughter.

But on one matter all seem to agree: the School for Guards' Cadets

[6] *MLN1*, 267. Presumably this was Beethoven's Op. 26.
[7] *MVS*, 16.
[8] Ibid.

could be a brutal place. It was a military training establishment with its own particular rigours, reflected not only in the daily routine but in a seven- to eight-week annual training camp. Moreover, like many an English public school, it abounded in those often ruthless practices through which the more senior members affirmed their lordship over the younger. 'The cadets in the senior class called themselves "cornets" and behaved arrogantly towards their younger comrades, dubbing them "vandals" ', recorded Kompaneisky. 'Besides his own serf-lackey, each cornet had at his disposal a vandal whom, on the grounds that "might is right", he submitted to various indignities. Thus, for instance, a vandal was obliged to carry his cornet on his back to the washroom.'[9] Semyonov-Tyan-Shansky was blunter. 'The first thing I found outrageous was the harrassment of new boys, which amounted to inhumanity . . . New boys were treated in ways that were demeaning; on every possible pretext not only were they mercilessly beaten but at times openly tortured.'[10] Another former alumnus was equally revealing:[11]

> The conducting of education in a totally military manner exacerbated the coarse customs to which serfdom had given birth or which it had fostered . . . Within the school these were joined with drinking bouts and scandalous revelry . . . The officers . . . already enjoying great credit [facilities] or counting on a rich inheritance, caroused up to the neck, and the young cadets who witnessed this rollicking existence of their elder brothers . . . tried, of course, to imitate them.

It is a notorious fact that the addiction to alcohol that was finally to destroy Musorgsky had its beginning in the four years he spent at the School for Guards' Cadets, and however overstated some of these recollections of the school environment may be, they point implacably to a situation in which any sensitive boy would have had phases of unutterable misery from which alcohol would have provided the swiftest and most ready means of temporary escape, whether in corporate imbibings within the school's walls or by himself during the brief periods of deliverance afforded by the parental home.

[9] *TDM*, 58–9.

[10] *MVS*, 15.

[11] From an anonymous contribution to *Russkaya starina* (1884), xli, 213. Quoted in *MVS*, 15–6.

Yet it was not all misery for Modest. He especially liked history, and in the senior class was to be attracted to German philosophers and to translating foreign languages. Academically he did very well, no doubt enjoying the occasional visits the school organized to galleries and museums, and having many close friends into whose homes he was invited. His skills as a pianist made him much in demand with his fellow-cadets for whom he would drum out dances interspersed with his own improvisations, and when in due course his voice developed into a light baritone he sang arias from Italian operas. He shared the universal affection for Father Krupsky, who visited the school to give religious instruction. Modest sang in the cadet choir during services, and Krupsky lent him church compositions by Bortnyansky and others for study. Later the composer himself declared that he had been even more indebted to Krupsky: 'Thanks to him, he [Musorgsky] succeeded in penetrating to the very heart of ancient church music, both Orthodox and Catholic', he noted, though the claim was certainly grossly exaggerated.[12] The piano lessons continued each Sunday. 'Herke familiarized the young Russian virtuoso exclusively with German piano literature', Kompaneisky recorded. 'Our virtuoso loved to improvise, guided only by his ear and imagination and having no notion of how to set down ideas on paper or of any of the elementary rules of music.'[13]

This deficiency did not, however, prevent him committing to paper a *Porte-enseigne polka* for piano, which he dedicated to his fellow cadets. This was in his first year at the school, and he allowed his father to have it published, a decision that later much embarrassed him. Pyotr Musorgsky certainly approved of his son's musical activities, and his death in 1853 must have been a sad blow, though we have no way of gauging just how close their personal relationship had been. With his mother it was certainly intimate. She was perhaps the most important woman in his life, and her death in 1865 was to strike him very hard.

In the summer of 1856 Musorgsky left the School for Guards' Cadets and followed family tradition by joining the Preobrazhensky Guards.

---

[12] *MLN1*, 267. In the French-language version of his *Autobiographical Note*, Musorgsky added 'Lutheran-Protestant' to 'Orthodox and Catholic'. But there is no evidence that this introduced Musorgsky even to the ancient Orthodox chants.

[13] *TDM*, 59.

There being currently no major wars to fight, there was little immediate prospect of real hardship, let alone danger, in army life. Musorgsky's duties were certainly not onerous, for they permitted a four-month period of leave in the middle of 1857, and he was able to live in his mother's apartment in St Petersburg when not on duty. There were things military to learn, there were drill and manoeuvres—but also, alleged Kompaneisky, 'visits, dances, cards, hard drinking, strategic *amours* in the hunt for a rich countess or, in an extremity, a merchant's wife with moneybags. Musorgsky acquired all the external qualities of a Preobrazhensky officer.'[14] True or not, this represented only one side of his activities, for his fellow-officers included some enthusiastic amateur musicians, both singers and pianists. Among the latter was 'Nikolay Andreyevich Obolensky . . . to whom Musorgsky promptly dedicated his little piano piece . . . *Souvenir d'enfance* . . . Musorgsky met frequently with all these musical companions and they occupied themselves with music. During all this they often had the most impassioned arguments and disagreements about music.'[15] For other musical pleasures Musorgsky went often to performances by the Italian opera company, and could play on the piano extracts from what he heard.

All this would have seemed a life he might have been content to prolong indefinitely. Yet he remained in the service only two years, and in 1858 the Tsar granted him his discharge. The official grounds for his application had been 'domestic circumstances'[16], but these were not the true reason. For all the unproductive routine of his service duties and the hollowness of part of his personal life-style, these two years had been among the most crucial and purposeful period of his whole existence, for he had made other contacts and begun other activities that had started to transform his present and would determine his future.

[14] *TDM*, 65.
[15] Vladimir Stasov, in *SMPM* (in *SSM3*, 54–5).
[16] *TDM*, 68.

CHAPTER 2

The Making of a Composer I

I N OCTOBER 1856 IT CHANCED THAT THE SEVENTEEN-YEAR-OLD, newly commissioned Musorgsky found himself duty officer at the second military hospital in St Petersburg where the duty doctor was the twenty-two-year-old, also newly qualified Alexander Borodin. The two men were quickly on good terms, and that same evening were invited to a soirée at the home of Popov, the hospital's chief doctor. 'At that time Musorgsky was totally callow, very elegant—to be exact, a mere sketch of an officer,' Borodin recalled in his brief memoir of Musorgsky written in April 1881, only days after Musorgsky's death:[1]

> His little uniform was spic and span, close-fitting, his feet turned outwards, his hair smoothed down and greased, his nails perfectly cut, his hands well groomed like a lord's. His manners were elegant, aristocratic: his speech likewise, delivered through somewhat clenched teeth, interspersed with French phrases, rather precious. There was a touch—though very moderate—of foppishness. His politeness and good manners were exceptional. The ladies made a fuss of him. He sat at the piano and, throwing up his hands coquettishly, played with extreme sweetness and grace (etc) extracts from *Trovatore*, *Traviata*, and so on, and around him there buzzed in chorus: 'Charmant, délicieux!' and suchlike. I met Modest Petrovich three or four times at Popov's in this way, both on duty and at the hospital.

[1] *MVS*, 86–7.

Borodin's precise sketch is precious for, taken in conjunction with the photograph of the same year (see plate 1), it affords a vivid image of the teenage Musorgsky. Three years later the two composers would meet again, but their very diverging professional paths were to ensure that contact between them would be rare. Far more critical for Musorgsky was his introduction later that winter to Alexander Dargomïzhsky, after Glinka the greatest living representative of that indigenous line of Russian composition that Glinka had initiated little more than two decades earlier. Dargomïzhsky was struck by Musorgsky's brilliance as a pianist, and the dapper young officer became an *habitué* of Dargomïzhsky's soirées. Nine years younger than Glinka, this son of an illegitimate nobleman, who had eloped with a princess who dabbled in poetry, had also begun as a dilletante. Some tuition from the older composer spurred him to write *Esmeralda*, a grand opera in the French manner based on Victor Hugo's *Notre-Dame de Paris*. But in the mid-1840s Dargomïzhsky had spent a period abroad during which, like Glinka while on an extended stay in Italy some dozen years earlier, he had been suddenly awakened to his own Russianness. Some of his songs had already shown a striking, if rough originality; in those that now followed he strove deliberately to reflect the inflections and intonations of Russian speech and the melodic features of Russian folk music. His opera *Rusalka*, produced in 1856, was a beneficiary of these experiments, establishing Dargomïzhsky as second only to Glinka within the native tradition.

However, the critics were cool towards *Rusalka*, and a deeply dispirited Dargomïzhsky promptly withdrew into a private, circumscribed existence. 'I pass the time quietly and pleasantly at home in a circle that is small but as sincerely dedicated to art as I, consisting of a few of my pupils and a few talented music lovers', he was to write in December 1859. 'We perform Russian music simply and sensibly, without fanciful effects. In a word, it is the kind of performance that our late friend Mikhail Ivanovich [Glinka] loved.'[2] These soirées were held on Mondays and Thursdays, and though the music given consisted mainly of romances by Glinka and Dargomïzhsky himself, on occasions pieces from Glinka's two operas, *A Life for the Tsar* and *Ruslan and Lyudmila*,

---

[2] Quoted in *SMPM* (see *SSM3*, 57).

were to be heard: above all, extracts from Dargomïzhsky's own *Rusalka*, 'sometimes superbly performed by Dargomïzhsky himself, for in both dramatic and comic scenes he was a great and inimitable master of musical declamation'—so Vladimir Stasov recalled.[3]

This was the milieu in which Musorgsky now passed a major portion of his leisure time, and the effect was immense; only now, declared Stasov, did he begin 'his true musical life'.[4] But it was not simply invaluable present experiences that Dargomïzhsky would afford Musorgsky. Dargomïzhsky's response to the death of Glinka in February 1857 would also, years ahead, prove momentous for Musorgsky himself. For all Dargomïzhsky's cordial relationship with Glinka, he had long smarted under the far greater public attention the latter had received. But suddenly his rival was no more; he, Dargomïzhsky, was now the unchallenged leading composer of the native tradition. The sense of liberation, of new responsibility—and also, perhaps, an awareness that some of the younger composers emerging around him both respected him yet already considered him *passé*—was to provide Dargomïzhsky with the stimulus to reanimate his pioneer instinct. In December 1857, in one of his most noted declarations, he gave a pointer to the direction his work would take: 'I want the sound to express the word directly. I want truth.'[5] A few years hence this could have been Musorgsky writing.

Yet even more important than the introduction to Dargomïzhsky was another effected at one of these soirées at the end of 1857; indeed, it proved to be the most important single musical contact of Musorgsky's whole life. Mily Balakirev was only two years older than Musorgsky, but already he was promising to become one of the most enterprising activists in Russia's musical life. Born in 1837 in Nizhny Novgorod, he owed his main musical education to a local teacher, Karl Eisrich, who arranged musical evenings for the wealthy Alexander Ulïbïshev, author of an early biography of Mozart. From 1851 Ulïbïshev engaged Balakirev as Eisrich's assistant in preparing and rehearsing performances, and opened to him his own music library. In the autumn

---

[3] Ibid.

[4] Ibid.

[5] Quoted in M. Pekelis, *Alexandr Sergeyevich Dargomïzhsky*, ii (Moscow, 1973), 261.

of 1855, after two years at Kazan University studying mathematics, Balakirev was taken by Ulïbïshev to St Petersburg. Here he met Glinka, who was profoundly impressed by the eighteen-year-old; never before had this greatest of living Russian composers found a man with, as he declared, 'views so close to my own on everything to do with music . . . In time he will become a second Glinka.'[6]

Little more than a year later Glinka was dead, and Balakirev confronted the destiny predicted for him. Yet though he was unaware at the time, he had already taken the first step in shaping the movement that would make him one of the most potent figures in Russian musical life in the 1860s, with influence extending beyond the causes he publicly espoused. Early in 1856 he had begun a close acquaintance with César Cui, a student at the Academy of Military Engineering in St Petersburg and, like Balakirev, a keen and talented amateur musician. It was from this meeting that Balakirev was to build the group of composers—the 'moguchaya kuchka', or 'mighty handful'—who would become the radical spearhead of the post-Glinka generation and produce many of the major creations of Russian music over the next half-century.

As critical for Balakirev as the meeting with Cui was the acquaintance he began at exactly the same time with Vladimir Stasov, also to be a very potent factor in Musorgsky's musical progress. Stasov was a rampant polymath with an insatiable appetite for all things creative, an appetite tempered only by the idiosyncracies of his personal tastes. A man of stupendous energy and force of character, the most visible sign of his activities was the stream of books, reviews and articles that poured from him to the end of his long life in 1906. Born in 1824, in 1854 he took a post in the St Petersburg Imperial Public Library, remaining there until his death. The demands of official work in no way affected the vigour and volume of his public utterances, nor did they cramp his zest for engaging in those boisterous, sometimes bruising polemics into which his enthusiasms, prejudices, and almost manic mental ferment so readily drew him. Nor did these demands diminish his more private

[6] As reported by Glinka's sister, Lyudmila Shestakova. Quoted in A. Orlova, ed., *Glinka v vospominaniyakh sovremennikov* [Glinka in the recollections of his contemporaries] (Moscow, 1955), 291.

interventions in the lives of those who came into his orbit and whose ideals and enterprises he approved. Balakirev, and those Balakirev was in the next few years to gather around himself, would discover this with a vengeance. Stasov was to stimulate, fire, cajole, bully—but always passionately support—this 'moguchaya kuchka' (it was he who had coined the label), pressing on its members subjects on which they might compose, proclaiming and sustaining their cause during their lifetimes, and penning the first biographies of Musorgsky and Borodin after their deaths.

It was at Dargomïzhsky's in December 1857 that Musorgsky encountered not only Balakirev but Cui, Stasov, and, in May 1858, Stasov's brother Dmitri, a lawyer by profession but also a first-rate amateur musician, who would the following year be one of the founders of the Russian Musical Society (RMS), which was to do so much that was fundamental for Russian musical life (though a great deal of which the kuchka did not approve, especially in its earlier years). However, it was Balakirev who had the immediate impact. If ever there was a right man in the right place, it was he. Though as a composer he was untaught, he seems to have had a unique ability, when practising and studying the music of others, to grasp its essence and technical means so swiftly and completely that he could at one leap cross the chasm between the brilliant amateur with a natural facility and the accomplished professional with an assured, if not all-embracing, technique. Even Glinka before him had hardly commanded this instant capacity.

This was the man who now took upon himself to shape Musorgsky's craft and guide his destiny, and within days of their meeting his campaign was under way. When Glinka had aided Dargomïzhsky some twenty-five years earlier, he had played with him piano duet arrangements of Beethoven symphonies and Mendelssohn overtures, dissecting them the while. This was the method Balakirev adopted, excusing himself from pedagogical teaching. 'Because I am not a theorist,' he remembered for Stasov in 1881,[7] 'I could not teach him [Musorgsky] harmony (as, for instance, Rimsky-Korsakov now teaches it) . . . [but] I explained to him the form of compositions, and to do this we played through both Beethoven symphonies [as piano duets] and

---

[7] Quoted in *MVS*, 89.

much else (Schumann, Schubert, Glinka, and others), analysing the form.' Up to now Musorgsky's musical horizons had been very narrow; according to Stasov he knew virtually nothing but piano music (and even here very little of Mozart and Beethoven), while his knowledge of more radical recent music was almost non-existent. Accordingly Balakirev set himself to fill these gaps by including among the 'others' Berlioz and Liszt, as well as Bach, Handel, Mozart, Haydn, and Beethoven.

With hindsight we may well wonder whether Balakirev should not at least have attempted formally to instruct Musorgsky in that basic musical syntax which he himself already commanded so naturally, though he seems to have advised his pupil to try to investigate some of these matters for himself. But to be confronted with great music, to have its mechanisms and the means that created the conditions for its greatness exposed through practical analysis, then to be sent away to attempt such things for himself, could be as stimulating to Musorgsky as it was testing, even though he often found the task set beyond his skills, and the more cerebral demands unpalatable (significantly he found composing scherzi more congenial than first movements). He accepted Balakirev's tuition avidly. But he also needed a new piano, and he asked Balakirev to choose the instrument. Balakirev did as requested, prompting the first of Musorgsky's letters to have survived:[8]

[St Petersburg, 27 December 1857]

Most precious Mily Alexeyevich,

I do not know how to thank you for choosing the instrument, and I am already persuaded that it is a good one . . .

I am giving you advance notice that, despite all my desire to spend the evening with you in musical activities, I cannot do so this Tuesday. I have to go to my relatives; they are exceedingly vexed with me, saying that I 'have forgotten them completely'.

If it suits you, then set the time of the lesson yourself—only let me know in a couple of days so that I may give you a reply.

But within that couple of days, with his family appeased, he could write more cheerfully:[9]

[8] *MLN1*, 35.
[9] *MLN1*, 35–6.

Most excellent Mily Alexeyevich,

The criminal is forgiven—and I await you with impatience on Thursday. Today, thank God, the fate of my so-long-desired piano was resolved. Tomorrow the most worthy Bekker will deliver it to us . . . Lay in by Thursday Beethoven's Second Symphony, and it will be destined to inaugurate the instrument.

Such terms uncover the close, enthusiastic tone of the new relationship and the swiftness with which it had consolidated. Over the next five or so years Balakirev would provide Musorgsky with the only guidance in composition he was to receive in his whole life. At first the lessons were paid for by Musorgsky's mother, who gave her younger son wholehearted support both financial and moral, buying him tickets for the opera and theatre, and entertaining his new teacher in the apartment she shared with her two sons. But before long Balakirev declined payment, insisting that their sessions should be as between friends. At their first encounter Musorgsky was unwise enough to exhibit his little piano piece *Souvenir d'enfance*, and Balakirev instantly dismissed the trifle, setting him to write a symphonic Allegro. It was a task beyond him, and within a month he was confessing it unfinished and himself 'sick to death of it'.[10] Unable to resist his own creative urges, he had also begun some original composition, perhaps sketching the prelude to an extended work he was envisaging on *Oedipus in Athens* by the early nineteenth-century Russian dramatist Vladisláv Ozerov, and which was to occupy him, though with few results, over the next three years. Neither did this piece come easily; 'such laziness and languor have descended on me that I don't know how to extricate myself from them. No, not for anything will I write eastern music; it's all contrivances', he continued in the same letter.[11] This is not the only hint in his early letters of that easy drifting into indolence that was to be one of his fatal weaknesses.

However, the impact of these new studies was swift and profound, for within only a few months of starting work with Balakirev Musorgsky had decided he must devote himself entirely to music. He would

[10] *MLN1*, 37.

[11] Ibid. The 'eastern music' may refer to the Introduction (which has not survived) to *Oedipus in Athens*.

resign his commission. Stasov, who could see no evidence that Musorgsky had the makings of a professional composer, did all he could to dissuade him: 'I told him that Lermontov had been able to remain a hussar officer and be a great poet . . . Musorgsky replied: "Lermontov was one sort of person—but I'm another. Perhaps he could cope with diversity—but me: no. My army service hinders me from devoting myself to what I must." '[12] His application was accordingly made, and on 17 June 1858 his discharge was allowed.

Musorgsky now had all the time he wanted for music, as well as the family resources to support him. But he was no Tchaikovsky, whose composing life was to be regulated by an ethic that imposed systematic, disciplined application, even when the promptings of inspiration were lacking. Musorgsky's working practices would always be fitful. When the inspiration was upon him he could apply himself with superhuman intensity for a sustained period, as when composing the initial version of his first and only completed opera, *Boris Godunov*. But between such internally driven bursts there could be far longer stretches of inertia. 'I haven't seen the Musorgskys for a long time and I don't know what they're up to', Cui wrote to Balakirev on 30 July. 'As before Modest is probably spending half the day thinking about what he will do tomorrow and the other half about what he was doing yesterday.'[13]

There is too little evidence of the course of Musorgsky's studies with Balakirev to gauge just how consistent was his application, what precisely was studied, or what (and how much) produced (or not). But he was far from completely idle. On 20 July, as he was about to leave St Petersburg to attend the wedding of Georgy Mengden, one of his fellow pupils from the School for Guards' Cadets, he listed for Balakirev his current musical activities:

I'm beginning to write a sonata (E flat major) and somehow I'm coping; I shall endeavour to see it comes out well . . . The scherzo is already prepared, and my practical occupations with harmony are going ahead in my spare time . . . We [Musorgsky and brother Filaret] played the B flat and C major symphonies of Schumann; he's in raptures about them and reads music magnificently . . . Yesterday [at Stasov's?] . . . I played the introduction to

[12] *SMPM* (see *SSM3*, 60).

[13] *TDM*, 69.

Oedipus and some themes for compositions. It seems they pleased Bach [i.e., Stasov][14]—which is nice.[15]

During his fortnight's expedition to the Mengden wedding Musorgsky succumbed to a curious nervous illness which persisted into the early autumn. Such nervous, transcendent eruptions were to mark his whole life and be a significant factor impeding his creative labours. He endeavoured to hide his condition from Balakirev, but the latter was given what may be an oblique pointer to his mental state in a letter sent towards the end of August:[16]

> Now in my leisure time I am translating Lafateur's letters on the state of the soul after death, a very interesting matter . . . Regarding the condition of the soul, he says that a dead man's soul communicates its thoughts to the man who is clairvoyant—thoughts which, being transmitted by the clairvoyant to the friend who has been left (by the soul) on earth, give the latter a notion of its condition after death.

Only a year later did Musorgsky try to describe more explicitly what had happened, and its effect:[17]

> As you know, . . . I was oppressed by a frightful illness which had begun very violently during my stay in the country; this was mysticism combined with cynical thoughts concerning the deity. This illness developed horribly on my return to St Petersburg. I managed successfully to conceal it from you, but you must have noticed its manifestation in my music. I suffered terribly, became terribly susceptible to impressions (even morbidly so). Then, whether in consequence of diversions or because I gave myself up to the fantastic dreams which had sustained me for a long while, the mysticism began little by little to abate; when I began to see the way my mind had evolved, I started taking measures to destroy it [mysticism].

One remedy he tried was bathing in the mineral springs at Tikhvin. Yet the rest of 1858 seems to have passed without further inner turmoils. He had decided to dedicate the E flat Sonata to Mengden and his bride,

---

[14] Stasov was given this nickname by Lyudmila Shestakova, Glinka's sister.
[15] *MLN1*, 38.
[16] *MLN1*, 40.
[17] *MLN1*, 46.

but the piece remained unfinished and he had started a second 'very unpretentious'[18] Sonata in F sharp minor. The latter has completely disappeared; what have survived from the rest of the year are two scherzos, one for orchestra, the other for piano, and three songs. To complement these creative labours he studied much music by other composers, reading through Gluck's operas *Alceste*, *Iphigénie en Aulide*, and *Armide*, Hérold's *Zampa*, and Mozart's Requiem, getting to know Beethoven's piano sonatas better, making a piano duet transcription of Glinka's Second Spanish Overture, *Recollections of a Summer Night in Madrid*, performing the entr'actes from that composer's incidental music to *Prince Kholmsky* in arrangements for two pianos eight hands, and playing with Cui piano-duet transcriptions of much Beethoven, Schubert, and especially Schumann, as suggested by Balakirev. Soon he was participating in domestic theatricals at the Cuis'. Stasov recalled a particular occasion early in 1859 when, in a performance of Cui's one-act opera *The Mandarin's Son*, Musorgsky performed the part of the mandarin 'with such life, hilarity, with such flair and so much that was comical in his singing, diction, posture, and movement that he made the whole company of his friends and comrades roar with laughter'.[19] Of experiences that the outside world afforded, the most important were performances of Glinka's second opera *Ruslan and Lyudmila*.

Excitement at an experience of a very different sort, though one that was more quintessentially Russian, was to come from his encounter with Moscow. In the middle of May 1859 he visited Glebovo, an estate to the west of Moscow. Stepan Shilovsky, its owner, was wealthy and welcoming, while his wife Mariya, an amateur singer, had made it something of a musical centre (a tradition that was to continue: in 1876 Tchaikovsky was to complete *Swan Lake* at Glebovo and, a year later, compose there the greater part of *Eugene Onegin*, with the Shilovskys' eldest son, Konstantin, having some part in the libretto). During his six-week stay Musorgsky was able to deepen his knowledge of Glinka by helping prepare the Shilovskys' domestic choir in choruses from that composer's first opera, *A Life for the Tsar*. By the beginning of July he

[18] *MLN1*, 40.
[19] *SMPM* (see *SSM3*, 60).

had moved on to Moscow. If he had passed through the city the previous September on his way to visit Nizhny Novgorod, he left no
record of his reactions. But this time Moscow proved a revelation. Instead of a modern metropolis like St Petersburg, planned on western
lines and moulded from western architectural styles, here was a city that
had grown with the centuries, permeated with influences from the east,
but whose heart was Russian:[20]

> I will give you my impressions [he wrote excitedly to Balakirev on 5 July].
> While still only approaching Jericho[21] [Moscow] I had already observed
> that it was unique; the belltowers and cupolas of the churches simply
> smelled of antiquity. *The Red Gates* are amusing and I liked them very
> much, between them and the Kremlin there was nothing specially remark-
> able—and then the Kremlin, the wonderful Kremlin—I approached it with
> involuntary awe. Red Square, on which so many notable unruly encounters
> have taken place, is impaired a little from its left side—from the bazaar. But
> [the Cathedral of] St Basil the Blessed and the Kremlin wall make you forget
> this disability: here is holy antiquity. St Basil affected me so agreeably, and
> at the same time so oddly, that it seemed to me that at any moment a boyar
> would pass by in a long, homespun coat and tall hat. Under the Spassky
> gates I bared my head; I like this folk custom. The new palace is magnif-
> icent, its best chamber is the former Granovitaya Hall . . . The Uspensky
> Cathedral, the Church of our Saviour, the Arkhangelsky Cathedral—they
> stand hand in hand with St Basil as representatives of the old. I made a tour
> of homage of the tombs in the Arkhangelsky Cathedral, among which I
> found ones before which I stood in reverence, such as those of Ivan III,
> Dmitri Donskoy, and even the Romanovs—at the latter I recalled *A Life
> for the Tsar*, and because of this halted involuntarily. I climbed the belltower
> of Ivan the Great with its wonderful view of Moscow . . .
>
> Strolling through Moscow I recalled Griboyedov ('all Muscovites have
> a special hall-mark'), and I saw the truth of this, at least regarding the
> common people. Nowhere else in the world are beggars and rogues such
> as these; moreover, I was especially struck by a certain oddness in their
> manners and by their fidgetiness.

---

[20] *MLN1*, 43–4.
[21] The nickname for Moscow used among the kuchka.

> Overall Moscow took me into another world—a world of antiquity (a world which, though also grimy, yet (though I don't know why) affected me agreeably) . . . You know that I have been a cosmopolitan—but now there has been some sort of regeneration; everything Russian has become close to me, and I should be disappointed if we did not treat Russia with proper ceremony in our present time. I am beginning, as it were, to love her.

For Musorgsky this encounter with Russia's old capital proved to be a crucial stage in awakening him to the heritage and culture of his native land. Already evident, too, is that alert observation of behavioural characteristics that would provide such fruitful stimuli in both song and opera.

Musorgsky continued his sessions with Balakirev throughout 1859. The year also produced a few original compositions. On 4 February 1859 he signed the completed manuscript of a chorus for the 'Scene in the Temple' from *Oedipus in Athens*, on 8 October he dated the manuscript of a piano piece, *In the Corner* (with which he intended at that time to open a suite, *Children Games*, but which in June 1860 he revised and renamed *Ein Kinderscherz*), and five days later he dated a second piano piece, *Impromptu passioné* (inspired by Herzen's novel *Who is to blame?*). Then, on 23 October, he completed the vocal score of a piece for tenor and bass soloists, chorus, and piano, to which the early Musorgsky scholar and editor Vyacheslav Karatïgin gave the title *Shamil's March*, and which used an Arabic text beginning 'There is no god but Allah.' For what precise purpose Musorgsky composed this piece is unknown, though it was doubtless somehow connected with the honourable surrender two months earlier of the Imam Shamil, who for a quarter of a century had been a thorn in Russia's side in the Caucasus, but who was now, in effect, pardoned, to be well accommodated for the rest of his days. During the year Musorgsky produced, it seems, only one song, *Sadly rustled the leaves*.

On the last day of October Musorgsky reviewed for Balakirev how their relationship had evolved over the past nearly two years:[22]

> Formerly: I recognized your superiority over me; in arguments with me I saw the great clarity of your opinion and your steadfastness. However mad

[22] *MLN1*, 46–7.

I was sometimes at myself and sometimes at you, yet I could not deny the truth. From this it is clear it was hubris that impelled me to behave stubbornly both in arguments and in my relations with you.

Subsequently: you know the former over-sensitivity of my character which marred my relations with people who deserved better. Once there had crept over me a feeling that my self-esteem had been wounded, all my pride rose up. Needless to say, I began studying people, and with this I developed rapidly and was on the alert regarding myself. But all the while I was not guilty of the slightest lapse concerning what is good and true. In my relationships with people I am greatly indebted to you, Mily; you have been wonderfully adept at jolting me when I have been nodding. Later I understood you completely, and wholeheartedly attached myself to you, finding in you, as it happened, an echo of my own thoughts—or sometimes the beginning and embryo of them. Our most recent relations have so strongly linked your personality with mine that I have come to believe in you completely.

Also in the autumn of 1859 Borodin again encountered Musorgsky. His 1881 memories record his fresh view of the man after a three-year gap:[23]

He had matured a good deal, had begun to put on weight, and his officer's ways had gone. His elegance of dress, manners, and such-like, were as before, but there was no longer the slightest hint of foppishness. We were introduced to each other—but we, for our parts, recognized each other immediately and recalled our first meeting at Popov's. Musorgsky explained that he had retired because 'he was making a particular study of music, and it was difficult to combine military service and art', and so on. The conversation involuntarily turned to music. I was still a fervent Mendelssohnian while still knowing hardly any Schumann; Musorgsky was already acquainted with Balakirev, and had nosed out all sorts of musical novelties I had never heard of. Seeing that in music we had found common ground for conversation, the Ivanovskys [their hosts] suggested we should play, as a piano duet, Mendelssohn's A minor symphony. Modest Petrovich knit his brow somewhat and said that he was very glad to—only that they should

---

[23] *MVS*, 87–8.

'spare him the Andante which was not at all symphonic, but one of the *Lieder ohne Worte*, or something of the sort, arranged for orchestra'. We played the first movement and the scherzo. After this Musorgsky began talking rapturously about Schumann's symphonies, of which I was at that time totally ignorant. He began playing me bits of Schumann's E flat Symphony; on coming to the central [development] section he stopped, saying: 'Now here begin the musical mathematics.' This was all new to me, and I found it to my liking . . . In passing, I learned that he himself wrote music. My interest was fired, of course; he began playing me some scherzo of his own (almost certainly the one in B flat); on coming to the trio he muttered through his teeth 'now this is oriental', and I was absolutely amazed at these unprecedented musical elements that were new to me. I won't say that I instantly found them particularly to my taste; rather, they took me aback by their novelty [but] having heard a little, I began to relish it a little. I admit I had at first received with incredulity his announcement that he wished to devote himself seriously to music; it seemed a bit like bragging . . . But having become acquainted with the scherzo I began to think: 'Should I, or should I not believe it?'

CHAPTER 3

The Making of a Composer II

IT MIGHT SEEM THERE COULD BE NO CHANCE THAT A COMPOSER whose background had included no formal training in technique, whose skill in many basic compositional tasks was still patently defective, and whose original compositions were as few in number as mostly they were slight in content, should gain a hearing in what was still the only series of professional orchestral concerts in Russia. Yet on 23 January 1860, through the initiative of Dmitri Stasov, Musorgsky's 1858 Scherzo in B flat, orchestrated with Balakirev's help, was played at a concert of the new RMS. Moreover, the conductor was Anton Rubinstein himself, one of the most internationally famed of pianists and now considered by many to be Russia's greatest living composer. The previous March Musorgsky had attended the première of Rubinstein's Second Symphony, *The Ocean*, and two years later he was to be blistering about the piece; 'O Ocean—O puddle!' he would write to Balakirev.[1] But Rubinstein as conductor was a different matter, and the performance of his piece delighted him. It was very warmly applauded, and Alexander Serov, the leading Russian music critic, while regretting that the scherzo was so short, wrote: 'It is remarkable that this symphonic extract by a composer as yet unknown not only lost nothing by being placed alongside music by an "outstanding" master [music for *Struensee* by Meyerbeer] but benefited very much from this.'[2]

[1] *MLN1*, 53.
[2] *TDM*, 82.

It was well Musorgsky revelled in this success, for within a month he had entered a second phase of psychological disturbance even more prolonged and severe than that of 1858. For all the confusion of the self-analysis that he poured out to Balakirev on 22 February, there is no doubting the desperation within his cry for help:[3]

You remember, my dear, how during the summer two years ago we were walking along Sadovaya Street (you were on your way home). Before this walk we had been reading [Byron's] *Manfred*. I had been so electrified by the sufferings of that lofty human nature that on the spot I had said to you: 'How I long to be a Manfred' (I was an absolute child at the time). It seems that fate has been pleased to grant my wish; I have become literally 'man-fredised', my spirit has overwhelmed my body. Now I am having to take every kind of antidote. Dear Mily, I know you love me; for God's sake, when we're talking try to keep a tight rein on me and don't let me destroy myself; for a while I must cease both musical occupations and every kind of intense mental labour so that I may recover. My prescription for myself is: everything that favours the physical side and, as far as possible, curbs the mental. Now the cause of my nervous irritation is clear to me; it is [not only the consequence of masturbation (this is almost a secondary reason) but] chiefly youth, over-driving enthusiasm, a terrible, irresistible desire for omniscience, exaggerated inner criticism, and an idealism that leads to me embodying my visions in manners and actions—those are the main reasons. At the present moment I see that, because I am only twenty, my physical side has not developed sufficiently to keep pace with my strong moral impulse [[(the reason for my physical underdevelopment is masturbation)]]; as a result my moral strength has stifled my physical development. The latter needs assistance; distraction and tranquillity (as far as possible), gymnastics, bathing: these should deliver me.

Today Kito [Filaret] and I went to the ballet (*Paquerette*), a very nice ballet: there were many beautiful scenes. But the music, Mily, the music was absolutely awful; Pugni is a musical Scythian. The music had a terrible effect on me; I was ill on the spot, when I got home I lay down to take a nap, I had the most tormenting dreams, but ones that were to such a degree

---

[3] *MLN1*, 48. The extended passages in square brackets are taken from the earlier, less rigorously censored source, *RKM*, 55; these passages were excluded from subsequent editions of Musorgsky's letters.

bitter-sweet, so ravishing, that to die in such a situation would have been easy. This was the end (fortunately) of my sufferings; now I am much better—at least, I am completely calm.

Musorgsky's sexuality has long been a subject for speculation—and such, in the absence of much hard evidence, it is likely to remain.[4] Anecdote and rumour have abounded. An early tale from his birthplace had it that he fell in love with a cousin who died young, and that she had requested his letters be buried with her. To Glinka's sister, Lyudmila Shestakova, Musorgsky was to declare repeatedly—and, she insisted, seriously—that if she read in the papers he had shot or hanged himself it would signify that the previous day he had got married. Vladimir Stasov, whose interest, both subjective and objective, in sexual matters was intense, alleged that Musorgsky suffered from a malformation of his sexual organs which inhibited, but did not prevent, sexual activity. Others have proposed homosexuality. Be that as it may, there is also hard evidence that points to him as heterosexual. Two years earlier, as he was about to set out for the Mengden wedding, Stasov had subjected him to mischievous and prolonged erotic teasing. 'Yesterday Stasov (Bach) suggested that at the wedding I should take a peep beneath the bride's corset', Musorgsky had reported to Balakirev. 'I rebelled against this, and this opposition was the occasion for a two-hour discussion of the secret parts of the human body, primarily female; illnesses were enumerated, the characteristics of "the queen of spades" (an apt name) were looked into, and all evening Bach asked again and again: will you take a look under the bride's corset? . . . I found it terribly boring.'[5]

Clearly Stasov judged Musorgsky not only heterosexual (in 1895 he would list Nadezhda Opochinina, Mariya Shilovskaya, and Alexandra Latïsheva—a singer at the Imperial Opera in the 1850s and 60s—as women to whom Musorgsky was attracted in the 1860s, all significantly older than him), but still sexually adolescent, as is powerfully suggested by Musorgsky's outpouring to Balakirev. Whether or not Musorgsky declared an indifference to Stasov's batings because his correspondent

---

[4] A speculative Freudian examination of the evidence concerning Musorgsky's (homo)sexuality, especially emphasizing a belief 'that the key to Musorgsky's baffling sexuality is masochism', is laid out in J. Turner, 'Musorgsky', *Music Review* xlvii (1986), 153–75.

[5] *MLN1*, 38.

was Balakirev, whose sexual attitude to women (whatever that might have been) was certainly less crude than Stasov's, it seems perfectly plausible that he found Stasov's heavy and insistent prurience genuinely distasteful and definitely embarrassing—though it may well be that he was about to move on to a new stage in active sexual experience.[6]

In early June Musorgsky left St Petersburg to spend the summer at Glebovo with the Shilovskys. During the earlier part of the year the frequent sessions with Balakirev had continued, but at the end of May Balakirev left for an expedition down the lower Volga to collect folksongs; it would be November before he returned to the Russian capital, and during this time contact between the two men would be lost. Back in St Petersburg at the beginning of October, Musorgsky hastened to discover Balakirev's current address from Stasov so that he might report his summer activities:[7]

My illness continued almost to [the middle of] August so that I could only give myself up to music at intervals. For most of the time from May until August my brain was weak and highly irritated. Nevertheless, I assembled some materials that would be needed later; *Oedipus* and the little sonata are proceeding. The sonata is almost ready, a little needs polishing in the middle [of the?] movement, the tail-piece works. Two choruses are being added to *Oedipus*: an Andante in B flat minor and a following Allegro in E flat, [both of] which will go into the introduction and are now being composed. In addition I have received a very interesting piece of work which I must have ready by next summer.

The work is this: a whole act on the *Bare Mountain* (from [Georgy] Mengden's drama *The Witch*)—*a witches' sabbath, different episodes for sorcerers, a triumphal march for the entire obscene rabble, a finale: glorification of this sabbath*

---

[6] A later letter from Musorgsky may provide a further pointer to his sexuality. Writing to Stasov on 30 October 1872 after reading Darwin's *Descent of Man, and Selection in Relation to Sex*, he makes a curious comparison between Darwin's hold on him and a lover's embrace. 'If a strong, passionate, beloved woman firmly clasps the man she loves in her embrace, that man, though he recognizes the violence, still does not wish to tear himself from that embrace because that violence is "bliss beyond measure", because from that violence "youthful blood's flame roars". I am not ashamed of this comparison: however much you twist and flirt with truth, he who has experienced love in all its force and freedom—that man *has lived* and remembers that he *has lived wonderfully*, and he will allow no shadow upon a bygone bliss.' (*MLN1*, 140).

[7] *MLN1*, 49–50.

which in Mengden is made incarnate in the master of the entire festive act on the Bare Mountain. The libretto is very good. I already have some materials for it; it could come out a very good piece . . .

Mily, you would rejoice in the change in me which, without question, is powerfully reflected in my music. My brain has grown strong, has turned towards reality, my youthful fire has cooled, everything is in perspective—and now *of mysticism not a whisper*. My last mystical piece is the B flat minor Andante (a chorus) in the introduction to *Oedipus*. Praise be to God, Mily; I am completely cured.

Dmitri Stasov, who had engineered the performance of Musorgsky's B flat Scherzo, now persuaded the committee of the RMS that one of the *Oedipus* choruses should be rehearsed and, if Musorgsky agreed, performed at another of its concerts. Musorgsky was highly flattered, but doubted the wisdom of exposing to the public a piece that was *agitato* and short, and would therefore need to be preceded by an Andante.

But there was a further reason for his hesitation; the politics of confrontation had begun in Russia's musical life. Despite Balakirev's respect for Dmitri Stasov, he was deeply suspicious of what the RMS under Anton Rubinstein offered, and especially what it threatened to become. Like Balakirev, Rubinstein was a young activist of boundless energy. Born in 1829, he had become famed not only as one of the finest of the century's pianists, but also as a composer of great facility and prodigious output. Yet he was still finding time, together with the Grand Duchess Elena Pavlovna (the Tsar's German-born aunt), to be the driving force behind the foundation of the RMS with its two-fold aims: to promote concerts, and to begin building a structure of musical education (at that time there was no advanced music school in Russia, nor even a textbook on harmony). To this latter end Rubinstein instituted classes in music theory—and so successfully that in 1862 these would grow into the St Petersburg Conservatoire with Rubinstein at its head (and a young civil servant, Tchaikovsky, as one of its first intake).

Already by 1860 Balakirev had perceived the threat this new, rapidly expanding organization could pose. Rubinstein was a musical conservative trained in the West, and his own post-Mendelssohnian music presented styles that Balakirev saw as inimicable to the ideals and objectives that he, Glinka's appointed heir, cherished. Russia would again become no more than an outpost of Europe; he feared, too, that the RMS's classes would inculcate a conservative compositional technique that would stifle true creativity in their students. In fact, time would show that the incompatibility of Rubinstein and Balakirev was much less absolute than at first appeared. But in the early 1860s Balakirev saw Rubinstein as representing a mortal danger, and Musorgsky reflected his mentor's views: 'Is this disorderly company really making ready to teach me!' he fumed to Balakirev. 'The chorus will be returned and I am heartily glad, having avoided a clash with Rubinstein. Basta! I have had enough of the Society.'[8]

For Musorgsky the spell of Russia's old capital remained, and mid-January 1861 found him at the Shilovskys' in Moscow. The three-week separation from Balakirev prompted an informative clutch of letters. His musical judgements and attitudes were hardening, as frequently do those of the young when beginning to exercise their still insecurely founded taste. Anton Rubinstein as composer is an object of contempt, Chopin is out of favour, and the C major Fantasia of Schumann is 'weak', having been composed at 'the time of his passion for Mendelssohn'.[9] The F sharp minor Sonata, Op. 11, is preferable; 'the introduction's nothing special, the best parts are the two Allegros, especially the first'.[10] There are signs that Musorgsky has been pondering seriously Balakirev's earlier advice that he should give attention to matters of musical technique ('I'll work at part-writing, starting with three voices . . . It's a healthy *incentive* for me to think for a while that my *harmony* has something in common with *rubbish*', he had written to Balakirev only weeks earlier).[11] His admiration for the first Allegro of Schumann's Op. 11, with its dutiful motivic working of a kind that had a wide, if transient, appeal to other major Russian composers intent upon symphonic 'correctness' (notably Borodin and Tchaikovsky) is significant.

So, too, is his defiance of Balakirev's insinuations concerning the

---

[8] *MLN1*, 51.

[9] *MLN1*, 53.

[10] Ibid.

[11] *MLN1*, 51. This is supported by the memories of Nikolay Kompaneisky.

influence of the 'limited personalities' of the circle in which he is mixing in Moscow:[12]

> Your aspersions . . . demand a single answer: 'Tell me whom you love, I'll tell you what you are.' And so it follows that I must be limited . . . If I am to judge from your view that my disposition is limited—a view grounded upon knowledge (knowledge, because we've known each other five years)—then *I cannot comprehend* how I can be breathing in the atmosphere of these people [they being intelligent, talented, and thus not limited]—and, vice versa, they mine . . .
>
> As for me being stuck and having to be dragged out, I will say one thing: if there is talent in me I shall not get stuck, provided my brain is stimulated. Furthermore: if I have neither [talent nor brain], what's the point of dragging a splinter [like me] out of the mud? To speak plainly: I did once get stuck (not musically but morally): I crawled out (however, you will learn later what happened if our conversation should touch on this: there is a woman involved). Whatever the case, I know one thing: your letter was motivated by a misplaced vexation, for it is time you stopped regarding me as a child who needs propping up in case he should fall.

Musorgsky is steadily gaining in confidence and spirit of independence. It seems probable the 'woman involved' was Mariya Shilovskaya, who certainly had a penchant for men. The previous year Musorgsky had dedicated to her his song *What are words of love to you?*, and there had been ample opportunity for intimate contact between them during the last two summers. Whatever Musorgsky's part in the relationship, he had now withdrawn himself and was staying elsewhere in Moscow. Whether he may have experienced a sexual attraction of a different kind within the circle of young men with whom he was now mixing, and whether a suspicion of this had been a factor in Balakirev's strictures on his current social activities is even less certain—but Musorgsky was certainly much taken by Alexander Demidov, also a former guards' officer whom Balakirev had also known in his native Nizhny-Novgorod, and whom Musorgsky envisaged accommodating in the family apartment if Demidov should decide to come to St Petersburg to develop his musical gifts further.

[12] *MLN1*, 56–7.

But however much Musorgsky may have engaged in lively talk on a variety of topics with his new companions, he still found time to work on a Scherzo and Andante for a Symphony in D, to explore Beethoven's first Razumovsky Quartet, and revel in Schubert's C major Symphony. Back in St Petersburg in mid-February he rejoined the gatherings at Balakirev's, where extracts from the latter's incidental music to *King Lear* (in Musorgsky's piano transcriptions) were to be heard. Encouragement came from a second public performance of one of Musorgsky's own pieces: the chorus for the Temple Scene in *Oedipus in Athens*, given at the Maryinsky Theatre on 18 April at a concert conducted by Konstantin Lyadov, father of Anatol, the composer.

In December a naval cadet was added to the Balakirev circle. Though Nikolay Rimsky-Korsakov was only seventeen years old and musically as untrained as the rest, he had already assembled some materials for a symphony which Balakirev instantly proposed should be purposefully composed under his guidance. In his memoirs, written nearly half a century later, Rimsky recalled hearing at that time Musorgsky sing Farlaf in the scene with Naina in Act 2 of Glinka's *Ruslan and Lyudmila*, listening to Balakirev, the Musorgsky brothers and Cui perform Musorgsky's arrangement for two pianos eight hands of the Queen Mab Scherzo and the Ball at the Capulets from Berlioz's *Roméo et Juliette*, and absorbing the collective enthusiasms and prejudices of the group— for instance, their approval of Berlioz on the one hand and, on the other, their diminished regard for Dargomïzhsky, with whom contact had lapsed. Sometimes there were readings from Russian literature.

To set against such rich pleasures was an outside event that was to have the profoundest of consequences for the Musorgsky family. On 17 March 1861, soon after Musorgsky's return from Moscow, the decree liberating the Russian serfs was read out in churches. On acceding in 1855, Alexander II had set himself to ease many of the pressures that had built within society under the increasingly autocratic rule of his predecessor, Nikolay I. 'No Russian ruler brought so much relief to so many of his people', observed the historian J. N. Westwood.[13] Inheriting the Crimean War as well as the throne, Alexander had signed a

---

[13] J. N. Westwood, *Endurance and Endeavour: Russian History, 1812–1980*, 2nd ed. (Oxford, 1981), 72.

peace agreement in March 1856. Though not a liberal, he was a prag-
matist who recognized that emancipating the serfs was the pressing priority, better effected from above than enforced from below. This
achieved, he instituted wider reforms. Russian universities gained
greater academic freedom, trial by jury was introduced, censorship was
relaxed. Because the spirit behind such reforms fostered a more open,
vibrant society, it is no surprise that the 1860s proved, intellectually and
creatively, one of the most vital decades in Russia's history, nor that in
such an environment Musorgsky throve. But being landowners, Alexander's first measure had cataclysmic results for the Musorgskys collectively. A two-year period of transition to the Emancipation was
specified, and though Filaret, as the elder son, bore the brunt of over-
seeing the changes on the family estate, Modest had also disappeared
from St Petersburg by the beginning of July 1861, remaining away until
late October, and the supposition that he also spent the time at Karevo
seems plausible; there would have been much that demanded the whole
family's presence. In the following year, 1862, their mother gave up her
base in St Petersburg, compelling Modest in future to find his own
quarters in the capital. However, he spent the spring of that year at
Volok, where he intended to undergo medical treatment and where he
remained until at least mid-May. After this his whereabouts are unknown until the autumn, when he resurfaced in St Petersburg. One
thing seems clear, however: Musorgsky scarcely threw himself into the
urgent processes that effected the Emancipation any more than he
seems, up till then, to have shown much interest in the lot of the
peasantry in general. There is certainly no reason to doubt Filaret's
avowal of his brother's ability to relate to peasants as individuals, but
there appears to be no concrete evidence that he had ever troubled to
visit his birthplace since being taken to school in St Petersburg some
twelve years earlier.

Yet the sentimental concept of the peasantry as the very heart and
hope of Russian society for the future infected Musorgsky, as it did
many other Russians, in the wave of euphoria that followed the Emancipation. One beautiful, sunny winter day early in 1862 he witnessed a
scene which impressed itself deeply upon his imagination, with instant
results. A whole crowd of peasants was crossing the fields striding

through the snowdrifts, many constantly disappearing into the snow and then with difficulty scrambling out. Stasov recalled Musorgsky's further account:[14]

> This, taken all together, was both beautiful and picturesque, both serious and amusing. And suddenly . . . in the distance appeared a crowd of young peasant women, singing and laughing as they went along the level path. Suddenly in my head this picture took on a musical form, and unexpectedly, of its own accord, the first 'striding-up-and-down' theme à la Bach took shape; the happy, laughing peasant women presented themselves to me in the guise of a melody from which I later fashioned the central section, or Trio. But all this was 'in modo classico', in accordance with my current musical preoccupations. And that's how my *Intermezzo* came into the world.

The *Intermezzo in modo classico* is Musorgsky's first instrumental piece of significance, all the more remarkable considering how scrappy had been his musical output to date. According to the summary worklist he prepared in 1871 for Lyudmila Shestakova, in 1856 he had attempted an opera on Victor Hugo's first novel, *Han d'Islande*, but, as he added ruefully, 'nothing came of it because nothing could come (the composer was seventeen)'.[15] 1858 saw the first of the pieces (the prelude) prepared for his extended music for Ozerov's *Oedipus in Athens*, but this prelude, like the two choruses projected in 1860, has disappeared, though it seems probable the latter were recycled in the mid-60s for use in the opera *Salammbô*, as was the chorus for the Temple Scene, composed in 1859, scored in 1860, and performed in 1861. Also from 1859 was *Shamil's March* and *Lord of my Days*, presumably a choral piece; the latter has vanished. Of orchestral pieces there were the B flat Scherzo (1858: it may originally have been a piano piece) performed at an RMS concert in 1860, and an *Alla marcia notturna* (1861), though a note on the latter exposes its purely functional purpose: 'an attempt at orchestration; lesson on Wednesday'. There was a series of what also proved no more than exercises to fortify his technique, and which were left in various

[14] *SMPM* (see *SSM3*, 63).

[15] *MNL1*, 263.

states of incompleteness: piano sonatas in E flat (sketches only) and F
sharp minor (lost: both 1858), and in C major (for piano duet, four
movements projected, two extant: 1860), and portions of a Symphony
in D (1861). The remaining handful of piano pieces were more creatively motivated, though hardly original. It could scarcely be expected
that the thirteen-year-old who created the *Porte-enseigne polka* (1852)
for his fellow students would produce more than a cheerful trifle whose
instant appearance in print would later cause him embarrassment, but
neither is it surprising that Balakirev should have scorned the harmonic
and melodic repetitiveness and feeble climax of *Souvenir d'enfance* (1857).
Nor are the pleasantries of *In the Corner* (1859; rev. 1860 as *Ein Kinderscherz*) of greater substance. What is significant in both pieces is Musorgsky's attraction to the world of childhood; as already noted, the
latter piece was planned as part of a set, and two more *Souvenirs d'enfance*
were to come in 1865. In this Musorgsky was following Schumann,
who was also an influence behind the ruminative, sometimes clumsy
Impromptu passioné (1859).

Of the piano pieces of the 1850s the C sharp minor Scherzo (1858)
is of most interest.[16] More Russian in its vigour and in some of its
melodic phrases, and less primitive in facture, it is a natural precedessor
of the *Intermezzo in modo classico*. And with this rugged piece Musorgsky
passed out of the world of the salon, and gratuitous ornamentation was
banished. He recognized the *Intermezzo* reflected some of his current
preoccupations with the music of other composers, and the 'à la Bach'
first melody (Ex. 3.1), like Balakirev's at the opening of his much later
Piano Sonata, is a curious mixture of the Russian and the baroque. But
whereas Balakirev was to move on into a fugue, Musorgsky's use of
counterpoint is simpler, less consistent, and totally devoid of formality.
In any case, the whole piece seems fundamentally more indebted to an
indigenous source: the opening of Glinka's *A Life for the Tsar*, where
peasant men enter to a sturdy tune, to be joined by peasant women
singing a brighter melody combined in due course with the men's
(though in Musorgsky's *Intermezzo* elements of the men's music is forth-

---

[16] Edward Garden has suggested that the coda to this scherzo may be as much by Balakirev
as Musorgsky. For a full examination of Balakirev's impact on his pupil, see E. Garden,
'Balakirev's Influence on Musorgsky', *MIM*, 11–27.

Ex. 3.1

Grave. Pesante

with mingled with the women's). That said, however, the piece is entirely Musorgsky's own, and he retained sufficient pride in it to add,
perhaps in 1863, a central Trio only very distantly derived from the
women's melody; then in 1867 he revised and orchestrated the whole
piece, making a re-transcription for piano (from which Ex. 3.1 is taken).
With the recurrence of the slightly shortened first section, the length
of the *Intermezzo* was now more than doubled.

In fact, the *Intermezzo in modo classico* apart, these earliest compositions are of interest only for the record. Musorgsky was still far from
discerning how he would compose operas, for though he would evidently consider a portion of his *Oedipus* music worth salvaging for his
uncompleted *Salammbô*, he would subsequently refashion yet further his
operatic style through the radical experiment of *The Marriage* before
presenting it fully formed in *Boris Godunov*. His first attempts at larger-
scale instrumental music had been little more than pastiche, and their
fruits would prove far more meagre; except for *St John's Night on the
Bare Mountain* Musorgsky would compose no significant orchestral
piece, nor any further piano music of real importance, save *Pictures at
an Exhibition*. But song-writing would be a very different matter. In
this genre his first batch of totally characteristic pieces would be

produced—and swiftly, too. So far he had composed only a half-dozen songs, but all have some interest and collectively they give pointers towards the greater achievements to come. It is with these that the closer study of Musorgsky's music must begin.

The Early Songs I

TWO OR THREE YEARS BEFORE HIS DEATH IN 1911 THE FRENCH musicologist Charles Malherbe, archivist-librarian and avid collector of musical autographs, came into possession of a bound manuscript of Russian provenance. The acquisition surprised him, for Russians were not accustomed to sell their manuscripts and, as Louis Laloy explained,[1] this one was no sketch but a carefully written autograph copy. Moreover, the composer was a major one: Musorgsky. It was entitled, in Musorgsky's own hand, 'Years of youth: a collection of romances . . . (from 1857 to 1866)', and the composer himself had been responsible for having it bound in St Petersburg.

Though internal evidence indicates the manuscript cannot have been begun before 1861, precisely when and why Musorgsky compiled it and how it subsequently found its way to France and into Malherbe's hands are likely for ever to remain mysteries. It contains sixteen songs as well as an operatic aria and a duet arrangement of a slight Italian piece; only one of Musorgsky's songs composed between 1857 and 19 January 1866 is not included.[2] Though four of these songs were published in Musorgsky's lifetime and five more have survived intact in other manuscript sources, for the remaining seven of these sixteen, quite

---

[1] In *Bulletin français* of the International Musical Society (May, 1909), 286–7. The manuscript is now in the Paris Conservatoire.

[2] *Meines Herzens Sehnsucht*, a simple setting of an anonymous German text, dated 18 September 1858 and dedicated to Malvina Bamberg a month before her marriage to Cui.

certainly Musorgsky's first compositions of real significance, this manuscript is our only complete source. Its importance therefore can hardly
be exaggerated.

By Musorgsky's time song composition in Russia had a century-long
history built by a substantial gallery of practitioners, though the worth
of its products remained slight until Alexander Alyabyev and Glinka
emerged in the 1820s. Seventeen years older than Glinka, Alyabyev was
likewise an amateur of independent means. He composed some 170
songs which exemplify mostly the two main types that had become
established by then: the sentimental 'drawing-room' romance much in-
fluenced by bel canto, and the 'Russian song' conditioned by folksong.
Alyabyev broadened the stylistic and technical base by enriching the
harmonic palette and devising more ambitious accompaniments and
structures, but his harmony often limps and is sometimes plainly defective, while his melody can all too easily falter. As a composer of songs
Glinka was from the beginning altogether more fluent—but also more
cautious, for those he wrote when barely out of his teens were mostly
uncomplicated sentimental romances, and though he continued to compose songs for the rest of his life, it was with diminishing productivity
and little broadening of style. His later songs do show rather more
variety, but to the end his most typical examples unfolded elegantly
expressive melodies which might be 'sung from the heart', supported
by clear bass lines, with harmonic filling supplied through simply patterned quaver accompaniments. Only rarely (though sometimes star-
tlingly) were there sorties beyond the conventional stylistic and
expressive bounds of the salon.

The truth is that Musorgsky began almost as though the songs of
Glinka, Alyabyev, and even Dargomïzhsky up to the time when Musorgsky first had contact with him, had scarcely existed. Yet to have had
direct acquaintance with a composer of such restless enterprise as the
last must have fortified his confidence in following his own creative
impulses. Rough Dargomïzhsky's technique might at times be (like Alyabyev's) and his style uncertain, but what might otherwise be banal
could be enlivened by asymmetries of phrasing, by harmonic experiment, and by an alert instinct to grasp at any opportunity for dramatic
projection. In this they are the opposite of the fifteen or so songs Ba-

lakirev composed between 1858 and 1860, his period of closest contact with Musorgsky. Always these are polished, rounded conceptions which treat the text decently, but there are few signs of the true song composer's response either to the actuality of the words or the resonances within them. Indeed, the definition set out earlier of the typical Glinka romance could well fit many of Balakirev's early songs.

Not so with Musorgsky. True, of the score of songs composed before the epoch-making *Darling Savishna* of 1866, seven are explicitly designated as romances; all set love poems. But the music of few of the others could sit comfortably within this category. Three are marked 'pesnya' (literally, 'song'), a label used for tougher-toned songs, in these instances a remembrance of a dead beloved, a sombre nature description, and an heroic monologue. Some others are given individual labels: 'a musical tale', 'fantasia', 'a study in folk style', 'an experiment in recitative', and so on. Their variety, both in the subjects treated and in their treatments, is remarkable. In fact, the main point in observing the song tradition Musorgsky inherited is to underline how swiftly he became independent of it. And yet, paradoxically, his earliest surviving song (designated in one source 'rustic song') does appear to owe a heavy debt to Balakirev. It is also one of the most interesting—and one of the most problematic. *Where art thou, little star?*, Nikolay Grekov's lament of a lover for his beloved, was composed 'for the album' of Isabella Grunberg, the song's dedicatee and a singer who had won Glinka's plaudits for her performances of his songs. Musorgsky had met Isabella through Dargomïzhsky. In the Paris manuscript of *Where art thou, little star?* Musorgsky inserted '1857', but the grossly inferior version designated for Isabella's album is yet more precisely dated ('30 April 1857'), and it was this version, slightly revised, that Musorgsky orchestrated in June 1858. Several scholars have been troubled by this choice, and Richard Taruskin is surely right to suggest that the Paris version, while recording the original year of composition (as was Musorgsky's custom when making later copies), was in fact a drastic and textually shortened revision prompted by examination of Balakirev's much later transcriptions and arrangements of genuine Russian folksongs,[3] was undertaken

---

[3] These were published in 1866.

no earlier than 1864, and was copied into the Paris manuscript in early 1866.[4]

Yet *Where art thou, little star?* is not an arrangement but an original composition, though heavily conditioned by that genre of folkmusic which, to the outsider, sounds the most intrinsically Russian: the 'pro-tyazhnaya pesnya', or 'melismatic song'. In such songs the phrases are much varied in rhythmic structure and may be highly ornamented, though a new phrase is often built around an earlier contour, just as the first two in Musorgsky's central section (Ex. 4.1*b*) reflect the outlines of those that open the song (Ex. 4.1*a*), but with their order now re-versed. While Musorgsky's rate of harmonic change is mostly slow and measured (a characteristic at times reinforced by pedals), there are also dislocations which emphasize that the harmonic rhythm may be sub-ordinate to the judgement of what best suits each in this trail of one-bar phrases—for instance, the bass drop on the second half-beat in bar 1 of Ex. 4.1*c*, which strongly foretells the chord change on the following quaver, or the sudden burst of harmonic activity in the following bar. True, neither the piano's modulation to the relative major for the central section, nor the cadence into a clear F sharp major phrase as the voice part finally dies, nor the touches of word-painting (a dark diminished triad on 'threatening', an octave plunge on 'cold') are of a folk culture, but their intrusion is hardly disruptive.

Where art thou, little star? must rate among Musorgsky's most shapely songs, and even in its crude original form it was a notable venture for so inexperienced a composer who had not yet come under Balakirev's tutelage. None of its immediate successors can match it for imaginative boldness. Musorgsky dedicated his roistering setting of Koltsov's *Hour of Jollity* (a 'drinking song') to Vasily Zakharin, a naval officer and am-ateur singer whom he was to introduce into the Balakirev circle in May

---

[4] See R. Taruskin, ' "Little Star": an Etude in the Folk Style', *MIM*, 57–84 (repr. in *TM*, 38–70). In instances where another autograph offered a different version of a particular song Pavel Lamm, in his edition of 'Years of Youth' (Moscow and Vienna, 1931), either recorded in footnotes the variants in the non-Paris version(s) or else printed both versions in full, always describing the Paris text as the 'first version'. In fact, in three instances (*Where art thou, little star?*, *Hour of Jollity*, and *Kalistratushka*) Lamm's 'second version' is almost certainly the earlier. In three cases, however (*King Saul*, *Night*, and *Lullaby*), the 'second version' is based on the text printed by Bessel in 1871, the proofs of which Musorgsky himself corrected. Here the order is the true one.

Ex. 4.1a

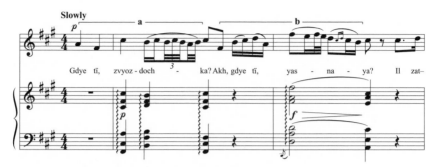

[Where art thou, little star? Ah, where art thou, bright one?]

Ex. 4.1b

[Where art thou, maiden? Where art thou, beautiful one?]

1859 and at whose home he enjoyed musical assemblies that supplemented those at Balakirev's. One manuscript source assigns the song to 10 May 1859, but the Paris version, though dated 1858, must be a later revision, for it pursues a less inhibited tonal course and has a more characterful accompaniment.

In sharpest contrast *Tell me why*, dated 12 August 1858 in St Petersburg on Musorgsky's return from the Mengden marriage and inscribed to the bride's mother, Zinaida Burtseva, is an old-fashioned sentimental romance. Perhaps Musorgsky felt his dedicatee, whose daughter had just quit the parental home, might be especially sensitive to the predicament of a young girl reflecting sadly on the imminent departure of her beloved for a distant land; whatever the case, it drew from Mu-

Ex. 4.1c

dru - ga mi - lo - vo, dru - ga mi - lo - vo ne - na -

glyad - no - vo?

[[Or have you deserted] your dear friend, your dear beloved friend?]

sorgsky a flow of gentle and touching invention and became among the earliest of his songs to be published (in 1867). Its most characteristic feature is the extended pedal that closes the central section. Even more prophetic are some of the tiny pedal passages in *Sadly rustled the leaves* of 1859. To conjure Pleshcheyev's nocturnal, graveside world in this 'musical tale' Musorgsky employed the quietest of barely moving textures haunted by the gently varied ghost of a measured, funereal phrase; only the brief recall of the burial itself momentarily breaks the surrounding stillness. Alyabyev's generation had become aware of Schubert, and one root of *Sadly rustled the leaves* drew up elements of the German lied tradition; certainly this song inhabits a world beyond the cosy walls of the salon. Also to a small degree redolent of the lied is the setting of the first part of Ammosov's at first bitter, then tender, love lyric, *What are words of love to you?*, though Schumann is the composer whose presence might—though only momentarily—be suspected here. Composed in 1860 and dedicated to Mariya Shilovskaya at whose Glebovo home Musorgsky had passed much of the summer, this highly charged romance may well have autobiographical resonances.

For a composer still as inexperienced as Musorgsky these first songs are even more impressive collectively than singly, for they already reveal a song composer of rare instinct, capable of tackling a very wide range of moods, sentiments, and manner. He seems to have written no more songs for some three years, and when he did resume there had been a marked shift in his style. Stasov attributed the decline in his productivity between 1861 and 1863 to the distractions produced for the family by the Emancipation. But Musorgsky was certainly not entirely unproductive, and at Volok from March to May 1862 he laboured on at his D major Symphony and began a two-piano transcription of Beethoven's Quartet in B flat, Op. 130. He also read philosophy, prattled by post to Balakirev about the effect of a change of environment on his mental condition and about the need to work—and awaited the eruption of the Russian spring. He struck up an acquaintance with the Prussian tutor to his landlady's children, a tolerable pianist who enthusiastically played Bach fugues for him (which must have been the source of those 'current musical preoccupations' which had conditioned his *Intermezzo in modo classico*), who sent him a spring rose and a poem on his birthday, then took him for '*promenades monstres*' through deep snowdrifts to counter the sluggish circulation to which the Prussian attributed Musorgsky's semi-somnolent condition.

Despite Musorgsky engaging in one of his customary bouts of self-analysis at Volok, there is little sign that he was in need of medical treatment either of body or mind, and this consolidates the suspicion that he may have been avoiding the trials that would have confronted him in the upheavals at Karevo, where Filaret had been in charge since his own resignation from the army in 1860. Where Musorgsky passed the summer is unknown, though he reappeared in St Petersburg in October, just ahead of Balakirev. The latter had spent the earlier part of 1862 launching the Free Music School (FMS) which, with the composer and choral conductor Gavriil Lomakin, he had founded in rivalry to the RMS as a base for musical tuition and concerts; exhausted from his labours, Balakirev had left St Petersburg for a cure in the Caucasus and been absent until late October. Now the two men's meetings and their more corporate musical occupations could resume. In November, as a newly graduated midshipman, Rimsky-Korsakov left on a cruise which would take him away from Russia for two-and-a-half years, but his place was filled for a while by Borodin, who had just met Balakirev and whom the latter immediately set to compose a symphony. Only now did Borodin confess to Musorgsky that he also composed.

In 1871 Musorgsky set down for Lyudmila Shestakova a brief account of his creative progress to date. Of 1862 he wrote simply: 'I set my brains in order and furnished them with valuable pieces of information'.[5] Certainly it seems to have been a year of consolidation, the fruits of which were also reflected in his piano playing which impressed Borodin with its new brilliance and intelligence. The only other visible product was a transcription for voice and piano of Balakirev's song with orchestra, *Georgian Song*; this was published before the year's end. But 1863 was to be very different. Musorgsky's personality was rapidly beginning to manifest traits that could prove wearisome, even exasperating, to others. By early March Cui was begging Balakirev to come and deliver him and his wife 'from the over-dose of Modinka with which we are threatened'.[6] His creative independence was also becoming disconcerting. 'Modinka has created a kind of musical monster, supposedly as a trio for his scherzo', Cui wrote to Rimsky-Korsakov on 4 May. ' . . . There are interminable ecclesiastical melodies and the usual Modinka pedals and such-like; all this is inarticulate, strange, clumsy, and just not a trio.'[7] In May Stasov encountered Musorgsky at the theatre and was appalled by the banality of his conversation. 'Everything about him is flabby, colourless. I think he's a complete *idiot*. Yesterday I could have hit him. I think that if you left him without someone to look after him, suddenly plucked him from the sphere into which you have dragged him by force and gave his own inclination and tastes their freedom, he would quickly grass over like everybody else. There's noth-

[5] *MLN1*, 263.

[6] *TDM*, 104.

[7] A. S. Lyapunova, ed., *N. Rimsky-Korsakov: Polnoye sobraniye sochineny: literaturnïye proizvedeniya i perepiska* [Complete edition: literary works and correspondence], v (Moscow, 1962), 246. The trio in question appears no longer to exist.

ing in him.'[8] Balakirev was hardly less sparing: 'Musorgsky is almost an idiot', he replied.[9]

In fact, Borodin had barely joined the kuchka than it became apparent that the group's high season was over. While Balakirev found on the one hand that the new FMS was making growing demands on his time, on the other he was realizing increasingly that he had no true personal closeness with Cui, that Musorgsky was growing musically incompatible with him, and that he had lost Rimsky-Korsakov for a very long period. Borodin, who had already laid the foundations for a distinguished scientific career, had received an appointment in the Medico-Surgical Academy and was becoming more and more absorbed by scientific commitments. Only Stasov remained close to him.

Musorgsky spent the summer of 1863 on home ground at Toropets and then at Volok. The previous year Filaret had married and settled in St Petersburg, and it was Modest upon whom supervision of the affairs of the estate devolved during the middle months of 1863, the year of the actual Emancipation. The problems he now had to confront were daunting. In the new social structure that had developed he observed the peasants with healthy respect. '[They] are far more capable than the landowners of setting their self-government in order. In meetings they come straight to the point of their business and *in their own way* discuss their interests sensibly', he wrote to Balakirev on 22 June. His view of their former masters was very different. 'At assemblies the landowners quarrel, get on their high horses. The aim of the assembly and the business are set aside.'[10] To Cui he described in detail the disorder that still prevailed, unleashing the full force of his feelings about his own class's behaviour, and describing the consequences for himself and his work:[11]

> I had thought to occupy myself with respectable matters, but here it's conducting *investigations*, making *enquiries*, and dragging oneself around a variety of government departments, both police and non-police . . . If mother weren't also in Toropets I would go quite crazy from this ridiculous situa-

[8] *TDM*, 106.

[9] Ibid.

[10] *MLN1*, 70.

[11] *MLN1*, 70–2.

tion. It's only this lady who keeps me tied down here; she's terribly pleased I'm here with her, and it gives me pleasure to give her this happiness. And what landlords we have here—what planters! They exult in the club they've established in the town, and they congregate there almost every day *to make noise*. The business opens *with speeches*, with *declarations* to the *gentlemen of the gentry*, and every time it comes near to blows so that you feel like calling the police. One of the main ranters has constant squabbles with the mediator, this mediator being his scapegoat; the ranter drives around the town and collects (for Christ's sake!) signatures for the removal of the mediator. Lacking powers of persuasion, another ranter *whose wits are afflicted* reinforces his arguments by raising his fists in the air which sooner or later *land on their target*. And all this takes place at the assembly of the gentry and you meet with these people every day, every day they tearfully torment you with *their lost rights, their total ruin*. [It's all] howling and groans and scandal! The gentry are allowed to assemble—and *they assemble*: they are allowed to stand up for their own affairs and the affairs of the *zemstvo* [district council]—and they *stand up*—what's more, with fists and strong words. *Make a fool pray to God, and he'll [end in] beat[ing] in his forehead!* And likewise they'll go on talking about their lost rights. True, there are decent young *fellows*, but I rarely see them; these young people are the ones who *do the negotiating*, and so they're always on their travels. And I, great sinner that I am, spin round in *this above-mentioned, lavatorial atmosphere*. A lavatorial atmosphere rarely touches the finer instincts; you think only of how not to make a smell or suffocate (how can you think of music here!). And so you try to go rarely *to the lavatorial club*; if you do go, then only *out of necessity*. Forgive the comparison.

The other day I came across some short verses by Goethe; I rejoiced— *and set them to music* . . . I shan't be able to compose anything more; thanks to the manager, my head finds itself *at the police department*—though composing small pieces is possible.

The 'small verses by Goethe' were the second of the Harper's songs (*An die Türen*) from *Wilhelm Meister*; the translation may well have been Musorgsky's own. He was proud enough of one six-bar phrase (bars 18–23) in *Old Man's Song*, as he called it, to quote it in full for Cui in a letter of 4 July, then add: 'The subject of Goethe's words is *a beggar*, I believe from *Wilhelm Meister*; *a beggar could sing my music without dis-*

comfort.[12] Already Musorgsky sensed he had succeeded in forming an idiom that might faithfully project the very essence of one of humanity's outcasts of a sort who daily confronted him in real life and who would soon become a central concern in his creative life.

Musorgsky could certainly take much pride in a good deal else in this setting. Thus instead of the first quatrain being set squarely as four two-bar phrases building a conventional eight-bar sentence, the third phrase is echoed (though newly directed) by the piano, delaying the fourth by two bars and producing an asymmetry which 'opens up' the end for the piano to take over and extend very naturally this final phrase into an unexpected central climax. Yet it is perhaps the tone of the piece that is most significant; already the composer of *Boris Godunov* is in prospect.

The Paris autograph, the only complete source of *Old Man's Song*, bears the date 25 August 1863. By then Musorgsky had left Toropets; two days later he was back in Volok, where he had spent some time early in 1862. On that day (27 August) *But if I could meet thee again*, a romance to a text by Kurochkin, was finished. The preamble is muted, even hesitant, and the powerful span that singer and pianist go on to build could scarcely be predicted from so modest an opening; clearly this song will be less formal than any of its predecessors. The preamble returns, the singer now uncovering its deeper meaning as he at last takes up the words of the song's title, then briefly shifts to a more declamatory, breathless manner before a climactic arching phrase of anguish prompts a further return of the song's opening plea. For Musorgsky the text is becoming less a secure framework for a rounded musical form than an equal partner in shaping a structure in which expressive shifts or details may be more pointedly presented. It is left to the piano to provide, Schumann-like, the last stage in an extended coda that insists freely upon the singer's yearning phrase.

I have many palaces and gardens, also labelled a romance (the lyric is by Koltsov), could scarcely be in greater contrast. The drinking song *Hour of Jollity* had shown Musorgsky capable of straightforward, robust melody, but his handling of this outburst from a potentate rich in possessions but poor in love is far more characterful. Its strength comes

[12] *MLN1*, 72.

from an accompaniment in which driving quavers are the dominant feature, though the melodic shapes these trace are restlessly changing and the impetus is constantly dislocated. The governing principle is two-part counterpoint (or heterophony) between voice and piano; full triads are sparingly used, and when an harmonic texture occurs it never so thickens as to impede momentum. *What are words of love to you?* had also turned suddenly from impassioned rhetoric to pained self-disclosure, but the initial virility of this new song makes the vulnerability suddenly uncovered in the concluding slow section the more contrasting and arresting.

I have many palaces was composed in St Petersburg—whether in the earlier or later part of 1863 is unknown, though the latter seems more probable. *King Saul*, a setting of Kozlov's translation of Byron's *Song of Saul before his Last Battle*, was written at some time between the end of August and mid-October while Musorgsky was at Volok, and was one of three songs that would be published eight years later. Writing in 1881, Stasov described *King Saul* as 'the best and most up-to-date romance of his [Musorgsky's] first period. Twenty [in fact, eighteen] years have already passed since then, but the impression of strength, passion, beauty, and vitality present in it remains unchanged in our own time. It is repeatedly performed in concerts by all our best singers.'[13] The song was a real gift to such: the declaration of a ruler who is heroic, yet human. Stasov's singers would, of course, have known only the published edition, but the Paris autograph presents a version that is far bolder and already—as is clear from the directions for scoring that it contains—envisaged as with orchestral accompaniment, an intention Musorgsky finally realized in January 1879. We can only assume that in 1871 caution (or pressure from the publisher Bessel) persuaded him to tame his 1863 original and also compress it. As published, the piece was transposed down a tone, and the more formidable difficulties of the piano part were eased. But it was not just a question of thinning notes or rewriting textures: harmonic structures were altered and bars deleted, and both the words and music of the last stanza (Saul's address to his son) were virtually rewritten, as was the coda, which was drastically shortened to end *fortissimo* instead of dying away. 109 bars became 82.

---

[13] *SMPM* (see *SSM3*, 64).

Enough remained, however, to alarm the more nervous: the chords in bars 2–3 of Ex. 4.2b, for instance. Yet the original was more uncompromising still, as Ex. 4.2a, the link corresponding to that in Ex. 4.2b, shows. Even allowing for Stasov's partisan hyperbole, it is clear that there were performers and audiences who could take Musorgsky's music on its own terms, but there were others, even enlightened musicians, who clearly thought that such passages exceeded the degree of tolerance allowable within current musical syntax. Such passages may no longer trouble us, yet it seems the issue is not entirely settled. So with these two extracts before us, this seems as good a moment as any to grasp the nettle, though this is but one tiny example from among a multitude that might have been sifted from Musorgsky's output.

Above all, it is Musorgsky's harmony that has caused most upset. It has been described rightly, as empirical: but is it arbitrary, in that, how-

Ex. 4.2a

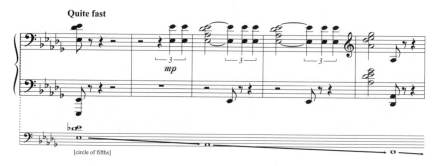

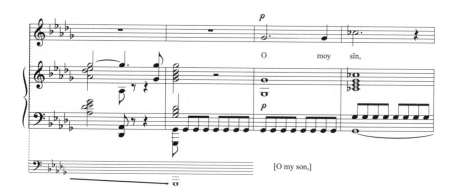

Ex. 4.2b

[O my son, my heir! Already to battle...]

ever often the experience is repeated the ear cannot come to accept its rightness? The answer is: rarely, if ever. True, individual dissonances may be employed as momentary expressive shocks, and seconds and seventh chords (and especially that of the added sixth) may be elevated to autonomous status. But in most instances what may initially appear irrational can be heard as a reasonable, if radical extension of established syntax. Approached thus, few problems will be encountered in the revised passage (Ex. 4.2b), since each dissonance finds its ultimate resolution by step: the A♯ appearing in bars 2–3 can be taken as a long-held upper auxiliary to G♯ with its note of resolution continuing to sound; the D♯ in bar 1 is the first intimation of a dominant being formed (confirmed by the bass G♯ in bar 2); the D♯ in bar 3 is an appoggiatura resolving conventionally to C♯ in bar 4.

But Ex. 4.2a is a tougher nut to crack. It begins with a partially formed dominant seventh of A♭, but when A♭ is inserted into the middle of the texture in bar 3, D♭ remains unresolved (this will ultimately turn out to have become an internal pedal), and in bar 5 the addition of a further dissonance, G♭, introduces for half a bar a suggestion of a dominant seventh of D♭, with a raised third. This receives some support at the half-bar, where the bass drops to D♭. But the repetition of this bar helps suggest an alternative function: that the prevailing harmony may be a dominant eleventh of G♭—which is precisely what the next bar confirms, for it is a G♭ triad that emerges as the long-term destination of the whole passage.

But there is a further intriguing point about this passage. The diad of A♭ and D♭ in bar 3, though harmonically incompatible with E♭, nevertheless introduces the two intervening pitches in a circle of fifths targeted on G♭ (see the editorial stave in Ex. 4.2a)—and in bars 5 and 6 these two pitches become the fifth in the LH that engineers the shift of key to G♭. Did Musorgsky (un)consciously choose these two pitches for vertical use in bars 3 and 4 because he had this impending, time-honoured function in mind for them? No one can say. Yet the possibility should prompt us to be cautious when assuming a degree of unmitigated empiricism in some of Musorgsky's more radical harmonic procedures. Whatever the case, his ear (and almost certainly he would have composed this at the piano) knew perfectly well what it was doing.

King Saul was a landmark—a creation whose eruption into this world could hardly have been guessed from Musorgsky's earlier songs, for all their variety and lively enterprise. Even in the revised, domesticated version there was much to make pundits shudder. One thing is certain: in this song the Musorgsky who, five years hence, would begin creating *Boris Godunov*, opens a vein of tragic heroism that would be mined further in that masterpiece.

Salammbô

ONE CONSEQUENCE OF THE PHENOMENAL EXPANSION OF MU-
sic history studies since World War II has been the toppling of
those titans who were once confidently credited with having, unaided,
created a form or founded a movement. No one today asserts, as some
did within living memory, that Monteverdi invented opera, Haydn (or
C. P. E. Bach) devised sonata form, or that Beethoven created Roman-
ticism. Yet to say that Mikhail Glinka singlehanded laid the foundations
of the Russian musical tradition as a distinct component of Western
music is nothing other than the truth. It was an achievement the more
remarkable because Glinka's list of seminally important works is so meagre: two operas, plus incidental music for a play, four brief orchestral
pieces, and a clutch of songs. Nor would Glinka have seemed capable,
either through force of personal character or depth of musical mind, of
such influence. Born into the landowning class in 1804, he received no
more than a fitful, unsystematic instruction in music while at school in
St Petersburg, and he exercised his musical talents in the 1820s mainly
as a composer of attractive, neatly turned piano pieces and affecting
romances to be performed privately for friends or within the city's salons
and coteries.

Glinka's Rubicon was crossed, appropriately, in Italy, where he headed
in 1830 to gratify his passion for Italian opera. Within two years he had
discovered that neither Italy nor Italian music was truly for him: 'a longing for my own country led me gradually to the idea of writing in a Rus-

sian manner', he recalled some twenty years later.[1] In 1833, now 29, he delayed nearly six months in Berlin for the only systematic training in composition he ever undertook. Yet within three years of his return to Russia he had given his 'dear compatriots' the opera in which they would feel 'at home'. And with *A Life for the Tsar*, the tale of how a Russian peasant, Ivan Susanin, sacrificed himself to save the founder of the Romanov dynasty, the true Russian musical tradition was born.

Yet what fired Glinka's imagination was less the patriotism reflected in this incident than its simple, stirring, and touching drama. And what so impressed the next generation of Russian composers about the resulting opera was not that it was monarchist[2] or even pointedly national, nor that it incorporated folksongs, or was the first Russian opera to dispense with spoken dialogue, but that in it music penetrated to every level of the drama, and that its melodic content was impregnated with a Russianness whose source might lie in folksong but had been so transmuted that its products were far from being folksong pastiche. It was the *musical* precedents and suggestions that others might follow or evolve for their own purposes that made Glinka's first opera one of the most seminal of all Russian compositions.

His second opera, *Ruslan and Lyudmila*, was to show in every way a more polished, assured, sometimes brilliant musical mastery. The work's problems lay in the scenario whose defects, and sometimes plain absurdities, are self-evident to any audience. No matter: Pushkin's *Ruslan and Lyudmila* was an enchanted tale that stimulated parts of Glinka's protean imagination which the real-life story of Ivan Susanin could not reach, and the result was music that was bolder still: fantastic, dazzling, sultry, at times passionate, at others touching, on occasion brilliantly bizarre. If *A Life for the Tsar* had established a many-sided 'human' style firmly grounded in the real world, *Ruslan and Lyudmila* created more extravagant, exotic idioms

---

[1] M. Glinka, *Zapiski* [Memoirs]. Printed in A.S. Lyapunova [edit.]. *M.I. Glinka: Literaturnïye proizvedeniya i perepiska* [Literary works and correspondence], i (Moscow, 1973), 260.

[2] This story was, of course, a splendid vehicle for furthering 'official nationalism', the doctrine of monarchical glorification invented by Nikolay I's minister of education, Sergey Uvarov, and this accounts for much of the court's enthusiasm for the piece. But if, in recognizing this, we learn much about the motivations of the poet and courtier, Vasily Zhukovsky, who proposed the subject to Glinka and wrote some of the libretto, we learn precious little about Glinka.

conjuring a kaleidoscopic realm of fantasy; it presented heroic and oriental idioms, it paraded examples of creative musical caricature, and it evolved further structures appropriate to the particular needs of Russian composers. All this was avidly devoured by the next generation, each member—Balakirev, Borodin, Rimsky-Korsakov, Tchaikovsky—taking from Glinka what he needed. And Musorgsky too, especially now that he was about to venture upon his most ambitious project to date.

But in 1863 even more crucial for Musorgsky was the première in May of another opera—*Judith* by Alexander Serov. Serov has remained unknown outside his native Russia, but for some Russians of his own time he was (or was about to become) their greatest living composer. Half German and with some Jewish blood, he had been born in 1820 and until 1851 had held a government post, confining his musical activities to those of a talented dilettante. During the 1850s, however, he began supporting himself as a music critic, building a huge reputation for being both readable and contentious. But it was *Judith* that made Serov truly famous. Its plot was from the Apocrypha: to defeat the Assyrians who were besieging the Jews in Bethulia, Judith, a chieftain's widow, enters the enemy camp, seduces and decapitates their leader, Holofernes, then returns to her own people to display the head on Bethulia's walls so that the demoralized Assyrians flee. The story was strong religious meat, the opera's reception was rapturous—and the piece was thoroughly digested by Musorgsky, who wrote a lengthy critique of it to Balakirev. This required that any enthusiasm should be guarded, for two years earlier Serov had passed the score of the first act of *Judith* to Balakirev for comment, and had received a devastating verdict. But it is clear that Musorgsky, having attended the première, had been more taken by the piece than he cared to admit. Certainly he had returned for a second performance, and in writing to Balakirev from Toropets he could recall the whole opera very precisely, even quoting bits. True, his preamble was blistering enough to reassure his correspondent that *Judith* had not seduced him, but his acknowledgement of the opera's significance ('all the same, *Judith* is the first seriously composed opera on the Russian stage since [Dargomïzhsky's] *Rusalka*'[3])

---

[3] *MLN1*, 64.

confirms that it had aroused not only his interest but his respect. There can be no doubt that it was Serov's piece that would decide him before the year was out to attempt operatic composition for himself.

Meanwhile there were pressing problems in Musorgsky's broader existence in consequence of the Emancipation. Since 1862, when his mother had given up her apartment in St Petersburg, he had been forced, when in the capital, to live with Filaret and his new wife. But that was not the end of his problems, and in March 1862 he had confessed to Balakirev that, besides intending to devote himself to composition, he was 'looking for a further kind of occupation where I would be useful'.[4] Maybe idealism had first motivated this urge to contribute constructively to the emergent new society, but within a year more material pressures were operating; the loss of estate income had been disastrous, and paid employment became a necessity. Back in St Petersburg in the autumn of 1863 he searched for a possible post, and in December became a civil servant with the rank of collegiate secretary in the Central Engineering Directorate.

In his life style an equally abrupt change occurred which Stasov recorded in his biography:[5]

> In the autumn of 1863, on returning from the country, he moved with several young comrades into shared accommodation which they jokingly called a 'commune', perhaps in imitation of that theory of communal living preached in *What is to be done?*, the novel [by Chernïshevsky] that was famous at that time. Each comrade had his own separate room which none of the other comrades dared enter at any time without special permission, and there was also one large common room where, once they were free of their own occupations, they all gathered of an evening to read, listen to reading, to converse, argue—finally, simply to talk or listen to Musorgsky playing the piano or singing romances and extracts from operas. At that time there were not a few such small communes in St Petersburg, and maybe in the rest of Russia also. In the present circle there were six comrades in all ... All were highly intelligent and educated people; each of them engaged in some favourite scientific or artistic occupation despite many of them working in the Senate or [one of the] Ministries; none of

[4] *MLN1*, 59.
[5] *SMPM* (see *SSM3*, 65–6).

them wanted to be intellectually idle, and each viewed with disdain that sybaritic, empty, idle life which, till now, the majority of Russian youth had so long led . . . Their [former] family life—semi-patriarchal, with its old-fashioned hospitality, its provision of food and entertainment as the priority of life, as almost a sacred rite, with everything familiar, with dropping-in-from-having-nothing-to-do—was over. There began a life of the intellect, active, with real interests, with aspirations to work and apply oneself to the task. And these three years which these young people lived through in this new way were, by their own accounts, one of the best times in their whole lives. For Musorgsky in particular. The exchange of thoughts, of knowledge, of impressions from what was read, built up for him the basis upon which he lived out his remaining years; at this time that unclouded view of what was 'true' and 'false', what was 'good' and 'bad', became for ever established—a view that he never subsequently betrayed.

There is a Utopian glow to Stasov's view of this communal existence, with its sweet purposefulness. Nor does this image of Musorgsky, the unswerving epitome of all that was ideal and virtuous, fit easily with the bald facts of his later life—or, indeed, with Stasov's own recorded observations during Musorgsky's lifetime. But just as saints are commonly easier to live with after they are dead, in 1881 Stasov could quietly grant Musorgsky canonization; the dross could be brushed away and the ikon burnished so that its surface might reflect such positive tones as Stasov chose to project upon it.

It was in this new environment that Musorgsky set about his opera *Salammbô*. Gustave Flaubert's novel was hot in every sense. It had been published in Paris only the previous year, but had been instantly translated into Russian. *Salammbô*, however, was not only new; it was sensational. Though its setting and most of its main participants were drawn from the historian Polybius's account of the conflict between Carthage and her mercenaries following the ending of the first Punic War in 241 BC, Flaubert made the central action of *Salammbô* derive from the obsession of Mâtho, a Libyan freeman, with the Carthaginian priestess, Salammbô (the one major character of the book who was Flaubert's own invention). After political rupture has led to the mercenaries laying siege to Carthage itself, Mâtho, guided by Spendius, a runaway slave, secretly re-enters the city to see Salammbô again, and also to steal the mantle of Tanit (the goddess of love and the moon), which is the talisman on which Carthage's security depends. Mâtho is cursed by Salammbô as he snatches the mantle, and in her turn she penetrates the enemy camp to ensnare Mâtho and regain the talisman (the parallels with *Judith* are unmissable). After the mercenaries' defeat, the captured Mâtho is loosed to the vengeance of the populace. On the verge of death from their assaults, he finally comes face to face with Salammbô, who is awakened to the ambivalence of her own feelings, and perishes with him.

Yet *Salammbô* is much more than just an historical romance. To describe it as a *War and Peace* of the ancient world would be absurd—yet, as in Tolstoy's as-yet-unwritten novel, the events that these characters create or into which they are caught unfold against a background of cataclysmic conflict, epic descriptions of which comprise a large part of the book. The virtuosity of these vast yet detailed, accurate yet artificial, spectacles is extraordinary, recalling less the mammoth, lifeless canvases of great historical or mythical events favoured by Flaubert's compatriot painters than the panoramic, choreographed set pieces of the biblical epics once beloved of Hollywood. But, accurate as may be their broader content, as processed by Flaubert they are as synthetic as these cinematic creations, their stylized orderliness distancing them sufficiently from brute reality for revulsion to yield to fascination. Without such softening, some of the descriptions of battle or of the dreadful scene in which the desperate Carthaginians burn their own children alive in sacrifice to Moloch would be insufferable. It is no surprise that Flaubert's novel was condemned by some as sadistic.

And these titanic events in turn condition the individuals whose destinies are fated to evolve within them. Flaubert's characters emerge as both larger yet simpler than life, less flesh-and-blood mortals than emblems of heroism or cruelty, subterfuge, decadence, lasciviousness, sexual allure, or desire, able the more easily to grab the attention of young men in search of exciting new experiences and sensations. Together the members of the commune devoured the novel, and Musorgsky saw in it a splendid subject for an opera. The settings could be magnificent, the opportunities for spectacular and powerful crowd scenes were abundant, and each major character, while being well outlined, was without that diversity of trait that might have demanded more subtlety and understanding than he yet had it in him to provide. Whether he mapped out a full scenario is unknown, but, like Glinka before him, he clearly set about scenes or incidents as they fired his imagination. He devised his own libretto as he went along (though drawing in verses by Zhukovsky, Maykov, and Polezhayev), and before 1863 was out he could sign the vocal score of the scene in the temple of Tanit, which he designated as the second scene of Act 2. The following year saw the completion of the first scenes of Acts 3 and 4. After this, however, Musorgsky's enthusiasm crumpled, and only fragments of the remainder are extant, the last from early 1866. Most were left unorchestrated.

Nevertheless, well over an hour's music was composed in full, enough to tell us much about Musorgsky's basic operatic instincts and gifts, and to uncover some of his characteristics. A list of surviving materials follows. All are in vocal score (dates of completion are given where recorded by Musorgsky at the end of each, and the existence of a full score is also noted). To provide a context, portions of plot left uncomposed, but which Musorgsky could not possibly have passed over, are given in square brackets:

Act 1 [The Feast. In Hamilcar's garden in Carthage the mercenaries are celebrating the anniversary of their victory at Eryx.] During this is heard the 'Song of the Balearic Soldier' (August 1864)[6] and, presumably, the 'Libyan War Song' for men's chorus (22 April 1866; full score, 29 June 1866). [The mercenaries' discontent with their recompense grows. Meeting of Mâtho and Spendius. Mâtho's first sight of Salammbô, daughter of Hamilcar, high priestess[7] of Tanit and guardian of the goddess's sacred mantle. The Numidian prince Narr'Havas is also attracted to her. Mâtho and Narr'Havas quarrel, but are reconciled.]

Act 2, Scene 1 [Revolt of the mercenaries. Spendius reveals to Mâtho that Tanit's sacred mantle is a talisman guaranteeing the security of Carthage. He tells Mâtho of a secret route to the temple of Tanit. Mâtho resolves to see Salammbô again and steal the mantle.]

Act 2, Scene 2 This entire scene survives (27 December 1863). The interior of the Temple of Tanit in Carthage. Night. As the moon appears, Salammbô invokes

---

[6] There exists also a piano transcription of the first half of the 'Song of the Balearic Soldier'. Whether this was intended as an orchestral interlude is unknown.

[7] In Flaubert's novel Salammbô is simply a priestess of Tanit.

Tanit, bows down before her image ('Ritual Scene'), then falls asleep on the catafalque. Her priestesses enter singing a hymn to Tanit. Mâtho and Spendius appear, then hide until the priestesses have withdrawn. Mâtho is enchanted by Salammbô then, urged on by Spendius, he snatches the mantle. Salammbô awakes and Mâtho pleads his love. Seeing he has the mantle, Salammbô curses him. She invokes the goddess's vengeance, and Mâtho and Spendius leave. Salammbô strikes the alarm and her twelve priestesses rush in, followed by more women and soldiers. Salammbô recounts what has happened. All call for vengeance, curse Mâtho, and beg Tanit's protection.

Act 3, Scene 1 This entire scene survives (at the end of the adoration of Moloch: 4 August 1864—at the end of the whole scene, 22 November 1864). *The Temple of Moloch.* In front of the temple a gigantic statue of Moloch, and on the right the sacred grove of Eschmoun. On stage the people, priests, musicians (an onstage orchestra), and children who surround the high priest, Aminakhar. A storm in prospect. The priests of Moloch and the children who are about to be sacrificed to appease Moloch beg the god for mercy. The people join in. The storm draws nearer, then breaks. The statue of Moloch begins to glow red, and the people in terror take refuge in the grove of Eschmoun. Suddenly the storm abates. The high priest declares Moloch will give them victory, the priests line up in procession with torches, then leave. Alone, Salammbô bewails the loss of Tanit's mantle, calling down vengeance on the thief. The crowd hear her prayer and reappear. Salammbô resolves to go to the enemy camp to recover the talisman. The crowd are impressed, their confidence begins to return, and they pray for her safety as she leaves.

Act 3, Scene 2 [In Mâtho's tent. Salammbô arrives to recover the mantle, seduces Mâtho, and leaves with it. Probably ends with the Carthaginian attack, Narr'Havas's treachery, the defeat of the mercenaries, and Mâtho's capture.]

Act 4, Scene 1 This entire scene survives (8 December 1864; full score is undated). *A dungeon beneath the Acropolis.* Mâtho in chains. He laments his predicament and Spendius's death while defending him, curses Narr'Havas for betraying him after Hamilcar has promised the Numidian Salammbô's hand in marriage, and even more bitterly reproaches Salammbô for her treachery. But he will confront his fate with fortitude. Aminakhar and priests

enter to reveal the terrible end that awaits him. They leave, and Mâtho
reflects grimly on what he will face.

Act 4, Scene 2 'Chorus of Priestesses' (20 February 1866). The priestesses
comfort Salammbô as they array her in her wedding clothes. [Torture of
Mathô, his last encounter with Salammbô, and their deaths (all this perhaps
in a separate scene)]

Salammbô could never have been a masterpiece, and there need be no
regrets it remained a torso. But, that said, what strikes so strongly is its
sheer precocity. Set the music of *Salammbô* beside that of *Judith*, and the
gulf separating the dramatic gifts of Musorgsky and Serov is instantly
exposed. *Judith* may have prompted Musorgsky to try operatic composition for himself, and its subject certainly conditioned his own
choice, but of musical debt there is virtually none (curiously, such direct
influence as *Judith* did have on him may be detected more in *Boris
Godunov*). There is no trace of the Italian tradition, and though the
prominence of choruses might point to a French model, Musorgsky is
as likely to have been prompted to these by the example of Glinka's
operas, reinforced by the recent experience of *Judith*. Indeed, the only
clear ancestors of *Salammbô* are those two cornerstones of the whole
Russian operatic tradition, Glinka's *A Life for the Tsar* and *Ruslan and
Lyudmila*.

Yet anything learned from these is much transformed. In fact, since
Salammbô is already so individual a creation, its interest lies less in what
it drew from the past than in what it presented to the future—and not
just because, as is well known, some few years later Musorgsky raided
it freely for passages in *Boris Godunov*. That is proof enough that he
came to recognize that as early as 1863 he had been writing music that
was fully characteristic. Only three fragments from outside the three
completed scenes are extant. It may seem odd that a composer working
in St Petersburg should shift his musical idiom yet further eastwards
towards the sultry orient of *Ruslan* when characterizing the inhabitants
of the western Mediterranean and north west Africa. But Musorgsky
must have judged that, for Russian ears at least, such colouring would
give the amorous yearning of the Balearic soldier and the melancholy
of Salammbô's priestesses arraying their mistress for her wedding a lan-

guorous, exotic quality that would set them apart from the persons more actively involved in the violent or excruciating events that are the opera's main business. But the warriors of the third fragment, the 'Libyan War Song', are given a powerful, if Russian virility. By exploiting his gift for fertile thematic variation and composing a piece that is essentially monothematic, Musorgsky achieved an impressive precision in projecting this single dramatic group, and also usefully asserted what will be the thematic identity of the Libyan connection, for (as with many Russian folksongs) a single protoshape generates a wealth of foreground phrases, not only in this chorus but elsewhere in the opera, to underpin Mâtho's appearances. It is a process worth noting, if only to emphasize that, though the music of *Salammbô* is, short-term, sometimes untidy and, long-term, insecurely planned and realized, the mind creating it already displays a powerful instinct for articulating personality and drama through the very stuff and procedures of music itself. The 'Libyan War Song' is an excellent character chorus, the music of which Musorgsky thought worth salvaging eight years later when sketching his vocal/orchestral piece *Jesus Navin*.

Of the three completed scenes, that in the temple of Tanit (Act 2, Scene 2) is the weakest; significantly, it was the first part of the opera to be composed. Parts of Salammbô's B major opening invocation suggest all too obviously improvisation at the piano. The off-stage orchestral interlude of the 'Ritual Scene' is undistinguished, while the ensuing women's chorus ('Hymn to Tanit') is really too slender to sustain the span of action demanded of it. Chernomor's enchanted maidens in *Ruslan* must surely have played some modest part in conditioning this music of Salammbô's priestesses, though Glinka's exquisite delicacy gives way to more saturated ornamentation, to judge from the elaborate parts for piano duet, bells, and harps that Musorgsky notated in detail in his vocal score.

Yet there are also some splendid passages in this opening section— Salammbô's extended, flat-key invocations flanking the 'Ritual Scene', for example; six years later Musorgsky would find the second of these worthy of adaptation in Boris's farewell to his son, just as he would give almost note-for-note the music setting Mâtho's first words on entering this seductive world to the Pretender in the Fountain

Scene in Act 3 of *Boris*. But the passage between Mâtho and Salammbô was beyond Musorgsky, for as yet he had not learnt how to use music's own resources to project a dramatic conflict such as now erupted between an importunate Libyan and a confused, frightened priestess. Yet Salammbô's fury when she perceives what Mâtho has done suddenly found Musorgsky on securer ground, for here was a single, largely unencumbered declaration, and this, too, would be reused extensively in *Boris* (in the final Kromy Forest Scene, when the crowd swoops on the two Jesuits). For the end of the scene Musorgsky drew on the chorus devised four years earlier for the crowd in *Oedipus in Athens;* with its driving quaver accompaniment, secure tonal control, and effective handling of three separate choruses (priestesses, other women and boys, and warriors) as background to Salammbô's lamentations and anger, it delineates very efficiently a situation seething with alarm, fear, and fury.

In early October 1860 Musorgsky had reported to Balakirev the composition of two more choruses for the introduction to *Oedipus in Athens* ('an Andante in B flat minor and an Allegro in E flat'),[8] and Gerald Abraham suggested that the first chorus in the Temple of Moloch and the procession later in the scene may be reincarnations of these. The keys certainly fit, the speeds and dramatic contexts seem similar, and the mood of the first also seems plausible (Musorgsky had described it as 'my last mystic piece'[9]), though both must surely have needed adaptation to fit their new situations. The opening stretch of this grim scene confirms Musorgsky's flair for the tableau chorus (again employing three groups—priests, boys, and the people), and especially in its first part—lean, lapidary, awesome; this is another section that would have been well worth resurrecting in a later work. The mood is one of solemn invocation, the soloist (the high priest) going on to intone a phrase that would become the very heart of the Tsar's monologue of self-revelation in Act 2 of *Boris*. But as in the exchanges between individual characters in the preceding scene, Musorgsky had not yet developed the flexibility needed for the dramatic chorus, and the music sinks into longwinded, often mechanical extension of old

[8] *MLN1*, 49.
[9] *MLN1*, 50.

material, until the long-approaching storm erupts with implausible abruptness.

The scene ends with Salammbô in dramatic alliance and colloquy with the people. There is much beautiful music here (one of the orchestral themes Musorgsky thought worth using in 1872 for his second version of *St John's Night on the Bare Mountain*, which he rewrote as part of his contribution to the abortive opera-ballet *Mlada*); there is also some of Musorgsky's boldest.

But some of the least spectacular music in this scene is also among the most prophetic, and it is worth scrutinizing in some detail. Musorgsky may still have been unequal to the challenge of active drama, but monologue was a very different matter, and in the high priest's address to the people (Ex. 5.1) he employs a plain yet eloquent idiom with complete assurance. Though his model is that recitative/arioso style which Glinka had devised to make *A Life for the Tsar* the first Russian opera in which every word was set to music, Musorgsky has already transformed this into something very much his own. In Ex 5.1 the collaboration of melodic line and harmonic structure is integral throughout. As in Glinka, the singer's part is almost syllabic, but it is measured out with constant pliability in rhythm and phrase length; the accompaniment is equally sober and mostly chordal, but is now consistently sustained and harmonically active, though unhurried and flexible. Throughout the harmony is mainly triadic, toughened by seventh chords and magisterial suspensions; chromatic touches (mostly secondary dominants) never threaten its sense of direction. And so the high priest's first two bars are answered by a wide ranging phrase that might have concluded in bar 7 (with the sustained A flat chord) were it not that the unfinished sense of the words urges an extension. Yet after these three extra bars the verbal sentence still flows on, and the A flat chord in bar 10, by thwarting the perfect-cadence resolution that an E flat chord would have provided, drives the music on into the following bar. Here the singer resumes with a two-bar phrase which both links with the past (its second bar echoes bar 10) and affords the opening of the following phrase (bar 13), which swiftly and sonorously moves to the sentence's climactic word: 'Vengeance!', highlighted by a chromatic twist. Finally, a quiet minor-triad-with-added-major-sixth (bar 16, a chord much beloved of Musorgsky; it has already been heard in bar 8) both accommodates the final verb and propels the monologue into its second half.

This is masterly. But the use of formal reminiscence themes in *Salammbô* would seem to be tentative, though it is possible that the uncomposed parts of the opera would have employed such themes more intensively and might also have shown that certain themes in the surviving portions have more point to them than is at present discernible. The many-faced Libyan theme is the only one we know ranges widely, twice turning up in the last scene Musorgsky completed (Act 4, Scene 1: Mâtho languishing in captivity), first as Mâtho recalls his fallen compatriots, then as a further forlorn memory in the wisp of a march during the brief orchestral coda. Though the first two bars (and the key) of this scene suggest strongly that Musorgsky was momentarily haunted by an earlier victim of brutal incarceration, it was less Florestan at the opening of Act 2 of Beethoven's *Fidelio* than Susanin in his Act 4 monologue in *A Life for the Tsar* that provided the model. Mâtho's formal aria lacks that lean strength of outline that Glinka managed with his doomed hero (though Musorgsky was to think it worth reworking as the central section of his *Jesus Navin* chorus). But what precedes it is a very different matter. Like Susanin facing imminent death, Mâtho recalls those who have been central to his past, prefacing each with what is (or surely must be) a reminiscence theme: first his fellow Libyans and Spendius, then Narr'Havas who had betrayed him (very curiously opening with the same first bar as the *Intermezzo in modo classico* for piano—see Ex. 3.1), and finally Salammbô herself (two themes evidently, neither traceable elsewhere). The most impressive music of all springs from Mâtho's hatred of Narr'Havas, a section that replaces the measured manner of the high priest's pronouncement (see Ex.5.1) with a stream of vivid and explosive imagery. This Musorgsky would transfer to Shuisky in the death scene of *Boris*, just as earlier in that same Duma Scene he would allow the assembled boyars to raid freely the music to which Aminakhar and the priests of Moloch enter to tell Mâtho of the fate in store for him.

Young composers are not to be reproached for sometimes choosing unwisely, for failure reveals with precision what still needs to be learnt. That was certainly the case for Musorgsky with *Salammbô*. Fortunately, the remains of the opera are too fragmentary for any well meaning

Ex. 5.1

[My blessing upon you! With secret trembling, in the grove of

Eshmoun,...before the gaze of the almighty gods, you offer up

prayers for your wives and children.

You beg for vengeance. May the enemy in [bloody battle]]

devotee to attempt a plugging of the gaps so that its technical roughnesses and stylistic insecurities may be publicly staged. That said, however, *Salammbô* is a work of profound interest not only to those curious
about Musorgsky's road to maturity but also to those seeking a more
complete perspective on his whole creative life, for it reveals not so
much what he needed to learn as how much he already instinctively
knew and could do. Then in 1866, immediately after composing his
last piece for *Salammbô*, the nature of his dramatic music changed
abruptly, to be followed by yet another shift when he launched into
Boris Godunov in November 1868. It has always been recognized that
in *Boris* Musorgsky looked back increasingly to his own past, especially
readmitting something of the lyricism that he had softened and on occasion entirely banished in the intervening years. In fact, it is not only
in a good deal of the solo writing in *Boris* that Musorgsky built directly
upon the foundations already firmly laid in *Salammbô*; viewed within
this perspective, his creations of the intervening years appear more as a
digression. In fact, the main route that led to *Boris Godunov*, albeit a
lengthy one, came direct from *Salammbô*.[10]

[10] Musorgsky made the following transferences of music from *Salammbô* to *Boris Godunov*
(this list includes instances already noted in the main text). References are to the Oxford
University Press publication of the vocal score in Pavel Lamm's edition, with English translation by David Lloyd-Jones (London, 1975):

Act 2

    Boris's monologue, p. 185, bar 6 to p. 190, bar 3. Built almost entirely from three extracts
    in the chorus to Moloch (Act 3, Scene 1), both directly adapted and reused (three bars
    of one of these appropriations also supports Shchelkalov's preliminaries (p. 328) at the
    opening of *Boris*, Act 4, Scene 1).

Act 3, Scene 2

    1. Pretender's address to Marina, p. 292, bar 9:16 bars. Adapted and condensed from
       priestesses' chorus (Act 2, Scene 2).
    2. ibid., p. 294, bar 1:9 bars. Direct adaptation of Mâtho's reaction to the Temple of Tanit
       (Act 2, Scene 2).

Act 4, Scene 1

    1. Introduction, p. 327, bar 1:18 bars. Orchestral part (expanded by two bars) to priests'
       chorus (Act 4, Scene 1).
    2. Boyars' chorus, p. 332, bar 8:15 bars. Adapted from priests' sentence upon Mâtho.
    3. Shuisky's monologue, p. 340, bar 8:20 bars. Directly adapted from Mâtho's denunci-
       ation of Narr'Havas (Act 4, Scene 1).
    4. Boris's farewell to his son, p. 359, bar 8:19 bars. Condensed from Salammbô's invo-
       cation to Tanit (Act 2, Scene 2).

Act 4, Scene 2

1. The crowd swoop on the two Jesuits, p. 404, bar 4:30 bars. Adapted and slightly condensed from Salammbô's denunciation of Mâtho (Act 2, Scene 2).

2. Pretender's march, p. 409, bar 1:28 bars. Directly adapted from three extracts from the priests' procession (Act 3, Scene 1).

The reasoning behind these transferences (and also some other of Musorgsky's inter-work adaptations) are examined in 'The Mediterranean element in *Boris Godunov*', in G. Abraham, *Slavonic and Romantic Music* (London, 1968), 188–94.

CHAPTER 6

The Early Songs II

ONE CRUCIAL FACT MARKED OUT THE CHILDHOOD YEARS OF
Glinka and Musorgsky from those of the other major figures of
nineteenth-century Russian music. Balakirev, Borodin, Tchaikovsky,
and Rimsky-Korsakov all grew up in urban environments; by contrast,
Glinka and Musorgsky were bred on rural estates, thus imbibing folk
culture to a degree probably denied the others during their most formative years. It is not merely that monodic folk melody would have
been a normal element in their existence; so would 'podgolosnaya'
performances of folksong, a uniquely Russian practice in which members of a choral group (usually women) improvised simultaneously on
a folksong, thus adding an harmonic dimension, but one saturated with
rough and arbitrary dissonance. Conditioned by these sounds in their
earliest years, it is no surprise that Glinka and Musorgsky should have
had especially ready ears for a degree of gritty, sturdy, at times strident,
even empirical, dissonance more than was usual among their respective
contemporaries, or that heterophony should have been a small but recurring weapon in Musorgsky's compositional armoury, even though
he made no effort to emulate folk heterophony itself.[1] Just how natu-

---

[1] Curiously, the one composer who did selfconsciously stylize folk heterophony in an original
composition (though based on a folksong) was Borodin (in the peasant chorus in Act 4 of
Prince Igor). But harmonically Borodin made no effort to match the degree of harsh dissonance
characteristic of the authentic article, confining himself almost exclusively to the occasional
unresolved dissonant quaver on a crotchet half-beat.

rally Musorgsky could turn to folk culture to provide one stylistic strand within an original work had been demonstrated in his very first song, *Where art thou, little star?*, and his strong, if sentimental identification with the world of the newly emancipated peasantry was the impulse behind the finest of his early instrumental works, the *Intermezzo in modo classico*. Now, from 1864 (for *Salammbô* had by no means monopolized his creative attentions during that year) songs would begin to come in which this deeply engrained side of his creativity, fortified by social conviction, would declare itself with a new and compelling mastery.

Not that he would confine himself to such songs, and of the three composed in the spring of 1864 two, *The wild winds blow* and *Night*, are sharply contrasting nature pictures; only the third, *Kalistratushka*, looks forward to this new kind. All are worthy successors of *King Saul*. Each is substantial, clearly characterized, and breaks fresh ground. Like *King Saul*, both *Night* and *Kalistratushka* exist in two versions. Those of *Kalistratushka* differ only in details, but *Night* was very heavily revised, presumably in anticipation of publication, and of the three new songs it was the only one to be printed in Musorgsky's lifetime (in 1871).

Variously entitled 'Romance-fantasia,' 'Fantasia', and 'Improvisation', *Night* (signed: 22 April) was certainly the one most likely to engage the public's ear, and it was to prove the most popular of all Musorgsky's lyrical romances during his lifetime, even though he was to receive censure for the very free prose paraphrase of Pushkin's poem devised for the first half of the published version. In other songs he showed no compunction about modifying his chosen texts, but the operation this time was unusually draconian. An urge to compress was one reason for rewriting and, there being no obvious structural need for this, might suggest (as, perhaps, with *King Saul*) pressure from a publisher intent upon cost-cutting as well as customer-friendliness. But Musorgsky's original setting of Pushkin's text had been gauche in its opening and middle sections, and a paraphrase of that text, now fitted to a completely new vocal line may have seemed the best way of salvaging some music of remarkable character. Certainly *Night* is one of the most hauntingly atmospheric of Musorgsky's early works, already revealing his love for harmonic richness achieved both by striking progression and a plentiful use of seventh, ninth and eleventh chords that foretells the legacy he would bequeath Debussy.[2]

The wild winds blow (a 'song': dated 9 April) is as romantically stormy as Koltsov's verse, and its musical manner much like that of *King Saul*. But there is a difference. The marching bass that launched the earlier song had generated the harmony; by contrast, the bass at the opening of *The wild winds blow* shadows the vocal part. This might pass unnoticed in a piece by Musorgsky, who freely used such passages (the bass also shadows the voice in parts of the central section), were it not that the remaining quaver-dominated piano strand also reflects, if far more freely, the melody's outline (Ex. 6.1). There had already been patches of heterophony in Musorgsky's earlier, also epic-toned *I have many palaces and gardens*, but heterophony is more fundamental to this opening; the dissonances in the second half of bar 1 could scarcely be accommodated within traditional harmonic practice.

Nevertheless, the style of *The wild winds blow* is entirely Musorgsky's own, and apart from its modality (and a suggestion of accompaniment by a *gusli*, a kind of folk psaltery, in the central section) it has few resonances from folk music. But in *Kalistratushka* (dated 3 June) the relationship with a folk milieu is explicit and pervasive. Subtitled 'a study in folk style' (and elsewhere described as 'first attempt at comedy'), it sets a poem by Nekrasov who from the later 1850s had made the plight of the peasantry a particular theme of his work. In real life Musorgsky had already contrasted the peasants' behaviour with that of their former masters in the aftermath of the Emancipation and, despite that event's dire consequences for himself, had joined in the broad wave of idealization of the former serfs—an idealization now engaged in all the more easily within the secluded walls of commune existence than in the sharper reality at Karevo. Kalistratushka recalls the utopian prediction of his mother's lullaby, then surveys the present predicament of his wife, children and himself. Musically the locale is set in a longdrawn, metrically free line (see Ex. 6.2*b*) modelled directly on the melismatic 'protyazhnaya', like the genuine article constantly turning back

---

[2] Nancy Basmajian has noted the tendency to rate Musorgsky's lyrical songs as less characteristic (and therefore less worthwhile) than his more realist examples. For her defence of Musorgsky's lyrical songs, see 'The Romances', *MIM*, 29–56.

Ex. 6.1

[The winds blow,

buy - nï - ye;

the tempestuous winds.]

upon itself in four variants on a fundamental contour (Ex. 6.2*a*). The suggestion of a homely lullaby underlying the ensuing monologue sharpens the irony. Except for one livelier diversion early on, the song now extends to its total structure the principle already presented in microcosm in Ex. 6.2*b*, proceeding for the most part as a series of very free variations around a Russian folktune (later also used by Rimsky-Korsakov in his opera *The Maid of Pskov*) in the piano part, the singer mostly left to shape and inflect his own line. In the process lullaby becomes dance; dream progressively confronts actuality.

No such transformation marks *Cradle Song* (dated 17 September 1865), and the tension between reassuring crib-side musings and bleak reality in Ostrovsky's text (from his play *The Voyevoda*) is barely reflected in the music. Yet this is no cosy lullaby. The dorian-mode insistence on natural-sixth-with-flattened-seventh conjures unease at the opening,

Ex. 6.2a,b

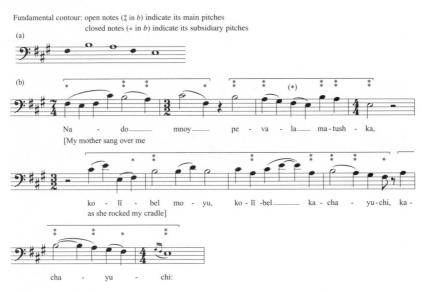

Fundamental contour: open notes ($\frac{o}{o}$ in *b*) indicate its main pitches
closed notes (* in *b*) indicate its subsidiary pitches

(a)

(b)

Na - do—— mnoy—— pe - va - la—— ma-tush - ka,
[My mother sang over me

ko - lï - bel mo - yu, ko - lï -bel—— ka - cha - yu-chi, ka -
as she rocked my cradle]

cha - yu - chi:

just as the lydian raised fourths which brighten the concluding invocation to angel-guarded sleep are opposed by the restless alternation of sharpened and flattened sevenths in the accompaniment. Weariness underlies the gentleness of *Cradle Song*. Again two versions exist, the published one shorter and replacing the original inconclusive end with the security of a formal tonic-major chord. As in *Kalistratushka*, a species of variation is fundamental, the three minor-mode 'verses' (in the original version) being interrelated. Following the example of some of Dargomïzhsky's songs, the original had incorporated 'stage directions' as supplementary guidance to the singer: 'she dozes', 'she awakes', and so on (though in this instance they may have been envisaged as stage directions for a production of *The Voyevoda*).

Gopak, composed nearly a year later (dated 12 September 1866), is a natural companion to *Kalistratushka*—this time a blunt outburst from a peasant wife tired of her pitiable, drink-sodden husband, herself escaping to the tavern in search of diversion, remembering her courtship, berating her husband, demanding he care for his family, then again recalling her younger, carefree days. The verse is Mey's translation of a Cossack song by the Ukrainian Taras Shevchenko, whom Musorgsky would have met through Balakirev in 1859, two years before the poet's death. Curiously, to one manuscript source Musorgsky added a revealing note: 'A kobza-player. The old man sings and dances to his own accompaniment.' Yet it is surely as right to let it be a woman's piece. Set as a racy dance song with explosive verbal exclamations added by Musorgsky, its pace shifts with the moods, which embrace anger, high spirits, bitterness, and touches of sentiment—even a residual tenderness. In brio and energy *Gopak* vividly anticipates Varlaam's set-piece Kazan song in the Inn Scene in *Boris*; more importantly, it reveals more clearly than anything in *Salammbô* Musorgsky's extraordinary flair for catching in musical terms both the physical mien and emotional convolutions of a human being. Couple the extroverted drama of this song with the introverted lyrical disclosures of *Cradle Song*, and an opera composer of enormous potential can be foreglimpsed.

Musorgsky had dedicated *Cradle Song* to the memory of his mother. Yuliya Musorgskaya had died in the spring of the preceding year, and a few weeks earlier, on 14 February 1865, her son had inscribed to her a second song, *Prayer*. We may only guess whether he felt that Lermontov's tender intercession with the Mother of God for an innocent, lonely girl could serve as an oblique expression of his own hopes for a dying mother; whatever the case, there is a touching directness in his setting and, as so often in his later music when treating subjects or emotions of deep but uncomplicated humanity, a tenderness that never becomes mawkish. There can be little doubt that Dargomïzhsky's *Still a prayer* (1861) had some influence on Musorgsky's song, both in general manner and in its brief echo of Orthodox church music. But Musorgsky is the more consistently flexible in declamation, harmonically more sophisticated, and bolder in the quiet disquiet of his unresolved coda.

The Outcast followed on 17 June. This, too, is an intercession, though this time for a woman from the more brutal world of the underprivileged. Musorgsky described it as 'an experiment in recitative'. Whether the example of Dargomïzhsky could have been behind this song also is uncertain. In the early 1860s the kuchka's relations with the older composer had cooled as he had become increasingly 'sullen and sulky' (Stasov's words) at the public's neglect of his *Rusalka*. But since returning from a successful European tour early in 1865 he had resolved to fulfil an ambition he had for some while cherished: to set *The Stone Guest*, one of Pushkin's 'little tragedies', exactly as it stood in a way where 'truth' (i.e., the word, with all its meanings and resonances) would remain supreme, music its servant. Finding the rejuvenated Dargomï-zhsky no longer the dyspeptic hypochondriac from whose soirées they had withdrawn, the kuchka began resuming relations with him. Certainly by June 1865 he had begun work on *The Stone Guest*, and though he still kept it very much to himself it seems unlikely that Musorgsky would not have got wind of the project, scenting enough to interest him in attempting an experiment based on similar principles for himself. Syllabically set primarily in quavers, to a simple, dissonantly pointed accompaniment, the success of *The Outcast* depends above all on the singer's declamation. But compared with Musorgsky's later ventures in this direction, the song seems timid.

Musorgsky's two songs from the earlier part of 1866 return explicitly to the world of the romance. Both are lyrical, and both are inscribed to women friends. The setting of Pleshcheyev's *Why are thine eyes sometimes so cold?* (also known as *Malyutka* 'Little One': dated 19 January) was given to a certain L.V. Azareva, and *The Wish* (a translation by Mey of Heine's *Ich wollt, meine Schmerzen ergössen*) was cryptically dedicated on 28 April to Musorgsky's close friend Nadezhda Opochinina, 'in memory of her verdict upon me'. Both songs are attractive, though breaking no new ground. Nine years later Tchaikovsky would set the same Heine text, opening with a phrase uncannily close to Musorgsky's. But there the parallels cease. Tchaikovsky, unsurprisingly, is the more polished but cautious, using the music of the first stanza for the second, and fabricating a closed ternary structure by repeating the opening stanza–plus–music to end. But Musorgsky's setting evolves musically, passing into a lengthy piano postlude that suggests Schumann—if only for its fleeting affinity with the dying end of that composer's *Papillons*. A third romance, *From my tears* (another Heine setting, *Aus meine tränen*: dated 13 September), was dedicated to Nadezhda's brother, Vladimir. It is the least interesting of the three. Borodin was to treat the same text, and this time Musorgsky is the loser, Borodin displaying an exquisite delicacy that ensures every note tells. Beside such intimacy and point Musorgsky sounds prosaic and prolix. Yet the very next day, 14 September, he would sign a song, *Darling Savishna*, that could not be in greater contrast and which would signal a radical new stage in his development.

Though clearly much had happened in his inner life, the surviving evidence of Musorgsky's outer existence during the last two or more years is thin. His civil service duties had absorbed a very significant portion of his time, and such snippets of information as we have suggest that, at least initially, he worked diligently; in February 1864 he was promoted assistant to the chief clerk in the department's barracks' section, and in April he was awarded the Order of St Stanislav (third class). But from the autumn of 1863 his stream of letters had dwindled, drying up completely throughout 1865. Though the contacts with friends continued and he appeared at various musical evenings with his old associates, there were occasions when he disappeared altogether. When he did resurface and reveal his newest compositions the results were not always found reassuring. 'Modinka's risen again', Cui reported on 26 June 1864 to Balakirev. 'He is visiting me weekly. He's composed two romances and Nekrasov's *Kalistratushka* (*Tableau de genre musicale*). There's a new musical form for you! None of it's without good things, harmonies, ideas—but in toto it's thoroughly nonsensical'.[3] But then Musorgsky dropped out of sight again.

1865 is even more sparsely documented. The death of his mother certainly took him to Toropets during the early spring. On 4 May, in the immediate wake of this blow, he signed the manuscript of *From Memories of Childhood*, two slight piano miniatures (the second uncompleted) entitled 'Nurse and I' and 'First Punishment: Nurse shuts me in a dark room', both dedicated to his mother's memory. Two more pieces would follow in the summer, both composed on others' themes: a dreary *Rêverie* (dated 3 August) on a melody by Vyacheslav Loginov, one of his commune companions, and the neat *La capricieuse* (signed four days later) on a tune by Login Heyden, an amateur musician and pupil of Balakirev. But not until October is there any specific indication of his personal life, when he resumed attendance at various of the gatherings of the circle around Balakirev, who had returned after a summer spent away from St Petersburg. Whether Musorgsky had now left the

---

[3] *TDM*, 116.

commune is unknown, but by the end of the year he had certainly withdrawn. 'In the autumn of 1865', Filaret later wrote to Stasov, 'my brother fell seriously ill. A terrible nervous illness was in the offing [probably the result of dipsomania following their mother's death]. In consequence of this my wife spared no effort to make him move out of the commune to us.'[4] Musorgsky was, according to Stasov, initially reluctant to leave, but quickly settled back into normal family life, remaining with his brother and sister-is-law until they left St Petersburg in 1868.

1866 began with a new acquaintanceship that would prove of enormous personal importance to Musorgsky. Lyudmila Shestakova was Glinka's sister. Twelve years younger than her brother, she had become the beloved confidante of his last years, outliving him by nearly half a century—and Musorgsky by a quarter. In 1863 her only child had died, and for a while grief made any musical experience unbearable for her. Now she was emerging again, and on 14 January, at Stasov's, Musorgsky was introduced to her. The immediate consequence of this meeting was that members of the kuchka were very soon invited to Shestakova's own twice-weekly soirées. Later she recalled briefly her impressions of Musorgsky:[5]

> From our first meeting I was struck by a certain special delicacy and gentleness in his manner of address; this was a man remarkably well bred and self-possessed. I knew him fifteen years, and during all this time I never saw him allow himself to flare up or so forget himself as to say an unpleasant word to anyone. And more than once when I commented upon his self-control, he replied: 'For this I am indebted to my mother; she was a saintly woman.'

Musorgsky's commune existence had been by its nature a private world, but Shestakova's memories remove any suspicion that he might have emerged from it coarsened in character or that, to the end of his life, he could be other than courteous and civilized in manner when the occasion demanded.

It was at Shestakova's that Musorgsky made another, and crucial ac-

[4] *SMPM* (see *SSM3*, 78).
[5] *MVS*, 106.

quaintance—with Vladimir Nikolsky, an historian and literary scholar, and a professor and inspector at the Alexandrovsky Lycée and the St Petersburg Ecclesiastical Academy. The attraction between the two men was mutual, and within months Musorgsky had affectionately made Nikolsky the butt of one of his raciest, most earthy songs, *You drunken sot*. Nikolsky's later gift to Musorgsky was yet more precious: not only the idea for an opera on Pushkin's *Boris Godunov* but much practical help during that opera's creation.

Nikolay Chernïshevsky's novel *What is to be done?*, published in 1863, was one of the most widely read books in Russia during the 1860s and 70s, being especially popular with the young for the novel ideas it propagated (today it might still be applauded by some as a testimonial for feminism). Musorgsky was no doubt as excited by it as any other young man. Vera Pavlovna, raised in an oppressive family environment, is offered escape by marriage to Lopukhov, a medical student. Motivated by the fashionable concept of rational egoism, they establish a system of living in which Vera, as much as Lopukhov himself, may enjoy personal freedom and fulfilment. In what is never more than an impersonal marriage Vera also works and earns—for money is power, and thus she is safe from Lopukhov's domination. Each has his/her own room for living (and sleeping) which the other enters only with permission. A third room is for meals and receiving guests (the only times Vera and Lopukhov meet regularly). Neither asks questions of the other; to do so would be intrusive. The rights and freedoms of each are absolute.

The parallels between such a life style and the recent commune existence of Musorgsky and his companions, as described by Stasov, are self-evident. But there is no sign that Musorgsky was stirred by the concept of Vera's working cooperative or by Chernïshevsky's rosy vision of an ideal society, and *What is to be done?* could contribute nothing to his creative development. This was to come from other sectors of Chernïshevsky's philosophy. In the 1850s, notably in his thesis *Aesthetic Relationships of Art to Reality*, Chernïshevsky had confronted the nature of beauty, rejecting the concepts of idealists or transcendentalists who believed that, while beauty might be met with in nature, this was only by chance and most likely would be transient—whereas nature, as mediated through the eye of the artist, could, in a considered selection and ideal arrangement of objects and phenomena, present a permanent, even greater beauty. Instead Chernïshevsky arrived at the baldest of conclusions: 'Beauty is life . . . That being is beautiful in whom we see life such as it must be according to our understanding; that object is beautiful that manifests life, or reminds us of life.'[6] Art was to be a reflection of some aspect of reality and human experience. Chernïsh-evsky's definition of beauty begged many questions (how is 'life' to be defined, for instance?). It recognized that 'understanding' (an individ-ual's natural intuitive response) of 'life' was not an absolute but would vary between social groups—that what, for instance, constituted fem-inine beauty would be very different for the peasant and the prince (in the spirit of the times Chernïshevsky inclined towards the fresher, more natural image favoured by the lower class).

Agree or not, such a definition could be readily understood in the visual arts whose business was still the reworking of images from the outer world. Nor did its application to some areas of literature in the choice and treatment of subjects pose difficulties. But music was dif-ferent, and Chernïshevsky's attempt to make his system engage with it by arguing that music copied life disclosed his total failure to understand the nature of music beyond its most basic forms. 'Thus instrumental music is an imitation of singing, its accompaniment or surrogate; in singing itself, singing as a product of art is only an imitation and a surrogate to singing as a product of nature. After this, we have the right to say that, in music, art is only a weak reproduction of the phenomena of life that are independent of our strivings for art.'[7] Just what that means in practice is anyone's guess.

The trouble was that, as with the late-sixteenth-century Italian Ca-merata, theory and musical reality could not directly and profitably engage. But what such ideas could do was stimulate composers to seek out and explore (but on music's own terms) new possibilities which, unprompted, they would never have envisaged. It is impossible to be-

---

[6] 'Esteticheskiye otnosheniya isskustva k deystvitelnosti' [Aesthetic relationships of art to re-ality], in N. Chernïshevsky, *Polnoye sobraniye sochineny*, ii: *Stati i retsenzy, 1853–1855* [Complete edition: articles and reviews] (Moscow, 1949), 10.

[7] Op. cit., 63.

lieve that discussion of theories such as these was not a major element in the communal life of Musorgsky and his companions. And it was not merely that, through the stimulus of closely observing ordinary life—that is, life that was most 'truthful' (i.e., most natural) and yet had remained unexplored by musicians on its own terms—new creations might arise. For just as Chernïshevsky had claimed that society understood more of the native Americans' way of life through Fenimore Cooper's novels than ethnographic presentations, so the insightful representation of (for instance) the Russian peasant and his/her world through the imaginative resources of music might do more to acquaint Russian higher society with its lower ranks than even the most scrupulous sociological investigation. What emerged might be not only art that entertained, but truth that illumined.[8]

It was surely within a world of such ideas that *Darling Savishna* (subtitled 'an imbecile's song') was born on 14 September 1866. Stasov, recalling Musorgsky's own testimony, fixed the song's moment of conception a year earlier in the summer of 1865, when the composer was staying with his brother at Minkino, near St Petersburg. From a window Musorgsky had observed a commotion:[9]

> a wretched imbecile was making a declaration of love to a young peasant woman he fancied, was imploring her, yet was himself mortified at his own ugliness and wretched plight; he himself well knew there was nothing in this world for him, especially the joy of love. Musorgsky was deeply affected, the strange character and the scene imprinted itself strongly on his mind, instantly there appeared distinctive forms and sounds for the embodiment of the images that moved him profoundly.

However instantly Musorgsky may have conceived the musical embodiment of this incident, a number of other songs, including *Cradle Song* and *Gopak*, intervened before *Savishna* was committed to paper. In this instance Musorgsky had to be his own wordsmith, and the text was his free recollection of the idiot's babble, cast in ten-syllable lines to fit the 5/4 metre. From the very first bar of (Ex.6.3) the essence of

---

[8] For a broader examination of the socio-philosophical theories and movements of Musorgsky's time, see R. Hoops, 'Musorgsky and the Populist Age', *MIM*, 271–306.

[9] *SMPM* (see *SSM3*, p. 79).

Ex. 6.3

[My light, Savishna, radiant falcon,

fall in love with me, witless one, caress me, unlucky one.

Is it possible, my falcon, radiant falcon, beautiful Savishna, Ivanovna, my light]

the whole song is exposed: a bare repetitive piano part with constant dissonance from appoggiaturas and especially pedals, and equally unbroken single-syllable crotchets from the singer (but with highly detailed, often unpredictable inflexions demanded by the composer; the style of the vocal part, with its tight one-bar cells and repetitiveness, was related closely to that of authentic beggars' songs). Taken by itself, the unremitting patter of 235 rapid crotchets ensures a breathless delivery, its fluency further impaired by the limping metre, which tends to a musical comma at each barline. The accompaniment, also a one-bar rhythmic ostinato, is the closest of allies. For all the sudden outbursts, there is no trace of definable 'meaning' within the music itself, but heard through the words (and given a singer with a lively declamation), the tiny phrases reveal a life of their own not possessed by functional recitative, and the song has surprising impact, for all its brevity.

Savishna was an extraordinary conception, the first of Musorgsky's thoroughly 'realist' songs. Here was Chernïshevsky's ideal of creative truth mediated in musical terms such as he himself could never have envisaged. The peasant monologues among Musorgsky's earlier songs had been highly individual, radical extensions of existing types (*Cradle Song* of the romance, *Kalistratushka* and *Gopak* of the dance song) in which lyrical expression and musically determined form had still remained paramount. But in the new brand of dramatic monologue the words could be all-determining, and they might be the only means of decoding the music.

Nevertheless, more normal human personalities, even of the humbler kinds who for a while were to be Musorgsky's main preoccupation, had more sides to them than the imbecile of *Savishna*. They had complexes of loves and hates, pleasures and pains, which produced a range of clear and powerful sentiments, and in his following songs Musorgsky readmitted a degree of lyricism, though only insofar as was required for the faithful projection of the individuals whose monologues they were. Merciless psychological dissection and uncompromising illumination are abetted by leanness of texture and sharpness of sound. Though extensive stretches of quaver or crotchet patter especially permit the pace of normal speech, a wider variety of syllabically set note values allows greater variety, and the invasion of the prevailing mode by other pitches helps suggest a wider range of verbal inflexion. The fitful phrasing and dynamic, as well as the tonal wrenches, graphically mirror the turbulence of a verbal flow that often reflects an emotional torrent. Pedals at all levels proliferate, the harmony sometimes taking on an unprecedented harshness beyond the norms of nineteenth-century practice, yet the rightness of which in performance disarms criticism. As Musorgsky would have said: 'Minimum of stylization, maximum of realism'. And, one might add, 'maximum of objectivity'. Yet however detached the approach, it is not one of indifference. Humorous some of these songs may be, even satirical, but always they seem compassionate. Equally, pity never seeks to create a manifesto—for truth eloquently presented can perfectly well be its own advocate.

While *Darling Savishna* retains the aura of the prototype, the two longer songs that swiftly followed are arguably of greater interest as music. Here also the texts were Musorgsky's own, hovering between rough verse and vernacular prose, though inclining far more to the latter. The first, *You drunken sot* (dated 4 October), seems, as noted earlier, to have been a jest at the expense of its dedicatee, Vladimir Nikolsky (the piece is subtitled 'from the adventures of Pakhomïch', Musorgsky's nickname for Nikolsky), and was never intended for publication. The joke (the point may be lost on us, but it was no doubt grasped by Nikolsky's close associates) is couched in a tirade against a drunken husband, the turbulent wife being a well-established figure in popular Russian culture. It seems more bitter than *Gopak*; unlike the latter, *You drunken sot* has no explicit dance element, despite its drive, for this peasant woman has no avenue of escape from domestic drudgery. But the torrent of abuse and reproach yields to pleading, drawing from Musorgsky a lyrical eight bars that would be given a public life in the Tsar's farewell in *Boris*. There follow faint echoes from a church idiom as the wife recalls the broken promises of her 'Pakhomïch', and her onslaught briefly abates, only to be abruptly resumed.

That Musorgsky intended *You drunken sot* for consumption only within his own private circle may account for its especially unbuttoned rumbustiousness and, at times, harmonic anarchy. Beside it *The Seminarist*, (dated five days later) perhaps sounds cautious. Again the words are Musorgsky's own. Its subtitle, 'a picture from nature', seems to support Nikolay Novikov's suggestion that the poor, distracted Latin scholar of Musorgsky's monologue, struggling with his Latin third declension nouns while his thoughts stray ineluctably to the charms of the priest's daughter and the painful consequences he has already felt for his attentions in that quarter, grew from Musorgsky's memories of a certain Vasily Molchanov, a seminarist from his home region whom he might well have encountered when visiting Karevo the previous year to attend his mother's funeral. The young novice's triple preoccupations—dreary duty, seductive fantasy, and moral unease—are reflected respectively in three kinds of music: monotonous quaver patter, melody filled with healthy folky resonances, and chunks of quasi-chant, from alternations of which the song is built. But not only from alternations: the monotonic chanting of declensions may weaken, then collapse under the pressure of erotic thoughts, and these in their turn may be intruded upon by the churchy idiom. There are some nice ironies here. *The Seminarist* may lack the kaleidoscopic swirl of invention that makes *You drunken sot* so invigorating, but this is no criticism; a peasant scold under full sail and a sexually repressed theology student are very different creatures. In *The Seminarist* the vagabond monks of *Boris*, Varlaam and Missail, can already be foreheard.[10]

Savishna (dedicated to Cui), *Gopak* (dedicated to Rimsky), and *The Seminarist* (inscribed to Lyudmila Shestakova) were published soon after composition, the first two in 1867, the latter in 1870 in Leipzig[11] in its revised version (shortened by the excision of some recitations of nouns, with revisions of detail elsewhere). Years later their reception by some listeners would draw from Musorgsky an impatient reaction which may still sound a necessary caution for us: 'not so long ago *Savishna* and *The Seminarist* were laughed at until some musical person explained that the leaven in both musical scenes was tragedy'.[12] Russian creators have always had a particular flair for taking characters, often from the lower strata of society, and highlighting their outer characteristics through brilliant caricature which may turn them into comic grotesques, yet without for one moment mocking their humanity or masking their pains or tribulations. Among writers Gogol had been supreme in this; among composers Musorgsky was proving himself Gogol's equal. For (as in parts of, say, Mozart's *Figaro*) within monologues such as these there are richly expressive—and deeply human—ambivalences, layers of pain and turmoil beneath their vivid surfaces that move (or should) the sensitive listener to 'smile through tears'. One thing is certain: in these songs Musorgsky is crossing the line dividing the brilliantly talented from the great composer.

[10] Compare, for instance, *The Seminarist* (revised version), bars 37–42, with the Inn Scene in *Boris*, p. 80, bars 4–9.

[11] The censor would not allow publication of this song in Russia (see pp. 194–5).

[12] *MLN1*, 235.

CHAPTER 7

St John's Night on the Bare Mountain: More Songs

During the 1866–7 season my friendship with Musorgsky developed further. I used to visit him where he lived with Filaret, his married brother, near the Kashkin bridge. From his [opera] *Salammbô* he played me many times extracts which delighted me greatly. I think that was when he played me his fantasia *St John's Night* for piano and orchestra, prompted by [Liszt's] *Danse macabre* . . . Musorgsky also played me his romances, which had not enjoyed success with Balakirev and Cui. Among these were *Kalistratushka* and the beautiful fantasia *Night* . . . During my visits to Musorgsky we talked freely, unmonitored by Balakirev and Cui. I was bowled over by much of what he played me; this delighted him, and he freely divulged to me his plans. He had more than I did. One of his compositional projects had been *Sadko*, but he had long since given up this idea, and suggested it to me.[1]

Rimsky-Korsakov's memory was far from faultless, but this provides some of the best overall information we have on Musorgsky's musical life in the period following the creation of *Savishna*. Its glimpse into the situation within the kuchka confirms what earlier evidence had suggested: that though it still convened, as a coherent group it had fallen apart and that, as the two youngest members, Rimsky and Musorgsky were now looking more to each other for stimulus and support. Most interesting of all, it reveals that what prompted Musorgsky to set about composing *St John's Night on the Bare Mountain* was hearing Liszt's

[1] *RKL*, 64.

Totentanz, first performed in Russia in March 1866 and instantly taken up at meetings of the Balakirev circle—though there is no corroborative evidence that Musorgsky ever envisaged his own piece for the same forces as Liszt's. Yet it is quite possible that he may have intended this initially and that, like Balakirev with *Tamar* or Borodin with his *Prince Igor* overture, he could play much, perhaps all of it at the piano before committing it to paper in its first, but not final form in 1867.

Musorgsky passed the summer of 1866 at Pavlovsk, returning to St Petersburg by the end of September. During the first two months of 1867 Balakirev was in Prague to prepare and conduct performances of Glinka's *Ruslan*, and the gatherings at Shestakova's became especially important for those left behind. Balakirev absent was easier to cope with, and now that he was briefly removed, all the affectionate gratitude Musorgsky felt for this browbeater to whom he owed so much came out in a couple of lengthy supportive letters which supplemented the corporate letter of goodwill compiled at one of Shestakova's assemblies. In a way that affected many of Musorgsky's letters when he was in a state of high excitement the tone is heightened, the language sometimes flowery, explosive, and discursive, its meaning at times so masked by its highly personal style and idiosyncratic use of vocabulary as to be almost impenetrable. But it is the thread of musical xenophobia that winds its way through these documents that is most significant. Anger would impel Musorgsky to deny entry into Russia to German and Italian musicians—and Jewish (no doubt with Anton Rubinstein in mind). 'Make me sing (not as a joke) *Lieder* by Mendels[sohn]', he continued to Balakirev on 7 February, 'and I will turn from a gentle and polished individual into an out-and-out boor. Force a Russian peasant to like Volkslieder from the foul German—he won't like them.' At least the Russian peasantry were true to their roots, he believed. Elsewhere the French, even the English, are berated, nor do the Czechs (Musorgsky's fellow-Slavs) escape a drubbing. That Russia must be herself is now an imperative:[2]

A people or a society that does not sense those sounds which, like memories of one's own mother, of one's closest friend, must make all the vital strings within a man vibrate, awaken him from deep sleep, recognize his own

[2] *MLN1*, 84.

individuality and the oppression that lies upon him and which, little by little, kills that individuality—such a society, such a people is *a corpse*, and the elect of that nation are the doctors who must, through a violent electro-galvanic shock, jerk the members of that *nation-corpse* before it turns into a physically decayed carcase.

That this whole letter is thick with prejudice fortified by ignorance and half-truths matters less than what it tells us about the degree of Musorgsky's commitment (at least, at this stage) to the ideal of an ethnically pure Russian music. All other members of the kuchka had written, or would write, symphonies or quartets in which there was no escaping contamination from alien western forms and procedures. Henceforth Musorgsky was, he himself declared, irrevocably putting such things behind him. From the moment *Savishna* had been born his own creative mission as a Russian composer had become clear to him, and his pursuit of it would be singleminded.

Early 1867 brought one more song (and also promotion to the civil-service rank of titular councillor). For *On the Dnieper*, as for *Gopak*, Musorgsky turned to Shevchenko's *Haydamaki*, whose subject was the Ukrainian insurrection against the Polish gentry in 1786, setting *Yarema's Song* from this much longer poem. To match this heroic vision of a free Ukraine Musorgsky composed music as stouthearted as the poem itself. Its opening and closing sections are founded on a Ukrainian folktune which Musorgsky transformed from what originally could have been a species of mazurka into a noble *largamente* invocation, initially in 7/4. At the song's head he wrote 'Populare'; in the central Allegro risoluto, with its confident procession of themes, the composer who had recently so perceptively projected individual peasant types now showed himself adept at catching the corporate spirit of a people intent upon creating a Ukraine 'free to the sea. No Polish landowners, no monks! The Dnieper has borne away their bones.' *On the Dnieper* anticipates the epic grandeur of 'The Field Marshal' in the *Songs and Dances of Death*—that is, assuming Musorgsky had not totally transformed the song when he revised it in 1879 (only this later version has survived). In this manuscript the song is subtitled 'My Journey through Russia', prompted by Musorgsky's concert tour that year with the singer Darya Leonova (their route took them through the Ukraine).

During 1866 work on *Salammbô* had finally petered out, and by the beginning of 1867 Musorgsky realized that this project was dead. But something of the musical spirit of the abortive opera lingered, to resurge in a choral-orchestral setting of the first three stanzas of Byron's *The Destruction of Sennacherib* ('The Assyrian came down like the wolf on the fold'). Alexey Tolstoy had translated into Russian this most cele-brated of Byron's *Hebrew Melodies*, and Gerald Abraham thought it more probable that Stasov rather than Musorgsky concocted the prose para-phrase which the latter used as his text. Presumably the piece was com-posed with the concert of the FMS on 18 March in mind. When precisely Musorgsky began composition is unknown, but by 4 February he was scoring his 'chorus à la magyar', as he characterized it to Bala-kirev, who was to be its dedicatee. Six days later all was finished.

Eight days after the first performance Cui's review appeared in the *St Petersburg Gazette*. Some Russian criticism of the period is especially noteworthy for its detail and precision, pointing to a lively, thinking readership, and also to the aural alertness of the critic (though in this instance Cui had the advantage of an open rehearsal the previous day). As specimens of such criticism his and a hostile critic's reports are worth quoting:[3]

> The chorus, *The Destruction of Sennacherib*, is very definitely not bad, with bold eastern colouring. Its centre, a bit like a Jewish chorale, is weaker, but the first part, repeated after the chorale, is wholly good. Its first bars would seem to recall a little the beginning of the martial song of Holofernes [in Serov's *Judith*], but this resemblance is purely *superficial* . . . In character the Jewish chorale in the middle is much of a piece with Mr Serov's Assyrian music, only incomparably more musical; inserted into *Judith* it would be an ornament to it, almost its very best number.
>
> The orchestration is excellent—effective and colourful; the basses are of remarkable richness; the use of the brass, especially the lower notes of the tenor trombone (its bass F is a lovely soft sound) is most successful; in sound the orchestra recalls that of Mr Serov. I will note the following shortcom-ings. As regards composition, the first theme is repeated too often; repeated for the fourth time it already begins to wear; the end of the chorus is too compact and brief. In the orchestration misuse of the cymbals was noticeable

and, in the middle section, the ineptly applied pizzicatos of the cellos and basses in octaves are extremely ugly.

Criticism could be unsparing, too, with aesthetic and journalistic politics breaking through. Accusing Balakirev, who conducted part of the concert, of 'unwarranted fetishism' and his 'disciples' of trying to put him on a pedestal, Feofil Tolstoy, one of the most prominent of St Petersburg critics, protested his own inclination to praise Musorgsky, but then affected perplexity at the

> high-flown praises from the heralds of the group whose organ is the *St Petersburg Gazette*. 'This chorus', exclaims its correspondent, '*inserted* into *Judith*, would be an *ornament* to it, almost *its very best number*'. How, after this, are we to regard Musorgsky? As a novice composer showing both knowledge and talent we would welcome him with pleasure; but suddenly we learn that with one small chorus he has outdone the five-act *Judith* . . . It emerges that already we cannot treat a piece by Musorgsky leniently, but must scrutinize it with all rigour as a piece not only fully mature but also worthy the honour of being set up as a model.[4]

The threat is unmissable. Nor would hostile criticism come only from those wedded to tradition or reaction, or with some personal axe to grind. Cui himself, the main spokesman for the kuchka, would on occasion prove himself the most disconcerting of commentators when some kuchka piece was performed—and increasingly so as his own inability to match the creative achievements of his colleagues became more apparent. But in this instance he had got things about right. *The Destruction of Sennacherib* was no more than a nicely turned piece capably presented, with no trace of the radicalism so brilliantly exhibited in some of Musorgsky's recent songs. Certainly one aspect of its structure also aroused Stasov's irritation: the ternary design with both music and words of the first section repeated—and as for the middle, 'what an indispensible trio in a classical manner', he snorted, 'and what an imitation, albeit unintended, of western chorales!'[5] But it was 1874 before Musorgsky heeded this censure, shortening the end, using a new text, and replacing the central section with rewritten words set to music

[4] *TDM*, 133–4.
[5] *SMPM* (see *SSM3*, 85).

which, nevertheless, Gerald Abraham said 'must be amongst the most banal Musorgsky ever wrote'.[6] Fortunately, the original version had already been published in 1871.

Abraham made one further observation about *Sennacherib*: that it was 'essentially orchestral music with vocal *obbligati*'.[7] In fact, while this chorus was being composed Musorgsky had been gestating a purely orchestral piece of far greater import. It is unlikely that the plan for an opera on Gogol's *St John's Eve*, drawn up corporately by a group including Musorgsky and Balakirev in 1859, can have contributed anything to this new project, but the seed for what would become a multi-version *St John's Night on the Bare Mountain* had surely been sown as far back as 1860, when Musorgsky's old school friend Georgy Mengden had commissioned him to compose 'a whole act on the *Bare Mountain* (from Mengden's drama *The Witch*)—*a witches' sabbath, different episodes for sorcerers, a triumphal march for the entire obscene rabble, a finale: glorification of this sabbath'*.[8] By October it was rumoured Musorgsky had begun *A witches' chorus for the Bare Mountain*, but nothing more was heard of this. As noted earlier, it was probably encountering Liszt's *Totentanz* in March 1866 that fired him to revive the *Bare Mountain* subject, though this time it would be embodied in an orchestral piece. 'I've begun sketching the witches—have got stuck with the devils—Satan's procession still doesn't satisfy me', he reported to Balakirev on 2 May.[9] But he was still tinkering with *Salammbô*, and this retarded progress. On 26 August he told Balakirev that he longed to have a talk with him about the witches, and even without Rimsky's testimony we might reasonably guess that Musorgsky had worked out the whole piece at the piano during 1866–7. Its final stage is fixed by a note on the surviving score: 'Conceived in 1866. Began writing it out for orchestra 24 June 1867, finished work on St John's Eve, 5 July 1867'.

For information on witches' sabbaths Musorgsky had turned to Matvey Khotinsky's newly published *Sorcery and Mysterious Phenomena in Recent Time*. His letter of 24 July to Nikolsky described the back-

[6] *CAM*, 181.
[7] Op. cit., 180.
[8] *MLN1*, 50.
[9] *MLN1*, 77.

ground and outline of the piece, as well as his own view of what he had created:[10]

> If my memory [of what I have read] does not deceive me, the witches congregated on this mountain . . . gossiped, engaged in debauchery, and awaited their lord—Satan. On his arrival they (i.e., the witches) formed a circle around the throne which their lord mounted in the form of a goat, and lauded him in song. When the witches' praises had brought Satan to a sufficient frenzy he would order the Sabbath to begin, during which he would pick out the witches who caught his fancy to satisfy his wants. I have done it thus. At the head of the piece I have indicated its content: 1. The assemblage of witches, their talk and gossip; 2. Satan's procession; 3. The obscene glorification of Satan—and 4. The Sabbath . . . The form and character of my piece are *Russian and original*. Its tone is inflamed and disorderly . . . I have (in the programme) named the episodes separately to make the musical form more easily grasped—because it is new.
>
>   . . . You know something of my musical convictions—and you will not dispute that for me the truthful representation of folk fantasy in whatever form it may appear is an important matter—if, of course, it is amenable to musical treatment . . .
>
>   I composed *St John's Night* very quickly, straight out into orchestral score without corrections . . . I did not sleep at night and I finished the work dead on the eve of St John's Day, something so seething in me that I simply didn't know what was happening to me—that is, I knew, but did not need to know; if so, I would have got a swelled head. In the Sabbath I deployed the orchestra in separate, different groups, which will be easy for the listener *to take in* because the colour of the winds and strings are quite appreciably contrasted . . . I am prattling rather too much about my *Night*, but that, I suppose, is because I see in my sinful prank an original Russian composition, not dusted with German profundity and routine but, like *Savishna*, flowing from our native fields, and reared on Russian bread.

It is obvious this score has disappeared, for in a letter to Rimsky of 17 July Musorgsky quoted two themes, one of which has no place in the extant 'first' version, while the other is modified. David Lloyd-Jones's suggestion that the extant score must be a revised copy is surely

---

[10] *MLN1*, 89.

correct (as noted with earlier compositions, the fact that it records the original composition dates is no obstacle to this). And a very revised one it is, for the latter parts of Musorgsky's more detailed account of the work itself simply do not fit the first version as he had described it to Rimsky:[11]

> The piece's form and plan are quite original. The introduction is in two parts (the witches' gathering); then a theme in D minor with a little development (the gossip) linked with Satan's procession in B flat (I have deftly avoided an *Hungarian* march style), [and then] the theme of the procession without development (with the [witches'] response in E flat minor—the debauched character of E flat minor is very diverting) finishes with the *chemical scale* [Musorgsky's idiosyncratic nickname for the whole-tone scale] in full flood in contrary motion on D. Then B minor (the glorification) in a Russian manner developed as variations and a semi-ecclesiastical quasi trio, a transition to the Sabbath, and finally the Sabbath (first theme in D minor), also Russian, with variations. At the end of the Sabbath the chemical scale intrudes and figures from the two-part introduction, which makes a rather good impression. The Sabbath will be almost new to you—it has come out very compact and, in my view, passionate. The form of disjointed variations with interspersions is, I think, the most appropriate for such a commotion.

Whether this last sentence refers only to the Sabbath is unclear, but it is a not unfair description of the earlier parts also. But the order of the E flat minor section and the first appearance of the 'chemical scale' have now been reversed, and beyond this there is little discernible relationship between the verbal account and the music that has come down to us.

When and why these changes had been made will probably always remain a mystery, though there must be some suspicion that Balakirev, to whom *St John's Night* was dedicated, had a hand in them. Certainly he had strong reservations when he was shown the piece, and he had certainly pressed Musorgsky to include in the witches' glorification a passage in F sharp minor like one in Liszt's *Dante Symphony*. But beyond this we know nothing of his requirements. Musorgsky's response in early October, while admitting the depression Balakirev's refusal to

[11] *MLN1*, 87.

endorse his new piece had produced, is resolute: 'I considered, do consider, and shall not cease to consider that this piece is respectable and, to wit, the one in which, after standing on my own feet in small pieces, I have for the first time stood on my own feet in a large-scale piece.'[12] There is no evidence that Musorgsky ever revised this as a purely orchestral piece, and it was never performed as such.

When it seems that a work has been created, perhaps exclusively, through improvisation at the piano over more than a year, there is no way of knowing whether the product finally committed to paper differs radically from the original conception. That is the condition of *St John's Night*. Indeed, Musorgsky's own words to Nikolsky ('something so seething in me that I simply didn't know what was happening to me') make clear that even this final stage may have involved an element of active composition. *Totentanz* may have provided the initial stimulus, and that work's scheme of variations on the 'Dies irae' plainsong, punctuated by cadenzas and extensions, may have suggested to Musorgsky his 'variations with interspersions' form and his choice of key (D minor). From Liszt, too, he may have caught the idea of repeating the entire introduction in another key; nor should some pervasive influence from Liszt's newly published *First Mephisto Waltz*, already a favourite of the Balakirev circle, be excluded. But if the Hungarian composer's music afforded some genes, the nearer ancestors of *St John's Night*, like those of Balakirev's first significant orchestral compositions, were Glinka's last three orchestral pieces, his two Spanish Overtures and *Kamarinskaya*—and explicitly the last, that virtuoso exhibition of how intensive variation, applied with sufficient inventiveness, may sustain an extensive piece. Yet whereas in Balakirev's pieces the debts to Glinka declare themselves explicitly, Musorgsky's are redeemed by his very individual application of what he borrowed. The final physiognomy of *St John's Night* proved to be thoroughly Musorgsky's own.[13]

The first thing that impresses is the flair and resourcefulness of the orchestration, the more so since, except in his handful of modest exercises for Balakirev, Musorgsky had had no practice whatsoever in scor-

---

[12] *MLN1*, 94.

[13] For a highly detailed commentary on *St John's Night*, see E. R. Reilly, 'The First Extant Version of *Night on the Bare Mountain*', *MIM*, 135–62.

ing and only three brief opportunities of hearing how his own orchestration sounded. True, most nights he could have studied such orchestral effects as were required of the pit bands in the St Petersburg opera houses—as Tchaikovsky certainly did. But orchestral concerts, though now promoted by both the RMS and FMS, were not that numerous, and the sureness of Musorgsky's instinct, as displayed in *St John's Night,* is the more impressive. His orchestral style is firmly within that native tradition established by Glinka and which remained strong even into the twentieth century. Put at its simplest, its foundation was the timbre of the individual instruments. The string section will, of course, produce an homogeneous sound. But (to generalize) whereas Brahms for example, built woodwind and brass textures as if thinking of these groups from the beginning as choirs, with the constituent instruments interlocking vertically to produce a blended sound (and also when using a tutti of both groups: Ex. 7.1*a*), Musorgsky assembled his tuttis as though he was grouping together solo instruments (or pairs), with each occupying its own level in the texture, a level that might be widely separated from that of the other nearest instrument (as, for example, between clarinets and bassoons in the coda of *St John's Night*: Ex. 7.1*b*). He thus ensured that each instrument's timbre was not entirely subsumed into a generalized corporate sound, and that the texture was 'well aired'. Significantly, perhaps, Musorgsky here did not employ horns to supplement the bassoons and thus consolidate the blend in the lower part of the chord, as did Brahms. Clarity, brightness, and transparency of sound were Musorgsky's priorities.

As for content, *St John's Night* presents an abundance of ideas, and throughout its course fluctuating accidentals within themes may impart

Ex. 7.1a

Brahms, *3rd Symphony*

Ex. 7.1b

Musorgsky, *St John's Night*

a new 'modal' colouring to an old phrase. The harmony is often striking and may be non-functional, sometimes pungent, and even highly abrasive—never more so than at the headlong opening with its whirring upper-string ostinato matched heterophonically by a four-note motif delivered by, amongst others, three timpani (suggested, surely, by their similar use at the opening of *Totentanz*). The initial stretches in particular are excellent, grabbing the listener into a vivid, intimidating world conjured with uncompromisingly brutal directness and energy. Nothing that follows quite lives up to this—for, despite all its qualities, *St John's Night* is a very uneven piece. Musorgsky's inventiveness may falter and in some of the latter half run out of steam or mark time. Some of the 'obscene glorification' of Satan sounds positively wholesome, and after the work's fearsome opening much of the Sabbath appears genial; though it does have some spine-tingling passages, its graphic uncertainties are consummated when the very end recalls all too clearly the sparkling coda of Glinka's *Ruslan* overture. As for the 'chemical scale' passages, these are crude (again, compare Glinka's coda, with its brilliant application of the whole-tone scale, with Musorgsky's).

As it stood *St John's Night* was therefore as gauche as it was original. No matter: Musorgsky had produced a trail of unprecedented orchestral imagery which five years later he could adapt for another context—the witches' Sabbath in his share of the (abortive) opera-ballet *Mlada*, commissioned for the Imperial Theatres from Borodin, Rimsky-Korsakov, Cui, and Musorgsky. Musorgsky was nothing if not thorough in his 1872 revision, ruthlessly purging the cruder ideas and passages and removing irregular barring, recomposing over two-thirds of the piece, adding choral parts throughout and a new and haunting postlude that completed a transformation whose achievement could never have seemed possible in 1867.

Disaster now struck in Musorgsky's personal existence. Suddenly on 10 May 1867, evidently because of reorganization within his civil service department, he lost his post. His immediate reaction to this is unclear, but it seems he was not over-distressed, for he was still living with Filaret and his wife, he would not immediately starve, and suddenly his time was entirely his own. Significantly the rest of the year saw a notable increase in his creative activity. Except for a few weeks in St

Petersburg during September and October, the period from June to November was spent with his brother and sister-in-law at Minkino near St Petersburg, where the cost of living was lower. With the scoring of *St John's Night* completed on 5 July, 'during the night of 23/24 July' he finished orchestrating his *Intermezzo in modo classico,* which he had composed for piano in 1862 and to which he now added (as he informed Rimsky three days later) a trio[14] 'in the character of the trio from [Beethoven's] Ninth Symphony'. This done, he retranscribed the whole piece for piano. The result pleased him, even though 'it is nothing other than a tribute to the Germans, and I have dedicated it to Borodin. Anyway, I'm very glad I've done it, for it would be senseless for this B minor piece, which is quite respectable, to be wasted.' He continued:[15]

Now I'm settling myself to a [symphonic] poem on Poděbrad the Czech. In many places the *Standpunkte* already exist. The theme of the introduction goes like this:

The first part of the introduction is heard twice, second time in C sharp minor; then comes a slavonic-style *cantilena* as if it were an extension of the theme, and it ends with a tremolando from all the strings against an orchestral tutti; the crescendo by stages grows to an *ff* (an explosion), then everything gets quieter and quieter. Poděbrad's theme (the introduction depicts the sad plight of Czechiya under German oppression) is as follows:

The papal anger at Poděbrad emerges very energetically and maliciously (this bit's still at the piano-strumming stage). At the end of the poem, after a rushing about by all the strings *ff* on an A major scale and a little slavonic

[14] In fact, it is possible the new trio dated from 1863.

[15] *MLN1,* 90–1.

fanfare on the brass, there's the theme that you know (I am arranging it *a la guerra*—Poděbrad—*the king*—Slavdom has triumphed):

—and so on. Thus the poem begins in F sharp minor, ends in D major.)

What prompted Musorgsky to make a fifteenth-century Czech king the subject of his second major orchestral work is unknown. The most likely spur was Balakirev, whose personal triumph as conductor of *Ruslan* in Prague had been as great as that of the opera itself (with the consequence that his opinion of the Czechs had soared), and whose own musical tribute to the Czech people, the overture on Czech themes *In Bohemia*, had received its première only two months previously. But for all the independent spirit of the Bohemian King George of Poděbrady who, as a Hussite, had opposed the challenge of the papacy (Catholic politicking was a theme that always roused Musorgsky, as *Boris Godunov* would show), there seems little reason why he should have found much to retain his sympathy, and the project lapsed.

If Balakirev upset Musorgsky that autumn with his reservations about *St John's Night*, he handsomely offset these with active concern for the real-life plight of his protégé, now that the latter had been nearly six months without income. But a grateful Musorgsky remained convinced that he could survive adequately until into the New Year, when it might be possible to secure a permanent position. Meanwhile he spent the middle of August making piano transcriptions of various quartet movements by Beethoven 'for Saturdays at the Opochinins'[16] and—of much greater significance—between June 1867 and April 1868 composed eleven more songs.

Three are romances. *Hebrew Song* (dated 24 June 1867), a setting of Mey's paraphrase of an extract from the Old Testament *Song of Solomon*, is a two-way love song dedicated to Musorgsky's brother and sister-in-law. Rich in simple chromaticism and dissonance, and in quasi-oriental ornamentation (more so than any other song by Musorgsky), this modest but rapt two-strophe romance is as affecting a gift as the two family members, closest to him both by relationship and day-to-day living,

---

[16] Op. 59, no. 2, 3rd movement; Op. 131, 5th movement; Op. 135, 2nd and 3rd movements.

could have wished. *The Garden by the Don* (dated December 1867) is equally beautiful, if less intense—and rightly so, when the emotion is that only lightly stirred by a chance brush with a young girl as recounted in Koltsov's verse. For a moment it might appear that, like *Hebrew Song*, this will be a two-strophe piece, though here the modifications in the second strophe are more radical, and this expands greatly before all ends with a re-run of the piano introduction, the singer repeating the opening words against it. The whole song has a pervasive colour that stems above all from its delicate chromaticism, and especially its extensive use of the flattened sixth/sharpened fifth degree of the scale, to which Russian composers since Glinka had showed special favour. As with *Hebrew Song*, the individuality within the simplicity is striking, and the two songs stand as the peaks of Musorgsky's lyrical style in the later 1860s. The third romance, *Child's Song* (dated April 1868), is a song-epigram as charming as Mey's poem: Naninka in her chocolate-box cottage is safely swathed in her parents' love while she falls asleep (to judge from the inconclusive dominant-seventh ending). When the song came to be published in 1871 all but one of its unproblematic changes of bar length were removed in favour of 4/4 throughout; more important, details were trimmed, an already tiny song losing nearly one fifth of its length. But the essence of an epigram is economy, and this is one instance where Musorgsky's decision to revise was well judged. Delicious as it is (especially in some of its harmonic touches), *Child's Song* is no more than a sweetly lyrical piece that reflects an adult's sentimental view of childhood, giving not a hint of those so-illuminating real-life projections soon to come from Musorgsky in his set of songs *The Nursery*.

Three more songs are highly contrasting descriptive pieces. Musorgsky himself described *The Magpie* (dated 7 September 1867), which interleaves portions of two poems by Pushkin, as 'a joke'. It is in two unequal parts, the second a truncated repetition of the first with some reshuffling of text and music. The song is a little nonsense fantasy, set as a species of dance-song made up of four-bar phrases, standing alone or grouped in two-phrase sentences, which unfold, in effect, as a series of variations. Only the vocal entry of the gypsy dancer disrupts the racy gopakish rhythm with a more cantabile manner and five-bar phrases. The text presents a series of little images, and any chance for unforced pictorialism is grasped—the magpie chirping, the little bells tinkling, a lift from F to a brighter A major as the crimson dawn tints the snow, the dancer leaping and drum-beating. Other major—minor oscillations and abrupt key changes further enliven the piece. Already the clapping-game song early in Act 2 of *Boris* is to be heard—perhaps even, very faintly in the future, something of the bustling Shrovetide fair of Stravinsky's *Petrushka*.

Various writers have drawn attention to the relationship of the thematic nuclei of *Savishna* to the characteristic melodic turns of traditional beggars' songs and to the melodic world of the old Russian narratives, the *bilini*. Musorgsky himself was fully aware of something intrinsically Russian achieved in *The Feast*, a 'tale' setting another Koltsov text; writing to Rimsky-Korsakov on 16 October, soon after completing the piece, he copied out the first eight vocal bars, explaining that '6/4 and 5/4 constitute the entire *chic* of this morsel, and have turned out just as naturally as the 5/4 rhythm of *Savishna*. This I consider . . . both Russian and, I make bold to think, musical.'[17] Only twice is the measured tread of crotchets setting Koltsov's eleven-syllable lines momentarily disrupted. The piano part has matching economy, quietly inflecting the vocal metre by its very flexible harmonic rhythm; the key shifts in the central section afford patches of contrasting colour, but tonally the piece is firmly grounded, the formality of the magisterial ternary structure as right here as it is explicit. If *The Magpie* had foreshadowed the future, *The Feast* links with the past; peasant feast this may be, but there is a restrained epic tone to the music which establishes an affinity with the noble festivities of Svetozar's court in the first act of *Ruslan*. The dedication to Glinka's sister was therefore particularly apt.

In sharpest contrast, *The He-goat* (dated 4 January 1868), subtitled 'a worldly story', is a satirical narrative. Maiden encounters he-goat ('old, bearded, wicked—a right devil!')—and flees; same maiden encounters man ('old, bearded, wicked—a right devil!')—and marries him. Here Musorgsky was his own poet, devising parallel structures for the two halves of the story so that, when embodied in two strophes, identical or related music heard in the second might resonate with an effortless irony. A slighter piece than some of its companion songs, *The He-goat* is nevertheless a delicious example of Musorgsky's ability to catch char-

---

[17] *MLN1*, 96.

acters and physical movement in simple but vivid musical imagery—
and offer the singer splendid opportunities to exploit his dramatic sense
as narrator.

Gathering Mushrooms, composed five months earlier, had also concerned a young woman with an elderly husband, a theme common in
Russian culture; in 1880 Tchaikovsky would treat it poignantly in one
of his most national-style songs, *Was I not a little blade of grass* (it is worth
noting Gerald Abraham's shrewd observation that this subject had
'moved Tchaikovsky as far as he was capable of being moved in the
direction of Musorgsky').[18] Whether or not Mey intended the youthful
wife to be taken at her word, Musorgsky presents her displaying energetic relish at the thought of poisoning her aged spouse with mushrooms. His setting blends dance-song with monologue, employing most
of the time the crotchet patter of *Savishna* with its declamatory potential, but building from this conventionally structured melody encased
within a ternary form, though on its recurrence the opening section is
transformed by expansion and a redesigned piano part as the young
woman's thoughts turn to the young man she fancies. Symmetry
heightens the masterly tautness of the piece; not a note is wasted, thus
allowing the myriad harmonic touches—tiny, surprise progressions that
individually pass so quickly as to be almost unnoticed—to tell cumu-
latively. The challenging harmonic rhetoric of *King Saul* has gone; but
if there has been loss in audacity, the gain is in precision. If proof were
still needed of Musorgsky's totally 'professional' competence, this song
alone would suffice. *Gathering Mushrooms* was published in 1868, together with *Hebrew Song* and *The He-goat*.

Of the remaining four songs setting monologues *The Classicist* (dated
11 January 1868) is the odd-one-out and the least significant. Described
in the first of its two versions as composed 'in reply to an observation
by Famintsïn apropos the heresy of the Russian school of music', it was
a riposte to that critic's assault on Rimsky's newly performed orchestral
picture *Sadko*. The young, Leipzig-trained and highly conservative Alexander Famintsïn had for three years been professor of music history
and aesthetics at the St Petersburg Conservatoire and was to be an

---

[18] G. Abraham, 'Russia', in *A History of Song*, ed. D. Stevens (London, 1960), 367; repr. in
G. Abraham, *Essays on Russian and East European Music* (Oxford, 1985), 28.

implacable enemy of all the Balakirev group represented. Musorgsky devised his own text: 'I am simple, I am serene . . . I am a spotless classicist . . . I am the bitterest enemy of the newest artifices . . . their noise and hubbub . . . I see in them the grave of art. But I, I am simple—but I, I am serene . . . '—and so on. Musorgsky's music is the most archly chaste of classical pastiches—that is, until the central section, where the *Sadko* 'sea motif', which had given particular offence to Famïntsïn, erupts in the accompaniment. *The Classicist* is significant as the first example of such a lampoon in Russian music (in 1870 it was published) and one whose success would prompt Musorgsky to a far more ambitious assault on Russia's conservative musical forces in *The Peepshow*. Otherwise it is now merely of documentary interest.

Eremushka's Lullaby (dated 28 March 1868) is a fully lyrical piece and, in returning to the theme of peasant infancy in a world of hardship, is in direct line from Musorgsky's earlier *Cradle Song*. But while Ostrovsky's nurse had offered her grandson a prospect of survival through unremitting toil, Nekrasov's nurse can only counsel submission and then, in the gentle F sharp major final stanza, which varies music that had soundly so bleakly in the first, fantasize on escape for her orphan charge. Yet lest we doubt her irrepressible awareness of hope's hopelessness, Musorgsky's music quietly reinstates reality; the reassuringly harmonious triads and dominant sevenths drop away as her dream reaches its bare conclusion, and the minor thirds with which Musorgsky had supported her lulling refrain at the song's opening (Ex. 7.2*a*) are replaced by harsh seconds (Ex. 7.2*b*: these were expunged in the published version). The precision with which Musorgsky could now apply musical resource to illumine emotional process is deadly accurate. *Cradle Song* had remained primarily a lyrical piece exploring a single expressive world; the very different treatments given the three verses of *Eremushka's Lullaby* transform this into a muted dramatic monologue, ultimately of despair. Appropriately, it was dedicated to that 'great teacher of musical truth', Dargomïzhsky.

By contrast *The Ragamuffin* (dated 31 December 1867) is the bluntest of dramatic monologues. Clearly a blood relative of *Savishna*, it also differs sharply from it. For this is not an imbecile's hollow prattle but the verbal torrent of a sharp-witted urchin well able to fortify with shifts of metre, pace and manner the insults he directs at an ugly old

Ex. 7.2a

Ex. 7.2b

[Lullaby]

crone. He may (as Musorgsky requires) mutter 'quietly', bark out crucial words 'hurriedly', draw out 'at the top of his voice' a specially insulting phrase, then hold back in pace and volume to mouth contemptuously some offensive jibe, all the while weaving and ducking, if not always successfully, his victim's blows. The piano part likewise abandons the studied repetitiveness of *Savishna* to abet precisely the ragamuffin's every word and move. Of all Musorgsky's songs of this period, this most graphically projects a tiny, action-filled drama between two specimens of lowly humanity. Witnessed in real life, it might prompt responses ranging from anger through revulsion to thoughtless laughter. But, as in *Savishna*, Musorgsky gives no hint of personal viewpoint, neither condemning nor condoning, neither actively soliciting our pity nor suggesting personal indifference. Yet again truthful representation will be advocate enough. And since, in this truthfulness, the evolution of the drama is as crucial as its details, the song takes its shape from that evolution, in its unconcern with matters of formal musical structure going further than any other of Musorgsky's songs to date.

The Orphan (dated 25 January 1868), also to Musorgsky's own words, is the natural companion to *The Ragamuffin*. Both are dramatic monologues for street children,[19] but with crucial differences. *The Ragamuffin* had been an urchin's thoughtless taunting; *The Orphan* is a cry of pain

[19] Richard Hoops has pointed out that 'Sirota', Musorgsky's title for this song, can mean not only 'orphan' but 'peasant', and that 'the subject matter [of the song] and the manner of its treatment imply an ethical issue of broad dimensions' (R. Hoops, 'Musorgsky and the Populist Age', *MIM*, 282).

Ex. 7.3

Not very fast

Ba - rin moy, mi - len-ky, ba - rin moy, dob - ren-ky, szhal - sya nad

[Dear sir, kind sir, take pity on

bed - nen-kim, gor - kim, bez - dom - nîm si - ro - toch - koy. Ba - ri-nush-ka!

a poor, wretched, homeless orphan. O sir!

Kho - lo - dom, go - lo - dom gre - yus, korm - lyu - sya ya;

With cold, with hunger I warm, I feed myself;]

from a starving child. *The Ragamuffin* had discarded regularity of metre, and musical form as such; *The Orphan* is regularly barred, has a ternary structure, and is packed throughout with two- or four-bar phrases, each forthwith repeated. Above all, where *The Ragamuffin* had rejected all expressiveness except that which might arise from the singer's vivid declamation of music designed to allow every inflection and meaning within the text to be conveyed, *The Orphan* has wholeheartedly reinstated lyricism. The result is that, where *The Ragamuffin* can impress, even dazzle, *The Orphan* can engage our deeper responses. Modality contributes strongly; the opening (Ex. 7.3) is aeolian, a later passage is lydian, and an intervening phrase (Ex. 7.3, bars 12–15) employs an eccentric mode evidently of Musorgsky's own invention (C-D♭-E♭-F-G♭-A♭-B♮). Pictorialism is unobtrusively employed; there is a suggestion of a tolling bell in the central section's ending, a suggestion absorbed into the musical process when the song's opening music returns.

Of these songs *The Orphan*, though by no means the most radical, is as prophetic as any. If *Salammbô* had looked ahead to *Boris Godunov* (and had already unwittingly 'composed' parts of that opera), so does a song such as *The Orphan* in presaging that alliance of realism with lyricism which would produce some of the best pages in that opera.

CHAPTER 8

The Marriage: Towards *Boris*

PUSHKIN'S FOUR *LITTLE TRAGEDIES* HAVE BEEN RATED AMONG literary critics as his most remarkable dramatic creations. Concentrated dramatic vignettes, the longest only some 500 lines of blank verse, they are so fleeting it is difficult to envisage them staged. But their very concentration, their mingling of the colloquial with the poetic, their economy and precision in character delineation, and their structural tautness made them gifts to the opera composer—provided each was accepted on its own terms. In due course Rimsky-Korsakov would set *Mozart and Salieri*, Cui *A Feast in Time of Plague*, and Rachmaninov *The Covetous Knight*. But first in the field was Dargomïzhsky with *The Stone Guest*. Its subject was the final stage of the Don Juan legend. With his servant Leporello the Don returns secretly to Madrid from exile to renew his liaison with the actress Laura. Outside a monastery he sees Donna Anna, widow of the Commander whom Juan had killed in a duel; then at Laura's he encounters Don Carlos, the Commander's brother, who challenges him and is also despatched. Juan's new objective is Donna Anna. Disguised as a monk, he lays siege to her in the cemetery beneath the Commander's statue, professes himself a languishing lover, and extracts from her a meeting next day at her house. Before leaving he invites the Commander's statue to stand guard while he seduces the widow. The statue nods assent. At Anna's house the Don reveals his identity, yet succeeds in overcoming Anna's horror. But the Commander's statue intrudes and drags him down to hell.

What *The Stone Guest* offered Dargomïzhsky was a miniature play concise enough to be set as it stood, and requiring of music no more than substantiation of the event or sentiment of the moment. But for a composer in 1865 this was still a major challenge, for nothing in Pushkin allowed for formal arias and ensembles which, in addition to their time-honoured potential for emotional amplification or heightened drama, had also afforded structural landmarks. But what could be more 'truthful' than to allow the text itself to provide the substance and the form, everything musical being accomplished through a shifting between recitative and varieties of arioso? This would, of course, require unprecedented resourcefulness if the result were not to sound starved. But, given good singers, the reward of such self-denial would be an unobstructed presentation of Pushkin's miniature tragedy enhanced by those special insights into human feeling and behaviour that music can offer.

Dargomïzhsky began work in 1865, but progress was initially painfully slow, and by 1868 he was a sick man with less than a year to live. But while failing health added urgency to his task, the intense interest now shown by his younger colleagues also further fuelled his zeal and boosted his confidence, and on 17 March the scene at Laura's was performed at his home, with Musorgsky as Don Carlos, Alexandra Purgold as Laura, and her sister Nadezhda, soon to become Rimsky-Korsakov's bride, at the piano. It drew great enthusiasm, and such sessions became almost weekly events, each newly composed bit being tried out with Musorgsky adding Leporello to his roles and Dargomïzhsky himself taking the part of the Don. By the end of April the opera was three-quarters done. But soon other distractions intervened; work finally ceased, and after Dargomïzhsky's death the following January the piece was completed, as he had wished, by Cui and orchestrated by Rimsky.

The Stone Guest has sometimes been dismissed as no more than an interesting curiosity. In fact, though there was little in the musical style and technique that had not been foretold in Dargomïzhsky's most recent opera *Rusalka* and some of his most characteristic songs, neither this particular novel experiment nor the achievement it would represent could have been predicted, and on the stage it works perfectly well. Despite the setting being syllabic almost throughout, there is little plain recitative; rather, Dargomïzhsky's style is a shifting arioso or cantilena

which Cui characterized as 'melodic recitative'. Though Dargomïzhsky's skills were sufficient to achieve some modest character dif-
ferentiation in dialogue, what brought out the best in him were those
passages where Pushkin's poetry is charged with human feeling; when
challenged by these, Dargomïzhsky's arioso can fill out, sometimes with
the sustained expressive intensity expected of an aria—as, for instance,
in the scene between Laura and Don Carlos, where Carlos's solicitous
warning to Laura of the transience of youth turns out as tender as
Laura's ensuing monologue on the loveliness of the night is beautiful.
Only the very end of the opera disappoints, the music becoming
bogged down in mannered reiterations of the whole-tone scale (of
which there has already been a large dose at the end of the preceding
scene) as the Commander exacts retribution.

Musorgsky was impressed; he had to try something of the sort for
himself, and by 8 May 1868 he could present a radically new song to
'that great teacher of musical truth', as he put it in his dedication of
the piece to the older composer. The text of *With Nurse*, in which a
child pesters his nurse for a story, constantly changing his mind about
which one it shall be, was of Musorgsky's own devising. Now it was
Dargomïzhsky's turn to be impressed; 'That's outdone me!' Rimsky
recorded him as saying.[1] Indeed it had. Again a child speaks, but this
time it is not the unrelenting abuse of the hectoring street arab in *The
Ragamuffin* or the importunate pleading of the starving waif in *The
Orphan*, but a bubbling stream of childish prattle, turning this way and
that through humours, questions, and entreaties—the most ingenuous,
uncoordinated chatter, demanding constant shifts of musical mood,
tone, and intonation.

The result is a miniature, virtuoso dramatic monologue. Though it
runs its course mostly to syllabically set crotchets, the phrases are designed, through contour, interval, and the twenty-six changes of metre
in fifty-three bars (abetted by Musorgsky's minutely detailed expressive
indications), to ensure the singer can reflect every verbal inflection and
tone. Though the words may give the impression of being almost ca-
sually compiled, it seems highly plausible that Musorgsky created text
and music in tandem, for the former in no way cramps the latter's own

[1] *TDM*, 153.

resources, successive verbal phrases on occasion making up couplets (perhaps with unobtrusive rhyme endings) that encourage pairs of balanced musical phrases (Ex. 8.1, bars 6–9). The melody ranges from quasi-recitative (bars 1–3) to moments of disarming lyricism (and especially of grotesquerie as the child envisages the 'terrible bogeyman', bar 5, then relishes the frisson afforded by his consumption of children) or pictures later in the song, with the piano's mimetic collaboration, the hobbling king and his queen whose sneezes shatter the palace windows. The harmony is rarely functional (though not undirected), being where necessary fragmented and dissonant to make it the closest of allies to the voice, whether concerned with atmosphere, emphasis, emotion, or mimicry. Equally novel is the compensatingly firm control of extensive stretches through a succession of 'pivot pitches' to create phases of local stability. A pivot pitch, which sometimes operates for only a few bars but at others for a more prolonged period, differs from a pedal in rarely being present at every moment in a passage and in freely migrating to different levels in the texture. While lacking the unbroken presence of the true pedal, each pivot pitch becomes an unobtrusive anchorage for a stretch of music, and may (unlike a true pedal) exercise a strong, if not absolute control on the chords employed. Thus, throughout the first section of thirteen bars of Ex. 8.1, B♭ is rarely absent, later D is for a while important, and in the second half D♭/C♯ underpins some nine bars. Pivot pitches as fundamental structural agents were to be exploited further in stretches of *Boris*.

But a single song would not satisfy Musorgsky. Prompted, it seems, by Dargomïzhsky and Cui, he embarked on his own experiment in Dargomïzhsky's new kind of opera, choosing as text Gogol's two-act comedy *The Marriage*. Podkolesin, a court counsellor living with his servant Stepan, is a prospective but reluctant bridegroom. A marriage broker, Fyokla, has selected his bride but after three months is impatient for a decision from the suitor. Podkolesin's friend Kochkaryov decides to take over. Matters are complicated when it emerges that Podkolesin is only one of five potential bridegrooms lined up by Fyokla. By a series of stratagems Kochkaryov manages to dispose of the four rivals, then brings Podkolesin to the point of agreeing to go through with the ceremony. But left to himself for a moment, the latter's nerve fails him and he escapes matrimony through a window.

Ex. 8.1

[Tell me, nanny, tell me, my dear, about that,

about that terrible bogeyman; how that bogeyman wandered through the woods,

how that bogeyman carried children into the wood, and how he gnawed their white [bones]]

Musorgsky began work on *The Marriage* on 23 June 1868, and within nine days his first scene was finished; then, having shown what he had done to both Dargomïzhsky and Cui, who urged greater simplicity, he left St Petersburg to join his brother and sister-in-law at their new country home at Shilovo, near Tula, to the south of Moscow. Here during the daytime he withdrew to a hut on the estate, and by 14 July had roughed out the second scene, even though he was without a piano (he would set everything in order when he returned to St Petersburg, he told Cui). The next day he summarized for Cui his objectives: 'The first act can serve, in my view, as an experiment in *opera dialogué* . . . [In it] I am trying to delineate as sharply as possible those shifts of intonation which occur in the characters' dialogue, evidently for the most trivial of reasons and in the most unimportant words, but in which, it seems to me, is hidden the power of Gogol's humour.'[2] On 18 July the third scene was done, on 20 July the fourth was signed, and Act 1 was complete, though unorchestrated.

For the moment Musorgsky decided not to proceed with *The Marriage*. Perhaps it was imperative he rested: 'I worked intensively: that was how it worked out—but intensive work tells on one', he wrote to Rimsky on 11 August. 'Any speech I hear, whoever is speaking (but, more important, whatever is being said)—already my brain is working out a musical statement of that speech.'[3] And so he relaxed in country pursuits—raking in the hay, and making jam and marinades—and pondering much the meaning of art, and the conditions that should govern its creation. The letters from his nine weeks at Shilovo are peppered with statements about his ideals, aims, and methods. Striking is the self-confidence with which he trenchantly sets out for Rimsky what he now sees as the creator's responsibility—and his freedom to decide what should result:[4]

> Now, my dear Korsinka, listen to one thing: creation carries within itself its own laws of refinement. Their verification is inner criticism: the artist's instinct determines their application. If one or the other is not present, there is no creative artist: if there is a creative artist there must be both one and the other—and the artist is a law unto himself.

To Nikolsky he went back to the ancient world in justification of his new credo, a precedent probably suggested to him by the work of the German literary scholar Georg Gottfried Gervinus, whose *Händel und Shakespeare: Zur Aesthetik der Tonkunst* had appeared in the same year as

[2] *MLNI*, 97–8.
[3] *MLNI*, 102.
[4] *MLNI*, p. 107.

The Marriage and whom Musorgsky would cite in his *Autobiographical Note* of 1880[5] as having been an influence upon him:[6]

> The Greeks worshipped nature, which means man also. Both great poetry and the greatest of the arts sprang from this. I continue: in the ranking of nature's creations man constitutes the highest organism (at least on Earth), and this highest organism possesses the gift of speech and voice unequalled in earthly organisms generally. If you will sanction the reproduction by artistic means of human *speech* with all its most subtle and capricious shades, represent it naturally as is required by man's life and constitution—will this not come close to the deification of the human gift of speech? And if it is possible, with the simplest of means, to tug at the heart strings simply by strict submission to artistic instinct in catching the intonations of the human voice, ought one not to devote oneself to this? And if moreover it is also possible to catch the intellectual faculty, then is it not fitting to devote oneself to such a pursuit?

To Shestakova a fortnight earlier he had been yet more specific about what all this meant (and, indeed, had already meant) in practical terms in his own music:[7]

> This is what I would like—that my characters should speak on stage as living people speak—but moreover, so that the character and strength of intonation of my characters, supported by the orchestra which provides the musical framework for their mode of speech, should achieve their aim directly—that is, my music must be the artistic reproduction of human speech in all its subtlest inflections, that is, *the sounds of human speech* as the external manifestation of thought and feeling must, without exaggeration and forcing, become truthful, precise *music*, but artistic, highly artistic. This is the ideal towards which I strive (*Savishna*, *The Orphan*, *Eremushka*['s *Lullaby*], *The Child* [*With Nurse*]).

And, above all, in *The Marriage*. But realizing he would have to win over his fellow-musicians not through the validity of his theory but

---

[5] For a discussion of the Musorgsky/Gervinus relationship and a highly detailed examination of *The Marriage*, especially in regard to text setting, see R. Taruskin, 'Handel, Shakespeare, and Musorgsky: the Sources and Limits of Russian Musical Realism', *TM*, 71–95.

[6] *MLN1*, 102–3.

[7] *MLN1*, 100.

from what they made of his music when they heard it, he wrote the same day to Rimsky:[8]

> I worked as best I could. You will all judge whether I have succeeded: I am on trial. Only one thing I will say: if you renounce operatic traditions in general and imagine to yourself musical conversation on the stage—as just unblushing conversation—then *The Marriage* is an opera. I wish to say that if the expression in sound of human thought and feeling *through simple speech* is truly reproduced by me *in music* and this reproduction is musically artistic, then it's in the bag. This is what you have to discuss, and I will stand aside.

In the meanwhile, he wasted no time in his search for material that might serve in future compositions, scrutinizing intently the human world around him at Shilovo. 'I am observing peasant men and women—I have found some appetizing examples', he wrote to Cui:[9]

> One peasant is the image of Anthony in Shakespeare's *Julius Caesar*—when Anthony is making his speech in the forum over Caesar's corpse. A very intelligent and, in his own way, malicious peasant. All these will come in useful—and the peasant women types are simply a treasure. With me it's always thus: I notice certain kinds of people and then, when the occasion arises, I pull them out.

The trial run of *The Marriage* before the kuchka and company took place soon after Musorgsky's return to St Petersburg after 5 September. Rimsky remembered the occasion. '*The Marriage* provoked not a little interest. All were startled by Musorgsky's task, were delighted by his characterizations and many of his recitative phrases, were perplexed by some of his chords and harmonic progressions.' In the performance Musorgsky sang Podkolesin, Alexandra Purgold was Fyokla, Konstantin Velyaminov was Stepan, and Nadezhda Purgold accompanied. Kochkaryov was taken by Dargomïzhsky, who was so enthusiastic that he copied out the part for himself. Reactions were mixed. 'Stasov went into raptures. Dargomïzhsky sometimes said the composer had gone a bit too far. Balakirev and Cui saw in *The Marriage* merely a curiosity

---

[8] *MLN1*, 101–2.
[9] *MLN1*, 105.

with interesting declamatory moments.'[10] Borodin was to take a similar view.

The Marriage is certainly an extraordinary piece, and its mixed reception no surprise. Even if Musorgsky and Dargomïzhsky had not been very different creative personalities, both in kind and stature, the former's choice of text would have been guarantee enough that what resulted would be very different from the opera that had prompted it. Pushkin's *The Stone Guest* was a tragedy in verse set in an aristocratic past, Gogol's *The Marriage* a contemporary comedy in colloquial prose, peopled by such as merchants and civil servants. And while Dargomïzhsky's *The Stone Guest* is remarkable not for its novelty of sound but for its unprecedented application of a limited number of familiar forms and styles to the exclusion of others, Musorgsky's *The Marriage* is a piece whose very idiom was radical. Its roots, as Musorgsky recognized, lay in his post-*Savishna* songs, but even these were scarcely preparation for what confronted his listener in this 'Experiment in dramatic music in prose', as Musorgsky himself labelled it.

Ex. 8.2 points up the fundamental differences between the two composers. Ex. 8.2*a* comes from early in the first scene of *The Stone Guest*, Leporello's opening three bars a snippet of Dargomïzhsky's simple kind of quasi-recitative. But the use of a (presumably) wellworn expression of the Don's draws from Leporello a pointed emphasis and a filling-out of the musical substance. The Don's rejoinder displays a sudden buoyancy (he has emerged from melancholy reflections on an earlier love, Ineza, now dead). Having declared a vigorous intention of calling on Laura, he is momentarily struck by the thought that another lover may already be there, and reflecting on how to cope with this causes disruptions to his flow of words (bar 16—the orchestra now sustaining the musical framework). But quickly the Don's gaiety returns (bar 19—*forte* orchestral chord), for he will bid his rival exit via the window. And, as the final orchestral descent indicates, that will settle that!

Ex. 8.2*b* is the opening of *The Marriage*. While Dargomïzhsky throughout had reflected the shifts of tone and emotion with a detailed fidelity and consistency unprecedented in nineteenth-century opera, Musorgsky homes in on the words themselves as spoken by Gogol's

[10] *RKL*, 82.

Ex. 8.2a

Dargomïzhsky, *The Stone Guest*

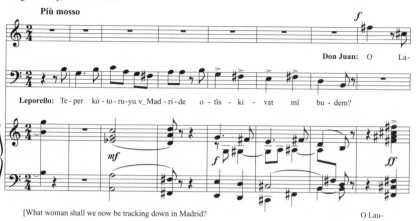

[What woman shall we now be tracking down in Madrid?

O Lau-

ra! I am running to her to present myself.

An affair. Straight to her door, and

if someone is already with her—

I'll ask him to jump out of the window!]

Ex. 8.2b

Musorgsky, *The Marriage*

Rather slowly—lazily

Podkolesin: Vot, kak nach-nyosh e-tak o-din na do - su-ge po-du-mĭ-vat, tak vi-dish,

[Well, when you begin reflecting on it at leisure, then you see that

shto toch-no— na-do zhe-nit-sya. Shto, v_sa-mom de-le?

yes, you should marry. What, indeed?

Zhi-vyosh, zhi-vyosh, da ta - ka-ya, na-ko-nets, skver-nost sta-no-vit-sya.

You live, you live, but in the end it becomes highly unpalatable.]

characters, with their myriad details of verbal nuance, pitch, and pace, reproducing these with as much flexible exactitude as was possible within the arithmetically related durations of conventional musical notation and the precise pitches of the chromatic scale (where Gogol's text did not suit his purpose exactly he had no hesitation in making modifications). *With Nurse* had attempted nothing as finely tuned as this. But it is also the outer man as perceived by the eye as well as the inner man revealed in his words that is Musorgsky's concern. The opening discovers Podkolesin reclining on a couch smoking a pipe, his two-bar theme burdened with the inertia and lassitude of a hopelessly indecisive bachelor. The ponderously slurred pairs of notes in bars 3–4 reflect perhaps a lazy fidget as he tries to get himself comfortable, the resolution onto a relaxed C major in bar 6 signal the attainment of total ease, where blissful puffing may begin and he can muse, cosily cushioned on leisurely chords, upon what he has to do, untroubled by any instant pressure to get on and do it. And when he begins his train of drifting consciousness, the phrases are sluggish, broken, yet fastidiously rhythmicized; only as he approaches the mention of marriage and an image of hard reality begins emerging through his mental mists does his voice rise in pitch and power. A brief pause, with a reference to his thematic identity card, and his soliloquy abruptly resumes with clear evidence of mounting agitation (his sudden *mf* entry, the prominence of the tritone, the steep rise and fall on 'you live, you live' which at the top is dissonant with the orchestra, the excruciating discord on 'skvernost,' literally 'nastiness'). Even more than in *With Nurse* the accompaniment throughout *The Marriage* is often fragmentary, perhaps merely a tiny detail in substantiation of the word(s) of the moment. Tonal reference and functional harmony play a minimal role; as in *With Nurse* major and minor seconds can have autonomous status. Economy is Musorgsky's watchword, both in voice and orchestra.

Each of the other three characters in the portion of Gogol's play set by Musorgsky has his or her characterizing theme. All suggest movement, Stepan's the lumbering, stumbling gait of an evidently aged (or just lazy?) servant, while Fyokla's and Kochkaryov's personify activity. Fyokla is introduced by three roughly energetic ideas suitable for a character for whom it was 'only one step from bragging gossip to rudeness or a shrewish trick',[11] while Kochkaryov whizzes in to a semiquaver scalic theme that proclaims an irrepressible activist upon whose schemes and manoeuvrings Podkolesin will be tossed until, inescapably confronted with his matrimonial destiny, he will commit perhaps the most decisive act of his whole life, and jump out of a window. Not surprisingly it was these two characters who immediately captivated the first private audience. Where Podkolesin and Stepan are passive and outwardly drab (though in fact it is the revelation of Podkolesin in soliloquy and in his relationship with his servant that is perhaps Musorgsky's most notable single achievement in *The Marriage*), Fyokla and Kochkaryov are extravert and more obviously projected. The matchmaker is a peasant type; Fyokla's introduction has a whiff of folksong about its final idea (in fact, just as Fyokla the matchmaker will produce the bride, so from this phrase is mothered the tender little orchestral idea later associated with the bride-to-be). Her breathless listing of the dowry provisions is the nearest thing to a set-piece monologue, and the opera's most explicit anticipation of the world of *Boris*; the hostess in the Inn Scene is in direct line from Fyokla.

Though like *The Stone Guest*, *The Marriage* dispenses with key signatures, and though functional harmony plays a diminished role, key still retains some real importance. Ex. 8.2*b* offers a strong initial suggestion of C-centred music launched from a tonic base, with a resumption from the dominant in bar 13, and though there are plenty of stretches to come that have other tonal allegiances (or none at all), C as a centre has an obstinate if intermittent pull throughout the first scene, and it is the key in which the act will decisively end. Meanwhile C major has become something of a tonal badge for Podkolesin, just as A major will become Fyokla's (though, routed by Kochkaryov, she exits in A minor), and an even firmer F major Kochkaryov's; these, too, will exercise a modest pull throughout the scenes in which these characters appear.

The music of *The Marriage* revealed a wide ranging and devastatingly precise comic dramatist at work. And while still occupied with Act 1 Musorgsky was planning ahead for the rest of the opera. One project confided to Cui gives some insight into his musico-dramatic intentions,

[11] *MLN*1, 98.

in this instance the manipulation for dramatic purposes of a theme associated with a specific event.[12]

> I have invented for Podkolesin a very successful orchestral phrase which I can use to best advantage in the match-making scene:

> Dargom[izhsky] seems perfectly satisfied with it, and it appears for the first time in the conversation with Stepan at the words 'Well, and didn't he ask?' and so on . . . in a word, about the marriage. This, as you see, is a fragment of a theme; the whole will appear intact at the moment of the formal matchmaking in Act 3, when Podkolesin has already decided to get married.

Already fragments of this theme, or derivatives from it, have haunted the orchestral part in Act 1.

Taken as far as it went, *The Marriage* is a modestly entertaining experience. But Musorgsky had set only about one fifth of Gogol's text, and since it depended so entirely on the detailed projection of the minutiae of minute-to-minute existence, to have pursued this for a further couple of hours or so could have left the spectator feeling that Act 1 had really been enough, much as some readers of James Joyce's *Ulysses* (a not dissimilar kind of enterprise) may feel after a few hundred pages that the author has done something very original but by now has made his point. Certainly Musorgsky realized (or came to realize) that what he was engaged on could be only a modest-scale experiment and had already served its purpose. But 'if God grants me life and strength, I shall speak on a large scale; after *The Marriage* the Rubicon is crossed'.[13] And his final objective was clear. 'Through the gloom of uncertainty I see, nevertheless, a bright point of light', he declared to Nikolsky, 'and that point of light is the complete rejection by society of former (though, however, still existing) operatic traditions.'[14] So though at Shilovo he conducted a thorough review of what he had already composed, he would add nothing more.

[12] *MLN1*, 97.
[13] *MLN1*, 100.
[14] *MLN1*, 103.

The early autumn of 1868 saw several private performances of *The Marriage* within Musorgsky's circle of friends. Otherwise we have very little information about his personal life over the next year, though this would see the completion of the first version of his greatest creative enterprise, on which he would embark within only weeks of returning to St Petersburg. Exactly why and when Musorgsky set about his opera based on Pushkin's drama *Boris Godunov* is unclear. In his *Autobiographical Note* he wrote that 'the friendly contact with Professor Nikolsky at Shestakova's was what caused the grand opera *Boris Godunov* to be composed',[15] and in early November Shestakova presented Musorgsky with a volume of Pushkin's works containing the play, with blank pages interleaved on which he could devise his own libretto. What is certain is that by early November any thoughts of continuing *The Marriage* had finally evaporated, and by 16 November the first scene of Musorgsky's masterpiece had already been composed.

Yet *The Marriage* retained a unique place in its composer's affections. On 14 January 1873, Stasov's birthday, at a time when Musorgsky was feeling increasingly isolated from his fellow kuchkists, he presented his faithful friend with the manuscript of this experiment. 'How may one provide some little amusement for a man who is dear to you?' he wrote in the covering letter. 'Without the slightest hesitation, as with all hot-heads, the answer comes: give him your very self. And so I do.'[16]

[15] *MLN1*, 268.
[16] *MLN1*, 144.

CHAPTER 9

Boris Godunov: Composition and Production

W ITHOUT NIKOLAY KARAMZIN RUSSIAN LITERATURE MIGHT
have evolved very differently. In the dying years of the eigh-
teenth century the young Karamzin sought selfconsciously to transform
the Russian written language, giving it a Gallic elegance, converting
French words and phrases into Russian, banishing increasingly archaic
Slavonic words, lightening the syntax, and bringing a French sensibility
to bear upon his subjects. *Poor Liza*, his sentimental story of a girl
seduced, then abandoned, who finally drowns herself, became a cult
bestseller. In verse, too, he refined the Russian language and began
probing man's inner emotional world; as D. S. Mirsky put it, his reforms
'facilitated the coming of an age of *classical* poetry: the ultimate justification of Karamzin's language is that it became the language of
Pushkin'.[1]

Yet having established himself as a man of letters, in 1803 Karamzin
abandoned literature to become the court historian, and in 1818 he
issued the first eight volumes of his massive *History of the Russian State*.
Three further volumes (and an uncompleted fourth) followed, bringing
the narrative through the tsardom of Boris Godunov to the threshold
of the accession of the Romanov dynasty which would rule Russia
from 1613 until the 1917 Revolution.

---

[1] D. S. Mirsky, *A History of Russian Literature*, ed. and abridged by F. J. Whitfield (London,
1968), 60.

Like Gibbon's *Decline and Fall of the Roman Empire* from nearly half a century earlier, Karamzin's history swiftly achieved classic status. A close friend of the reigning Tsar, Alexander I, Karamzin believed that the state, to be strong, demanded autocracy. What had shaped Russia's past were her rulers, not their subjects, and it was on these that he focussed. But he was no dry pedagogue; his historical record benefitted from the resources developed in his literary experiments, his narrative being informed by a lively sensibility that could operate all the more readily when the lives of his principal players were often so eventful, even turbulent. When the occasion offered, he had no hesitation in turning story-teller or prose dramatist. Yet propagandist as he was, Karamzin preserved a strongly moral view of his subjects, judging strictly, if sentimentally, their virtues and failings by the standards of his own time.[2]

What he told, therefore, was a very human tale. So it is no wonder that in September 1825, when creating his own 'romantic tragedy' on Boris, Pushkin could write to a friend: 'You want to know the *plan*? Take the end of the tenth and the whole of the eleventh volume [of Karamzin's history], and there you have it', even describing Karamzin's work as 'palpitant comme la gazette d'hier'.[3] A contemporary critic would be even more explicit: Pushkin's play was just 'bits of Karamzin divided into scenes and conversations'.[4]

But in writing *Boris Godunov* in 1824–5 Pushkin was less interested in history than in literary reform. While Russian tragic drama into the early nineteenth century had mostly followed the magisterial neoclassical French tradition, Pushkin now envisaged a Russian tragedy modelled on Shakespeare, with freedom from constraints of time, situation, or language, where poetry and colloquial prose, Tsar and beggar, the

[2] For a summary of the historical events on which Musorgsky's opera was based, see C. Emerson: 'Tsar Boris in History' *MBG*, 3–11. For an investigation of Musorgsky's direct debt to Karamzin, see A. Orlova and M. Shneerson, 'After Pushkin and Karamzin.: Researching the Sources for the Libretto of *Boris Godunov*', *MIM*, 249–70.

[3] From, respectively, letters to Pyotr Vyazemsky and Vassily Zhukovsky. Quoted in T. Wolff, *Pushkin on Literature* (London, 1971), 160, 158.

[4] Quoted in J. Bayley, *Pushkin: a Comparative Commentary* (Cambridge, 1971), 180. Bayley's examination of Pushkin's play is invaluable, as is C. Emerson, 'Musorgsky's Literary Sources, Karamzin and Pushkin', *MBG*, 12–34.

tragic and comic, might freely coexist. His drama, in its complete version, unfolded in twenty-four scenes:

1 The Kremlin Palace: 4 March 1598. Princes Shuisky and Vorotïnsky discuss Boris's outward reluctance to become Tsar. Shuisky is convinced Boris was behind the murder of the infant Tsarevich, Dmitri, at Uglich seven years earlier, and that he will ultimately agree to take the throne.

2 Red Square. The populace lament their leaderless state. Shchelkalov, secretary to the Duma, reports that on the morrow the Patriarch will lead a further attempt to persuade Boris.

3 The Maiden's Field, Novodevichy Monastery. The crowd await Boris's decision. Finally they learn he has agreed to take the throne.

4 The Kremlin Palace. Boris addresses the Patriarch and boyars, and invites the whole nation to a feast. Shuisky expediently counsels Vorotïnsky to forget their earlier conversations.

5 Night. A cell in the Chudov Monastery. The aged monk Pimen is concluding his chronicle with the death of the Tsarevich. The young, ambitious novice Grigory questions Pimen about this, and Pimen discloses that Boris is a regicide, having been responsible for the death of the infant Tsarevich at Uglich. This greatly excites Grigory.

6 The Patriarch's Palace. The Patriarch is furious to learn from the Father Superior of the Chudov Monastery that Grigory has absconded, declaring he will become Tsar.

7 The Tsar's Palace. Two servants discuss Boris's preoccupation with sorcerors and fortune-tellers. Boris enters and, alone, laments the inner misery of his six-year, otherwise peaceful if not untroubled, reign. At the end he reveals obliquely what burdens him: the murder of the Tsarevich.

8 An inn on the Lithuanian border. Two vagabond monks, Varlaam and Missail, with Grigory, now in secular dress. The hostess tells Grigory that the road leads to the frontier and that someone who has fled Moscow is being sought. Police officers enter with a description of the wanted man. Grigory escapes through a window.

9 Shuisky's house in Moscow. Afanasy Pushkin [an ancestor of the poet] informs an alarmed Shuisky that a pretender has appeared in Poland and is gaining support.

10 The Tsar's Palace. A domestic scene between Boris and his children, Feodor and Kseniya. Subsequently Shuisky reports the appearance of a

pretender claiming to be the murdered Dmitri. Alone, Boris reacts strongly, but determines to stand firm.

11 Wisniowiecki's house in Cracow. Grigory, now known as Dmitri, discusses religion with Father Czernikowski, then meets a motley group of his supporters.

12 In the Wojewoda [Governor] Mniszek's castle at Sambor his daughter, Marina, is being dressed to meet Dmitri, and talks about him with her maid Ruzia.

13 In a suite of lighted rooms in Mniszek's castle a ball is in progress. Mniszek envisages his daughter as the Tsaritsa. Marina dances with Dmitri and arranges a *rendez-vous* later beside the fountain.

14 Night in the garden beside the fountain. Dmitri, in love with Marina, confesses he is a runaway monk. The ambitious Marina declares she will marry him only when he has ousted Boris.

15 The Lithuanian border (28 October 1604). Dmitri, with Polish troops, approaches and crosses into Russia.

16 The Tsar's Duma. Boris talks of the measures taken against Dmitri. The Patriarch, to Boris's visible agitation, tells of a blind shepherd whose sight was miraculously restored at the Tsarevich's grave at Uglich, then counsels that the child's remains be brought to Moscow and exhibited to counter any pretender's claim. Boris's agitation is widely noted, and Shuisky diplomatically rejects the Patriarch's proposal as untimely, and says that he personally will appear before the people and scotch the rumours.

17 A plain near Novgorod-Seversky (2 January 1605). A battle. Russians flee in disarray. A victorious Dmitri disengages his forces.

18 The square before the cathedral in Moscow. Inside the cathedral the anathema is being pronounced against the Pretender. Outside a crowd of urchins torment the Simpleton. When Boris emerges the Simpleton asks him to kill his tormentors 'as you murdered the little Tsarevich'. Boris protects the Simpleton from the incensed boyars, and begs for his prayers. But the Simpleton declares he cannot pray for a 'Tsar-Herod'.

19 Sevsk. Dmitri interrogates a Russian prisoner—and learns, to his amusement, that the Russian camp consider him 'both a criminal and a good fellow'.

20 A forest. Dmitri has lost a battle and sets up camp for the night. As he falls asleep his companion, Pushkin, remains optimistic.

21 The Tsar's palace in Moscow. Boris has heard that Dmitri's fortunes have recovered. He appoints Basmanov his commander, then withdraws to receive foreign guests. Outside he suddenly collapses, is brought back in and, alone, gives his son advice and bids him farewell. The boyars return and swear allegiance to Feodor. Boris takes the tonsure as he prepares for death.

22 A military headquarters. Pushkin tries to persuade a very ambivalent Basmanov to defect.

23 The place of execution in Red Square. Pushkin reports that the 'true Dmitri' is approaching and that Basmanov has now joined him. The crowd hail Dmitri and condemn the Godunovs.

24 Boris's house in the Kremlin; guards at the entrance. Feodor and his sister are prisoners. The crowd are divided about them. Boyars enter the house. Noise within. A boyar comes out to report Feodor and his mother dead from poison. The crowd are ordered to proclaim Dmitri. They remain silent.

Pushkin set great store by *Boris Godunov*, yet it is one of his least satisfactory works. As the preceding summary shows, its scenes veer unceremoniously between the various protagonists and social groups from whose actions the plot accumulates. Interaction between the main characters, the source of Shakespeare's greatest dramatic achievements and the means through which his characters not only declare themselves but grow, scarcely exists. Indeed, Boris never confronts his arch-enemy the Pretender, appears in only six of Pushkin's scenes, and reveals himself only insofar as circumstances may force on him a personal participation or permit a soliloquy. Events, not personalities, fix the course of Pushkin's play; the result is less an organic human drama than a decorative historical tapestry woven to record a succession of critical incidents.

In fact, for Musorgsky this made the task of devising a scenario all the easier, for an organic drama could not have been dismantled without threatening its integrity. As it was, the selection of a number of the more crucial incidents from Pushkin (but embracing all six scenes in which Boris had appeared), with conflation and amplification elsewhere, could result in a scenario as dramatically viable as that of its source. Indeed, in his first version of *Boris* Musorgsky based only three scenes directly on Pushkin (while making revisions in all of them) and drew material from only seven others, even amputating all four consecutive scenes dealing with the Pretender's Polish interlude. The libretto was in part drawn from Pushkin's original either exactly or adjusted, in part of Musorgsky's own devising.[5] No doubt to signify that his new creation was no conventional opera, Musorgsky headed it 'Musical representation in four parts and seven scenes'. It was organized as follows:

PART 1
Scene 1 A courtyard of the Novodevichy Monastery. A crowd implores Boris to accept the crown. Shchelkalov emerges to report that Boris still refuses, and enjoins the people to pray for Russia and Boris. A procession of pilgrims appears and enters the monastery. A police officer instructs the crowd to go to the Kremlin next day and await orders. The crowd, dispirited, disperses. [Based on Pushkin, scenes 2 and 3]
Scene 2 Red Square (Coronation Scene). The crowd sing Boris's praises. The newly crowned Tsar emerges from the Uspensky Cathedral, reflects on his inner turmoil, then invites all to his coronation feast. The crowd renew their praises. [Boris's address largely drawn from Pushkin, scene 4; otherwise the scene is Musorgsky's invention]

PART 2
Scene 1 Night. A cell in the Chudov Monastery. Pimen is concluding his chronicle with the death of the Tsarevich. Grigory questions Pimen about this, and Pimen reveals the truth. This greatly excites Grigory. [Based on Pushkin, scene 5]
Scene 2 An inn on the Lithuanian border. Varlaam and Missail, with Grigory. The hostess tells Grigory that the road leads to the frontier and that a runaway from Moscow is being sought. Police officers enter with a description of the wanted man. Grigory escapes through a window. [Based on Pushkin, scene 8]

PART 3
The Tsar's Palace. Kseniya, comforted by her nurse, laments her dead betrothed, while Feodor studies a map of Russia. Boris enters, talks with his

[5] For a meticulously detailed examination of Musorgsky's use (and otherwise) of Pushkin, see 'Musorgsky's *Boris* and Pushkin's' in G. Abraham, *Slavonic and Romantic Music* (London, 1968), 178–87.

children, then laments the inner misery of his six-year, otherwise peaceful if troubled, reign—how he has tried to serve his people, but how his efforts have been thwarted by misfortunes for which his people have blamed him. A boyar appears and suggests that Shuisky is conspiring with Poles against Boris. Shuisky in turn enters and reports the appearance of a pretender claiming to be the murdered Dmitri. Boris orders that the borders with Lithuania and Poland be closed, then grills Shuisky about the on-the-spot investigation he had conducted into the death of the Tsarevich. Increasingly agitated, Boris dismisses Shuisky, then imagines the ghost of Dmitri rising before him, and collapses onto his knees. [Based on Pushkin, scenes 7 and 10]

PART 4

Scene 1 The square before St Basil's Cathedral in Moscow. Inside the cathedral the anathema is being pronounced against the Pretender. The crowd discuss the authenticity of the Pretender, then openly turn on Boris until cautioned to silence. A crowd of urchins torment the Simpleton, who sings a song before the urchins steal a kopek from him. As Boris emerges the crowd beg food from him, and the Simpleton complains about his stolen kopek, exhorting Boris to kill his tormentors 'as you murdered the little Tsarevich'. Boris protects the Simpleton from the incensed Shuisky, and begs for his prayers, but the Simpleton replies that he cannot pray for a Tsar-Herod. All leave except the Simpleton, who adds a second verse to his song [Based on Pushkin, scene 18]

Scene 2 The Great Hall in the Kremlin. An emergency meeting of the Duma. Shchelkalov reports the emergence of the Pretender. The boyars support Boris's decree of dire punishment for him. Shuisky enters and tells of having secretly observed Boris's uncontrolled reaction to news of the Pretender's emergence. The boyars' incredulity is dashed by the sudden entry of Boris as though pursued by a spectre. As the Tsar begins, when more composed, to address the boyars, Shuisky announces that Pimen would speak with him. The old monk tells of a blind shepherd whose sight was miraculously restored at the Tsarevich's grave at Uglich. Boris collapses and orders Feodor to be summoned. Alone with him, Boris gives him advice and bids him farewell. Against a death knell and a monks' choir, at first offstage, Boris dies. [Based on Pushkin, scenes 16 and 21.]

The speed with which Musorgsky composed the initial version of *Boris* was prodigious, and seems the more so, considering that in the mornings during most of this period his work in the Forestry Department demanded his presence. Yet such dispatch was far from unique in a Russian composer, for whom the impulse to create could be as violent as it was sudden; the flood of inspiration could be almost uncontrollable and, moreover, sustained until the whole piece was done. As Tchaikovsky described the process: 'you forget everything . . . you are totally incapable of keeping up *at all* with your spirit's impulse, time passes literally unnoticed. There is something *somnambulistic* in his condition.'[6] Something like this now seems to have possessed Musorgsky; moreover, what issued from his creative faculty was totally unprecedented in character, yet remarkably self-assured. Having completed the first scene of *Boris* by 16 November 1868, he had ten days later finished the Coronation Scene. A further three weeks (17 December), and the Cell Scene was done. Evidently Musorgsky was far from secretive about his new project, for by early December the RMS gave notice of its intention to give extracts from various as-yet-unperformed operas by native composers, including Musorgsky's *Boris*. Exactly when the Inn Scene was finished is uncertain, but it must have been by the middle of January 1869, for both Stasov and Nadezhda Rimskaya-Korsakova (formerly Purgold) remembered that Dargomïzhsky, who died on 17 January, heard this and the opera's opening scene and had observed that 'Musorgsky has gone even farther than I'.[7] Progress now seems to have slowed—and not surprisingly, for it was now, on 2 January, that Musorgsky re-entered government service, this time as assistant to the head clerk in the third division of the Forestry Department. Nevertheless, 3 May apparently saw the completion of the scene in the Tsar's Palace and 3 June that of the scene before St Basil's Cathedral. By 30 July, after only nine months' work, the whole opera was ready in vocal score. Musorgsky wasted no time in scoring the opera, completing this on 27 December.

Yet it would be more than four years before *Boris* would be produced, and the version that would finally reach the stage would be very different from the one Musorgsky had initially composed. The first

[6] For Tchaikovsky's fuller account of his compositional processes, see D. Brown, *Tchaikovsky: a Biographical and Critical Study*, ii (London, 1982; repr. 1992), 232–8.

[7] *MVS*, 97.

barrier could prove to be the censor. True, the stage performance of Pushkin's play had at last been sanctioned in 1866, but even if the censor made no objection to Musorgsky's text, there would remain the problem that the law expressly forbade the representation of a Tsar on the operatic stage. Nevertheless, Musorgsky's first encounter with the director of the Imperial Theatres, Stepan Gedeonov, seems to have been encouraging. In July 1870, before a large audience at Stasov's dacha at Pargolovo, portions of the opera (certainly the Inn Scene, as well as the opening and/or St Basil Scene(s)) were given a private performance, and in the autumn Musorgsky submitted his opera to the selection committee, only to learn in February 1871 that it had been rejected by six votes to one.

This was little cause for surprise. As Cui promptly observed in the *St Petersburg Gazette*, of the seven members of the selection committee, only Nápravník was a musician with any competence to judge in a case such as this. The remainder were merely jobbing conductors or orchestral players, four barely spoke Russian, and Musorgsky himself had not been summoned, as was usual practice, to play his opera to the committee. With a work as novel and as text-dependent as *Boris* it could hardly be expected that it would not be decisively rejected by such a team, and perhaps with a vehemence that would have discouraged any hope of subsequent redemption. In fact, though a variety of reasons for the rejection were advanced by various individuals both at the time and subsequently, there seems to have been only one objection of real substance: the absence of any major female role.[8]

Shestakova was the first to learn of the decision, and promptly invited Musorgsky and Stasov to come that very evening (22 February) so that she might break the news as gently as possible to them. Musorgsky's reaction must have surprised her, for while Stasov 'with passionate enthusiasm began talking over with Musorgsky the new bits to be introduced into the opera . . . Modest Petrovich himself set about

---

[8] The process through which *Boris* was revised and finally accepted is examined intermittently in Taruskin's 'Musorgsky versus Musorgsky' in *TM* (especially pp. 249–61), and in systematic detail in Robert Oldani's 'History of the Composition, Rejection, Revision, and Acceptance of *Boris Godunov*', *MBG*, 67–90. Both writers convincingly dispose of widely disseminated allegations and inaccuracies that have been associated with the fate of the opera.

improvising a variety of ideas, and a very lively evening was spent'.[9]
Certainly Musorgsky took the news remarkably well, for he seems to
have concluded that if he remedied its one clear shortcoming *Boris*
would be accepted. But the Pargolovo performance of extracts had
forewarned him that other aspects of the opera would need rethinking.
Boris had been composed in the immediate wake of *The Marriage*, and
though Musorgsky had already drastically softened the naked realism at
which he had aimed in that pioneering work, the divided reaction of
the Pargolovo audience to his musical presentation of the peasants, some
finding 'that this was *bouffe*(!), while others saw *tragedy*',[10] must have
reinforced the point that the whole of musical truth could not be conveyed in the faithful imaging of their everyday speech—indeed, that
such imaging could actually lead to ambiguity. Music's lyrical and rhetorical resources for defining the inner world of emotions were also
indispensible.

Marina, the Wojewoda's daughter, is the one substantial female role
in Pushkin's drama, and the only way in which Musorgsky could satisfy
the selection committee's main demand to incorporate the Pretender's
Polish episode.[11] Accordingly he interpolated a new act after the Tsar's
Palace scene. This comprised two scenes. Because these were based only
on suggestions from Pushkin, and included incidents (and even a major
new character) that were Musorgsky's own invention, Musorgsky had
to invent the new dialogue, freely paraphrasing Pushkin's text where
he used it:

> *Scene 1* Marina's room in Sandomir Castle. Young girls sing as Marina's maid
> Ruzia dresses her mistress's hair. Left alone, Marina ponders the attractions
> of Dmitri and reveals her burning ambition to be Tsaritsa. The Jesuit Ran-
> goni appears and presses the case for a Roman Catholic Russia, urging a
> horrified Marina to persuade the Pretender, by seduction if necessary, into
> submitting to the authority of Rome. [Suggested by Pushkin, scene 12,
> which had been omitted from the 1831 edition, but was published later:

---

[9] *MVS*, 103.

[10] *MLN1*, 117: letter to Rimsky-Korsakov, 4 August 1870.

[11] Stasov claimed that Musorgsky had composed an almost complete Fountain Scene for the
initial version of *Boris* but did not include it.

Rangoni was Musorgsky's invention, prompted perhaps by Father Czernikowski in Pushkin, scene 11]

Scene 2 A moonlit night in the garden (with fountain) of Mniszek's castle
at Sandomir. The lovesick Dmitri awaits Marina. But Rangoni appears as
her messenger; she is suffering calumny because of her love for the Pretender. Dmitri promises she shall be Tsaritsa. Rangoni urges Dmitri to make
him his confidant when he becomes Tsar. He counsels Dmitri to remain
hidden as a group of guests, Marina among them, emerge from the castle
and dance a grand polonaise, then re-enter the castle. An inflamed Dmitri
resolves to speed his campaign for the throne of Russia. Marina returns and
demands how soon he will be Tsar. She torments him until he declares that
he will carry through his intention, and that she will then bitterly regret
having rejected him. Marina yields, and a love scene ensues. Unnoticed,
Rangoni watches in triumph. [Built on suggestions from Pushkin, scenes
12 and 13]

The vocal score of the first Polish Scene was virtually complete by 22
April 1871. Musorgsky then began the second, but he also directed his
attention to changes in the Tsar's Palace Scene. The opening was largely
recomposed; only the first twenty-one bars of the nurse's exchange with
Kseniya after her lament remained essentially unchanged. Feodor's examination of the map of Russia, which had interlaced with Kseniya's
lament, became a silent operation, its music now compressed and
adapted for his words of comfort to his sister. Kseniya's lament itself
was rewritten, with a new chiming-clock incident appended—an idea
that, like the later incident of the parrot, came from Karamzin's record
of these gifts having been presented respectively to Boris and Feodor
by the Austrian ambassador to the Russian court in 1597. A large stretch
of fresh action (the scene of the nurse and the two children, with its
two songs) was inserted before Boris's entrance. Nevertheless, a substantial portion of Boris's scene with his children (from his G major
address to his daughter) was retained in essentials, as were the first
twenty-nine bars (as notated in the revised version) of his monologue,
though with some revision of detail.[12] But the rest of the monologue

---

[12] A five-chord motif, unique to the initial version of *Boris*, had to be excised immediately
before the monologue itself.

was almost completely new—except that most of it was taken from *Salammbô*, with the ending now anticipating some music from the Tsar's hallucination scene at the end of the act. After the monologue were added the off-stage rumpus occasioned by the escaped parrot and Feodor's song about the incident. Although occasional brief incorporations from the initial version follow this, little of Shuisky's original exchange with Boris remained in the revision, and Boris's hallucination scene was largely new, the chiming-clock music being incorporated to chilling effect.

The vocal score of the new second act was completed by 22 September. But even before this revisions elsewhere had been contemplated and acted on. From an incident narrated by Karamzin a whole new scene (the Kromy Forest Scene) was envisaged in place of the St Basil's Cathedral Scene. This depicted the anarchy fermented by the Pretender's incursion and included the humiliation of a boyar and the apprehending (stoked up by Varlaam and Missail, who had now joined the Pretender) of two Jesuits in the Pretender's retinue, followed by the entry of the Pretender to claim the throne. From the St Basil's Cathedral scene the part of the Simpleton was salvaged, his brush with the urchins now following on the boyar's humiliation, his concluding song likewise providing the ending for the new scene.[13]

Apart from the Inn Scene, the original *Boris* had been almost unremittingly sombre, and the new insertions in the Tsar's Palace Scene had introduced a measure of liveliness, while the tone of much of the new Polish act was relatively unstrained, colourful, and near its end quietly rapturous. There were other smaller revisions. The conclusion of the first scene (the 64 bars after the exit of the pilgrims), where the dispirited people mutter, and receive instructions for the next day's coronation, was lopped off. At Stasov's suggestion, a song for the hostess was added to open the Inn Scene; by contrast, the preceding Cell Scene lost Pimen's long account of the infant Dmitri's death but gained the first two interventions from an off-stage chorus of monks. In the Duma Scene Shchelkalov's report of the Pretender's emergence was excised. Exactly when each of these changes was carried through is unknown; what is

---

[13] Taruskin has argued plausibly that the Kromy Forest Scene was composed between late September and November 1871.

certain is that, with the completion on 26 December 1871 of the love duet ending the Polish act, the vocal score of the second version was finished. Only one major decision was taken at a later stage: at Nikolsky's inspired suggestion, the Kromy Forest Scene, originally sited (like the scene it replaced) before the Duma Scene, was switched to the opera's end. Thus in the final form of this 'Opera in four Acts with a Prologue', as Musorgsky now labelled it, the original Parts 1–3 became the Prologue and Acts 1 and 2, the two Polish scenes followed as Act 3, and the Duma Scene and Kromy Forest Scene made up Act 4.

Musorgsky launched forthwith into scoring the opera. The five existing scenes that he retained required little work, but each of the other four was a major operation. Nevertheless, the Tsar's Palace Scene was completed on 23 January 1872, the two Polish Scenes on 22 February and 10 April respectively, and the Kromy Forest Scene on 4 August.

Well ahead of this Musorgsky had been preparing the ground for the opera's resubmission. There had remained the problem of the stage personation of a Tsar, but in April this had been finally sanctioned by Alexander II himself. Meanwhile, as was common practice, the public's appetite had been whetted by concert performances of excerpts; on 17 February the Coronation Scene had been heard at a concert of the RMS, to encouraging audience response, and on 15 April, at a FMS concert, Balakirev had conducted the polonaise from the Fountain Scene. On 18 May the selection committee had reconvened to decide the fate of *Boris*. Until recently it has been believed that once again the opera was rejected. The primary evidence offered for this is a statement by Cui, as well as the claim made in 1885 by the soprano, Yuliya Platonova, that in 1873 *Boris* remained unaccepted and that it was Platonova's insistence that this opera should be mounted for her benefit performance that led Stepan Gedeonov, the Imperial Theatres' director, to override the committee and authorize the production of *Boris*. But Robert Oldani has argued plausibly that Platonova grossly overstated her part as the opera's good fairy, pointing out that, since the full score was not yet finished, the committee could give only a provisional approval which Cui subsequently, for his own purposes, chose to view as a non-acceptance tantamount to rejection. As it was, the production schedule for the coming season was already well filled. Nevertheless, the publisher Bessel had already negotiated for *Boris* to be engraved, which he was unlikely to have done had he not been confident that the opera's production was secure.

Nevertheless, it is still possible that the final authorization for a full performance had not been issued at the time of the partial presentation given on 17 February 1873 as the benefit performance for Gennady Kondratyev, the chief producer at the Maryinsky Theatre; indeed, this may have been sanctioned as a useful way of testing the waters before the directorate took the final plunge. Three excerpts were given: the Inn Scene and the two Polish scenes. The costumes and sets were those designed for the première of Pushkin's play, which had finally taken place three years earlier. Public reception was very enthusiastic and critical reaction at this stage encouraging, sufficient for Darya Leonova, who had sung the Hostess in the Inn Scene, to choose to repeat the Inn and Fountain Scenes for her own farewell benefit four days later instead of excerpts from Verdi's *Il trovatore*, (though this intention was to be frustrated by the illness of another of the singers).

The première proper of *Boris* took place on 8 February 1874 as the benefit for Yuliya Platonova, who had already sung Marina in the partial presentation.[14] The singers were the best the Maryinsky could muster, and Musorgsky himself drilled them in their parts. The costumes and scenery were again those created for the 1870 production of Pushkin's play, and Eduard Nápravník conducted. Nápravník, who had cast the single vote in favour when *Boris* had first been submitted to the selection committee, was an excellent musical director whose reign at the Maryinsky would last nearly half a century, during which he would prepare and conduct the first performances of most of the major Russian operas of this period, including five of Tchaikovsky's (the première of the first of these, *The Oprichnik*, would take place only two months after that of *Boris*). Nápravník was notorious for introducing cuts, and Musorgsky's friend, the minor poet Arseny Golenishchev-Kutuzov, confirmed that he was behind the omission of the entire Cell Scene (with Pimen now converted into a hermit for the Duma Scene), as well as various other excisions on dramatic grounds, including the in-

---

[14] For a detailed account of the first production of *Boris* and its fate until it was withdrawn from the repertoire in 1882, see R. Oldani: 'A Tale of Two Productions—St Petersburg (1874–1882), Paris (1908)', *MBG*, 91–107.

cident of the parrot and the two interventions of the chiming clock in the Tsar's Palace Scene, and the final brief trio in the Fountain Scene. The opening two scenes were merged into a single unit under the title 'The Call of Boris to the Throne'; taken with the following Inn Scene, this constituted Act 1.

The public's enthusiasm for the new opera was extraordinary, Musorgsky taking eighteen to twenty curtain calls (according to Stasov). Press reaction was a different matter. Russian musical criticism had acquired a far broader base in the quarter-century since Serov had begun laying its foundations. A good deal of musical criticism remained essentially of a dilettante nature, but in the 1860s, at the very time that the more liberal climate favoured the emergence of a more lively, disputatious press, the newly founded conservatoires had begun producing a first generation of domestically trained professional musicians capable of making more considered and informed judgements. However bumpy might be the critical ride for the young composer of the 1870s, the one thing he needed never to fear was that most stultifying of reactions: indifference. By the time of the *Boris* première Bessel had published the vocal score, and a number of critics showed clearly that they had already done their homework.

In fact, critical reaction to *Boris* was not as unrelievedly hostile as has sometimes been represented (and Musorgsky must have found grim amusement in the sometimes blatant disagreements among the critics on the quality of separate scenes and incidents). True, Nikolay Solovyev, in the *Stock Exchange Gazette*, described the opera as 'cacophony in five acts and seven scenes', then censured Musorgsky's own words in the libretto, and pronounced his harmony, counterpoint, and structures to be 'weak to the point of absurdity. His lack of artistic instinct, combined with his ignorance and his wish to be ever new, results in music that is wild and ugly. His orchestration is very uneven.'[15] In a second review however Solovyev did commend a few details: Shchelkalov's monologue in the Prologue, Pimen's narration in the death scene, and the portrayals of Varlaam and Missail in the Inn Scene. In *Musical Leaflet*, also in a two-part review (under the epigraph 'La grammaire est l'art de parler et d'écrire correctement'), Alexander

[15] *TDM*, 336–7.

Famintsïn was equally damning about Musorgsky's music, which he found to be saturated with 'crude grammatical errors' and remarkable for its 'dazzling lack of musical logic in its counterpoint and harmony', all of which he attributed either to Musorgsky's 'inadequate knowledge of the elementary rules of harmony or to his total contempt for them'.[16] Nevertheless, with some specific reservations, he complimented Musorgsky on his choice of subject, the general effectiveness of his scenario, his word-setting, and his accompanying orchestration, to all of which he attributed the opera's popular success. Famintsïn also singled out some particular contexts (mostly 'set pieces' and therefore least unconventional) as effective.

In *The Voice*, Herman Laroche, a conservatoire fellow-pupil and life-long friend of Tchaikovsky, who would establish himself as one of the most intelligent and stylish of Russian music critics, largely concurred with Famintsïn (despite having previously given the three performed scenes a remarkably enthusiastic review, though this had been partially explained by Laroche's having gone to the theatre expecting worse). Though Musorgsky 'has a talent for recitative, for characterization, he is a very weak musician . . . The very composition of his opera testifies to dilettantism and lack of skill, though it shows powerful flashes of a nature that is gifted'.[17] Mavriky Rappoport, writing in *Theatre and Music*, pointed the finger directly at the source of Musorgsky's problems.[18]

> In all fairness I must say that I find Mr Musorgsky has great potential and a brilliant future if he directs his talent correctly and decides to abandon his servile, somehow slavish dependence upon the [Balakirev] circle. In his opera he reveals brilliantly his theatrical talents, skill in deftly employing scenic effectiveness; a poetic element is also clearly apparent in places, the structure is serviceable.

Like a majority of other critics, he found the Inn Scene a high point of the opera. But if, in his view, the death scene was the boldest passage in the opera, 'capable of moving a large audience', the Kromy Forest Scene was 'absolutely incomprehensible'.

[16] *TDM*, 362.
[17] *TDM*, 337.
[18] *TDM*, 341–2.

However, one critic, Vladmir Baskin (writing under the pseudonym 'Foma pizzicato' in *The Musical Courier*), did display a genuinely and markedly open mind, less deaf to what Musorgsky was about than his colleagues. He recognized Musorgsky's creative credo but was not fazed by it:[19]

> Clearly he [Musorgsky] belongs to a specific school and maintains an orientation towards realism in his music. Many contexts in his opera impress through their novelty and originality, while being outstanding also for their detailed finish and the breadth of their overall design. Everywhere is evident an exceptional, major talent, a thorough knowledge of music, an ability to make the orchestra bend to his will and to use it successfully, though you cannot fail to notice that the orchestration of the composer of *Boris Godunov* is too heavy—but all the same, effective and without crude effects. One must attribute Mr Musorgsky's undoubted merits to his striving *after truth*, the absence of the commonplace [in his music], and an independence that carefully avoids triteness.

But like some at the opera's trial run at Pargolovo, Baskin saw humour in places where we do not. It is however perhaps over-easy for us to fault such a perception in an audience for whom a lively syllabic delivery by lower-class individuals had been so often associated with comic characters, and, after all, however we may today view the Simpleton, to the urchins in *Boris* he appeared an object of mirth (though having seen the two vagabond monks on-stage in the final scene, it remains difficult to understand how Baskin could have perceived them as comic).

For all its gaucheries, Musorgsky must have read Baskin's review with some satisfaction. But the one on which he pinned the greatest hope of an understanding verdict was that of his musical associate—and friend—Cui, writing in the *St Petersburg Gazette* ten days after the première. What emerged shattered him. Cui began with a blast against the libretto:

> It has no subject, there is no development of character conditioned by the course of events, there is no integral dramatic interest. It is a succession of . . . disconnected, uncoordinated scenes, not organically connected with

[19] *TDM*, 338–40.

anything . . . You could shuffle these scenes, re-arrange them; you could throw out any of them, introduce new ones, and the opera would not be changed, because *Boris Godunov* is not an opera but only a succession of scenes—a musical chronicle perhaps . . . As for the separate scenes, all of them present very interesting musical tasks. It is a pity only that Mr Musorgsky did not stick more closely to Pushkin . . . Many of Pushkin's most superlative lines have been replaced with others that are extremely mediocre, occasionally tasteless.

Cui approved of Musorgsky launching straight into the first scene without an introduction:

> The first scene is superb. The principal theme is very successful with a purely folk character, and expresses beautifully the people's entreaty, forced on them by the police-officer's staff. . . . The phrases which the people exchange with one another are also beyond reproach, alive, neat, truthful, characterful, musical . . . Shchelkalov's speech is musically beautiful, but its excessively poetical quality and a certain degree of 'Schumannism' make it inappropriate for the personality of Shchelkalov. The beautiful chorus of the passing pilgrims is effective, very characteristic and musical.

But the Coronation Scene was the weakest in the opera, the orchestral representation of the bells was ineffective, and the treatment of the folksong most clumsy. Boris's address to the people was better, but the whole left the impression of a 'weak, unsuccessful essay'. The Cell Scene (which Cui knew, of course, only from the score) was also bad: a very good beginning and an even better ending, as well as one or two other good spots, but as a whole it was unsuccessful not because it was incorrectly handled or set out, 'but because there is very little music in it and its recitatives are not melodic'; instead there were only 'scrappy chords, at times harshly dissonant, and upon them chopped recitative without musical content. Inspiration is not needed for the creation of such recitatives; you need only routine, craft'. In signalling the Pretender through a special theme the baleful influence of Wagner was to be detected.

And so on. Cui had studied the opera thoroughly, his dissection was precise and highly detailed, and adjectives proliferated. The Inn Scene and the concluding Kromy Forest Scene were the best in the opera; for the former Cui claimed that 'such a sustained, broad, realistic, varied, superb comic scene exists in no other opera'. There was a lot of excellent detail in the Tsar's Palace Scene: Kseniya's lament was filled with pain, her brother's response was warm, the nurse's address to Kseniya was very nice, the song about the gnat not bad, the clapping-game much weaker. Boris's reflections, 'expressed in the form of an arioso', were not bad either; 'his music is attractive, dignified, and beautiful; moreover the composer had a very well-founded wish to make his music melodious', though the end was less satisfactory because the melody was concentrated in the orchestra and there were too many words. However, Feodor's song about the parrot oustripped perfection (Cui could have known this only from the vocal score or earlier private performances); these were 'the most beautiful and musical pages in *Boris*', and Boris's response to his son was also excellent. Yet there was little good in what followed, and the act in general left a feeling of dissatisfaction 'because one impression is forthwith replaced by another, and they cancelled one another out'.

The Polish act was a mixture. Cui liked the opening chorus, Marina's 'mazurka' song even better. About Musorgsky's intentions in his musical characterization of Rangoni Cui was uncertain. The Polonaise was the best thing in the act; by contrast, Musorgsky had failed completely with the Pretender. 'During his monologue by the fountain we are seduced by the beauty, the poetical mood, the enchanted sound of the orchestra—that is, the background—but are brought down to earth by the absence of musical thoughts in the Pretender's speeches'—though the ending of his love duet with Marina almost made Cui forget the preceding shortcomings. The first part of the Duma Scene (the duma and Shuisky's narration) was weak, the second half (Pimen's narration and Boris's farewell to his son) incomparably better, but the ending (from the first sound of the funeral bell) 'is imbued with such realism, is executed with such mastery, that it makes upon the audience just about the strongest impression of the whole opera'. The Kromy Forest Scene was 'very strongly and broadly planned, full of life; in it there's much superb music . . . It makes a bold and aesthetically satisfying ending to the opera'. Cui then summarized his overall impressions of the opera and its composer:[20]

[20] *TDM*, 355–60.

Mr Musorgsky is a powerful and original talent, richly endowed with many qualities necessary for an opera composer, devoting himself with enthusiasm to the demands of contemporary opera. His colours are vivid, at times crude; he is especially disposed to the representation of folk scenes, to spontaneous outbursts. He is less disposed, though also able, to represent passion when it is expressed in gentler, more refined forms. *Boris Godunov* is an immature piece (in justice should we demand maturity in a first opera?); in it there is much that is superb and much that is weak. This immaturity declares itself in everything: in the libretto and in the piling-up of minute effects to such a degree that cuts had to be made, and in an enthusiasm for [musical] onomatopoeia and the debasement of artistic realism to an anti-artistic reality (in the first folk scene there is laughter, and before the last there is a hubbub without defined notes—consequently, without music)—finally, in the mixing of beautiful musical thoughts with paltry.

There are two chief shortcomings in *Boris*: the disjointed recitative and the lack of coordination in the musical ideas which makes parts of the opera like a pot-pourri. These shortcomings do not stem from Mr Musorgsky's creative feebleness, certainly not; . . . these shortcomings stem from his very immaturity, from the fact that the composer is insufficiently self-critical, from his undiscriminating, complacent, hasty compositional process . . . There is another deficiency from which Mr Musorgsky will hardly ever free himself; this is his incapacity for symphonic development . . . But for all these shortcomings, in *Boris Godunov* there is so much that is fresh, good, strong, that even in its present form it can occupy an honourable place among outstanding operas.

Musorgsky was furious and bitter, as he made clear to Stasov the same day:[21]

The tone of Cui's article is hateful . . . And this reckless attack on the *complacency* of the composer! That modesty and humility, which have never left me and never will while my brains in my head are not completely burnt out, means little to one without brains. I see nothing behind this mindless attack, behind this notorious lie; it's as though soapy water has been sprayed in the air, clouding everything. *Complacency! Hasty compositional process! Immaturity!* Whose? Whose? I'd like to know.

[21] *MLN1*, 176.

In her manuscript recollections of her musical *soirées* Shestakova pondered the matter:[22]

> I don't know how to designate this action [of Cui's]. Many asserted that it had been written out of envy. I do not allow this idea because, after *Ratcliff* [Cui's opera produced at the Maryinsky in 1869] Cui had no need to be jealous of anyone—even though, it must be said, *Boris* was received much more warmly by the public than Cui's operas in general. But should we really pay attention to that?

Whether Oldani was right to detect a touch of sarcasm in Shestakova's words, he was surely right to see Cui's reaction as fired primarily by envy. Cui's own opera, *William Ratcliff*, had enjoyed little success during its brief run at the Imperial Opera five years before. But it was not only that *Boris* had now encountered an incomparably warmer reception at its run in 1874, and that just a year earlier Rimsky's *The Maid of Pskov* had also been well received in the same theatre; Musorgsky was now veering away from the principles of truth and realism which Dargomïzhsky had embodied in *The Stone Guest* and on which, even more radically, Musorgsky himself had created some of his most startling songs and *The Marriage*. But in the last especially Musorgsky clearly went too far for Cui. For Cui, melodic values remained paramount. The vocal line should always be inventive and musical, whether its business was, on the one hand, the truthful presentation of an evolving situation requiring the lively declamation of everyday speech (as Cui considered Musorgsky had managed so well in the first and last scenes of *Boris* and, above all, in the Inn Scene) or, at the other extreme, with situations of narrative (Feodor's song about the parrot), inner searching (Boris's central Act 2 monologue), or intense personal emotion (the Pretender/Marina love duet) where truth demanded rich—or simply beautiful—lyrical melody to match the words. For Cui's ears too much of the vocal line in *Boris* (the Coronation Scene and much of the Cell Scene, for instance) seemed to have achieved neither of these ideals. But it was not just this. Ever since Balakirev's withdrawal from the Russian musical scene in the early 1870s Cui had fancied himself the leader of the kuchka, but now he could see not only that his ideological grip had

[22] *TDM*, 360.

slipped, but that others in the group were more successful and (more galling still) more talented composers than he.

Boris was given eight times in the 1874–5 season, was omitted from the following, but was heard four times during that of 1876–7, though now with the Kromy Forest Scene also omitted. During the following two seasons it was performed altogether five times, then never again during Musorgsky's lifetime. None of these performances ever included the Cell Scene, which was first heard at a FMS concert in January 1879. With Musorgsky's death in March 1881 there was a brief revival of interest in the opera, and early in the 1881–2 season it was mounted four times with much apparent enthusiasm. But after a single performance in the following season had enjoyed little success, on 20 November 1882 it was officially withdrawn from the repertoire.

There has been much debate about which version of *Boris* Musorgsky himself considered to be definitive. Three clear versions are extant: an initial full-score version of 1869, the revised version of 1872 as represented by the changes in the full score, and the final version as published in the vocal score of 1874. In 1928 the vocal score of the 1869 version was published, and for some years the balance of informed opinion favoured this initial version, it being assumed that the subsequent revisions were made only because of outside pressures. Yet in fact Taruskin seems totally justified in dismissing the belief of some earlier scholars that Musorgsky had set about his revision of *Boris* unwillingly.[23] There is every sign that, on hearing of the rejection of the initial version, he was undismayed and immediately applied his mind not only to satisfying what seems to have been the selection committee's sole requirement— an extra scene incorporating a significant female role (in fact, the committee got a whole new act)—but also to revising the whole. The experience of the run-through at Pargolovo, where many had taken

---

[23] For a full presentation of Taruskin's case, see 'Musorgsky versus Musorgsky: the Versions of *Boris Godunov*', *TM*, 201–90. Performances that reinstate the St Basil Scene before the Duma Scene are sometimes given. Certainly the quality of some of the music in this scene fully supports its inclusion, and its loss deprives us of the powerfully charged confrontation between Boris and his accuser, the Holy Fool. But since it also contains the latter's two interventions, which Musorgsky subsequently transferred to the Kromy Forest Scene, a ludicrous tautology results. Nevertheless, this double version still receives performances. Taruskin is also very informative on the context within which Musorgsky's *Boris* was created, its musical antecedents, and its precise relationship to Pushkin's play.

the peasants to be buffa characters, may have played a critical part in this, for it had pointed to a problem fundamental to the whole opera, at least in a contemporary audience's perceptions: that the realism which was sought through a truthful declamation of the text produced an effect of comedy. But *Boris* was a tragedy, and to do justice to the subject required the reinstatement of a rhetoric that could conjure an epic aura, and of a lyricism that might uncover the complexes of character and feeling in very human beings. Without sacrificing the best in what had already been created, the whole piece needed to be rethought and re-wrought. Musorgsky knew it and set about doing it.

But while it is fair of Taruskin to believe that a version published under the composer's personal supervision, as was the 1874 vocal score, has a special authority, especially since Musorgsky is not known to have made or contemplated any later changes, this does not signify that it truly represents *his* ideal version. It differs from the 1872 score princi-pally in its deletions, but we do not know how much these may have originated with Eduard Nápravník, who prepared and conducted the first performance and who, as noted earlier, was notorious for de-manding cuts. At the time Musorgsky may have been persuaded of the practical force of some of Nápravník's requirements, but that does not signify that he may not have accepted some very unwillingly, or have later regretted them. Be all this as it may, the following examination of the opera will take into account the complete text of the 1872 version, ignoring the cuts in the 1874 vocal score. And since in recent years the 1869 version has received occasional performances, the often excellent music that was sacrificed during Musorgsky's revisionary process cannot be passed over entirely. For convenient future reference these versions will be described respectively as the revised and the initial version.

CHAPTER 10

Boris Godunov: The Music

CHAIKOVSKY'S *EUGENE ONEGIN* AND MUSORGSKY'S *BORIS Godunov*, for most musicians the two greatest of nineteenth-century Russian operas, have much in common. Both are founded upon major poetical works by Pushkin; in both the scenarios and libretti were devised by the composers themselves, using Pushkin's text as far as it suited their requirements. And both operas run as a series of stage pictures, sometimes spectacular, sometimes intimate, each presenting a single crucial stage in the drama with perhaps massive time gaps between. Though these may require the spectator to guess at intervening events, in practice this proves no more of a problem than do the equally discrete moments in a strip cartoon.[1] Such a structure means that though events may move on within a scene, perhaps raising the level of emotional or dramatic intensity, less store is set by those sudden frisson-producing twists or wrenches of plot that are a fundamental element in many other operas. Certainly there are such moments in *Boris*—but the most precious passages here, as in Tchaikovsky's *Onegin*, are those where Musorgsky could focus upon the emotions, shifts of mood, or psychological trajectories of the character(s) or group(s) within a situation, and present these with all the intensity and vividness of which his insight

---

[1] Since both composers were targeting their work at a Russian audience and were setting what by the 1870s were classics from the most revered of Russian writers, they could reasonably assume a prior knowledge of the missing action.

and musical language were capable. The result is that the degree to which the characters and their predicaments can enlist the spectator's personal engagement, whether of sympathy or revulsion, is such as in few operas in the repertoire.

However, that extreme doctrinaire subordination of music to text pursued in *The Marriage* could have no place here, for while Gogol's comedy had exposed the most prosaic of Russians speaking in the most vernacular and self-revealing prose, Pushkin's play paraded epic figures controlling or influencing nations, driven by grand ambitions, creating awesome events, racked by savage torments, who spoke through a poet whose mastery of the Russian language was unsurpassed. And, as noted earlier, to conjure the grandeur of such a dramatic context and lay bare the inner worlds of such humans demanded the reinstatement of all the resources of rhetoric and sentiment that music possessed. Yet there were times when the method of *The Marriage* had some relevance, most obviously in the Inn Scene. Though Pushkin's prose here made no attempt to match the colloquial informality of Gogol's, its free rhythms and swift exchanges encouraged Musorgsky to exploit something of the dramatic 'truthfulness' of his earlier experiment, even though the orchestral context for the characters' exchanges, by returning towards a more harmonically formalized language, far less fragmented and sketchy and with fewer and briefer intervening silences, curbed an absolute freedom of metre, pacing and phrase structure in the vocal parts.

In fact, fixing the musical ancestry of a work as unique as *Boris* is not easy. As regards debts to other Russian composers, the Coronation Scene copies the ternary pattern of the Epilogue to Glinka's *A Life for the Tsar*, where choruses in praise of the Tsar flank a central movement mostly for soloists, though there is a sharp contrast between the enthusiasm of Glinka's crowd for their sovereign and the dutifulness of Musorgsky's. The girls who sing their mistress's praises at the opening of the Polish Act of *Boris* are descendants of Chernomor's houris from *Ruslan and Lyudmila* (backed, perhaps, by the water maidens of Dargomïzhsky's *Rusalka*), though the real-world court of which Marina's attendants are part could have no place for the more delicate spells of enchantment their ancestors had spun in the evil dwarf's magic gardens. From *Ruslan*, too, came the changing background treatment whereby a melody is repeated intact to ever-varying accompaniments, Musorgsky adapting this device for use at the opening of *Boris* and in three of the five self-contained songs that occur later (the Hostess's *drake* song and Varlaam's Kazan song in the Inn Scene and, less consistently, in Feodor's parrot song in the Tsar's Palace Scene). Even more literally anticipated in *Ruslan* were the tritone-connected dominant sevenths that constitute the coronation motif in *Boris* (see Ex. 10.2*l*), though Musorgsky's exploitation of these as appurtenances of Boris's royal status, both waxing and waning, could scarcely be farther removed from their employment as identity card for Glinka's witch Naina.

However, Musorgsky could as easily have acquired his coronation motif from the recurrence of this same harmonic cell in the royal hunt in Act 3 of Serov's *Rogneda*, first heard in 1865. Gerald Abraham believed Boris's hallucination scene was 'probably suggested—dramatically, not musically'[2] by Holofernes' in Serov's *Judith*, just as it seems the idea for the clapping game in the Tsar's Palace Scene may have come from an incident in that composer's *The Power of the Fiend*, first performed in 1871, just four months before Musorgsky added the dance-songs to *Boris*.[3] Abraham also noted Serov's liking for ending a scene dying away (*cf* the end of *Boris*) and for constantly varying the number of singers delivering each voice part during a dramatic chorus to create a greater realism (*cf* Musorgsky's peasant choruses).

Though in its broadest terms *Boris* was in the tradition of Meyerbeerian grand opera, the western composers most likely to have had a gift for Musorgsky were Wagner and Verdi. Nevertheless, any influence from the former was likely to be such as from Serov: that is, insights and suggestions that might be gathered from particular dramatic situations and contexts rather than pervasive musical influences. For, on the musical level, a gulf divided Musorgsky from both composers. From Serov he was separated by the disparity of their musical gifts; the older composer might point to what could be done, but Musorgsky's ability to do it was so immeasurably greater that the final result was bound to be very much his own. From Wagner he was yet further separated by

[2] G. Abraham, 'The Operas of Serov', in J. Westrup, ed., *Essays presented to Egon Wellesz* (Oxford, 1966), 171–83; Repr. in G. Abraham, *Essays on Russian and East European Music* (Oxford, 1985), 40–55.

[3] For a more detailed examination of Serov's influence on Musorgsky, see R. Taruskin, 'Serov and Musorgsky', *TM*, 96–122.

musical style and technique, and by savagely differing objectives in pacing achieved through radically differing mechanisms. However much Musorgsky may have been impressed by Wagner (much more so than perhaps he cared to admit to Stasov and the like), the magisterially spun harmonic web that had become so much the foundation of the German master's music was not for him. Musorgsky's harmonic inventiveness could be bold, sometimes stunning, but that was mainly exploited in individual incidents and short-term structures. For him the characters remained his paramount concern and their vocal lines, as both the compliant bearers and the attentive interpreters of the uttered word, his priority.

Verdi might have been a rather different matter. At least here was a composer who also centred his attention on the singer and his text. The evidence suggests that Musorgsky knew the current repertoire of Italian operas very well, though he was unlikely to have confessed openly any great partiality for it. Not only were Verdi's operas fundamental ingredients in the Russian repertoire: *La forza del destino* had been written for St Petersburg and first performed there in 1862. Besides observing parallels between Verdi's and Musorgsky's treatments of recurring themes, which (*pace* the Dmitri/Pretender theme in *Boris*) are each normally re-used only two or three times by both composers, Robert Oldani cites parallel contexts in Verdi and Musorgsky: the pilgrims' choruses in *Forza* (Act 2, Scene 1) and *Boris* (Prologue, Scene 1), the offstage chorus of monks behind both Leonora's 'Madre, pietosa Vergine' in *Forza* (Act 2, Scene 2) and Grigory's dream in *Boris* (the Cell Scene), and 'the similarities in pacing'[4] between the army camp scene in *Forza* (Act 3, Scene 3) and the Kromy Forest Scene in *Boris*. He also finds parallels between *Don Carlos* and the revised *Boris*: the women's choruses that open the scenes outside the St Just monastery in *Don Carlos* (Act 2, Scene 1) and *Boris* (Polish Act, Scene 1), and, more significantly, King Philip's aria 'Ella giammai m'amò' in *Don Carlos* (Act 4) and Boris's central Act 2 monologue. And Taruskin has detected an intriguing parallel between the openings of Act 3 of *Don Carlos* and the Fountain Scene in *Boris;* in both the lover begins by repeating to himself the instructions for a tryst—'At midnight . . . in the garden . . . by the

---

[4] *MBG*, 236.

fountain'. Taruskin suggests that *Don Carlos* may have been a pervasive influence on *Boris*; it had its Russian première on 1 January 1869 while Musorgsky was engaged on his initial version.

But none of these instances displays any hint of a direct musical connection; at most something might not have been heard in the way it was in *Boris*, but for the prompting of something in Verdi. All of which re-emphasizes the newness of Musorgsky's opera. For the music of *Boris* grows naturally from that which Musorgsky himself had already created—from the music of *Salammbô*, now modified and enriched by genes implanted from certain of the songs and *The Marriage*, and animated by an insight and sensibility beyond Musorgsky at the time of that earlier extravagant piece. And if doubts remain, the affinities are convincingly confirmed by the amount of *Salammbô* music that Musorgsky absorbed essentially unaltered into *Boris*.

Despite its seemingly unorganic scenario which drew Cui's censure, *Boris* gives no impression of structural slackness. Musorgsky himself, having composed the first draft of *The Marriage*, clearly felt he had confined too drastically the accompaniment's potential for character support and for giving shape to the whole, and in the second version (the one subsequently published) he had amplified the accompaniment, providing clear thematic labels for most characters. In *Boris* this is carried far further and applied with much more sophistication, for absolutely fundamental to the opera's musical organization (especially in the initial version) is a network of recurring themes, which may relate either to individuals or to activity and which are instantly recognizable, for all the modifications made to some of them from context to context. Foremost among those relating to activity are two tiny four-note cells which erupt during incidents of crowd restiveness or police enforcement. There is the semiquaver figure (Ex. 10.1*a*) forewarning, even before the curtain has risen, of the crowd's turmoil and the police officer's vigorous attempts to retain control; it returns in the Inn Scene to underpin the intervention of a second police officer and, (notated in quavers) during the earlier crowd music in the rejected St Basil Scene. A second, trenchant, sometimes angular four-quaver cell (Ex. 10.1*b*) also runs through the Inn Scene, acting as one of Varlaam's appurtenances by punctuating his more robust utterances. As a bass it fortifies mightily the element of physical energy in this turbulent monk's Kazan song—

Ex. 10.1a   **Ex. 10.1b**

and also in the latter part of the Hostess's opening song about a drake, where it alerts her to Varlaam's approach. It will resurge in the Kromy Forest Scene as Varlaam fans hatred against the two Jesuits. But most arresting of these pantomimic inventions is the tranquil theme that runs its semiquaver course intermittently through the Cell Scene as Pimen inscribes the last stages of his chronicle (Ex. 10.1*c*); a more gentle yet vividly visualized matching of a simple, measured activity can hardly be imagined.

Ex. 10.1c

Ex. 10.1d

Ex. 10.1e

Incomparably more important are the themes relating to individuals. Dominating these is that associated with both the murdered Dmitri and with Grigory as pretender (Ex. 10.1*e*, its first explicit appearance in the opera: it will go on to present innumerable modifications of detail). It is presaged within the solo (and very Russian) cantilena which opens the opera (Ex. 10.1*d*: see asterisks), and whose immediate double reiteration against changing backgrounds confirms the opera's Russian provenance and establishes the subdued yet uneasy mood about to be revealed on stage, and it lurks darkly beneath Boris's first words (Ex. 10.2*i*[5]—for it is the ineluctable memory of the dead Tsarevich that breeds his 'irrepressible terror'. But it exposes itself explicitly only in the Cell Scene during Pimen's narration of events at Uglich, an account that gives instant focus to Grigory's ambition. This is the opera's first defining moment, for though the canker that consumes Boris, making his degradation inevitable, is guilt at the Tsarevich's murder, it is Grigory as pretender who will now begin shaping a train of events that will undo him. The theme is the more important, seeing that, from the instant of his escape through the inn window until his brief reappearance to claim the throne of Russia at the opera's end, the runaway novice is seen only during his marginal interlude as lover in Poland. But, absent in person, his presence is signalled in every subsequent scene through his thematic surrogate, which, according to the situation it finds itself in, artfully modifies its contour and rhythmic structure without for a moment compromising its identity. It displays every variety of character—insouciant (in the Inn Scene as Grigory feigns casualness to mask his identity), intimidating (its defiant capping of Shuisky's first narration in the Tsar's Palace Scene), gently insinuating (as its shadow falls across the girls' chorus in the first Polish Scene),[6] languorous (during Grigory's amorous musings that open the second Polish Scene), then vaunting (as he attempts to crush Marina later in that scene), suggesting a quiet martial resolve (the people reflecting on his approach in the excluded St Basil Scene), assuming a more assertive mien (as, in the Duma Scene, the boyars ponder the threat he represents), striking terror into Boris when later in that scene it quietly insinuates itself as the crucial point in Pimen's narrative becomes clear, and finally vaunting itself triumphantly as the Pretender sets out for Moscow at the opera's end.

Only the theme of Pimen (Ex. 10.1*f*), the unworldly, worldly-wise

---

[5] This is the contour it presents during Grigory's final utterance in the Cell Scene, thus confirming its function as a reference theme.

[6] Especially from Figure 10, no doubt reflecting Marina's private thoughts about the one most welcome from among the band of suitors to which her attendants are referring. And did the first four pitches of his theme (as presented at the end of the Cell Scene) condition the opening bar-and-a-half of her ensuing mazurka (p. 238, bars 1–2)?

Ex. 10.1f

Ex. 10.1g

Ex. 10.1h

monk, also mutates significantly, thus reflecting his many sides as revealed in the colloquy with Grigory in the Cell Scene. Otherwise,
thematic recurrences provide labels of identity or recall. Shchelkalov's
two appearances[7] are signalled by the same music, and each of Boris's
children has a theme associated with him/her, that for Feodor (Ex.
10.1g) fresh and untroubled enough instantly to point the gulf between
the present tormented Tsar and the son who should succeed him, that
for Kseniya (Ex. 10.1h) a particularly tender invention, its harmony as
chaste as its melody. In the Inn Scene a slightly churchy tune (Ex. 10.1i)
is less a projection of the joint persona of the itinerant monks, Varlaam

---

[7] However, Musorgsky excluded the second of these (in the Duma Scene) from his 1874
vocal score.

Ex. 10.1i

and Missail, than a thematic garb in which they may clothe themselves, whether to affect an image of sanctity to impress the hostess or, later, as a shield from the police officer's attentions. Yet their melody is really as much from the world of folk music, and in the final scene they introduce themselves more honestly with a true folksong. But, as in the Inn Scene, they sing in duet, their vocal blend sufficing to identify them, though they sing a different tune.

Shuisky and Rangoni, operators both, have their very different badges. The latter, a reptilian subversive with an obsequious surface masking ruthless guile, has no consolidated theme, simply a smooth-descending, featureless chromatic scale above unrelated, mostly dominant-seventh type, chords (Ex. 10.1*j*). But while everything about Rangoni is unstable, Shuisky is an open political operator, parading a

Ex. 10.1j

Ex. 10.1k

plain-spoken theme (Ex. 10.1*k*), simple but clear enough to establish his identity while disclosing little of the man behind it—though the underlying trail of crotchets points to a perpetual machinator.

Pinpointing the precise dramatic function of other recurring or seminal themes can sometimes be difficult. The problem is exacerbated by the seeming family affinities between melodies that are otherwise independent. Calvocoressi long ago laid stress on the large part played in the opening folk scene by material freely extracted or adapted from the opera's initial theme, as well as that theme's importance as the womb from which the Dmitri/Pretender theme sprang.[8] In fact, all this is a microcosm of a procedure exploited, as though by second nature, by Musorgsky in this opera, for (as noted earlier) decoration is fundamental to Russian musical creativity. This is evidenced not only in countless folksongs, each of which evolves as a succession of phrases that are decorative variants of a common protoshape, but also in the 'podgolosnaya' method once used by peasant choirs in the performance of such folksongs where, by the singers simultaneously improvising decorative variants of the folksong, a multi-voice accompaniment was constructed—but one that was in nature heterophonic (i.e., decorative),

[8] See *CM*, 144–5. Calvocoressi, who took full account of the initial version of *Boris*, still remains worth reading on thematic matters. See also *CAM*, 111ff.

not contrapuntally regulated by a triadic harmonic structure (i.e., organic). It should be no surprise that a sophisticated Russian composer should show the same instinct and facility as the numberless creators of his nation's folk melodies, and that he should invent with seemingly inexhaustible resourcefulness ever-new melody against the background of existing material.

Indeed, such protean inventiveness, joined with a remarkable aptitude for applying that inventiveness to dramatic ends, was one of Musorgsky's greatest assets in creating the overall unity that most listeners seem to sense in a work which, in so many other regards, seems to set little store by more mainstream methods for ensuring shapeliness and clear, all-embracing structure. New themes may relate or be born to old ones; certain themes that appear to have a family kinship foster a particular aura without seeming to bear an exact message. Thus the broad melody that unwinds beneath Shchelkalov's first-scene address to the people (p. 20, bars 6ff.) is closely related to the three rising themes taken over from *Salammbô* for Boris's Act 2 monologue, the first of which (see Ex. 10.2*g*) earlier commentators seem to agree relates to the Tsar's majesty and power/authority. Shchelkalov's monologue in the Prologue is where the future Tsar's shadow first falls across the drama, and this theme intimates that shadow; it is aptly ironic that in the Duma Scene this 'majesty' theme, now sombrely recast and presented in a way that brings it so very close to the Shchelkalov theme, should reflect not only the stunned boyars' final memory of their Tsar, now that they view his corpse, but also mark his final exit.

But perhaps the most subtle, yet revealing, example of organic thematicism is the emergence of the Dmitri/Pretender theme during the Cell Scene. The process whereby Musorgsky arrived at this is all the more mysterious, considering that this theme was already embedded in the opera's very first sounds—but the workings of Musorgsky's musical mind were much more sophisticated, intricate and intensive than might have been expected from his perceived persona and day-to-day existence. It is during the Cell Scene that this theme progressively surfaces. It is first foreshadowed when Grigory confesses to Pimen how 'a diabolical dream has disturbed' his peace (Ex. 10.2*a*). The novice chaffs in the confines of his monastery cell; as his dream reveals, he is already racked by irrepressible ambition, and Ex. 10.2*a* is the musical proxy of this as-yet-untargeted drive. Ambition rouses envy of the adventurous, riotous past of Pimen who 'had beheld the court and splendour of Ivan' (Ex. 10.2*b*), and Grigory demands forcefully: 'And why cannot I revel in wars, and feast at the Tsar's table?' (Ex. 10.2*c*). And perhaps his ambition is already overleaping itself, for the end of his final phrase (x) virtually echoes that to which the newly crowned Tsar had ended *his* universal invitation to feast with him after his coronation. Be that as it may, Pimen will unwittingly point the road not simply to the royal court, but to the crown itself. The stealthy phrase (Ex. 10.2*d*) which, constantly transforming its detail but never losing its identity, stalks remorselessly through the old monk's re-telling of what he had seen at Uglich twelve years earlier is a paraphrase of the Dmitri/Pretender theme to come, though with its opening and close reversed. But at Pimen's first mention of the murdered Dmitri the ends are reshuffled and, with minimal adjustment, the initial version of the Dmitri/Pretender theme itself (Ex. 10.2*e*) leaps out in a form to which, in retrospect, Grigory's ambition theme (Ex. 10.2*a*) is heard to have been akin.[9] The uncontainable drive and the means to its fulfilment suddenly meet and merge; in an instant Pimen's recounting of the past has, through his solitary listener's response, created the future. One more mention of the murdered Dmitri—and another, yet franker form of the Dmitri/Pretender theme parades itself (Ex. 10.2*f*). Ambition has become mission, and the opera's course is set.

Such things, for all their cumulative importance, are too numerous to trace here. But six ideas particularly associated with Boris must be noted (Ex. 10.2*g–l*). Defining the precise significance of each of these

---

[9] The latter stages of this process were lost when Musorgsky dropped Pimen's narration from the 1874 vocal score. His decision to exclude it may have been taken as the result of pressures from others uneasy at the music's boldness—though in the end the decision, taken for whatever reason, was of no practical consequence since the scene was never staged during Musorgsky's lifetime. Taruskin, however, believes it was removed to deprive the Dmitri/Pretender motif in the opera's revised version of its association with the murdered Tsarevich, thus restricting its resonances to the first stages of Grigory's bid for the crown. Later, however, when the motif recurs in association with the murdered child (during the Tsar's Palace Scene in Shuisky's account to Boris of the scene at Uglich, and in the Duma Scene during Pimen's narration), Taruskin argues that these recurrences are prompted not by the speaker's train of thought but by what Boris, as listener, is thinking. This seems implausible (see 'Musorgsky versus Musorgsky', *TM*, 282–8).

Ex. 10.2a,b,c

Ex. 10.2d

Ex. 10.2e

Ex. 10.2f

can prove difficult. The 'majesty and power/authority' theme (Ex. 10.2*g*) has already been observed, and what seems to be the 'theme of foreboding' (Ex. 10.2*k*) emerges in the Tsar's Palace Scene as Boris gravely reminds his son that he may soon inherit the throne, then prefaces (first) his address to the boyars in the Duma Scene before Pimen is brought in to deliver the mortal blow and (second) his farewell to his son. The Tsar's 'distress'[10] theme (Ex. 10.2*i*(i)), which prefaces his address in the Coronation Scene, instantly communicates his prevailing

[10] Oldani labels it the 'anxiety' theme. For Oldani's table of recurring themes and motifs in *Boris*, see *MBG*, 232–3.

Ex. 10.2g

Ex. 10.2h

Ex. 10.2i

Ex. 10.2j

darkness of mood, returning to introduce his anguished central monologue in the Tsar's Palace Scene when, alone, he confesses his crime (and resurging in the excised St Basil Scene where the Simpleton uncovers before the people the truth no other had dared speak). The fourth theme (Ex. 10.2j), identified by Calvocoressi variously as connected with the Tsar's anger and remorse (though distress might seem equally appropriate) and with his preoccupations and fears, plays a very significant role in the Tsar's Palace Scene in the original *Boris*; but since

Ex. 10.2k

Ex. 10.2l

none of these occurrences survived when this scene was rewritten, its retention during the Duma Scene of the revised *Boris* (in Shuisky's address to the boyars and Boris's farewell to his son) produces no dramatic resonance[11]. The fifth Boris theme, which has three distinct forms (Ex. 10.2*k*), seems connected to his guilt and terror, the first (Ex. 10.2*k*(i)) appearing in his central monologue in the Tsar's Palace Scene, the second (Ex. 10.2*k*(ii)) in his later exchange with Shuisky as his fevered imagination fastens on images of dead children rising from their coffins—and also, during this interview, in its third, more controlled form (Ex. 10.2*k*(iii)); whereas its first two forms reflect Boris's inner emotional ferment, the third may direct his feelings outwards into hostility and rage at others. Between them the three forms dominate the remainder of the scene. In the Duma Scene the first of these themes twice erupts, first as a still-haunted Boris disrupts Shuisky's account to

[11] In fact, in the initial *Boris* it had loomed large at the end of the hallucination scene, the very moment Shuisky is recalling when this theme recurs in the Duma Scene.

the boyars of their Tsar's irrational behaviour, then as Pimen's narrative at last homes in on the murdered child.

But it is the sixth Boris-associated idea, the coronation motif (Ex. 10.2*l*), that is the most striking single invention in the whole score and, though it is heard on only two occasions,[12] these afford the most vivid aural memories which listeners new to the work are most likely to carry home with them from the opera house. It is the briefest of the motifs— a plain oscillation between two dominant-seventh-type chords related only by the two pitches they have in common. But its acquired label is misleading, for it also heralds Boris's death, and it can be heard not only as benevolent to Boris but also as malign, its first colourful self-presentation in the Coronation Scene merely a hollow homage, in re-ality ironic. We cannot know whether the sinister interval between these common pitches (C and F♯/G♭—the tritone, or *diabolus in musica*, 'the devil in music' of medieval theory) was fundamental to Musorg-sky's conception, though it seems not improbable.[13] Whatever the case, Musorgsky dressed the motif in two ways to devastating effect. First, it is decorated with colourfully imposing orchestral figuration and on-stage bells as ornament to Boris's ceremonial entrance from the cathedral after his coronation. But, as the new Tsar's first words reveal, he already takes little pleasure in this acclaim, and on its second occurrence, as Boris's death agony begins in the Duma Scene, it is denuded of orna-ment and its tritone is drawn out to oscillate relentlessly between bleak bass trombone and pizzicato strings, the former coloured by tam-tam and bells. Few sounds in opera are as stark and chilling as these.

In handling keys and their relationships nineteenth-century Russian composers had priorities very different from those of their western counterparts. If for such as Beethoven these had been primarily the

---

[12] The music of the chiming clock, which Musorgsky added when composing the second version of the Tsar's Palace Scene, is drawn from the coronation motif but acts only collat-erally. The quiet recurrence of this progression during the parrot song is coincidental.

[13] Tchaikovsky would certainly come to exploit the expressive and symbolic potential of the tritone in the central scene of *The Queen of Spades*, when Hermann demands of the Countess whether her secret of three winning cards is 'linked with a pact with the devil?', using the interval not only melodically but to determine the local tonal course (E flat minor to A minor). That Musorgsky was consciously exploiting this association is supported by his pow-erful use of the tritone in the St Basil Scene when Mitukha and the crowd speak of the anathema pronounced against the Pretender.

means for spanning out a structure, for Russians a key more likely afforded a colour or acted as a symbol. In opera a single key might be used to signify a particular character, group, dramatic force, or emotion, while juxtapositions of keys could heighten the contrast between differing dramatic forces or simply signal the move to a new stage in the drama. Musorgsky's broader procedures had little to do with the magisterial, all-embracing strategies of classical tonal practice—and not surprisingly for, as noted in the previous chapter, a Russian composer's creativity, once roused, could become almost uncontainable, and while the product of such mental ferment was being captured on paper there would have been little room for searching cogitation on widely spanned schemes. But that did not preclude clear-headed running decisions. We may debate whether there was any grander plan to Musorgsky's employment of key and key relationships,[14] and we can only speculate on whether the tonal organization of the Prologue in *Boris* was premeditated or worked out as Musorgsky went along. Be that as it may, it reveals that Musorgsky, who never wrote a single symphonic piece in his life except as an exercise in composition, could employ key more systematically than most of his compatriots as one means of directing a process to its destination, for such things contribute unobtrusively to the sense of dramatic evolution and culmination in the Prologue, especially when its two constituent scenes are run together (as at the première).

For while in the opera's opening scene Musorgsky distributed the bluster of the police officer and the interjections and mutterings of individuals and groups from within the crowd across his often spare but always pointed orchestral texture, he intersected these bursts of activity with more stable movements, each firmly establishing a clear tonal or modal area and each occupying more real time than its predecessor. True, the F-Aeolian first chorus is heard twice, but its repetition on F♯ (G♭) is more assertive and pointedly extended. Shchelkalov's noble declaration follows in E flat (first minor, ending major), the pilgrims arrive and leave in A flat; then, after the police officer has issued his final instruction and the grumbling crowd have dispersed, the whole scene

---

[14]Oldani sets out, as a main element in his very extensive examination of the music of *Boris* in *MBG*, 225–76, a highly ramified view of Musorgsky's key usage in this opera.

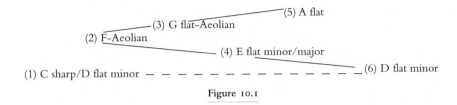

Figure 10.1

ends, as it had begun, in C sharp (D flat) minor.[15] Whether deliberately planned or not, the scheme of these tonal salients has a particular symmetry, masked only by the ambiguous notation. With the sharp-key notations reversed, a wedge emerges (Fig. 10.1).

The Coronation Scene that now follows opens with a diminished triad on the leading note of D flat, thus introducing the C which will provide the unbroken bass throughout the prelude and remain as the tonic of the entire scene, thus affording a final tonal anchorage for the Prologue and endowing this second scene, with its choruses that flank Boris's concise monologue (which sets out so firmly in C minor), with a firm sense of musical finality.

At a more local level, pivot pitches, already employed in the first of the *Nursery* cycle songs, play their part. Thus the initial C♯ (D♭), prominent in the opera's brief orchestral preamble that takes its character from the folky tune of Musorgsky's own creation, becomes operational when the police officer appears, running almost unbroken through a dozen bars, to be replaced by C which after nine bars is joined by F for the first nine bars of the crowd's first chorus. For the next ten bars E♭ and D♭ alternately vie for supremacy, the latter prevailing until C is restored for two bars. For the remainder of the chorus, F functions as an orthodox pedal. Such procedures run through the rest of this Novodevichy Scene and will be audible elsewhere, especially in the final Kromy Forest Scene. But during the opera's far more extensive stretches involving interaction between the principal players, pivot pitches are rare or absent, for their function seems to have been to give a succession of clear moorings to stretches of music which might otherwise, in

[15] This final section was not included in the 1874 vocal score. Thus the scene ended in A flat, which linked almost seamlessly with the first chord of the Coronation Scene (a diminished triad on C).

Ex. 10.3

Musorgsky's search for as realistic a presentation as possible of a disorderly situation, have slipped towards the incoherence of *The Marriage*.

The choruses of the Coronation Scene, founded on the Russian folksong[16] of which both Rimsky and Tchaikovsky also made enthusiastic use (not to mention Beethoven in his Second Razumovsky Quartet), are very different in outer mood from the same crowd's earlier collective lament, though the brevity of their acclamations suggests they are short on enthusiasm (Rimsky's decision to expand these in his own second version of *Boris* may have made for better opera but undermined dramatic truth). The gloom with which Boris reflects on the power that is now his foretells little joy for his future. The heavy brooding of his monologue's C minor opening and his ensuing plea to Heaven uncover the despondency of his inner condition (as well as hinting at its source: see Ex. 10.1*n*(ii), above); the wrench into A minor marks his return to awareness of present reality, first to pay due homage to his predecessors then, adjusting to the people's own C major, to summon all present to a more nourishing inauguration of his reign. At the scene's end Musorgsky capitalizes on the bell-like clang of a major triad with added sixth, which reflected a brand of tuning characteristic of peals of Russian church bells (Ex. 10.3).

Initial scenes must needs communicate the essentials for understanding what is to come. In practice this does not make for tidiness or tautness (as the preliminaries of both *Onegin* and *The Queen of Spades* demonstrate). Not the least virtue of the Prologue to *Boris* is that it

---

[16] For a detailed investigation of the role of folksong, folksong style and the bowdlerized church style of Musorgsky's Russian predecessors in (mainly) his operatic choruses, see V. Morosan, 'Folk and Chant Elements in Musorgsky's Choral Writing', *MIM*, 95–133.

proceeds straight to business, uncovering the role of the crowd through their response to their situation, Shchelkalov's monologue sufficient to apprise us (as well as them) of the state of affairs, Boris's address starkly defining the principal player and his view of his predicament. His monologue is little more than two minutes long and he will now disappear for two whole scenes. It speaks volumes for Musorgsky's razor-edged precision that when Boris re-emerges, perhaps an hour later, he seems already a familiar figure.

Act 1 above all shows the lingering influence of (as Taruskin has noted) Dargomïzhsky's *Stone Guest* and Musorgsky's own *Marriage* experiments, and it is here that Musorgsky drew most heavily on Pushkin's own words instead of inventing expedient text. Dargomïzhsky's influence is evident in the measured duologue in Pimen's cell, that of *The Marriage* in the lively exchanges in the rustic hostelry. The extended conversation between Pimen and Grigory, the future Pretender, in the Cell Scene was hardly likely to prove an audience rouser, which may be one reason it was never staged in Musorgsky's lifetime. But making the Inn Scene the Pretender's only sighting in the opera is unsatisfactory, for while initially it had been sufficient merely to establish Boris's presence (full self-revelation could be left till later), Grigory needs not only to be displayed but his motives and intents to be disclosed, for he will become the other of the two forces whose contention will drive the drama. In the initial version of *Boris* the course of this rivalry had not been pursued further, what followed being built exclusively from Pushkin's scenes in which the Tsar himself appeared; though the ostensible reason for adding the Polish Act was the introduction of a major female role, Musorgsky must also have perceived that there was a void in the listener's reasonable expectations if the Pretender disappeared before ever any portion of his career during which he actively challenged Boris had been revealed. Yet once this void had been filled, another remained unless the contest's result was supplied. And so though in the revised version these twin forces still never meet head on, their competing courses are delineated in parallel, Boris's decline being charted in Act 2 (the Tsar's Palace Scene) and the Duma Scene, the Pretender's rise in the Inn Scene and Act 3 (the two Polish scenes); the outcome is the final business of Act 4, the Duma Scene ending with Boris's downfall, the Kromy Forest Scene with the Pretender's triumph.

After the turmoil and grandeur of the Prologue, the tranquillity of Pimen's cell and the finely limned music that first mirrors the old monk's visible activity, then accompanies his self-revelation, impresses the more deeply. But Pimen had been no introverted recluse predestined for a secluded cloister; his past had also been of the world and its battles, and his final mission is fearlessly to put on record the crime of the usurper, now Tsar. And so the gentle D minor/dorian music fills out, shifts to the major, and adumbrates the theme that confirms the strength and steadfastness of this wise monk and which the orchestra presents in full (see Ex. 10.1f), then repeats as Pimen remembers his stormy past before resuming his writing. While Boris's address had shown Musorgsky's capacity to encompass succinctly a variety of shifting moods, the opening music of the Cell Scene presents magisterially a progressive revelation of character.

Pimen's drift of key is also part of Musorgsky's dramatic strategy. Though his key system has none of the rigidity of Tchaikovsky's in *Swan Lake*, where tonality would be an indicator of benignity and malevolence (the more powerful the presence of good or evil, the sharper or flatter the prevailing key), Musorgsky in this scene clearly colours things secular with a sharp-key brightness. Grigory, desperate to escape the fetters of the monastery, utters his first words as in B minor/dorian[17] and mounts his dream tower of ambition on steps that spiral dizzily sharpwards;[18] Pimen, confessing his own irrepressible memories 'now of wanton feasts, now of skirmishes of war', twice briefly lifts his theme out of its seemingly fixed D major into B major. Later, when Grigory's

---

[17] In the first version (before Musorgsky added the offstage choir) Grigory's entry had been heralded by the abruptest of wrenches from a D / dorian context to a chord of B major. Carl Dahlhaus commented on the harmonic boldness of this chorus, but his observation must be treated with caution. He claims that the 'last chord, C sharp minor, in the sixth bar from Figure 9, is simply inexplicable in terms of the rules of tonality as they were understood in the nineteenth century, except as the blunder of a dillettante' C. Dahlhaus, *Realism in Nineteenth-Century Music*, Cambridge, 1985, 77). That statement is debatable; but in any case there is no C sharp minor chord in bar 6 in either Musorgsky's vocal score or full score, only a bare C♯-G♯ fifth.

[18] Like Tchaikovsky in *Swan Lake*, Musorgsky may reverse his notation when reaching six sharps or more, as he does four bars after Figure 15. The sharp notation is resumed after six bars (though B♯ is still notated as C; two bars later, when the bass drops to E, is surely the point where B♯ reverts enharmonically to C).

confession of worldly ambitions threatens to get out of hand (to judge from the extreme sharpwards turn his outburst has taken, which even annexes recklessly his mentor's D major/B major music of worldly memories), Pimen responds in A flat, Musorgsky presumably viewing this abrupt shift as an enharmonic move back into more wholesome regions, imposed by the old monk to check a situation that might become unmanageable. Yet the centre of virtue, or simply of moral neutrality, seems to be among the 'white notes'. Twice Musorgsky shifts Pimen's theme into this region: first, when he recalls how Russia's rulers had sometimes sought peace by exchanging royal panoply 'for the monk's humble cowl and the holy cell' (Musorgsky still beginning Pimen's personal theme on D, though adjusting and reharmonizing it over a double pedal suggesting G while still taking care that all may be innocent of sharps); then, when he remembers how Tsar Feodor 'had transformed the Tsar's palace into a house of prayer' (this time both transposing and reharmonizing the theme).

Quiet as this scene is, it contains some of the opera's most powerful music whose uncompromising bluntness may be one reason it was removed from the revised version. The aged monk's chilling account of events at Uglich some dozen years earlier is unsparing, driving home not only the bestiality of what was done but the deed's unremitting potency in the present. Beside this narrative, Shuisky's later selective report to Boris in Act 2 sounds merely sentimental—though, in its dramatic context, absolutely right—for, conditioned by terror of his master at one of Boris's most fearsome moments, Shuisky chooses his words to soothe and reassure, putting into his music everything that may mitigate his account. The quiet opening of Pimen's narrative is deceptive, the stalking phrase of Ex.10.2*d* rapidly acquiring a formidable power. Its music can become by rapid turns poignant, stealthy, intimidating, electric, towards its end almost disorientated (Ex.10.4). It can be harmonically savage, in musical progress unceremonious. But what binds all these disparate elements is the theme that underpins Pimen's first words, and which goes on to show its ever-mutating fecundity in nearly every bar, through one line of evolution growing into the chaste image of the murdered infant (see Ex.10.2*f*), through another by exploiting its capacity to assume any form and character it chooses (see the three versions in Ex.10.4), suggesting an unstable, uncontainable potency that may still appal those who witnessed anything of the event itself and bring unendurable terror to any implicated in it.

In any opera, but especially in one depicting a series of critical moments spread over a very wide time span, it is likely that there will be a number of marginal characters, each indispensible for a particular scene but with no part to play in any other. What is striking in Russian operas is the musical prominence sometimes given such characters during their brief appearances. They may be furnished with an aria in no way required by their role, but which turns them from mere functionaries into living beings. Think of Liza's confidante, Polina, in the second scene of *The Queen of Spades*; even more, of Tatyana's husband, Gremin, whose noble expression of love in the ballroom scene is almost the largest aria in the whole of *Onegin*. Certainly the Hostess's song that opens the Inn Scene in *Boris* is a light-weight matter, but Musorgsky's decision to furnish this feisty lady with this self-introduction for the revised version etches her individuality firmly; also, after the orchestra has opened with a snatch of the Kazan song, as well as themes to be associated with the itinerant monks (see Ex.10.1*i*) and Grigory, who has now taken ostentatious possession of the Dmitri/Pretender theme (see Ex.10.1*e*), it establishes the lowly social stratum of this wayside hostelry's customers.[19] Varlaam's Kazan song, prescribed by Pushkin himself, is one of Musorgsky's most robust creations. With its opening phrase marked by an insistent flattened second degree, its accompaniment brilliantly inventive in both its textural variety and scoring, it provides a useful landmark dividing the scene's preliminaries from its main business.

[19] As an insight into one feature of the no doubt instinctive (and also very Russian) workings of Musorgsky's melodic faculty, it is worth noting that when he came to add the Hostess's song his inventiveness shaped the one-bar figure that introduces this addition (*b*) around the immediately preceding Dmitri/Pretender theme (*a*). This new figure was then promptly adjusted by the Hostess to become the song's fundamental melodic element (*c*).

Ex. 10.4

["Confess," the crowd roared:

and in terror beneath the axe

the villains confessed and named Boris.]

In this scene sharp and flat regions are no longer the respective domains of the world and the spirit (as in the Cell Scene) but of ease and anxiety, though white keys still seem to be a mark of virtue—at least, in their sanctuary Varlaam and Missail attempt (though without total tonal success) to seek refuge on the police officer's entry. Initially everything is to the sharp side, though the rogue-monks borrow Pimen's D minor/dorian for their theme until the curtain rises, they are seen for what they are, and the incongruity is exposed. There is nothing unbreakable in Musorgsky's key usage; nevertheless, until after the Kazan song, the music plunges flatwards only when attention is directed at Grigory's troubled brooding, the Dmitri/Pretender theme pointing us to his preoccupation.[20] In its strongly inflected vocal part and fitful, seemingly uncoordinated progress, the section after Varlaam's star turn shows as clearly as any passage in *Boris* the dividend reaped from composing *The Marriage*. Here also irritation with Grigory, who has refused to provide backing for Varlaam's performance, drives the monk's music briefly flatwards, but it settles firmly into F minor as he intermittently drones and dozes, his diminutive folksong winding its way, *cantus firmus*-like, as an intermittent thread through Grigory's and the Hostess's furtive colloquy as the former extracts travelling directions to the Lithuanian border. Events have taken a serious turn: hence, perhaps, this shift to deep flat regions. But after this the most significant tonal element is Varlaam's dogged determination to cling to Pimen's D minor/dorian as a mask of piety and probity, first when he pleads poverty to stir the police officer's sympathy, finally when he returns to his dozing theme as he laboriously summons up all his small literacy skills to avoid being hanged.

The prevailing impression borne away from the Inn Scene is of raciness, vitality, and informality. The music is more text-conditioned than any other single scene in *Boris*, its pace ensures it never falters and Musorgsky's inventiveness that it never loses its dramatic hold. There are also landmarks that help shape out a structure. Varlaam's Kazan song is the most obvious—but the monk also unwittingly has a certain stabilizing influence on a second substantial stretch through his drowsy

---

[20] The two-bar shift to flats five bars after 17 is simply a momentary reversal of notation, as are the flat-notated passages in the Kazan song.

repetitive chanting. Even his return to this simple theme at the end makes a tiny contribution to shaping the scene.

This is the point at which the two versions of *Boris* part company, to become very different operas. It is not merely that, of the remaining three scenes of the initial version, one was drastically rewritten with most of its music replaced and another was excised completely, only the final Duma Scene remaining mostly intact into the revised version; the whole nature of the drama was changed. The preceding four scenes had presented three virtually unconnected milieux and groups of characters. But if this might seem confusingly discursive, what followed was implacably singleminded, with all centring on Boris himself. For, above all, the first version of *Boris*, as Taruskin has cogently argued, was not a people-versus-authority epic but the tragedy of a just man who has committed a single crime and is destroyed by conscience, and it was this process of degradation that the remaining three scenes went on to trace with remorseless concentration. Certainly the initial Act 2 had no time for detours; Kseniya and Feodor were observed and their conditions defined, the former as the betrothed maiden lamenting the death of her beloved, the latter as Boris's heir absorbing the geography of his future realm. The Nurse had comforted Kseniya, and Boris had entered and praised, exhorted, then forewarned his son of what would confront him. Alone, in his monologue he had unburdened himself of his woes. The opening stretch of this outpouring, which had included the first quotation from *Salammbô*, was to be taken over into the revision, but beyond this the second part was different both in text and music. Musically the earlier version was integrated principally by recurrences in the orchestra of two themes, both from *Salammbô*, the first (Ex.10.2g) heard five times, the second (the anger and distress theme: Ex.10.2j) thrice; meanwhile the singer dealt with its lengthy text in an often quasi-recitative fashion. This plainness and consistent concern for a tight text-music relationship had marked the rest of the act, and while there may have been nothing in the monologue that immediately called to mind the more doctrinaire method of *The Marriage*, there were moments in the ensuing Shuisky/Boris encounter that certainly did. Yet what was most striking was the continuing thematic concentration in this first version. Once Dmitri's name had been spoken his theme, and the complementary one of Boris's anger and distress, had haunted the music; for compactness and singlemindedness there is nothing, perhaps, in the familiar *Boris* that quite matches these final stages of the initial version. Only Shuisky's narration of events at Uglich seems positively inferior to the music that supplanted it.

The following St Basil Scene had moved the tale from the personal to the corporate, through the crowd's participation linking the latter stages of the opera to its opening, dispelling the almost claustrophobic intimacy of the Boris/Shuisky encounter, but leading Boris to a second meeting—less awesome, but in its way as dreadful, for the Simpleton's words affirmed devastatingly for all to hear that their Tsar was a regicide and the road to absolution forever barred to him. Oldani has suggested that the opening, with its pizzicato string phrases punctuated by held wind chords, was modelled by Musorgsky on the 'Procession by Night', the first of Liszt's *Two Episodes from Lenau's Faust*. The treatment of the crowd's part in what had preceded the Simpleton's confrontation with the urchins was much like that which had opened the opera, but of all the choruses in *Boris*, the people's later plea that their Tsar assuage their hunger was the most moving. It had grown out of the Simpleton's wailing, then with equal smoothness had returned attention to that pitiful creature. To be deprived in the revision of this and the ensuing Boris/Simpleton confrontation is heart-breaking, but unavoidable— for the subsequent transference of the two Simpleton incidents, and especially of his final lament, to the Kromy Forest Scene renders insupportable the incorporation of the St Basil Scene into per- formances of the revised version (though this frequently still seems to happen).

Curiously, the initial version of Kseniya's lament that opens Act 2 (Ex.10.5a), with its rhythmic fluidity, aggressive modality (the scale of the opening two-and-a-half bars evidently synthesized by Musorgsky from two conventional tetrachords, the second in retrograde: Ex.10.5b), and, from bar three, its austere single-line accompaniment, had carried as many resonances from a peasant environment as anything in the preced- ing Inn Scene; with little modification this portion could have been ac- commodated in that vivid projection of a Russian peasant milieu, Stravinsky's *Les noces*. But Kseniya was a royal child, and Musorgsky, fore- warned by the wrong dramatic signal the audience at Pargolovo had caught from his 'buffa' peasants, must have decided that a more

Ex. 10.5a

Kseniya: Mi-lïy—moy zhe-nikh,— pre-kras-nïy— kor-o-le-vich, Ne— mne— tï do-stal-sya, ne svo-

[My dear betrothed, handsome son of a king, you have not claimed

yey— ne-ves-te, a sï-roy— mo-gil-ke na dal-ney, na dal-ney sto-

me, your betrothed, but a damp tomb in a distant,

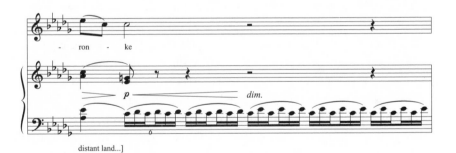

- ron— ke

distant land...]

Ex. 10.5b

Ex. 10.5c

[Where are you, my betrothed, my beloved! In a damp tomb, in a foreign land...]

regular melody (though originating in its predecessor) which was paired with the brand of functional harmony typical of the rest of the opera would be socially more indicative (Ex.10.5*c*). But his reworking of what followed was far more draconian. The act's length was nearly doubled with less than a third of the original retained; of the two largest transferences, only the closing section of the second (the opening portion of Boris's first monologue) was a passage of heightened dramatic tension. As for the remainder of the act, only a few fragments, mostly provided by Shuisky, will be familiar to those who know only the revised version. The introduction of the chiming clock near the beginning enabled Musorgsky to create a graphic musical image that could recur with chilling effect at the act's end, its two occurrences also providing an unmissable structural frame. The precision with which Musorgsky conjures the reality of the clock's ticking and whirring, especially on its recurrence, is as striking as it is simple. There are two two-note ostinati, one a ticking tritone oscillation outlined in quavers by cellos and violas pizzicato with horns (the first violins spinning a fleet chromatic line between these two pitches), against which the second ostinato, the preoccupation of a pair of bassoons initially alternating with clarinets, grates gently but unremittingly. There are also brief perfect-fifths from double basses and, increasingly, tiny stuttering interjections from oboes and flutes to suggest the machinery's creakings as it finishes its periodic ritual. Throughout the whole opera the scoring is always the minimum required, and at times the detailed local judgements are made with a chamber-music finesse; such exemplary economy of means marks, for instance, the touching scene between the Nurse and Boris's children. Musorgsky may never have attained that self-advertising virtuosity in orchestration which Rimsky would command, but in his sense of what was right—and what would work—he was almost unerring.

Whatever ambivalence may be felt about some of Musorgsky's later changes, his decision to expand this act's opening section further to create an aura of increasing lightheartedness was absolutely right, for its instant dislocation by their father's entry transmits the unease that even Boris's own children feel towards him. Almost before he has uttered a word he is instantly to be connected with the monarch whose inner torments we have already glimpsed, albeit briefly, in the Coronation Scene. The two interpolated songs that precede this disruption are gems. The exchanges of the children and nurse are homely, the latter speaking plainly and with her main advice set in a plain white-note region, though she picks up Kseniya's E flat and in kindly teasing plunges into its deep-flat but modally-spiced minor to tell her playfully ghoulish tale of the gnat killed with his own cudgel. But this song is more conventional than the double-act patter song in which she is Feodor's ally. Set in a bright G major, the perfect foil for Boris's heavily-flatted intrusion to come, its text is a babble of prattle, its music a chain of a dozen or so tiny melodic tags split between two verses; the refrain to the second verse takes a new tonal direction, and the growing impetus of what follows is seemingly uncontainable until the Tsar's presence is suddenly noticed.

Enough has already been written here to establish something of Musorgsky's view of keys and key relationships in *Boris*, and the present investigation need not pursue the matter further in detail. But for the Tsar himself, Musorgsky does seem to have selected three flats as a special tonal region. Boris's first words had been in C minor, and E flat is the key to which he gravitates most readily in the present exchanges with his children (though his most tender moment with his daughter tugs him abruptly back into a brighter G major). In revision Musorgsky rightly made only the most minor of changes in this intimate and warm-hearted interlude, but he did now permit Kseniya to reply to her father (in the original she had remained mute)—a tiny touch that for an instant allows Boris to react with a sensitivity and compassion that have no place elsewhere in the opera to reveal themselves so touchingly. More typical of his private world are the pain and loneliness of his ensuing monologue.

Here above all is the pointer to Musorgsky's central aim in his dramatic remodelling of *Boris*. Other commentators have analysed and described the radical changes he made when compiling the text for the revised version.[21] Pushkin could no longer serve as he had for the first *Boris*; there is no clearer indication that Musorgsky had in mind to create a very different kind of opera than the abundance of new text he himself now provided and his liberal rewriting of those portions of Pushkin that he did incorporate. In the initial monologue he had drawn almost exclusively on a little over half the Tsar's soliloquy in Pushkin's Scene 7, where Boris had lamented the woes of power—the ingratitude of his people, their blame of him even for natural disasters, how 'whoever dies, I am the murderer . . . ' It is the lament of a man raging at fate, a victim of (as Caryl Emerson has put it) 'the destructive power of *rumor*'.[22] But in the revised text these accusations from an ungrateful people vanish, and in their place, through Musorgsky's own words, comes the outpouring of a haunted soul besieged by plots at home and intrigues abroad, the scapegoat of all—and beset nightly by 'the blood-stained child', eyes ablaze, tiny fists clenched, imploring mercy. While the Boris of 1868–9 had remained an undiminished if intolerably oppressed figure, the Boris of 1871–2 exposes the man within the Tsar, now increasingly unable to bear the burden of guilt. Given this more human face and heart, Musorgsky could permit him to drop that detachment which had marked not only his public oration in the Prologue but also this present monologue in the initial version, where he had delivered himself obliquely, as so often in tragedy, as though to an audience of impartial listeners. Instead Boris now addresses each of us with a confessional frankness aimed not so much to win our understanding for efforts made and wrongs wrongly imputed as to gain our pity, even sympathy, for torments endured for a particular wrong bitterly regretted. There had, of course, been a fair measure of lyricism in the initial *Boris*,

[21] See C. Emerson, 'The *Boris* Libretto as a Formal, Literary, and Historical Problem', *MBG*, 183–224, and R. Taruskin, 'Musorgsky versus Musorgsky', *TM*, 201–90.

[22] *MBG*, 201.

and this monologue had already borrowed its two main ideas from that early venture into operatic melodrama made long before Musorgsky had fallen under the spell of realism. Now he returned to *Salammbô* again to raid it with a vengeance, for it had deployed that very brand of spacious and noble sentiment that the new situation required.

What is remarkable about the new *Salammbô* borrowings is how exact they are, and their extent; moreover, original keys are mostly preserved—though this suited well, for six flats (the signature of Musorgsky's first new borrowing) had become particularly associated in nineteenth-century opera with arias of deep inner emotion (for example, Gremin's aria in Tchaikovsky's *Onegin*, Polina's in *The Queen of Spades*). The monologue's preliminaries were taken over from the initial *Boris*, but whereas that monologue had gone on to extend the kind of music laid down there, these preliminaries were now followed by a re-run of Kseniya's theme (see Ex.10.1*h*): five more bars, and then began an arioso—for that is what Musorgsky now made it (openly, and perhaps a little defiantly, admitting as much to Stasov). The earlier version had assigned largely separate roles to the singer and orchestra: while the orchestra had presented fully worked-out music with nearly everything repeated or echoed at some stage, thus creating a rather haphazard design that nevertheless gave the piece a discrete musical identity, the singer had been increasingly concerned with a clear and functional delivery of his lengthy text, even when locked onto the orchestra's thematic material.

But now this dualism eases, and the lyrical phrase is Musorgsky's prime preoccupation. Simultaneously a design becomes clearer—a simple rondo, the first episode opening with the pulsing triplet quavers that begin in bar 10 and abruptly change the expressive tone, with the second episode (ten bars) entering at bar 27;[23] there follows an extension to accommodate the regicide's terror-filled recollection of nightly hauntings by the murdered child's ghost. And the monologue's expressive world is now more focussed, nearly three-quarters of the main arioso being compounded exclusively from *Salammbô* music, the two newly composed slivers marked less by heavy gloom than by a shud-

---

[23] Or perhaps the second episode begins six bars earlier, where the ritornello theme is abandoned.

dering chill as Boris's thoughts fasten on his torments. Nothing exemplifies more vividly Musorgsky's new readiness to renege on kuchkist principles when they were inadequate for the full revelation of an inner condition; the dramatic retreat, already beaten in the initial *Boris*, from the pedantic exactitude of *The Marriage* had simply not gone far enough for the revised opera's needs. The result is one of the greatest passages in this greatest of Russian tragic operas—and one that lends no help to the following off-stage 'parrot incident', which was the other major insertion in this scene.

This was Musorgsky's one major miscalculation in his revision. The motivation was no doubt the same as that which had expanded so drastically the earlier part of the act: to introduce a lighter episode as foil to the grimmer matters to come. There had been every justification for the earlier addition; after all, what more natural than that Feodor and the Nurse should have tried to lighten Kseniya's distress, and that Boris's entrance should thus bring a sudden and revealing change of mood? But the parrot episode was contrived, a trivial interruption unconnected with any dramatic thread and described in a formal song of much charm but, in this context, obstructive. Far better to have proceeded forthwith, as in the initial version, to the Boris/Shuisky encounter via news of the Polish conspiracy communicated by the boyar—though sadly this would have lost us Boris's tender response to his son's account of the parrot incident.

For what follows is the most tense one-to-one confrontation of the opera. If Boris's monologue had been the hinge on which this act turned, this exchange with Shuisky and its outcome is the hinge of the whole opera, for even without Pimen's intervention in the Duma Scene its impact leaves Boris doomed. Over it hangs the Pretender, first simply an anonymous threat but, once named by Shuisky as Dmitri, an imminent figure of terror that will shatter Boris's sanity. The Tsar's initial fury springs only from Shuisky's contacts with Poland, and his music, spiked with menacing trills and sturdy dissonances, with the harmony initially rotating in tight circles and all firmly grounded on a C♯ pedal, projects a rage that is dangerous but still contained (though the harmonic field opens as Boris reminds Shuisky of the punishment his former master, Ivan the Terrible, would have dealt him); then, when Boris suddenly smothers his visible fury to grant ironic forgiveness, the musical backdrop of a quiet yet strangely 'unsafe' structure of bald triads and less stable chords leaves no doubt that he is still as much to be feared, even when thus. This is one of those extraordinary moments in *Boris* the impact of which is totally out of proportion to its brevity.

Shuisky's weapons of diplomacy are the plain melody and reassuring consonance of the dutiful courtier. Faced with Boris's sustained outburst, he retreats into the protection of his most secure, well-practised persona (see Ex.10.1*k*), though his broken vocal line belies his outer poise, just as the disorientated trail of major triads to which he breaks news of a Pretender already points to the latter's identity (at least, for us—for do these not recall that progression to which a cell-bound novice had begun to confess his obsessive dream of worldly power in the Cell Scene?). Boris demands the Pretender's name, the serpentine bass communicating the underlying tension with which he awaits the answer to his almost whispered words. Recovering something of his composure, Shuisky procrastinates in identifying the claimant; the resources of prolixity exhausted, he tries another expedient, slowing his delivery until he can no longer withhold the name 'Dmitri', then crying it, *quasi adagio*, at the top of his range.

He could not have delivered the blow more devastatingly. What follows is virtually a monologue, with Shuisky merely the petrified onlooker. Brusquely dismissing his son, Boris orders the western border to be closed (echoing the music that had touched on foreign intrigues at the centre of his monologue), then focusses on the murdered child. Instantly his guilt-and-terror motifs gather. One had appeared in that Dmitri-obsessed extension to his monologue; now the remaining two for a while take absolute control, then yield to other music already heard as Boris retraces matters or moods in evidence earlier—his whispered Pretender-enquiry music, a portion of *Salammbô* music from his soliloquy, the Ivan-punishment music. Such cumulative concentration prepares for the act's last and, in human terms, cataclysmic event.

No scene in opera traces more brutally, and without the slightest alleviation through sentiment, the final stage in the demoralization of a human being. Shuisky paints the rosiest picture he can of the scene in Uglich as he had witnessed it. But, confronted with the graphic vividness of the courtier's description, Boris cracks; his second guilt-and-terror motif (Ex.10.2*k*(ii)) erupts again, unceremoniously abbreviating

Shuisky's description. What follows requires little further commentary; the clock again begins to strike, its chimes now wreathed in a shifting mist of whirring violins and flickering woodwind from within the shadows of which Boris images moving figures, the murdered child's ghost itself rising in accusation. Musorgsky's last musical touch is as revealing as any: as Boris falls helplessly to his knees, his third guilt-and-terror motif, which has just achieved its most savage-ever presentation as the Tsar's cries reached their peak, now too abates and, in the last bars, dissolves in the dying accompaniment.

The Polish Act confronted Musorgsky with two major problems. First: while the Pretender, now grown from a peasant in monk's clothing to a formidable schemer in courtier's garb, had ardour in plenty, Pushkin's Marina was a proud, calculating beauty, concerned only with the wealth, influence, and prestige that marriage might bring; her sole significant exchange with the Pretender was in the Fountain Scene, which she turned into a hard-headed contest on the politics of their union, with an absolute embargo meanwhile on passion. There were neither grounds nor materials here for a love scene. And second: though by 1871 a scene excluded by Pushkin from the 1831 edition was also available (Scene 12 in the play's complete version: Marina in her boudoir, with her maid Ruzia prattling about the Pretender's devotion and his uncertain origins), there was still insufficient appropriate material from which to build a dramatic framework in which this new relationship might not only be exposed but appear to have real relevance to events presented elsewhere in the opera.

To solve the first problem Musorgsky wrote the necessary lines himself (indeed, in the whole act there is little trace of Pushkin's own words), casting these in two scenes. Pushkin's Marina/Ruzia scene suggested the first, with Ruzia now a silent part and a chorus of attendants singing Marina's praises instead; the second scene dealt with the essential business of Pushkin's Fountain Scene (Scene 14), the idea for a polonaise lifted from his preceding scene. Then, to give this new act an organic connection with the wider business of the whole opera, Musorgsky invented a new character: Rangoni, a 'secret Jesuit' suggested perhaps by Father Czernikowski in Pushkin's Scene 11 (though taking his name from a real-life Count Rangoni, the papal nuncio responsible for the historical Pretender's conversion to Catholicism). Rangoni's political

Musorgsky in officer's uniform (1856)

Alexander Dargomizhsky

Mily Balakirev

Dmitri Stasov

Musorgsky, with brother Filaret (1858)

Nikolay Rimsky-Korsakov

César Cui

Alexander Serov

Musorgsky (1865)

Lyudmila Shestakova

Alexandra Purgold

Nadezhda Purgold

Vladimir Stasov

Viktor Hartmann

Musorgsky (1874)

Osip Petrov

Musorgsky (portrait by Repin, 1881)

Darya Leonova

manipulations on behalf of the Church of Rome—but primarily of himself—would add a religious-political strand exposed through his encounters with Marina and the Pretender in these two scenes, and this might later be picked up in the lynching of the two Jesuits in the Kromy Forest Scene.

With the Polish Act the opera enters a foreign land and the different musical world of a western-bordering and cosmopolitan-minded, if provincial, court. The mitigated tone of much of Musorgsky's musical language here is recognition of this, a consequence not of diminishing inspiration but of the necessary shift in cultural tone. Mazurka and polonaise stylizations appropriately abound in the music of the indigenous inhabitants. Yet the stylistic shift is only relative, and the charming opening chorus for Marina's attendants singing her praises in the Boudoir Scene could more probably have been conceived within a Russian context. Marina's soliloquy is a mazurka, but with none of the explicit, balanced compartmentalization familiar from Chopin; instead, its structure is free, its trail of a dozen or so different four-or eight-bar units and its open end relating it structurally, though not in style, to Feodor's patter song in the preceding act. It does not gain from the comparison, for though the frustration of an ambitious woman may reasonably be reflected in the obsessive reiteration of a one-bar rhythmic matrix stamped on a succession of ideas over most of 100-plus bars, the procedure also strait-jacketed Musorgsky's creativity, and some passages are nondescript.

But the Polish Act would have proved worthwhile for Rangoni alone. Musorgsky made him a studied antithesis of Pimen. Where Pimen, the devout Orthodox, is open, firm, yet compassionate, Rangoni, the guileful Catholic, is covert, ingratiating, yet ruthless. His intrusion ruptures Marina's increasingly unrestrained soliloquy, F minor abruptly clouding her sharp-key cheerfulness. If Marina now sounds to be seeking sanctuary in a Kseniya-style musical mantle, there is no refuge to be found there, once her confessor has set about his business. His tactics are well practised and his control of shifting posture absolute, his pace always unhurried but its pressure unrelenting, whether he is engaged in intimidation, entreaty or exhortation. Marina's musical responses now reveal her formerly masked personality as both vulnerable and spirited. But she is no match for Rangoni; when she defies his demand that she sacrifice her virtue if necessary, he crushes her through superstitious manipulation. Twice fleetingly during his earlier campaign he had allowed his own musical badge (see Ex.10.1*j*) to be spied; now victorious, he displays it again as a symbol of supremacy. Of the man behind the badge nothing shows.

After the tensions of this scene, the moonlit quiet of the Sandomir garden, in which the love-sick Pretender awaits Marina, is the more striking. If there is a brief eye to this opera's tempest, it is here. But it is to prove a scene of ironies. Rangoni, scheming to further the Pretender's relationship with Marina by listing to him the public and private torments she endures through love, recycles the music to which earlier he had urged *her* to inflame the Pretender. And especially ironies in key. Indeed, Musorgsky's enterprising use of E major (in this act very much the Pretender's key of love) during the Pretender's encounters both with Rangoni and Marina is further evidence that his musico-dramatic sensitivities were as alert here as elsewhere in the opera, for the key is used not only as the agent of the Pretender's passion but as a weapon against him. In the Boudoir Scene Marina herself had slipped into it in her monologue as she had begun setting out her campaign to inflame her lover 'with tears of burning passion'; now, in the second scene, Rangoni, who otherwise operates almost exclusively within the more shadowed world of flat keys, twice uses its sympathetic resonances to temper reassuringly any overreaction to his manipulations. Told by him of Marina's reciprocation, the Pretender had leaped ecstatically into E major to swear, with all the passion his own special theme could muster, that Marina would be his Tsaritsa, only to abandon the key angrily when questioning his informant's veracity. Seeking to reassure, the Jesuit quietly returns the music to E major to sweeten his rebuttal—then swiftly glides back into E flat to renew his assault on the Pretender's susceptibilities. Then later, having retreated behind the image of the humble, unworldly monk, Rangoni sets out his price for delivering Marina as bride: to be *confidant* to the Pretender, when Tsar. And so, again, a reassuring E major to open, before slipping back onto his own deep-flat ground to complete his condition.

This is a carefully crafted, taut duologue that evolves both dramatically and musically. Even the theme that will become the open emblem of the Pretender's love (Ex.10.6*b*) has been foreshadowed in his first

reaction to the news of Marina's love-lorn state (Ex.10.6*a*). The encounter is neatly joined on to the grand choral-orchestral polonaise that
bisects the whole scene and permits a touch of ceremonial ballet in a
score that otherwise offers only rough folkish dance. And a very distinctive piece it is, with the lydian raised fourth of its main C-centred
theme, its secondary tonal centres (E major and A flat major) balanced
symmetrically a major third on either side. The most striking detail
however, is the recourse, both at the opening and at the return of the
main theme, to a pentatonic sonority already used to end the Prologue
(see Ex.10.3).

The Pretender, reeling from a distant sight of Marina on the arm of
another during the polonaise, now musters all his resolve to pursue his
campaign in Russia itself, in so doing anticipating that quasi-polonaise
presentation of his theme which will accompany his exit towards Moscow at the opera's end. But on Marina's entry he relinquishes his flat-
key turmoil for the E major of love. Her identity mark is again the
mazurka, but its appearances will finally acquire a purposefulness absent
from the chain of ever-changing ideas of her earlier soliloquy, and her
final taunting challenge to her suitor's mettle (*Piu mosso poco a poco, alla
polacca capricciosa*) will display an uncompromising strength, with its
vaulting opening gesture (so different from the mild, even bland phrases
of her mazurka-soliloquy near the act's opening) and its firm pedal.
Again tonal irony is present, the music of her first address (*alla polacca*)
pitilessly picking up the Pretender's E major as she crushes any hope
that love might play a part in what she has to say—and it is brutally in
the key of love that she will set out her loveless condition for union:
the throne of Russia itself. The Pretender's response is all she might
have hoped, yet feared; initially rededication to his mission, but

Ex. 10.6a,b

with rejection of her as partner to his future triumph. Yet his dismissal is ambivalent for, with its unbroken pedal B asserting the pull of E major, the 'white note' music above soon readmits sharps and, for all the lover's anger, it is ineluctably back in E major, though with the bitterest of discords (Ex.10.7) that he ends his rejection. Marina recognizes his ambivalence and knows exactly what is required. First responding with the tersest of defiances, then instantly (as though hearing her D♯ as E♭) changing her tone, she yields with the most melting of declarations, and opens a love duet as quietly rapturous as any in western opera. The key and mood of the Fountain Scene's opening return, to be consummated when the six-note descending ostinato that had there underpinned the Pretender's theme is now coupled with her new love theme. But just as that most peaceful of openings had proved the backdrop for ruthless intrigue and emotional cruelty, so the sly appearance of a gloating Rangoni at the love scene's end is forewarning enough that the course of this new affair will not be smooth.

There are bruising confrontations in the Polish Act, but its more refined tone is deliberately calculated, its presentation far more accomplished and appropriate than some would have us believe, and dividends are reaped when the opera's central train of events is rejoined in the final act, for the reversion to an earlier tone is striking. In the Polish Act there had been two modest appropriations from *Salammbô* during the Pretender's music in his scene with Marina,[24] but the borrowings become greater in Act 4. One preludes the act and the boyars' initial exchanges, and a second serves well for setting out the dire fate the boyars have in mind for the Pretender, once caught; a third, already familiar from Boris's Act 2 monologue, companions Shchelkalov's preliminaries as he addresses the Duma. Also more numerous are the recurrences of music already heard. In the Polish Act the only imported theme had been the Pretender's, but in Act 4 such recurrences proliferate. Even before the recollection from Boris's monologue already noted, Shchelkalov's music from the opera's opening scene had supported his appearance before the assembled boyars, as will some of Shuisky's from Act 2 when he too appears. Throughout the whole

---

[24] See Chapter 5, n.10.

Ex. 10.7

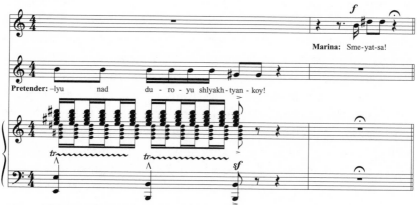

[I shall order all to deride your folly! Deride!]

O tsarevich, I beg you not to curse me for my wicked words.]

Duma Scene there is a relentless sense of moving towards a culmination. Threads are drawn together and tied—though what follows in the so-contrasting Kromy Forest Scene will deny the wider drama any final resolution.

While the paramount factor contributing to the dramatic coherence of *Boris* may be its inner psychological thrust, its outer musical form can be equally crucial to its dramatic impact—and nowhere more so than in the Duma Scene, for fundamental to the impression of an implacable momentum driving towards the solemn nemesis of Boris's death agony is not only Musorgsky's assured pacing of the drama but also the whole scene's clear, balanced structure. The masterly design was

Musorgsky's own, the only portion based with any real focus on Pushkin's text being an extract from Pimen's narration. The whole scene is planned as three stages (Fig. 10.2): the powers of this world (the Duma) gather and learn the truth; the agent of God—or fate—(Pimen) in a tone of pitiless serenity performs the lethal act; and the victim's death throes are ritualistically observed. The first two stages have the same microstructure which clamps events firmly in their place, the rigour of this double deployment reinforcing the impression of a fate, talon by talon clawing the Tsar into its grip. Each of these stages has a midway landmark, then a concluding intervention from a distraught Boris, his uncontainable horror at what he has witnessed in a previous scene, or hears in this one, transmitted through now familiar material (his first guilt-and-terror theme: see Ex.10.2k (i)), each time succeeded by identical music to launch an address from the Tsar as inauguration of the next stage. Yet these addresses quietly but starkly expose how events move on, for after a couple of bars they part company. The first (Ex.10.8a), to his boyars, is formal, spacious, the pronouncement of a Tsar in whom some hope yet remains. The second (Ex.10.8b) is intimate, direct, the preface to the last words of a doomed man with much to say and little time to say it, where there is no room for the dignified sequence laid out in bars 3–4 of Ex.10.8a; instead the bass passes, stepwise, to the middle of bar 6. The opportunity for the kind of broad, sequential phrase in the last four bars of Ex.10.8a has gone; here, and in what immediately follows, the short-winded, broken phrases are absolutely right.

Basic also to the effect of the whole scene is Musorgsky's tonal strategy, quite different from that of the Polish Act which, as noted earlier, had at its horizontal axis a single key, E major. In the Duma Scene everything is unrelentingly in flat keys, except for four passages in which Musorgsky pointedly lifts the music into a brighter sharp-key world: (1) very briefly, as Shuisky seeks with wide-eyed openness to counter the boyars' deep doubts about his motives, a calming stratagem he returns to (2) as a precautionary sedative for Boris when informing the Tsar of Pimen's wish to speak with him; (3) as Pimen enters, and then begins his tale; and (4), most potently, as the old monk's narrative turns to the miracle wrought at Uglich, at which point the move sharpwards becomes a veritable stampede, culminating in C sharp major (for

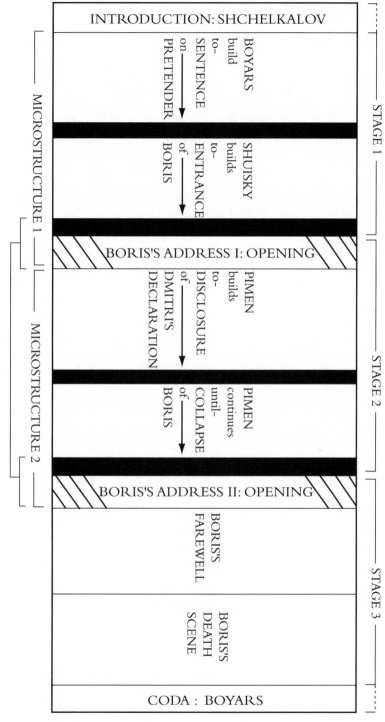

Figure 10.2

Ex. 10.8a

[I have summoned you, boyars. I rely upon your wisdom:

in a time of troubles and terrible trials, you are my helpers, boyars.]

the last four bars Musorgsky reverses the notation)[25] and giving this passage a luminosity unique to an otherwise sombre scene.

The extensive participation of the chorus (albeit men only) in the opening stages of the Duma Scene suffices to make it distinctive, since—except for the brief offstage contributions in the Cell and Tsar's Palace Scenes, the sweet treble sounds of Marina's girls at the start of the Polish Act, and the guests' scrappy contributions to the later polonaise—there has been no choral sound since the Prologue. Though the deliberations of boyars in session will have more order than the

[25] The four-bar shift into sharps during Boris's farewell (p. 357, bars 5–8) is also a reversal of notation. As for the choruses of the death scene itself, to the ear these simply pick up, after the intervention of the keyless coronation motif, the D flat major in which Boris had concluded his farewell now turned into the minor. Reversing the notation here was obviously a practical imperative.

Ex. 10.8b

[Farewell, my son; I am dying. Forth with you will

begin your reign.]

grumblings and banter of a peasant crowd, Musorgsky's choral method
is the same as in the first scene, and equally effective, especially when
abetted by magisterially shifting blocks of orchestral colour, and in particular by some striking wind sonorities, once the boyars have got into
their stride. And just as a new element has been brought into the opera
by this section, whose end forms the midway landmark of the first stage,
so the ensuing situation uncovers more of Shuisky. Confronted with
Boris in the Tsar's Palace, he had been defensive, then intimidated; here,
among his equals, his superior experience and skill as a consummate
politician tells. As the bearer of sensational news that he fully intends
to break as effectively as he knows how, yet whose very shockingness
could render his hearers' reactions dangerous, he first underplays to gain
their confidence and to relish for a while the impact of what he will
disclose. And so initially he lightly brushes aside their innuendoes of

duplicity, giving a studied casualness to his music until he begins his report. Once again, as with the boyars' malevolence towards the Pretender, Musorgsky salvaged a stretch of powerful and dissonant music from *Salammbô* to launch Shuisky's graphic description of Boris as last seen. Threatened as his listeners' mounting disbelief turns towards anger,[26] Shuisky almost shouts to be heard above the hubbub. The Tsar's entry saves him. But a further danger opens. Boris, regaining some hold of himself, insists Dmitri still lives (to the Dmitri/Pretender motif in its chastest guise), accuses Shuisky of slander, and threatens him with death. Then, recovering himself further, he turns to the boyars (see Ex.10.8*a*), and Shuisky reports Pimen's wish to have an audience. Hoping for comfort in what he will say, Boris assents.

Boris contains no deeper irony than in the plainness and simplicity of the old monk's devastating telling of the blind shepherd whose sight was restored to him at the grave in Uglich. There is no earthly reason why Pimen should intervene at this time[27]—but fate has set its sights on Boris, and fate needs its messenger. Or, to put it as in the original *Boris* when the St Basil Scene was still in place, while the Simpleton in that earlier scene had pointed to the sentence, Pimen now appears as executioner. Yet he remains as we had observed him in his cell, for the theme (Ex.10.9) that runs through his narration is, in profile if not in character, a relative of that likewise ever-changing invention (see Ex.10.2*d*) which had underlain his earlier account of events at Uglich given to the future Pretender. Sometimes the orchestra presents this as no more than a single line in counterpoint with the singer, at others an inner pedal ensures poignant dissonances in this open texture (as in Ex.10.9). The tone is dispassionate and the music itself almost white-note. But when Pimen comes to Uglich, the intermediary landmark of the act's second, central stage approaches; accidentals accumulate, adding new tonal colours, and Pimen's voice acquires epic strength. A brief return to his earlier music, a second lift in intensity—and Boris's self-

---

[26] As noted earlier, this 'anger' motif (see Ex.10.2*j*) had been prominent during the Tsar's Palace Scene, but had been totally excluded in the revised version. Thus its occurrence here carries no significant dramatic resonance.

[27] In Pushkin's play Pimen's narration is delivered by the Patriarch as a preliminary to suggesting that Dmitri's relics should be brought to Moscow and displayed to undermine the Pretender Grigory's claim. Boris's death occurs five scenes later.

control breaks, his first guilt-and-terror motif erupting for the second time. Realizing he can bear no more, he orders his son to be summoned and his farewell begins.

This is Boris's third set-piece of self-revelation. In the public declaration at his coronation he had intimated his inner condition; alone in his palace monologue, he had bared this, withholding nothing. Now, at the prospect of imminent death, there is no time for self-justification, only an inventory of advice to the son who will inherit his poisoned legacy. Pushkin offered a lengthy ready-made text, but this could never have served. The urgency of his situation denied Boris the broad sweeps of his earlier soliloquy; instead this farewell proceeds initially in spurts, and only a few tiny fragments were lifted from Pushkin. There are some thematic recollections. Feodor, about to become the lawful, untarnished Tsar, hears his own theme now given a white-note presentation; Kseniya's theme is lovingly dwelt on in its entirety, though only a ghost of

Ex. 10.9

[In vain was I treated with a potion and secret spell, in vain]

from founts of holy, healing waters my eyes were treated... in vain!]

the Pretender's emblem finds an allotted place.[28] But there is no sense, even after the coherence of Pimen's narrative, of structural disconnection; each detail leaves a clear image, and the impetus compacts a form. As it proceeds the sections become more substantial; then, having ranged through a catalogue of responsibilities and dangers confronting Feodor that has become increasingly intimidating, Boris turns to that close family life which had proved his one treasure in this world. Entrusting his daughter's welfare to his son, he invokes heaven's blessing upon his children to the music with which Salammbô had once prayed to Tanit.

This scene is really more notable than the death scene that follows. It was customary for a dying Tsar to be inducted into monastic orders and be invested with the *skhima* (or monastic habit), and to the approach of the officiating choir of monks, first heard off-stage, then entering, Boris utters his last sounds and death rattle. It makes for the most unblushingly theatrical incident in the whole opera, with some extraordinary orchestral sounds, though Musorgsky could hardly have envisaged it otherwise. The stunned boyars can only mutter the briefest of benedictions on Boris's soul as his power and majesty theme dies with him in the orchestra.

With the Kromy Forest Scene *Boris* comes full circle. The opera had opened with the people centre stage; they return to close it. As with the Duma Scene, there is the clearest of structures,[29] two large choral tableaux flanking a savagely contrasting central episode for the Simpleton and urchins, with all boundaries stark. Equally abrupt is the wrench when the two Jesuits are heard approaching, the ensuing scene and the Simpleton's wailing which closes the opera acting as flanks to the final historical event—the appearance of the Pretender, his brief address to the people, and their acclamation before they all leave. The whole scene's tonal scheme is also clear. The opening is D-centred, the Simpleton/urchins incident and the scene's close A-centred, but between these tonal points the move is almost always flatwards, as in the Duma

---

[28] In fact, this section was removed from the farewell in the published vocal score.

[29] Richard Hoops has noted that the Kromy Forest Scene appears 'in a form which might have served as a detailed synopsis of *Boris Godunov*'s closing scene' in Ivan Khudyakov, *Drevnaya Rus* [Ancient Russia] (1867). See R. Hoops, 'Musorgsky and the Populist Age', *MIM*, 289. Taruskin disagrees (*TM*, 183–5).

Scene (though with some reversed notation).[30] This Kromy Forest
Scene is considerably shorter than its predecessor but is as powerful in
impact, with outbursts of sustained, ferocious energy, abrupt contrasts,
and an ending so different from the sensational outcome of the Duma
Scene but, in what is foreseen, yet more dismal. As in the opening
Novodevichy Scene, pivot pitches are strongly in evidence, and lively
comments are initially thrown between different sections of the crowd
to thematic fragments that at times reflect the small change of folk music
or broaden into phrases that might have come from folksongs.

But it is a genuine folksong that opens the act of humiliation to
which the hapless boyar, Khrushchov, is subjected. And at this point
there begins a very significant shift in Musorgsky's dramatic method.
So far the crowd has been vocally fragmented in the old familiar cause
of maximum realism; now it becomes a chorus, the music structured
on three statements of the folksong (together with the free extension
that Musorgsky himself tagged on to pick up something of the mob's
aggressive ebullience). The folktune itself is too gentle to be denied at
least one accompaniment that cherishes its loveliness, and this second
hearing provides a tiny transcendent moment in an otherwise turbulent,
cruel environment. But by the third hearing the prevailing mood proves
irrepressible and the momentum is maintained, brought up abruptly
only by the appearance of the Simpleton with urchins in pursuit.

The 'yurodivy', or Holy Fool, was probably in most cases no more
than a pathetic figure whom we would once have described unpityingly
as 'mentally defective'. But in Russian society he had a very special
place. He was an object of both ridicule and reverence, for it was
believed that his pathetic inadequacy in relation to things of this world

---

[30] The notation in this scene can cause confusion. However, the opening of the revolution
chorus (p. 389) after Varlaam and Missail's entry in four flats is surely *heard* as in G flat minor
both here and on its return (p. 393) after the section employing a folksong. Interestingly,
when on this main section's recurrence Musorgsky sifts out its second theme (p. 396), he
retains the three-sharp key signature throughout a section doggedly notated in B flat/phry-
gian, despite the welter of accidentals this involves, before returning to three sharps when
the tonic of this whole massive section is regained. This seems to confirm that this shorter
section, whose notation proclaims its *true* key (A sharp minor would have involved even
more confusing accidentals), is nevertheless to be heard within the context of the prevailing
key of the music, however notated, to which it forms an interlude. Thus in a curious way
it confirms the context as G flat minor.

was balanced by God-given powers of insight into the beyond. To equate him with the Shakespearean fool is misleading, but in his capacity to glimpse the future he can take on almost Shakespearean stature. Yet here he is first seen in what must be his daily travail. There had been point to the urchins' filching his kopek in the St Basil Scene, for there it had provided the ground for his encounter with Boris; here it has none, and his distress is swallowed up in the crowd's curiosity at the sound of the approaching Varlaam and Missail. But he had to be introduced at some point if his role at the opera's end was to be understood—and on its expanded recurrence his song will sound, as will its new text, with a weightier and disconcerting resonance. Nothing shows more clearly Musorgsky's mastery of tonal colour for expressive ends than the wrench into a deep-flat region that breaks the white-note world of its opening, or the painful chromatic route traced on the way back towards the point of tonal departure, the Simpleton's thoughts seeming to trail off into forgetfulness before the children's taunts return him to reality. This is one of Musorgsky's tiniest songs—a mere eleven bars with introduction—yet as great as any.

The corporate pandemonium soon resumes. But this choral tableau is different. True, it picks up the method of its predecessor's ending as the rogue monks are heard approaching, for here again there is a folk melody,[31] and though the turn of events prompts a counterpoint of spontaneous curiosity among the crowd, it is the monks' four statements of the folktune against different backgrounds that generates the form. But with the monks' appearance on stage the individual is instantly subsumed into the corporate; doctrinaire realism is thrown to the winds and the method of the traditional operatic finale is embraced (this massive choral shout, sometimes called the 'revolution chorus', actually inclines to ternary form). By now Musorgsky knew this was no betrayal of dramatic verities any more than Boris's new Act 2 monologue had been—simply a recognition that when rabble-rousers concentrate into a single overwhelming emotion the individual discontents, prejudices, and hatreds within a crowd, and mob psychology takes over, the terrifying mass energy that results remains as rooted in the passions and

---

[31] Taken down, according to Stasov, by Musorgsky from the noted exponent of Russian *bilïnï*, Ivan Ryabinin.

Ex. 10.10a

[Daring bravery has been unleashed.]

Ex. 10.10b

personalities of the individuals that constitute the crowd as any personal muttered grouse or groan heard earlier: it is simply that the corporate utterance is more powerful than the sum of its parts. The new violence unleashed by the rogue monks is caught into a furious moto perpetuo phrase (Ex.10.10*a*) that runs, ostinato-like, through the orchestral part. At first the men merely ghost it, as though still missing the significance

Ex. 10.10c

[Oh, power, you daredevil power...]

Ex. 10.10d

[People, recognise the tsar...]

of what they themselves are saying. But confidence and resolve quickly grow; a powerful descending phrase (Ex. 10.10*b*) rounds off this section, and a new one begins, the women chattering in joy (to another folk-song: Ex.10.10*c*) at the prospect of escape from misery, the men then adding a virile purposefulness which draws in their womenfolk, before all return to their earlier music, the men now confident enough to bellow the whole strongly profiled ostinato phrase in mighty augmentation against its progenitor (Ex.10.10*d*). A sudden break and hush, a shift of key—and now it is the turn of the second theme of the opening section. The energy still pulses, for this pause was not hesitation through doubt, merely a moment to recharge hatred. This time, when the opening key returns, it is—significantly—the women who lead the pack. For a moment frenzy produces musical disorientation, but a clear sense of objective is swiftly regained. The ostinato phrase, now in daunting alliance with a descending phrase adapted from Ex.10.10*b*, generates a yet greater thrust which might have proved unstoppable but for the distraction produced by the intervention of the two Jesuits.

After this great tableau, which in terms of sheer dynamic energy is the climax of the opera, the new incident cannot but seem low-powered (this is no criticism). Varlaam revels in rabble-rousing, and a further substantial extract from *Salammbô* is recycled to prepare the lynching of the two priests. But the Pretender with his party is heard approaching (again ex-*Salammbô*), he is greeted and, to an extensive and varied parading of his theme, he responds before heading off with the crowd in tow, leaving the Simpleton the daunting responsibility of rounding off the opera. For what we have seen has provided no dramatic resolution. We have glimpsed the power of the people when roused, but we know how fickle can be the most violent and intimidating of such emotional waves, just as a power that may have seemed unshakeable can collapse with disconcerting abruptness on the death of one man. The preceding Duma Scene had merely closed the tragic tale of one such being. That death had been shocking enough—but the Simpleton's words are yet more disturbing for, addressing us again in his music of primal desolation which finally trails into nothingness, he foreglimpses the greater tragedy in store for the Russian people.

CHAPTER 11

Life alongside *Boris* I:
The Nursery Completed

IT IS NO SURPRISE THAT WHILE *BORIS* WAS IN THE MAKING Musorgsky had little time for other things, and not one of his letters survives from the period of its composition. Since September 1868 his permanent base had been with old family friends, Alexander Opochinin and his sister Nadezhda. Throughout the earlier part of 1869 there were occasional reports of him at the familiar musical gatherings at various friends' and colleagues' homes, where *Boris* was exhibited as it was composed, Musorgsky himself performing all the male parts, choruses, and recitatives, Alexander Purgold the female and boys' roles. But not until October 1869 do we have any direct evidence from the composer himself, when he wrote to Balakirev excusing himself from being a rehearsal pianist for an FMS concert on the grounds that he was too out-of-practice and would be a hindrance rather than help. Nor, as he explained in December to Karl Albrecht, one of Tchaikovsky's colleagues at the Moscow Conservatoire, did he have anything to hand that he could contribute to the anthology of choral pieces that Albrecht was compiling. Since Albrecht belonged to a musical establishment antipathetic to Musorgsky, the latter might have been expected to show no sympathy for this project, and it seems the more surprising that he should have promised to compose and despatch such a piece as soon as time permitted. But relations between the two main opposing groups in Russia's musical life were by now much easier. Tchaikovsky and Balakirev had long ago moved close; in 1868 the former had dedicated his symphonic poem *Fatum* to Balakirev, had accepted the justice of the latter's devastating (and well founded) criticism of the piece, and had gone on to compose the first version of his fantasy-overture *Romeo and Juliet* on a ground plan laid down by Balakirev. Dedicated to the latter, Tchaikovsky's first masterpiece had received warm approval from others of Balakirev's circle, and Stasov, on hearing the D flat love theme, had made his famed pronouncement to the kuchka: 'There were five of you: now there are six.' Tchaikovsky himself began occasionally to appear at musical gatherings with the group. Then in 1871 Rimsky would do the unthinkable by becoming professor of practical composition and instrumentation at the St Petersburg Conservatoire itself. And while there is every reason to think that Musorgsky had no enthusiasm for this rapprochement, it probably tempered his more outward manifestations of hostility. His promise to Albrecht may, therefore, have been simply a diplomatic delaying tactic, for it was never fulfilled.

There followed a further gap in Musorgsky's surviving letters for the first five months of 1870. But *Boris* was now completed, and it would be February 1871 before the selection committee's rejection of the opera would require Musorgsky to direct his creative energies into revising it. In the meantime, with his opera in limbo, he seems initially to have felt no inclination for composition, and only in June 1870 did he resume with a wickedly pungent 'musical joke' for voice and piano on a selection of his own *bêtes noires*, all collected together to provide *The Peepshow*, which he dedicated to Stasov, who had proposed the subject in the first place.

Musorgsky compiled his own text for *The Peepshow*, casting himself as master of ceremonies and enthusiastically summoning all to marvel at his parade of 'great musical commanders'. First, to the adapted strains of 'See, the conquering hero comes' from Handel's *Judas Maccabaeus*, appears Nikolay Zaremba, now director of the St Petersburg Conservatoire. Zaremba's ultra-conservatism had led him (allegedly) to proclaim that, while the major key could afford redemption, the minor key was the source of original sin—a charge Musorgsky picked up presumably from Balakirev, though a year earlier the latter had alleged to Zaremba's erstwhile pupil, Tchaikovsky no less, that it was rondo form that Zaremba had identified as precipitating man's first fall. Next comes 'Fif' (Feofil Tolstoy, music critic and failed composer), whose penchant for Italian opera and 'the divine Patti' is paraded in a trivial waltz-song, complete with ponderous coloratura cadenza. Alexander Famintsïn had already been the butt of Musorgsky's song *The Classicist* of three years earlier; now this critical arch-enemy of the kuchka plods in, begging that his 'stain' (an accusation of lying made by Stasov in an article) should be washed away. Once modest and self-effacing (here Musorgsky incorporated an extract from one of Famintsïn's own songs), he had suddenly become strong-willed, 'had spied his foe [Stasov], engaged in combat with him [instituted a libel action]—and perished [lost]'.[1] Finally comes Serov ('the Titan!'), hailed to a fanfare from his own opera *Rogneda*, then ridiculed for his vehement advocacy of Wagner. Stasov identified the other musical items Musorgsky pillaged from *Rogneda* for their creator's discomfort (the buffoon's song, actually based on a folksong from Act 3, and a chorus, 'Death to him!', from Act 1), and also clarified Musorgsky's more veiled verbal allusions—to Serov's anger at the RMS for denying him a press seat for its concerts, for not having invited him to a dinner in honour of Berlioz nearly three years earlier, and for not making him one of the RMS's directors. But an increasingly demented Serov is pulled up sharp by the descent, to the sound of a twangling harp (or gusli), of the Muse herself (the Grand Duchess Elena Pavlovna, who had been Rubinstein's ally in founding the RMS), to whom Zaremba, Fif, Famintsïn, and the Titan sing ('moderato, fervently, at the tops of their voices') a final votive prayer ('O most glorious Euterpe, great goddess, send down to us inspiration, stir us from our feebleness. . . . '), set to the buffoon's folksong, now blown up into long notes.

As music, *The Peepshow* may be of little importance, but as a lampoon it is devastating. Though by its very nature a piece of ephemera, it could be relished by all those familiar with its topical allusions, and in 1871 it was published for a wider audience. So also were the songs *King Saul, Night, Cradle Song, The Magpie, The Ragamuffin, Eremushka's Lullaby, Child's Song,* and *The Orphan.* Meanwhile, in the previous year *The Seminarist* had been issued though this was in Leipzig, publication

---

[1] Not strictly true. When the case had been heard in May 1870 Stasov had been cleared of libel but found guilty of abuse. The punishment prescribed had been very modest: a fine of 25 roubles and seven days' house arrest, an incarceration Stasov seems to have turned into a continuous house-party.

in Russia having been blocked by the censor (as Musorgsky informed Stasov) 'because of the seminarist's concluding admission that he was "led into temptation by the devil in the temple of God" '.[2] However, Musorgsky was allowed, upon a special petition, to distribute ten copies to his friends.

Fired by the success of his suggestion that Musorgsky compose *The Peepshow*, Stasov now reacted swiftly to an indication from Musorgsky that he was looking to begin another opera and came up with Friedrich von Spielhagen's recent drama, *Hans und Grete*. Characteristically, having laid hands on a copy of the play, Stasov had by the following morning not only read it, transferred it to a Russian setting, supplemented it, reworked it, then devised a scenario, but had prepared six pages of libretto. It was to be called *Bobïl* ('The landless peasant'). 'Musorgsky has already started the *divination scene* in his new opera; it's simply marvellous', Stasov could report on 1 September.[3] In fact, nothing more was to be heard of *Bobïl*, but without knowing it Musorgsky had made a tiny start on what would be his next opera—for what he had composed would provide Marfa's divination scene for Golitsïn in *Khovanshchina*.

Musorgsky's relationship with the Purgold sisters was close, and Nadezhda's diary entries from this period give intimate insights into the composer, some far from uncritical. Nadezhda realized that her sister Alexandra was attracted to Musorgsky, and back in St Petersburg in September Alexandra became a prey to depression and jealousy. Sometimes Nadezhda thought Musorgsky was becoming attracted to her sister, but then decided otherwise:[4]

> . . . or else he has an uncommon ability to hide his feelings and control himself. . . . He has a way, stemming probably from being too proud, of never talking with someone who does not address him . . . He only likes to talk with someone who considers talking with him a particular pleasure and who himself opens the conversation. It is the same in other matters: because of being too proud he never takes the initiative in offering to bring his own songs . . . [though,] particularly when he alone [of composers] is present . . . he usually comes with the aim of performing some piece of his

[2] *MLN1*, 118.

[3] *TDM*, 200.

[4] Entry for 10 Sept. 1870. Quoted in *TDM*, 202–3.

own, to show something new, and therefore now wishes that all attention should be directed exclusively at him, wishes exclusively to monopolize the whole evening. In a word, it emerges . . . that his most prominent trait is pride . . . I do not agree that, as some think, he is not intelligent. He has a peculiar, original, and very sharp mind. But it is this very sharpness that he sometimes abuses. Could it be from a wish to pose, to show that he is not as all others are but is completely special, or is this really his nature? The former is the more plausible . . . The nickname Sasha and I gave him (when we did the same to all the others)—namely, Humour—I find appropriate, for humour in fact is his prime mental characteristic. But in this he also lacks warmth, gentleness, of which, on the contrary, there is such an abundance in dear Sincerity [Rimsky-Korsakov, whom Nadezhda herself would marry]. It is even, perhaps, that he has no capacity for being overwhelmed, no capacity for love.

But Nadezhda remained uncertain about her analysis:[5]

Today Humour was very sweet, he talked so nicely, intelligently—sometimes especially so; today he was particularly on form. And he sang so splendidly! . . . I still cannot understand properly his attitude towards Sasha. Whatever the case, I think that she interests him and seems to him a sort of enigmatic, peculiar, capricious, but strong nature. But I do not know whether he is capable of falling for her, of falling in love. He is proud, terribly proud.

Reminiscences from this same period, though from a very different viewpoint, were provided by Stasov's niece Varvara, eldest daughter of brother Dmitri:[6]

I was seven when I began to notice his [Musorgsky's] appearance in my parents' home . . . All of a sudden he entered our children's life as Musoryanin, as all the grown-ups called him, and as we, the children, also at once began calling him, having decided this was his real name. He often visited us both in the city and in our dacha at Zamanilovka, near Pargolovo, and because he did not 'pretend' with us, did not talk in that unnatural way in which grown-ups usually talk with children at home when they are

[5] Entry for 12 Sept. 1870. Quoted in *TDM*, 204.
[6] *MVS*, 109–10.

friends of their parents, we not only quickly became attached to him but began also to consider him *one of us*. My sister Zinochka and I were particularly struck that, when greeting us, he always kissed our hands as with grown-up ladies, saying: 'Good day, *young lady!*' or 'Your hand, *young lady!*' and we thought this unbelievably wonderful—and amusing. But after that we talked to him with complete freedom, as with an equal. Nor were my brothers in any way constrained with him; they told him all that had happened to them, during which the youngest could still not even say his name properly and said 'Musolyanin'—and Musorgsky, when he was coming, would call out to us from the distance: 'Musolyanin's coming!' The musical pictures 'The Cat Sailor', 'To Yukki by Hobby Horse', and 'A Dream', after a story by Zinochka (unpublished, it seems, and I do not know whether it survives in manuscript, but played by Musorgsky on the piano), and also the fourth scene from a child's life ['With the Doll'(?)] must have been depictions of *our* childish stories.

Though Vladimir Stasov believed that it was cherished memories from Musorgsky's own childhood that accounted for his preoccupation with the nurse/child relationship (and Nadezhda Purgold that it was her sister Alexandra's incomparable talents as a performer of his music), it seems that his *Nursery* cycle was prompted by this present environment—and perhaps not only by the Stasov brood but by his own niece and nephew, Tatyana and Georgy, Filaret's children, to whom he dedicated 'With the Doll' ('Going to Sleep' was inscribed to Musorgsky's godson Alexander, Cui's child). In fact, besides (possibly) 'With the Doll', only one of the songs listed by Varvara ('A Dream') may have gone into the cycle itself (as the final one, 'Going to Sleep'; the remaining two date from two years later, when Musorgsky had envisaged them as part of a second such cycle). To open *The Nursery* Musorgsky incorporated 'With Nurse' from two years earlier, composing the remaining four songs in the last months of 1870 and publishing all five in 1872. The texts are Musorgsky's own, all in direct speech in that 'rhythmicized prose', as it has been called, which can on occasion slip towards regular poetic forms (as with the 'dream' quatrain in 'With the Doll'). Three are monologues for a child, two are dialogues with its nurse; the child in the second and third (and presumably the first) is a boy, in the fifth (and surely the fourth) a girl.

The four post-*Boris* songs in *The Nursery* are conditioned by the experience of composing that opera. Gone are the constant shifts of metre that had marked 'With Nurse', composed as Musorgsky was preparing to set about *The Marriage*, and when the text was still all-commanding. Only the nurse's anger at the end of her opening outburst in 'In the Corner' (no. 2; dated 12 October 1870) finally proves uncontainable within regular barring and disrupts the furious flood of unbroken quavers in the accompaniment. Having staggered into the corner, the child shows his tactical instinct. As he crumples beneath his nurse's verbal onslaught, he first adapts the Simpleton's two-note wailing figure (Ex. 11.1) as his weapon of injured innocence: it wasn't Misha's fault (a tiny touch of assertive protest in the high tessitura) but the cat's (a drop to a more self-effacing tessitura, with 'the pussy cat' twice emphasized by an exaggerated inflection and pointed dissonance). Misha is, in fact, spotless (the exaggerated inflection now on 'Mishenka', his growing confidence evident in the more securely centred vocal line, the shift to the brighter major, and the more stable, harmonically 'persuasive' accompaniment), and Nanny the real villain (spikiness, dissonance, and spat delivery). If any music manages vividly to convey a complex of shifting feelings without condescension, sentimentality, or exaggeration, but as coming from within the very child, this surely is it.

Nothing that follows quite matches this for its charmingly devastating 'truthfulness'. The breathless excitement at discovering 'The Beetle' (no. 3; dated 30 October 1870) sitting on the roof of a miniature twigs-and-leaves house prompts a rattling, prattling quaver piano part. But even when setting the scene for such an alarming tale a child will constantly change its tone; only when the beetle comes into the narrative does the voice draw out the awesome tale in long notes and wide, wide-eyed intervals, with the accompaniment chromatically creepy. Frisson turns to shock: the beetle flies at the child, striking his temple—but Musorgsky's piano textures, always very spare throughout the whole cycle, ensure this momentary terror is kept in proportion.[7] Fear passes as the beetle falls prostrate. Only the question remains: is it

---

[7] A longer variant of this central crisis point (21 as against 11 bars) exists, but Musorgsky rejected this when it came to publication.

Ex. 11.1

Ya ni-che-vo ne sde-lal, nya-nush-ka, ya chu-lo-chek ne tro-gal,

[I didn't do anything, Nanny, I didn't touch the stockings,

nya-nush-ka. Klu-bo-chek raz-mo-tal ko-tyo-no-chek, i pru-toch-ki raz-bro-sal ko-

Nanny. The ball was unwound by the pussycat, and the needles were thrown around by the

tyo-no-chek. A Mi-shen-ka bïl pa-in-ka, Mi-shen-ka bïl um-ni-tsa.

pussycat. But Mishenka was a good boy. Mishenka was a clever boy.

A nya-nya zla-ya, sta-ra-ya, i nya-nya no-sik-to za-pach-kan-nïy;

But Nanny's nasty and old, and Nanny's got a dirty nose;]

stunned or dead?—and the earlier music, extended, can serve perfectly well for musing upon this until it peters out because, presumably, the child's interest is straying elsewhere.

'With the Doll' (no. 4; dated 30 December 1870) is a lullaby. Bidden to sleep, the doll is clearly not to be seriously frightened by the brief threat of being devoured by a bogeyman or carried off by a grey wolf; Musorgsky treats these images very lightly compared with his graphic projection of similar terrors in 'With Nurse'. Rather, the doll is wished enchanted dreams to be shared with her mistress when she awakes. Harmony so impregnated with major seconds can never cloy, but their constant reiteration can prove appropriately somniferous (Borodin had already exploited this potential in two songs, *The Sleeping Princess* and *The Sea Queen*). A portion of patterned accompaniment, too, may encourage slumber. A final tiny touch: the 'bogeyman' music is heard in the piano during the final bars—maybe a momentary return to an earlier ploy for encouraging a will to sleep before a snatch of the more soothing music ends the song?

Another bedtime ritual is the subject of 'Going to Sleep' (no. 5; dated 1870). English listeners may be familiar with the subject from A. A. Milne's *Christopher Robin is saying his prayers*—that is, the child who nightly runs through a ritual catalogue of relatives and friends upon whom God's blessing should be invoked, but forgets to include himself. The nurse's gentle reproof at her charge's omission reveals her as of the same stock as the Nurse in *Boris*. As in 'With the Doll' there is nothing here of the dramatic realism of 'With Nurse' or 'In the Corner', nor should there be. Each slight shift in mood gets its fair acknowledgement, but otherwise both songs confirm quietly but firmly that lyricism can again play an appropriate part in Musorgsky's music—a further pointer to the direction to be taken in the revised *Boris*.

Two years later, possibly prompted by a visit to the Stasov family at Pargolovo, Musorgsky composed two further songs which he planned as part of a companion cycle to be called *At the Dacha*. But there would be no successors, and it has now become common practice to append these two waifs to performances of the official *Nursery* set. Both suggest a rather older child, and in both mother replaces the nurse as addressee. Though in *The Cat Sailor* (dated 27 August 1872) the child only recounts an incident, she relives it vividly in the telling, characterizing every detail: her busy hunt for the sun-shade, the sudden spying of the miscreant feline besieging the bird cage, the bullfinch's trembling, the cat-versus-girl manoeuvring, the mis-aimed swipe, and finally the lament to mother. What strikes most strongly in this piece is Musorgsky's economy of notes, much of the first part running simply as a line of quavers, the voice doubling in discrete heterophony. Even more is *On the Hobby Horse* (dated 26 September 1872) all action until near its end. Nowhere, even in *Boris*, does Musorgsky more consummately catch into music a stretch of vigorous, breathless, highly detailed activity than in his projection of the boy's reckless ride, or its disastrous conclusion. Yet simultaneously he achieves an effortless accommodation with more traditional procedures by stretching his music for the whole song over a frame of three substantial, harmonically structured paragraphs: the two, nearly identical, galloping passages that flank the summons to Vasya, and the soothing words from the mother before the brief resumption of the child's ride brings all neatly full circle. As in *The Cat Sailor* it is the absolute precision of Musorgsky's music that is its most impressive single feature. Taken together, these seven songs of childhood afford a vivid miniature conspectus of Musorgsky's evolution as a composer during the four years since *The Marriage*.

The revision of *Boris* was Musorgsky's chief preoccupation during 1871. But two other minor tasks were discharged ahead of this. The first was a neatly turned, bustling piano 'scherzino', *The Seamstress*, composed during January, a superior salon piece whose most impressive features are its polish and touches of refined chromatic decoration. Its occasional jerks and shifts of metre are surely prettily graphic reflections of the uneven pace of operations in this treadle-driven machine. The piece was to be published the following year in the monthly *Nouvelliste*, a periodical that specialized in musical supplements (four years later it would be responsible for commissioning Tchaikovsky's most famed piano work, his series of twelve miniatures usually known (inappropriately) as *The Seasons*, which appeared monthly throughout 1876). The other minor task was a song-epigram, *Evening Song* (dated 27 March 1871), dedicated to Sofiya Serbina, a natural daughter of Vladimir Stasov, who had already been a very young but eager spectator of the private musical circles in which Musorgsky himself flourished but whose circumstances compelled her to leave St Petersburg in the early seventies. Whether this song was a farewell offering cannot be said, but it would have served excellently as such, for it is as tender and affectionate as it is diminutive. It could almost be the twin of *Child's Song*, composed three years earlier.

On 22 February Musorgsky had learned of the rejection of *Boris* and promptly plunged into revising his opera. This in no way inhibited his participation in the usual round of musical evenings with various friends; indeed, he seems, like Glinka before him, to have had a peculiar ability to engage in the very act of composition while such activities were going on around him. Years later Rimsky told Ivan Lapshin, a professor of philosophy at the University of St Petersburg, of one instance at the Purgolds: 'In the course of the evening he [Musorgsky] kept going to the piano, strumming bits, and before his friends the whole [of Marina's] monologue gradually came into existence'.[8] On 1 May Musorgsky attended the première of Serov's opera *Hostile Power*. Serov had died three months earlier, but this did not enable Musorgsky to take a more kindly view of what his opera would prove to be, for while the libretto promised some 'excellent stage situations, . . . yet judging from Serov's general talent for vacillation and for *being suspicious* of a national character in opera, I anticipate, as regards music, caricatures in the vulgar meaning of this word. However we'll see and hear', he told Stasov.[9] In a spirit of genial self-mockery he declared, according to the poet and translator Dmitri Minayev (writing in the journal *The Spark*), that having composed *The Marriage* to Gogol's words, he now intended to compose two further operas; in the first he would set to music the judicial statutes 'and, in the second, *volume ten* of the civil laws. It is an excessively original idea—but I'll cope'.[10] His current work was going well. 'I have finished [the first Polish Scene]—for two nights in a row the Jesuit did not let me sleep', he informed Stasov on 30 April. 'That is good—I like this, that is, I like it when composition goes thus.'[11]

But there was one notable cause of deep disquiet within his circle. Balakirev was in a bad way. The report came from Stasov: the former

[8] Quoted in *KYM*, 151.

[9] *MLN1*, 121.

[10] *TDM*, 218.

[11] *MLN1*, 122.

benevolent autocrat had lost his voracious vitality and retreated into a silence which rendered almost all communication with him impossible. The depth of his depression was now truly alarming. 'Your lines about Mily knocked me sideways, my dear, even though I have not been eye-witness to his freezing up', Musorgsky replied to Stasov's report.[12]

> Because of my impressionability, I envisioned something more horrifying: your lines seemed to me a burial service over Mily's artistic embers—it's terrible if it's true and if, on his part, it is not a mask. It's too early: *too horribly early!* Or is it disenchantment? Well—perhaps it is this also, but where then is his manhood, and perhaps also his consciousness of his cause and artistic goals, which are never achieved without a struggle? Or was art merely a means, and not an end?

But does one detect a touch of *Schadenfreude* within this sympathy for a man who in the past had so tirelessly cajoled an inert Musorgsky into activity?

The condition of Balakirev was not only a personal predicament but also a pointer to the changed nature of the kuchka. It would be facile to see him merely as that not unfamiliar phenomenon: a brilliant young-ish man, but now with a great future behind him. Events had simply overtaken Balakirev. As a nineteen-year-old he had suddenly been nominated by Glinka himself as his successor in shaping and directing the destiny of a truly Russian music, and for a dozen or so years he had discharged that role magnificently; above all, he had gathered round himself some young men who happened to be prodigiously gifted and whom he had, in a way no one could have believed possible, turned into significant, even great composers. The chance conjunction of these particular men with this extraordinary catalyst is surely one of the most remarkable accidents in Western music.

At first in all this Balakirev had been their leader, accepted by all as such. But things had now changed. With the base of Russian music, which Balakirev had done so much to consolidate, now rapidly ex-panding, with the conservatoires of St Petersburg and Moscow begin-ning to produce a flow of professionally trained native musicians, Balakirev himself was becoming marginalized. In 1869 he was ousted

[12] Ibid.

from the conductorship of the RMS concerts, his FMS concerts the
following season made a loss, and a piano recital in 1870 in his native
Nizhny Novgorod, where he had hoped for a local-boy-made-good
triumph, drew a miserable audience. And in his more intimate musical
world his power had waned. That control of others' destinies on which
he had thrived in the 1860s had now slipped from his grasp, and his
despotic nature could not temper itself to this.

This, of course, would have happened anyway. But it was not just
the fading of his personal authority that dispirited him; he had little
sympathy with the independent directions that some of his former pro-
tégés—and above all Musorgsky—had taken. The problem was that
Balakirev, for all his pioneering work, had not that kind of creative
mind that, either through the force of some inner process or in response
to changing outer stimuli, evolves. In fact, this seeming radical was also
an innate conservative, and having established an immediate post-
Glinka stylistic base fortified by powerful elements from recent Western
music, he held to this base for the rest of his days—as is cogently
demonstrated in his First Symphony. He had abandoned this in 1866
with only part of the first movement completed, and he did not resume
work on it until 1893—yet it is impossible to identify with certainty
where the hiatus was bridged, for his style remained that of a quarter-
century earlier. By 1871 he was already becoming irrelevant, and he
sensed it. His intensifying depression made him fair game for anyone
who might seem to have an answer to his problems, and he fell under
the influence of a soothsayer, who turned him from a freethinker into
a fervent believer. A last attempt to re-establish himself in a series of
FMS concerts in the 1871–2 season failed, and in July 1872 he was
forced to take employment on the railways. For four years he withdrew
completely from Russian musical life and when, in 1876, his interest
revived and he showed signs of becoming active again, it was with
much diminished force and with no consequences for Musorgsky himself. That role which in the formative years of Musorgsky's musical
career had been so critical was now history.

On 8 June 1871 Musorgsky left St Petersburg for a four-week break
on the family estate at Shilovo. This moment also signalled the end of
his three-year residence with the Opochinins. On 6 July he was back
at his work in the Forestry Department where a year earlier he had

been promoted 'for meritorious service', and there followed a somewhat nomadic summer, including a series of brief stays at Pargolovo
before, in mid-September, he took a joint tenancy with Rimsky of an
apartment in St Petersburg—'or, rather, a furnished room . . . My living
with Modest was, I suppose, the only instance of two composers living
together', Rimsky later observed. At that time the latter was still composing his first opera, *The Maid of Pskov*, and the two friends settled
into a routine that permitted them both time for unimpeded work. 'In
the morning until noon Musorgsky usually used the piano, and I copied
or orchestrated something I had already fully thought out', Rimsky
continued:[13]

> Towards twelve he went off to his work in the ministry, and I used the
> piano. In the evenings the matter was settled by mutual agreement. In
> addition, twice each week I went off to the conservatoire at nine o'clock
> and Musorgsky frequently dined at the Opochinins—and nothing could
> have worked out more ideally. That autumn and winter we both produced
> a great deal, constantly exchanging ideas and plans.

For members of the kuchka this last sentence could have especially deep
implications. A culture of communal creativity informed the group;
without this Balakirev's interventions not only in another's creative intentions but even in the creation itself would not have been tolerated.
Earlier in 1871 Musorgsky had already provided Rimsky with the texts
for two girls' choruses in *The Maid of Pskov*, and though both that opera
and the revision of *Boris* were largely completed by the time the two
men began sharing accommodation, it is still highly likely that neither
opera would have come out quite the same were it not for the constant
active proximity of the other composer. Borodin's personal observations, if overstated, confirm this; writing to his wife in early November,
he noted that 'Modest has perfected the recitative and declamatory side
of Korsinka; he, for his part, has eliminated Modest's tendency to un-
couth originality, has smoothed out all his harmonic roughnesses, his
fanciful orchestration, his illogical structuring of musical forms—in a
word, has made Modest's pieces incomparably more musical.'[14]

[13] *RKL*, 96.
[14] *TDM*, 228.

In these new conditions Musorgsky quickly finished his revisions of the Cell Scene. It seems altogether to have been a very contented phase in his existence. Relations with Borodin were particularly close, and while the latter enthused over the other two's operas, they responded with warm approval of Borodin's new Second Symphony. Rimsky's recent appointment was a further sign of the better relations with the conservatoire circle. Currently Rubinstein himself was actively cultivating the kuchka, publically toasting the group and naming them individually at the ninth anniversary celebrations of the conservatoire (though he gave precedence, as composers, to Tchaikovsky—and Laroche) and arranging to play over to them his new opera, *The Demon*. Musorgsky himself was very flattered by this mogul's personal attentions: 'Rubin[stein] was *warm and absolutely charming*—a vital and excellent artist', he enthused to Stasov after their meeting.[15] Rubinstein's opera impressed less when he and brother Nikolay played it over to the group at Dmitri Stasov's at the end of September; far more warmly appreciated was Anton's subsequent piano playing. It was at this time that the artist, Konstantin Makovsky, drew a caricature (now lost) of Stasov and his circle, in which Musorgsky was portrayed. But while his image is lost, the knowledge of what it would have been is instructive: Musorgsky would have been portrayed as a strutting cock.

The vocal scores of both *The Maid of Pskov* and the revised *Boris* were finished before the year's end, and each opera received a preliminary performance for the Stasov circle. That of *Boris* on 24 November was not complete, omitting the Prologue, the duet that closed the Polish Scene (as yet unfinished), and, according to Borodin, the last act (presumably only the final Kromy Forest Scene which, like the Prologue, had a very large choral element). Nadezhda Purgold played the piano, while Alexandra sang everything her voice could manage, Musorgsky and Konstantin Velyaminov joining in where it could not (Boris, Pimen, the Pretender, together with Varlaam and Missail). Though the performance was not comprehensive, the impression created was enormous: 'A delight! What variety, what contrasts!' Borodin wrote to his wife two days later. 'How rounded and [dramatically] motivated everything now is. I liked it very much. In my view, as an opera

---

[15] *MLN1*, 125.

Boris is stronger than *The Maid of Pskov*, though the latter is richer in purely musical beauties.'[16]

The earlier part of 1872 was dominated by scoring *Boris*. On 28 February the première of Dargomïzhsky's *The Stone Guest* took place, Musorgsky having assisted at the rehearsals. A further private performance of *Boris* had been mounted at the Purgolds' in January. But more significant was the public performance on 17 February of the Coronation Scene at an RMS concert conducted by Nápravník. Alexandra Purgold noted in her diary that, though it had not gone well, Musorgsky had been twice called to take a bow. In his published review of the concert Cui condemned the folly of presenting excerpts from operas in a concert, especially when these operas were as yet unperformed and the audience would not know the context of an excerpt. He found the scene, as music, had some shortcomings, but thought it might prove very effective in the theatre.

Yet despite his continuing preoccupations with *Boris*, Musorgsky had found time to participate in another dramatic project. During the winter of 1871–2 Stepan Gedeonov, director of the Imperial Theatres, had proposed that Borodin, Musorgsky, Rimsky-Korsakov, and Cui should jointly compose music for a fantastic opera-ballet, *Mlada*, to a text by Viktor Krïlov. The business of these four would be the operatic and serious musical element, with Cui and Borodin assigned Acts 1 and 4 respectively, and Musorgsky and Rimsky sharing Acts 2 and 3. The routine dances would be provided by the official ballet composer, Léon Minkus. The project foundered because it would have proved too costly to mount, but not before a good deal of music had been composed, much of which was subsequently drafted by each composer into other works. In 1889–90 Rimsky would be drawn back to the subject to compose his own full version of this opera-ballet.

Mlada was based on legends of the Baltic Slavs. Voyslava, daughter of Mstivoy, Prince of Retra, has poisoned Mlada, wife of the Arkonsky Prince Yaromir, so that she may marry him. But Yaromir rejects Voyslava, and she turns to Morena, goddess of the underworld, whose magic now causes Yaromir to fall in love with Voyslava, though subsequently in a dream an incredulous Yaromir learns of Voyslava's crime. Act 2

[16] *TDM*, 229, 230.

opens with a lakeside betrothal festival outside the temple of Radegast: there is first a market scene, then a march for princes and priests. But each time the couple try to kiss, Mlada's spirit appears between them. Finally Yaromir rushes off in pursuit of Mlada, and Voyslava curses Morena. In Act 3 Mlada leads a repentent Yaromir up Mount Triglav, for to be forgiven he must endure a trial. A witches' sabbath begins, led by Chernobog and Morena, and a vision of Cleopatra is called up to tempt him. But a cock-crow heralds daybreak. In Act 4 a bewildered Yaromir seeks counsel from the priests of Radegast and is told to wait until nightfall. Spirits reveal the truth, and command him to avenge Mlada. Voyslava appears and confesses her crime. She pleads her love as excuse, but when Yaromir stabs her she calls upon Morena to avenge her. After a further spectacle in which the lake inundates the temple and the city of Retra, Yaromir's and Mlada's spirits are seen embracing.

Musorgsky completed three pieces for the collective *Mlada* and made fragmentary beginnings on two others. To open Act 2 he provided a market scene and a march for the princes and priests (the latter completed on 9 March); between these came a fist fight, schemed for three choruses and orchestra (only the first forty-eight bars of the instrumental part survive),[17] and after the march a priest addressed the people (eleven bars only extant). For the appearance of Chernobog in Act 3 Musorgsky returned to his still unperformed *St John's Night*, heavily rewriting it and adding chorus parts. None of these pieces was orchestrated, and all three were later adapted in varying ways for other uses; in 1880 the march, with a new *alla turca* trio, became the march *The Capture of Kars*, while the market scene and revised *St John's Night* were absorbed into *Sorochintsy Fair*, the former providing material for the opening market scene of Act 1, the latter the dream of Gritsko, the Ukrainian peasant.

Musorgsky's own view of what was required of him in his *Mlada* allocation was blunt. Stasov had been the Imperial Theatres' intermediary; now on 12 April he was the recipient of Musorgsky's angry sorrows, though one suspects that these were a *post factum* reaction of

---

[17] This was taken, with modifications, from a chorus for *Oedipus in Athens*, which had already been re-used in *Salammbô*. In its new incarnation, of the three four-part choruses one would be for women, and two for men representing respectively the Polab Slavs and the Novgorodians.

one who had discharged an undertaking and then suspected he had compromised himself.[18]

—but *Mlada*!
And beyond the damp tomb
There is for me no rest
From her, the dear departed (read: *stillborn*)
It is shameful to take my pen in hand to represent 'Saganu, chukh!' and such rubbish, written by so-and-so,[19] at some time or other, perhaps with drunken eyes and brain . . . The menial position of the collaborators on *Mlada*, the disgracefully crass evaluation of their work, the lack of any ethical principle in our worthy commissioner, the consequent moral *fiasco* (not far off) of our circle—that's what sickens me. My dear and good friend—you know I can't haul around trash and nurse it—and so I am taking up a positive position—plainer, more straightforward, and better. I explained (as cleanly and delicately as I could) to Korsinka and Borodin that, with the intention of preserving the maiden purity of our circle, wishing that we should not prostitute it, I shall *in the matter of our more menial labours* do the prescribing and not the listening: I shall not make the replies but ask the questions on Korsinka's, Borodin's, and my own behalf (but this, of course, only with their consent). As for the contractor, that's up to him.

I'm writing Chernobog, it's coming along very well, it's turning out excellently with voices.

While Musorgsky may by now have been looking back balefully at the negotiations that had led to his current preoccupations, sensing that in having submitted to another's prescription he might have compromised too much his own principles, the fruit of those preoccupations had turned out well enough. In the autograph of his march Musorgsky identified the borrowed material, the theme of the flanks being taken from no. 6 in Balakirev's folksong collection (a theme later made widely

[18] *MLN1*, 129.

[19] Though Musorgsky's use of nonsense syllables for the devil's creatures' utterances in the revision of *St. John's Night* must have been suggested by the 'demon language' that Berlioz invented for his devils in *La damnation de Faust*, Musorgsky here drew on the 'Sabbath Song of the Witches on the Bare Mountain', a folk-text built from the names of devils intermingled with nonsense sounds, as recorded in N. Sakharov, *Skazaniye russkovo naroda* [Tales of the Russian people] (St Petersburg, 1841).

familiar in the introduction to the finale of Tchaikovsky's Serenade for Strings), while 'the priest's theme [of the central trio] belongs to Rimsky-Korsakov'. Musorgsky's compact processional, which unfolds mostly as a succession of changing background variations against the borrowed tunes, would no doubt have served its context as efficiently as would have the preceding market scene. Audibly blood-brother to the folk choruses in *Boris*, the processional follows on a measured orchestral introduction based on a folky theme, which conditions the chorus's initial plea that Radegast should grant them a good day's profit, trading its beginning with the music that would later be recycled to open act one of *Sorochintsy Fair* (though there its more radical passages would be rigorously excluded). Competition turns to insult, tempers rise, the mixed chorus divides into its constituent parts, and the scuffle begins between Polab Slavs and Novgorodians. The thought of Minkus's balletic pap being heard alongside this racy, uncompromising music is bizarre.

But it is the revised *St. John's Night on the Bare Mountain* that is of greater interest. It had been thought that the manuscript of this was lost, but it is now accepted that later Musorgsky simply relocated it among the materials for *Sorochintsy Fair*, having made the necessary modifications and added the confusing date '22 May 1880' (in the opera, the piece covers the span from the moment the familiar opening of the *St. John's Night* music is heard up to the point where Gritsko, the young Ukrainian peasant (or Parubok), awakens). Assuming that the final dawn music had been conceived for Yaromir's awakening, it shows that in 1872 Musorgsky had already composed anew most of the piece, rather less than a third of his 1872 version being derived from that of 1867 (only the first choral-orchestral portion of the opening section up to Chernobog's vocal entry).[20] A theme (Ex. 11.2) salvaged from the end of the scene in the Temple of Moloch in *Salammbô* provides the main musical substance of the 'Worship of Chernobog' (and also contributes to the magical dawn music with which the piece ends), while the ensuing 'Sabbath', with its wild 'Ballet', mingles this theme with earlier

---

[20] With minor excisions and barring made consistent, this is adapted from the first 139 bars of the 1867 score, linked to some 20 bars drawn from the latter part of 'Satan's Procession' (bars 208–31).

Ex. 11.2

music. Since in his 1872 piano-duet transcription of the familiar portions from the 1867 version Musorgsky did not incorporate every detail from that full score, we may reasonably assume that he might also, if he had scored the new piano-duet music of his later version, have added extra significant detail; thus it is impossible to make other than a qualified comparison between his old music and that which he supplied in 1872. Yet the impression is certainly of less fierceness, for all the heady licence with which the various ideas press on each others' heels. But

Ex. 11.3

Musorgsky was certainly right to feel enthusiasm for what the chorus could now contribute, and the new and very extensive ending as dawn breaks and the voices of the Sabbath's participants fade provides the most memorable part of the whole. The new lyrical phrase in Ex. 11.3, formed from the drooping figure in its first two bars with, as appendage, the slurred-quaver arching phrase of Ex. 11.2 (bars 3–4), its wildness now purged, is one of Musorgsky's most haunting; its quietly insistent repetitions, finally intersected by the wonderfully fresh flute melody that is Gritsko's badge, make this ending one of the most memorable Musorgsky ever wrote.

CHAPTER 12

Life alongside *Boris* II:
Khovanshchina Begun

OUTWARDLY MUSORGSKY'S EXISTENCE FOR THE REMAINDER OF 1872 was uneventful. A modest promotion at work was cheering, and during the summer he often spent the weekend very pleasantly with Stasov and the history professor Platon Pavlov at Pargolovo, and the round of musical *soirées* continued. In July Rimsky-Korsakov's wedding to Nadezhda Purgold took place, Musorgsky acting as best man. It marked the end of the two composers' joint tenancy and, according to Lyudmila Shestakova, of their close friendship. Then in November Alexandra Purgold married a civil servant and art-lover, Nikolay Molas, with Musorgsky again as best man. This signalled the end of any romantic hopes Alexandra may have pinned on Musorgsky as husband, but fears that it would also mean no more musical gatherings at her home were instantly dispelled, for within weeks they were again flourishing and would continue to do so, sometimes two or three times a week. According to Musorgsky's *Autobiographical Note*, during the autumn of 1872 a complete performance of *Boris* was arranged at the home of the sisters' uncle, Vladimir Purgold, with singers and staff from the Imperial Theatres present, at which it was straightway decided to mount three scenes at the Maryinsky Theatre 'although the opera itself had only recently been rejected by the Theatres' directorate'—so Musorgsky recorded.[1] Be that as it may, the campaign on behalf of *Boris* was clearly progressing nicely.

---

[1] *MLN1*, 269. This statement seems to confirm that, while *Boris* may earlier (on 18 May) have been approved in principle for production, final acceptance remained conditional on

But Tchaikovsky was a less impressed listener when he encountered some of Musorgsky's work early in 1873. Back in October he had met members of the kuchka and had asked to hear *The Nursery* because Bala-kirev had praised it. His reaction is unknown, but it was natural that con-tacts should now develop between him and the group, for Tchaikovsky's current trend towards a self-consciously national style in his own work had been powerfully demonstrated in his recently completed Second Sym-phony ('Little Russian'), and the finale especially would be rapturously re-ceived at a *soirée* at the Rimsky-Korsakovs' on 7 January 1873. But two days earlier at Cui's Tchaikovsky had shown little taste for what Musorgsky had performed from his own recent work—with the exception, that is, of one piece. As Musorgsky reported to Stasov in that fanciful, sometimes el-liptical style into which he easily slipped when keyed-up:

> *The Nursery*—he did not agree with the type or the aim of the composition; he declared that the composer's performance sells it—otherwise, he says, it's nonsense.
>
> 'The tramps' [the Kromy Forest Scene from *Boris*]—a fiasco.
>
> 'The Tale about the parrot' [from Act 2 of *Boris*]—furore.
>
> Sadïk-Pasha [Tchaikovsky] was half dozing, dreaming of sherbet, and perhaps also of Muscovite leavened dough, into which he turned himself during the playing of these extracts from *Boris*. I always observe listeners (it is instructive), and having noticed in Sadïk-Pasha an aspiration to turn him-self well and truly (*seriously*) into dough, I awaited fermentation. Well, the dough fermented—that is, after 'the parrot' it fermented, and its bubbles began bursting with a dull, lazy and unlovely sound. From the sum of these bursting bubbles' sounds (there weren't many of them) I deduced: 'a strong man (you know who), but his forces are in disarray . . . could be usefully worked on . . . a symphony (*en forme*, of course).

That Tchaikovsky should have approved of the conventionally tuneful parrot song only increased Musorgsky's scorn, especially when he asked to hear it a second time. He continued to Stasov:[2]

the scoring (as yet unfinished) proving satisfactory. When this confirmation may have been forthcoming is unknown, though the final decision to produce the opera was taken as late as November.

[2] *MLN1*, 142. Sadïk-Pasha was Musorgsky's nickname for Tchaikovsky. It was the title by which the Polish writer Mikhail Czajkowski, who had joined Mickiewicz in raising forces

The strong man thanked Sadïk-Pasha—and that's it. Yesterday I happened to see Sadïk-Pasha at Bessel's . . . 'offer musical beauty—only musical beauty!' Balakirev arrived—I played Dargo[mïzhsky]'s *Finnish [Fantasy]* with him. Sadïk-Pasha didn't approve.

With the fate of *Boris* in the balance, and with Rimsky's *The Maid of Pskov* also a candidate for performance, the intrusion of a third competitor, Tchaikovsky's *The Oprichnik*, into the acceptance stakes was even more unwelcome. Though Musorgsky had not heard a note of *The Oprichnik*, this did not prevent him passing judgement. Yet there is a touch of respect for his rival's creative integrity, however misguided that might be:[3]

> *The Oprichnik* is written with the intention of winning public fame and making a name. The composer has ingratiated himself with the public's taste (O Pasha!), but at the same time has applied himself to his work very ardently and sincerely (O Sadïk!). First, tastes are fickle, secondly, the public demands something Russian from Russian artists, thirdly—it is shameful to play with art for personal ends. It emerges that Sadïk, like a true Pasha, is not without cynicism, and openly preaches the religion of absolute beauty.

The creative antipathy of Musorgsky and Tchaikovsky was mutual. But the latter, in return, recognized Musorgsky's creative gift. 'In talent he is perhaps superior [to the other kuchka members]', Tchaikovsky would write to his patroness Nadezhda von Meck in January 1878. 'But his nature is narrow-minded, devoid of any urge towards self-perfection . . . In addition he has a certain base side to his nature which likes coarseness, uncouthness, roughness . . . He flaunts . . . his illiteracy, blindly believing in the infallibility of his genius. Yet he has flashes of talent which are, moreover, not devoid of originality.'[4]

Nevertheless, all these activities were secondary to a new project that had been preoccupying Musorgsky since the spring of 1872. At the

---

to fight against the Russians in Turkey at the time of the Crimean War, became known after he had embraced Islam.

[3] *MLN1*, 143.

[4] P. I. Tchaikovsky, *Polnoye sobraniye sochineny: Literaturnïye proizvedeniya i perepiska* [Complete works: literary works and correspondence], ed. N. A. Viktorova and B. I. Rabinovich, vi, (Moscow, 1961), 329.

beginning of the year he had confessed to Nadezhda Purgold that two years earlier he had thought of composing an opera on an unspecified subject from Gogol, and now that the creation, if not the scoring, of the revised *Boris* was completed and he would be scouting for an idea for another opera, Nadezhda had again raised the same subject. But, as Musorgsky put it, it 'does not fit my chosen path; it doesn't sufficiently capture Mother Russia in all her simple-souled breadth.'[5] The ever-helpful Stasov came up with the answer to that need. It was what would become *Khovanshchina*. 'It seemed to me that the struggle between the old and new Russia, the passing of the former from the stage and the birth of the latter, was rich soil for drama, and Musorgsky shared my opinion', he later recalled.[6] Set in the early reign of Peter the Great at the close of the seventeenth century, the opera would trace the struggle between the young Tsar and the old order as represented by the boyar Prince Ivan Khovansky, the conservative sect of the Orthodox Church (the 'Old Believers'), with the monk Dosifey at their head, and the Europeanizers embodied in Prince Vasily Golitsïn. All would end with the ascendancy of Peter. But there was no existing drama ready for adaptation, not even a plot; everything had to be worked out *ab initio*. Stasov claimed (and there is no reason to doubt this) that it was he who worked out a scenario 'in its general outlines and most important details'.[7] But *Khovanshchina* would be no dry chronicle. 'On stage there will be the "streltsy" [Khovansky's militia] and the "raskolniki" [the Old Believers], and the German "sloboda" [a settlement exempt from state obligations] in Moscow', Stasov enthused to his daughter, 'with foreign officers, a pastor, German merchants, and a German girl, etc.— and Sophia [the regent], and the young ten-year-old Peter and his regiment of "toy-soldiers", and the self-immolating raskolniki, and so on. Musorgsky is delighted and is already getting down to composing the text and music.'[8]

Whether Musorgsky was meaningfully composing any music at this early stage is unlikely, but he was certainly soaking himself in the period

---

[5] *MLN1*, 126.

[6] *SMPM* [see *SSM3*, 111].

[7] *TDM*, 257.

[8] Ibid.

in general and in this subject in particular. The ferment of his excitement led to a spate of letters, some very long, to Stasov, on whom he had become almost passionately dependent, seeing him as the one being from the old Balakirev circle who could be relied on not only for ideas and stimuli but for absolute support. The letters chronicle the first conceptual stages of the opera, and much feverish inner searching to (re-) define—or (re)muster—Musorgsky's own creative creed and its practical embodiment as he prepared for the task facing him. His burgeoning excitement is palpable and his literary style, in its almost telegraphic jerks and leaps, its idiosyncratic syntax and vocabulary, makes decoding his precise meaning at times hazardous: 'It happens that, "though you are being pigheaded", you want to speak your mind. I am pregnant with something and I am giving birth—and to what I am giving birth you will behold, my dear généralissime [Stasov]', he wrote on 28 June 1872. 'And what if Musoryanin were to become earth-stained through Mother-Russia!' he continued six days later:[9]

> Not for the first time would I have begun to delve into the black earth, and I want to delve not into the tilled but the virgin earth—I thirst not just to become acquainted with the people but to be their brother: terrifying, but good! What then?. . . . The black earth's power will reveal itself when you delve to its very bottom. You can dig the black earth with a tool whose nature is alien to it, and at the end of the seventeenth century they dug into Mother-Russia with a tool *such* that she did not straightway recognize with what they were digging and, like the black earth, she *heaved* and began *to breathe*. And here she freely took on board various actual and privy state councillors, and they did not give her, the long-suffering one, time to collect herself and think: *Where are you pushing me?* They executed the ignorant and the confused: *force*! But officialdom still lives on and the search is the same as before the command; only the time is different: the actual and privy councillors prevent the black earth *from breathing*. The past in the present—that is my task.
>
> 'We have gone forward!' You lie. 'We're still there!' . . . Until the people can verify *with their own eyes* what is being cooked out of them, so long as they do not *themselves* will that, out of them, either this or that *should be cooked, 'we're still there'*! All benefactors are good at achieving fame, at con-

[9] *MLN1*, 131–2.

solidating their fame through documents, but the people groan and, so as not to groan, they drink—and groan more: *We're still there!*

But before anything could be achieved the subject had to be thoroughly researched. On 25 July he gave Stasov a report on progress:[10]

> By your return, dear généralissime, it is probable that all the materials for our future opera will have been assembled. I have put together a note-book and called it '*Khovanshchina*, a people's musical drama—materials'. On the title-page I have noted my sources: nine of them—not at all bad: I am inundated with information, my head is like a cauldron that absorbs everything. I have already sucked dry Zhelyabuzhsky, Krekshin, Count Matveyev, Medvedev, Shchebalsky and Semevsky; now I'm sucking at Tikhonravov, and then Avvakum—for dessert.

However, it was not simply a question of sources, but of medium and method; Musorgsky was reviewing his musical armoury and the principles and strategy that would determine its deployment. If there had been signs in his recent music that he might have been discarding his earlier credo, this had to be purged. That old conflict (as Musorgsky saw it) between technique and ideals/inspiration, between means and ends—between stifling pedantry and liberating realism—was resurging strongly, and his own stance had to be reaffirmed: 'the artist believes in the future because he lives in it', he had reminded Lyudmila Shestakova (and himself) two days earlier.[11] This was the more important because he recognized how the centrifugal paths being pursued by the kuchka's members were leaving him increasingly isolated—except, of course, from Stasov. Despite the others' enthusiasm for *Boris*, Musorgsky's longstanding sense of intellectual inferiority and his alienation from his old musical associates through his gaucherie in discussing technical matters with them are once again painfully evident:[12]

> Why, *tell me*, when I listen to the conversation of young painters or sculptors ... can I follow the workings of their brains, their thoughts, their aims— and rarely hear talk about technique, except where necessary? Why (*don't tell me!*) when I listen to our musical brotherhood, do I rarely hear a living

[10] *MLN1*, 134–5.
[11] *MLN1*, 133.
[12] *MLN1*, 136.

thought, but everything, rather, is from the schoolroom—technique and musical vocabulary?

Is musical art really young only because adolescent ignorami practise it? How many times have I inadvertently, *through my ridiculous habit*, initiated a topic (in a round-about way) with the brotherhood—and received either a rebuff, or something obscure—but, more likely, not been understood? Well, let us grant that I cannot *set out my thoughts clearly*—that is to say: present my brain on a salver with my thoughts printed on it (like a telegram). But what about themselves? Why don't they do the initiating? Evidently they don't want to . . . Could it be that I'm afraid of technique because I'm bad at it? However, there is someone [Stasov?] who will stand up for me in art—and in this regard also . . .

In truth—until the artist-musician renounces his cradle, his straps and braces, until then the *symphonic priests* will rule, setting up their *Talmud* 'first and second editions' as the alpha and omega in the life of art. Their little brains sense that their *Talmud* cannot apply to living art: where there are people, there is life—there's no place there for preconceived paragraphs and articles. And so they cry: 'Drama, the stage inhibits us—we want space!' So let us gratify our brains: 'The world of sounds is boundless!' But their brains are limited, so what is in it, in this sound of worlds or, rather, this world of sounds! . . .

I'm not against symphonies, but against symphonists—incorrigible conservatives. So *do not tell* me, dear généralissime, why our musicians talk more often about technique than about aims and historical tasks, for it is *because of that*.

Two days later the *Khovanshchina* notebook was despatched to Stasov, together with a full list of the materials Musorgsky had researched. Already it was decided the opera should be 'in five parts'. The accompanying letter was in itself an inscription. Nothing more eloquently uncovers Musorgsky's boundless gratitude to—or sense of dependence on—Stasov:[13]

In dedicating *Khovanshchina* to Vladimir Vasilyevich Stasov: For me the absence of precedents for a still non-existent work being already dedicated does not matter, nor should it. There is no fear in my heart that would

[13] *MNL1*, 138.

impel me to withhold this dedication and look back. I want to look forward, and not back. I dedicate to you that whole period of my life during
which *Khovanshchina* will be created; there will be nothing absurd in me
saying: 'I dedicate to you myself and my life for that period'—for I still
remember vividly: *I lived* Boris in *Boris*, and the time I lived in *Boris* is
recorded on my brain in precious and indelible marks. Now a new work,
your work, will boil—already I am beginning to live in it—how many rich
impressions, how many new lands to be discovered—splendid! And so
therefore I beg you to accept 'all my disorderly being' in the dedication of
Khovanshchina, whose inception came from you.

No doubt the weekends at Pargolovo with Stasov and Pavlov were
preoccupied with discussions around *Khovanshchina*. Any tiny detail that
Musorgsky chanced on that summer in his more casual reading and
which might contribute to *Khovanshchina* was carefully noted. He was
vastly impressed by Darwin's newly published *Descent of Man*, and he
thought he detected 'between its lines' confirmation of his own values.
The 'graceful delicacy' in ancient Greek art was 'gross', Italian painting
was 'repulsive like death itself. In poetry there are two colossi: coarse
Homer and refined Shakespeare', he continued to Stasov on 30 October:[14]

> In music there are two colossi: Beethoven the thinker, and Berlioz the ultra-
> thinker. . . . 'And our own?' Glinka and Dargomïzhsky, Pushkin and Ler-
> montov, Gogol and Gogol and again Gogol (no-one stands at his right
> hand)—all great generals who also led their armies of art to the conquest
> of good lands . . . Darwin has strongly confirmed for me my cherished
> dream which I have nevertheless approached with a certain dull-witted
> diffidence. The artistic representation of beauty alone, in its material sense,
> is gross childishness—art in its infancy. *The finest traits in the nature* of man
> and of *the mass of humanity*, the persistent delving into, and conquest of,
> these little-known regions—that is the artist's true calling. 'Towards new
> shores!' fearlessly, through tempest, shoals, and submerged rocks, 'Towards
> new shores!' Man is a social animal and cannot be otherwise; in the masses
> of humanity, as in the individual man, there are always the finest traits which
> elude our grasp, traits untouched by anyone: to observe and study these

[14] *MLN1,* 141.

through reading, observation, surmise, to study *with all one's inner being* and feed them to humanity as a healthy dish as yet untasted by it—that's the task! That's the rapture, the eternal rapture! We shall attempt this in our [*sic*] *Khovanshchina,* shall we not, my dear soothsayer.

It was this resurgence of all his old beliefs and values that would make his reaction to Tchaikovsky so contemptuous when they met early the next year, and would also account for the sudden access of affection for his earlier creation, *The Marriage,* whose more extreme realism he had relinquished, especially in the revised *Boris* and the later *Nursery* songs. The gift of the manuscript of *The Marriage* to Stasov on the occasion of his birthday on 14 January 1873 was as personal, heartfelt, and pointed a gesture as Musorgsky ever made in his whole life. First he reflected on what *Khovanshchina* would signify—and how it would be received:[15]

> *Yes, quickly to court!* It is joyful to dream of how we shall stand on the place of execution, thinking and living *Khovanshchina* at the time when they will be judging us for *Boris*; audaciously cheerful, we shall look into the far musical distance which beckons us forward, and judgement will have no terror for us. They will say to us: 'You have flouted divine and human laws!'. We shall reply: 'Yes!'—and we shall think: 'There's more to come!' They will croak of us: 'You will soon and for ever be forgotten!' We shall reply: '*Non, non et non, Madame!*' We have daring enough to face down all judges.

Then he turned to his present gift. We may wonder what we should infer from the cryptic, and seemingly reckless, invitation to compare *The Marriage* with the masterpiece he had already created and which is now generally held to be the greatest of all Russian tragic operas. Musorgsky's words are unlikely to change our relative evaluations of the two works, nor should they; but they alert us to a quality, or at least a special significance, in the earlier work that should temper, at

---

[15] *MLN1,* 144. The final reply quoted was that returned to the Empress herself by a pupil at a school in St Petersburg on the occasion of a prize-giving. The girls had been told that under no circumstances should they contradict anything the Empress said, but one of them did this in response to a factual error on the part of Her Majesty. Reproved by the Empress herself, the girl held her ground: '*Non, non et non, Madame!*'

least a little, an over-ready dismissal of it as no more than a brilliantly original experiment of nothing but historical interest: 'Take my youthful work on Gogol's *The Marriage*, survey my attempts at musical speech, compare them with *Boris*, *compare* 1868 with 1871, and you will see that I am giving you, irrevocably, myself.'[16]

The major event of early 1873 was the performance on 17 February at the Maryinsky Theatre of three scenes from *Boris*. Their success with public and press alike was both the most auspicious of auguries for the future of *Boris* and the keenest of spurs to proceed with the opera that was projected as its successor. If the theatres' directorate had still not given final approval for *Boris* to be mounted in its entirety, this must surely have been the most decisive factor on its road to final acceptance. Especially reassuring was the overwhelming success of the Inn Scene, far more radical musically than the two Polish Scenes. Yet for Musorgsky the single most memorable incident of the evening was probably seeing the 66-year-old Osip Petrov, the doyen of Russian singers who in 1836 and 1842 respectively had created the parts of Susanin and Ruslan in Glinka's two landmark operas and who was now singing Varlaam, leading the applause when Musorgsky appeared to take his first bow; so moved was the composer that he forthwith embraced him. After the performance there was a champagne supper at the Rimsky-Korsakovs'.

Musorgsky had never crossed the borders of Russia (nor ever would). Nevertheless, Stasov had now extracted his agreement to travel with him to Vienna where he might encounter, both in the theatre and concert hall, much new music that could not be heard elsewhere. 'He's already 34, his talent is at its peak, and he's beginning a new opera . . . It is absolutely essential that such a man should take a sniff at Europe', Stasov wrote to his daughter Sofiya on 29 March.[17] However, extra funds would be needed for this, and there was no immediate prospect of Musorgsky receiving money either from performances of *Boris* or from the printing of the vocal score; it was only in April that Bessel would open a list for subscribers to its future publication. Yet Stasov

---

[16] Ibid.

[17] *TDM,* 289–90.

seemed sure he could work out a budget that would allow them to
travel together, and Musorgsky was evidently taking the proposal very
seriously. By mid-May Stasov had widened their itinerary to include
Weimar and Liszt. Inevitably one speculates on what might have been
the consequences for Musorgsky had this trip ever materialized. Liszt's
voracious musical appetite, through the intercession of Bessel, was about
to be fed with a substantial dish of works by the new Russian composers. A year earlier, at Bessel's request, Musorgsky had underlaid a
copy of Dargomïzhsky's *The Stone Guest* with Friedrich Bodenstedt's
translation of Pushkin's Little Tragedy so that it could be presented to
Liszt; now, however, it seems the recent Russian piece that had won
Liszt's greatest admiration was Musorgsky's own *Nursery*. The report to
Bessel came from Adelheid von Schorn, daughter of an art historian, a
long-time resident of Weimar, and a prolific source of information
about the composer. Her gushing cry-by-cry account of Liszt's reaction
cannot be taken at face value, but Liszt was sufficiently impressed by
The Nursery to sit down and write to Musorgsky. The letter never arrived, however, and Stasov journeyed alone. Even from abroad he
maintained the pressure, dismissing Musorgsky's claim that his chief's
illness tied him to the department and instructing that his own salary
for August should be put at Musorgsky's disposal to cover his travel
expenses. All to no avail. As for Musorgsky, hearing of Liszt's response
to his *Nursery* from Bessel's brother who, spotting Musorgsky in the
street in St Petersburg, had jumped out of his cab to tell him about it
and of Liszt's intention to dedicate something to Musorgsky himself, on
4 August he wrote to Stasov in Vienna:[18]

> I never thought that Liszt who, with few exceptions, chooses colossal sub-
> jects, could *seriously* understand and appreciate *The Nursery* and, in particular,
> go into raptures about it; you see, all its children are Russian, with a strong
> local scent. What will Liszt say or think when he sees *Boris*, if only in the
> piano transcription? . . . God grant that he may live a little longer and per-
> haps, when the opportunity occurs, I'll slip across to see him in Europe and
> amuse him with novelties—though only in your company, généralissime,
> not otherwise. But now I am fated to wither and mope among the Chal-
> deans, to waste my time and effort on the kind of matter that would be

[18] *MLN1*, 155.

done even better without me. I am fated to realize the complete futility
and uselessness of my work *in the Forestry Department* . . . It's terrible!

With his growing sense of creative isolation from his kuchka colleagues, Musorgsky found all the more congenial his acquaintance with
two leading visual artists he had recently met through Stasov. Mark
Antokolsky would become one of the most popular of Russian sculptors
in the last years of the century, while Ilya Repin is, for most non-
Russians, the most famous painter of his generation, familiar for, if
nothing else, his portrait of Musorgsky himself painted only days before
the composer's death. Musorgsky had known both since at least 1871,
and the three naturally bonded through their mutual dedication to the
principle of realism. For Stasov they became his 'troika'—a symbol of
all that was best in Russian creative culture. In 1872 Repin had designed
the title-page for Bessel's publication of *The Nursery*, and the relationship
had quickly become personal, for by October Musorgsky was a guest
at the christening of Repin's daughter, subsequently entertaining the
company by performing Mozart and his own vocal pieces. Repin's admiration for Musorgsky was very genuine, but personal contact between the two men would be relatively shortlived, for Repin would
spend much of the next few years abroad.

The most significant single event for Musorgsky from the latter part
of 1873 was the final sanctioning at the beginning of November of the
production of the complete *Boris*. The first soloists' rehearsal would take
place on New Year's Day 1874. Early in January he composed the new
trio for his chorus *The Destruction of Sennacherib*, now transferring the
dedication to Stasov on the occasion of his fiftieth birthday. Being unable himself to orchestrate the new trio in time for the charity concert
on 2 March, at which Rimsky-Korsakov would conduct its première,
he asked Rimsky to undertake this task. But Stasov's delight at this
inscription was as nothing compared to his excitement at what Musorgsky had already composed for *Khovanshchina* during the previous
months.

Scarcely anything, however, was being notated, though bits were
being improvised and stored in his head. Musorgsky blamed the demands of government service for his failure to set these down on paper,
but there is already disturbing evidence of another, more ominous factor

lurking behind this. In mid-June 1873 his physical condition had given Dmitri Stasov some cause for concern. 'The other day Musorgsky himself told Volodya [Dmitri's brother, Vladimir] that on Whitsunday he had felt attacks of the kind of dementia he had already had some years before, but at the same time he insisted that he was drinking very little, though he loved to drink! It would be a misfortune if that should happen.' But now Dmitri had seen Musorgsky for himself. 'I found him significantly altered', he continued to his wife, Polixena, who was in Vienna. 'Somehow he has let himself go, grown sallow, and is notably quieter—but as before he is composing well.'[19] Polixena had promptly written Musorgsky the kindest of letters, giving him the best counsel she could in a situation at which she could only guess, and saying, in effect, that his music was far too valuable to lose for problems, to many of which his friends had solutions either through moral or financial support. Her letter affords the most vibrant proof of both the unique importance attached to his music by some of his friends and of the depth of their affection for him, a proof substantiated a few weeks later by her brother-in law, Vladimir, who was confidently scheming to have Musorgsky transferred that autumn to another department where members of the Purgold and Molas families were established and where Musorgsky could find more free time (and, indeed, by the year's end Musorgsky was promoted to the rank of court councillor in the Ministry of State Properties). Meeting him three days after noting his changed appearance, Dmitri found him looking better. Yet there can be little doubt that Musorgsky, for all his disclaimer, had again engaged in a bout of heavy drinking, a suspicion later reinforced by Borodin in a letter he would write to his wife, recounting how, during the summer, the family of one of Borodin's professional colleagues had seen Musorgsky 'completely drunk at Pavlovsk. He was causing a disturbance and it became a police matter'.[20] What had happened during the few weeks after Polixena had written is unknown, but there had been an ominous delay before Musorgsky had replied on 4 August, charmingly waving aside Polixena's fears, assuring her that it was only the endless burden of Forestry Department work that had depressed him, then

---

[19] *TDM*, 296.
[20] *TDM*, 311.

listing some of the things he had prepared or was preparing for the opera as proof that he had otherwise been profitably employed. 'I am living now in *Khovanshchina* as I lived in *Boris*, and I am the same Musoryanin, only I have become stricter with myself after my success which you crowned,[21] and more terrified in approaching people . . . But I want to create [in *Khovanshchina*] a people's drama—*that's what I want!*'[22]

But the alcoholic excesses were in progress even as Borodin was writing to his wife. 'Almost daily he sits in the Maly Yaroslavets restaurant on the Morskaya and gets drunk, sometimes till he's insensible', he continued his letter of 6 November. ' . . . Now he will periodically drop out of sight, then reappear uncharacteristically morose, taciturn. After a while he is again himself—sweet, cheerful, lovable, and witty, as always.'[23] Reviewing this period, Rimsky confirmed Borodin's report, though he placed the inception of Musorgsky's dipsomania a little later.[24]

> From the time when *Boris* was mounted Musorgsky began in general to appear amongst us rather less often than before, and a certain change became noticeable in him: a certain mysteriousness manifested itself and perhaps there was even a certain standoffishness. His self-esteem swelled to a marked degree, and his obscure and convoluted way of expressing himself, which had also been to a certain extent a characteristic earlier, became extreme. Often it was impossible to understand his stories, discourses, and smart observations, which aspired to be witty. From this time dates the beginning of his long sessions into the early hours in the Maly Yaroslavets and other restaurants, drinking cognac either alone or in the company of his newly acquired friends and acquaintances, who were unknown to us at that time. When dining with us and other common acquaintances Musorgsky normally refused wine almost completely, but later in the evening he was drawn to the Maly Yaroslavets. Subsequently one of his companions of that period,

[21] On returning home after the première of *Boris* to an apartment in darkness, Musorgsky had been alarmed when he pricked himself on something thorny, only to discover that it was a celebratory wreath sent to him by Polixena Stasova.
[22] *MLN1*, 153.
[23] *TDM*, 315–6.
[24] *RKL*, 111.

a certain Verderevsky, . . . once told me that, in the language of the company which Musorgsky was keeping at that time, there was a special term 'to wreck oneself with cognac', which they translated into practice. From the time when *Boris* was mounted began the decline of its highly talented composer.

This was the personal background against which Musorgsky set about *Khovanshchina*. Yet, as Borodin had noted back in the summer of 1873, he was still composing well. By mid-August Musorgsky reported to Stasov that the prelude and first part of the first scene were complete, though still nothing had been written down, partly because of the pressures of government work, partly because he was not satisfied that everything was yet as he wanted it. 'Sometimes you rush ahead—but no, stop!' he had written to Stasov on 14 August. 'The inner cook tells you the soup is boiling but it's too soon to put it on the table—it will be too watery, perhaps, you must toss in some more root or salt; well, the cook knows his job better than I do: so I wait. Then as soon as the soup lands on the table—*I'll devour it.*'[25]

Elsewhere Musorgsky seems to have been giving particular attention to the structure of the opera's end (the preliminaries to the self-immolation). His often massive letters to Stasov during the summer chronicle the debate seething within him about the issues involved and the psychology of his players, and he pleaded that the time and attention all this had absorbed was the reason he had been unable to travel abroad. Tangible proof that he had actually been composing was forthcoming during August and September when Marfa's Song and a portion of what followed in Act 3 was put on paper. Nevertheless, work on the opera seems to have ceased altogether by the end of September and would not be resumed for nearly a year. Creative exhaustion, the recourse to alcohol, and the news in November that *Boris* would be given early the following year must account for this. In December he saw his *Intermezzo in modo classico* and *Ein Kinderscherz* into print in an anthology of piano pieces.

Otherwise his 'creative' time was taken up proof-reading the vocal score of *Boris*, coaching the cast, and attending rehearsals. There were at least seven official singers' rehearsals, several orchestral rehearsals, and

[25] *MLN1*, 162.

seven full rehearsals, as well as, no doubt, much undocumented personal consultation with the composer. The day before the première he did not sleep but paced the room all night (so remembered Kutuzov).

As noted earlier, the première itself went excellently, Stasov claiming Musorgsky had to take between eighteen and twenty curtain calls, and the *St Petersburg Gazette* confirming that the greater part of the audience applauded loudly after each scene, calling out both performers and composer. All three of the season's subsequent performances were sold out, and Musorgsky's personal success remained enormous. The press reaction may have been very mixed, and Musorgsky was bitter at Cui's censure; yet *Boris*, unquestionably Musorgsky's greatest work, also provided him with his greatest public triumph. It was also the watershed in his life.

CHAPTER 13

Two Relationships: *Pictures at an Exhibition* and *Sunless*

MUSORGSKY HAD KNOWN THE ARCHITECT AND ARTIST VIK-
tor Hartmann since the late sixties. The two men had quickly
become friends, and in 1868 Hartmann had presented Musorgsky with
two of his sketches (of a rich and a poor Jew). In return Musorgsky
had dedicated to Hartmann the second song, 'In the corner', of his
Nursery cycle, and the artist had become a frequent presence at the
musical *soirées* of Musorgsky's circle. But suddenly, on 4 August 1873,
he had died. Musorgsky was deeply shocked; while walking with Hartmann in St Petersburg during the artist's last visit, he had seen him
suddenly taken ill with what was clearly some serious cardiac disorder
and was now full of self-reproach for having shrugged it off at the time.
The letter to Stasov in which he recounted his reaction is perhaps the
most consistently pain-filled he ever wrote. Stasov being currently in
Vienna, Musorgsky wrote a brief stop-gap obituary which appeared in
the *St Petersburg Gazette* three days later.

However, Musorgsky had not lost merely a personal friend, for Hartmann's creative comments had had some influence on his work; it was
Hartmann, for instance, who had been among the most insistent that
the Fountain Scene be incorporated into the revised *Boris*. Yet his
greatest service to Musorgsky would be rendered after his death,[1] for it

---

[1] For more information on Hartmann, see G. Abraham, 'The Artist of *Pictures from an Exhibition*', *MIM*, 229–36. The facsimile of Musorgsky's piano score, together with detailed

was the memorial exhibition of Hartmann's work, organized by Stasov
in late February 1874, that spurred Musorgsky to compose his piano
suite *Pictures at an Exhibition*. Commenting on Hartmann's pictures in
the *St Petersburg Gazette*, Stasov observed that they were[2]

> the lively, elegant sketches of a genre painter, the majority being of scenes,
> types, figures from everyday life, caught from the environment that swirled
> around him—on the streets and in the churches, in the Paris catacombs and
> Polish monasteries, in Roman side-streets and villages around Limoges, car-
> naval types *à la Gavarni*, workers in smocks and Catholic priests on donkeys
> with umbrellas under their arms, old French women at prayer, Jews smiling
> from beneath their skull-caps, Parisian rag-pickers, . . . country scenes with
> picturesque ruins, wonderful vistas including an urban panorama.

All the same, Stasov had reservations about Hartmann's talent, ad-
miring his originality as an architect but not placing him in the first
rank, and considering that he had been at his best when treating subjects
with some element of fantasy or something especially Russian in
them—that is, subjects that had stimulated his imagination and which
were the very sort likely to draw a response from Musorgsky. Since the
exhibition offered works for sale, a number of items that became Musorgsky's subjects have disappeared without trace. It is not known
whether Musorgsky had already stored in his head some of his own
Pictures during or in the immediate wake of the exhibition, but since
he had already proceeded thus with bits of *Khovanshchina*, it is possible.
Certainly by 24 June he was immersed in them. 'Hartmann is seething,
like *Boris* seethed', he wrote to Stasov.[3]

> The concept and sounds have hung in the air; now I am ingesting them,
> and I am so gorging myself that I can scarcely manage to scribble them
> down on paper. I am composing the fourth number. The links (in the
> 'promenades') are good. I want to get it done as quickly and reliably as
> possible. My physiognomy is evident in the interludes. I consider it suc-
> cessful thus far . . .

editorial commentary by Emiliya Frid (Moscow, 1975) and reproductions of Hartmann's six
surviving sketches represented by Musorgsky, is invaluable.

[2] *TDM*, 364–5.

[3] *MLN1*, 178–9. In fact, this letter may have been written on 1 July.

My nomenclature is curious: 'Promenade (in modo russico)'; No. 1: 'Gnomus'—intermezzo (the intermezzo [promenade] is untitled); No. 2: 'Il vecchio castello'—intermezzo (also untitled); No. 3: 'Tuileries (dispute d'enfants après jeux)'; [then,] right between the eyes,—No. 4: 'Sandomirzsko bydlo' (le télègue) (it goes without saying that 'le télègue' is not written in—that is between us). How well it's working out! . . .

PS. I want to add Vityushka's [Hartmann's] Jews.

Pictures was completed on 4 July. A note in Musorgsky's manuscript reads: 'For press', with the date, '7 August 74', but the suite was not published until 1886, five years after his death and now edited by Rimsky. The dedication was to Stasov. There is no record of it ever receiving public performance during Musorgsky's lifetime.

Pictures provides some of the clearest evidence so far of the growing breadth of Musorgsky's creative gifts. Till now he had produced only one large-scale instrumental piece, the orchestral *St John's Night*, in its original form an immature if prodigiously inventive work which, now it had been revised for the abortive *Mlada*, should be numbered among his theatre pieces. Furthermore, Hartmann had worked mainly as an architect before leaving for western Europe in 1864, and it was primarily as architect and designer that he was employed after his return in 1868; only during his nearly five years abroad had he really concentrated on painting, and in consequence the subjects of nearly all his paintings were non-Russian. The international spread of the subjects of *Pictures* is evidenced in the titles themselves, and that Musorgsky found congenial any challenge that this spread represented is perhaps confirmed by the variety of languages in which he chose to emphasize their national diversity: Latin and Italian, French, Polish, German inflected with Yiddish, as well as Russian.

But in fact not all the subjects in *Pictures* were drawn from the 1874 exhibition. ' "Samuel" Goldenberg und "Schmuÿle" ' was prompted by the two pictures Hartmann had given Musorgsky in 1868. Nor were all the sketches from life or nature. The opening piece and the final two—'Gnomus', 'The Hut on Hen's Legs (Baba-Yaga)', and 'The Bogatyr's Gate (in the ancient capital Kiev)'—were based on designs, the first made in 1869 for a grotesque nutcracker intended as a Christmas tree decoration, the second for a clock designed to resemble a hut on hen's legs (the traditional habitation of the Russian witch Baba-Yaga), while the last had been a competition entry from 1869 for a ceremonial gate to commemorate Alexander II's escape from assassination in Kiev in 1866. 'Ballet of the Unhatched Chicks' was a costume design made in 1870 for a ballet, *Trilby*. Apart from that for 'Gnomus', the pictures or designs that inspired these five pieces are all extant. But beyond these only the sketch for 'Catacombae (Sepulcrum romanum)/Con mortuis in lingua mortua' is also known to have survived. Help in decoding 'Limoges le marché (La grande nouvelle)' comes from the two overlapping verbal sketches Musorgsky pencilled into his manuscript; these vividly describe the personages and gossip he imagined when creating this musical scene, though subsequently he struck out both. For the rest we have to rely on the exhibition catalogue's descriptions (if these can be identified) and Stasov's memories of Hartmann's work as recalled in his preface to the first publication of *Pictures*.

Musorgsky's suite produces a more coherent impression than might have been expected from the variety of subjects depicted. The Soviet scholar V. Bobrovsky identified a symmetrical scheme in the subject matter of the pictures themselves (centering on the 'Unhatched Chicks')[4] and Michael Russ has offered evidence of systematic planning in Musorgsky's key sequence in the fifteen movements that make up the entire suite.[5] But crucial to the work's structural integrity are the five pieces not yet mentioned: the Promenades. Inserting these was a brilliant way of tightening the structure, as well as enriching the extra-musical content of the suite, for while the first three guide us in turn to the first three pictures, they also function as unifying quasi-ritornelli. But subsequently the rigid alternation is loosened, two pictures intervening before each of the remaining two Promenades is heard. The three central Promenades, all founded on the opening theme of the first, are briefer and more leisurely (*moderato* or *tranquillo*)

---

[4] Bobrovsky's proposal requires 'The Bogatyr's Gate' to be omitted. Yet if the initial Promenade is allowed in to balance this, the scheme in fact becomes more convincing, for this piece matches reasonably 'The Bogatyr's Gate'. For a comprehensive examination of *Pictures*, its various contexts, documentary materials relating to it, and an admirably detailed investigation of Musorgsky's musical materials and techniques, see M. Russ, *Musorgsky: Pictures at an Exhibition* (Cambridge, 1992).

[5] See Russ, op. cit., 33.

and depict Musorgsky wandering through the exhibition, observing attentively. They are also set in new keys (A flat, B major, and D minor aeolian respectively). But the fifth and final one is a lightly modified repetition of the first, back in B flat, thus neatly packaging the first six pictures. In a letter to Rimsky Stasov had described what now followed as *'the second part* [which] you do not know at all',[6] which, with the preceding part's neat framing by the virtually identical Promenades 1 and 5, raises a suspicion that this had initially been envisaged as an autonomous piece. Whether or not this is true, a sustained B♭ at the end of Promenade 5 now ensures no aural break, and material from the Promenades will continue to recur, though now incorporated into two of the pictures ('Con mortuis in lingua mortua' and the final 'The Bogatyr's Gate'); thus the two musical lines of *Pictures* merge to accomplish a creative union between spectator (Musorgsky) and artist (Hartmann). On both levels, structural and conceptual, Musorgsky exhibits in *Pictures* a control of large-scale musical space comparable to that displayed in the last act of *Boris*, a result the more impressive, considering that he seems to have composed the pieces straight off in the order presented.

That Musorgsky saw himself as the spectator in the Promenades is clear from his letter to Stasov, and Promenade 1 brilliantly suggests him walking purposefully into the room, though there is an ebb and flow in the phrasing that indicates that his gait is subject to constant slight irregularities, perhaps through momentary shifts of direction as he turns to give the pictures a preliminary survey. Far from being the solid, even stolid, piece this might at first sight appear to be, Promenade 1 is a remarkably sophisticated product of the kind of rhythmic flexibility that Musorgsky had assiduously begun exploiting in some of his songs (and in *St John's Night*). For now, though with no text to determine (or constrain) him, he proceeds, against the virtually unbroken crotchet tread, to devise an unprecedented assymetry and ambiguity in the phrasing that both animate and stimulate. It merits closer inspection.

The opening instantly establishes an affinity with the world of Rus-

---

[6] N. Rimsky-Korsakov, *Literaturnïye proizvedeniya i perepiska* [Literary works and correspondence], ed. A.S. Lyapunova, v. (Moscow, 1963), 351.

sian folk music, not only in the nature of the theme on which all the 'Promenades' are founded,[7] but in its presentation: a soloist leads, the chorus follows, repeating and harmonizing the theme. The phrase itself is in two clear parts, respectively of five and six crotchets (Ex.13.1a), the second a modified mirror image of the first. Musorgsky's barring has matched this division, and the two ensuing periods of 5+6 crotchets consolidate this structure. But now, except for one 5/4 bar, all is to be regularly presented as in 6/4 (see Ex.13.1b the second half of the piece). The pianist, of course, quickly realizes this is no reliable guide to phrasing—yet it is a meaningful barring, for twice a pair of bars, in which the second bar is a clear if modified echo of the first (bars 3–4 and 9–10 of Ex. 13.1b) do present a clear six-crotchet bar structure, and against such bastions of relative stability the irregularities of the intervening bars and those that conclude the piece are felt the more clearly. Bar 5 might be heard as embracing a three-crotchet repetition, were it not that the repeated portion is extended into the following bar in a varied repetition. There follows a clear eight-crotchet phrase (b), forthwith repeated, though now with a crotchet G as anacrusis. But bars 9 and 10 reveal that the three notes that created a bridge to the repetition of phrase b have an identity of their own (c), for in each of these bars they assert their autonomy, each time followed by an echo of their last two notes (d).[8] Yet the second echo itself turns out to be ambiguous, for it is also the beginning of a repetition of a from Ex.13.1a, which had opened the Promenade. Since a is eleven crotchets long, its immediate repetition in bar 12 is bound to begin a crotchet earlier, on the fourth instead of the fifth beat of these six-beat bars. As for this instant repetition, it is truncated by two beats (by removing the internal repetition) to end abruptly on the final beat of bar 13 with *attacca* following—as though Musorgsky has suddenly turned and the gnome has leapt, visually, out at him.

Among the pictures that ensue, only 'Il vecchio castello' (No. 2) is

---

[7] Indeed, the Soviet musicologist A. Shnitke traced a resemblance between the second theme of Promenade 1 and the folksong in the Coronation Scene in *Boris* (see A. S. Ogolovets, ed., *Voprosï muzïkoznaniya: Ezhegodnik. Vïpusk I (1953–1954)* [Questions of musical knowledge: Yearbook, 1, 1953–1954] (Moscow, 1954), 329.

[8] This might be heard differently, i.e., phrase *b* being identified as two crotchets longer, completing on the first beat of bar 8 and thus overlapping with its repetition.

Ex. 13.1a

purely lyrical and only 'Catacombae' (No. 8) purely atmospheric—
though by founding the second part of the latter ('Con mortuis in
lingua morta') on the main theme of his Promenades, Musorgsky
draws himself into the scene as observer. Otherwise it is primarily
through pantomimic means that Hartmann's pictures are evoked.
What makes the unpredictable 'Gnomus' (No. 1) so unnerving is the
sudden alternations of its three savagely differing musics—violently
convulsive, forcefully leaping and stumbling, menacingly creeping—
each marked out from the others as much by stark contrasts of texture as of melodic character. Grotesques of this sort have had a significant history in Russian music ever since Glinka created the dwarf,
Chernomor, in *Ruslan and Lyudmila*, though none is more brilliant
than Musorgsky's 'fantastic, lame figure on crooked little legs' (Stasov). The prominence of the augmented fourth (the *diabolus in musica*
of medieval musical theory) surely cannot be accidental. After this intimidating encounter, 'Il vecchio castello' seems almost too safe. Stasov wrote that Hartmann's picture included a minstrel, and the
melody that runs throughout the piece is presumably his song, a
blend of Italian siciliana with Russian melancholy. The patches of descending chromatic movement in the middle part over a pedal bass
are a distinctive feature frequently found in other Russian composers;
again the source of this idiom was Glinka.

For music composed almost certainly at the instrument by a very
capable performer, the piano writing in *Pictures* can sometimes seem
ungrateful. But 'Tuileries (dispute d'enfants après jeux)' (No. 3) is thoroughly pianistic. Stasov vouched for a group of children playing with
their nurse in Hartmann's 'Tuileries Garden', and Rosa Newmarch suggested that Musorgsky may have conceived the drooping two-note fig-

Ex. 13.1b

ure that opens the piece and runs insistently through the first section as the children calling 'Nyanya!' ('Nanny!') like the child in *The Nursery*. If so, Musorgsky allowed himself to hear these as Russian, not French, children (with, presumably, the following trails of semiquavers mimicking their competing appeals for the nurse's support). It seems plausible. Russ has suggested the children 'adopt an attitude of mock contrition'[9] in the central section. 'Tuileries' is a delicious piece, and a perfect background to 'Bydlo' (No. 4) as Musorgsky originally wrote it. However, in his 1886 edition of *Pictures* Rimsky changed the opening dynamic from *ff* to *p*, replacing the 'right between the eyes' impact Musorgsky had envisaged to Stasov with one that could, through progressive increase in volume, suggest an ox-cart approaching from a distance. But while the Russian word 'telega' ('le télègue' was probably one of Musorgsky's frenchifications) does mean 'cart', and though the title, presumably sanctioned by Stasov for the 1886 edition, was 'Polish Cart', the word 'bydlo' in both Russian and Polish means simply 'cattle'.[10] What Musorgsky's cryptic remark to Stasov concerning 'le télègue' was all about remains a mystery. Emiliya Frid, editor of the facsimile edition of *Pictures*, states that the melody of 'Bydlo' contains 'not so much Polish as Ukrainian features'.

The cute scherzino 'Ballet of the Unhatched Chicks' (No. 5) seems composed against the background of the trio to Chernomor's March in Glinka's *Ruslan*. As with 'Tuileries' in relation to 'Bydlo', it provides a foil to ' "Samuel" Goldenburg und "Schmuÿle" ' (No. 6). Stasov was responsible for the title under which this was published: 'Two Jews: rich and poor'. But Taruskin has claimed that 'the use of quotation marks [in Musorgsky's authentic title] points up the fact that the two *zhidy* have the same first name: one Germanized, the other in the original Yiddish. They are in fact one *zhid*, not two. The portrayal is a brazen insult: no matter how dignified or sophisticated or Europeanized a *zhid*'s

---

[9] Russ, op. cit., 39.

[10] The exhibition catalogue is unhelpful since it refers to no picture of a cart. But since Musorgsky in his letter to Stasov of 24 June proposed the title of 'Sandomirzsko bydlo', meaning 'Sandomir [i.e., Polish] Cattle', Russ has speculated cautiously that, 'given Musorgsky's Russophile tendencies [which would have included no love of Poles], the Sandomir cattle are the Polish people themselves' (Russ, op. cit., 40: see also 42–3). It is an intriguing suggestion.

exterior, on the inside he is a jabbering, pestering little "Schmuÿle".[11] This is implausible. Musorgsky had told Stasov he wished to include the two sketches given him by Hartmann, and though incorporating them into a single piece, the very distinct musical identities he retained for them argues against conflation. Like many of his class, Musorgsky had anti-Semitic tendencies, but there is no reason to imagine that a composer who had so often presented specimens of humanity in its less attractive forms without ever hinting at a moral posture should, in the present instance, be taking a disdainful view of what his piece would seem to be projecting: an impoverished Jew begging from a rich one. In inventing his polyglot title Musorgsky seems merely to have been clarifying the very different socio-cultural statuses of his personae.

' "Samuel" Goldenburg und "Schumÿle" ' is both a dual portrait and a dramatic incident. The characters are presented separately, the one insufferably overbearing, the other abjectly importuning. They confront each other, the former abruptly curtails the latter's supplications: a last cringing appeal, finally a peremptory dismissal. Such would seem to be the scenario of this vivid one-to-one scena. But the business of 'Limoges le marché (La grande nouvelle)' (No. 7) is an energetic crowd scene. Stasov described it as 'old women quarrelling at the fair in Limoges', but Musorgsky's own descriptions pencilled into the manuscript were more specific. 'La grande nouvelle:' reads the first. 'Mr Pimpant Panta-Pantaléon vient de retrouver sa vache "La Fugitive"; Oui, "Maàme", c'était hier.—Non, "Maàme", c'était avant-hier.—Eh bien, oui, "Maàme", la bête rôdait dans le voisinage.—Eh bien, non, "Maàme", la bête ne rôdait pas du tout—etc.' The second is more wide-ranging: 'La grande nouvelle: Mr de Puissangeout vient de retrouver sa vache "La Fugitive". Mais les bonnes dames de Limoges ne sont pas tout à fait d'accord sur cet sujet, parceque Mme de Remboursac s'est appropriée une belle denture en porcelaine, tandis que Mr de Panta-Pantaléon garde toujours son nez gênant—couleur pivouane.' But such a precise scenario was meaningless in what is manifestly a crowd picture of lively but generalized busy-ness albeit, as Musorgsky's semiquaver patter makes clear, with much corporate and increasingly

---

[11] TM, 382.

Ex. 13.2

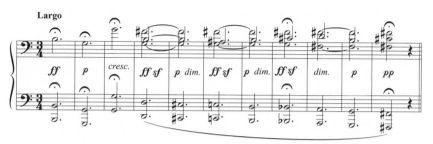

hectic detail, its vividness and vitality heightened by the disrupted phrasing.

The brutal contrast between this turbulence and the stillness of 'Catacombae (Sepulcrum romanum)' (No. 8; Hartmann's drawing is, however, of a Parisian catacomb) is only the first shock of this chilling piece, filled with dynamic contrasts as abrupt as they are extreme, the savage discord of bar 4 finding its bleak resolution only seven long bars later. This opening (Ex. 13.2) could almost be a distant echo of how *Tristan* had begun, Musorgsky now unceremoniously parodying Wagner's yearning for the most exquisite of physical pleasures in order to lay bare an experience of irrational terror that subsides with only painful slowness. The semblance of emerging order suggested by the line of melody that begins to grow in the piece's centre is to be ruthlessly subverted before the final chords, underpinned by an F sharp pedal, prepare for Musorgsky's own appearance.

This first part of 'Catacombae' is the weirdest piece Musorgsky ever created, and in 'Con mortuis in lingua mortua' the tension eases with the stabilizing of harmonic order and movement. Hartmann's sketch had depicted the artist himself and a friend or guide viewing a skull-stacked catacomb by lantern-light, and Musorgsky now imagines himself their companion. 'A Latin text would do well: the creative spirit of the dead Hartmann leads me to the skulls, apostrophizes them; slowly the skulls begin to glow', he wrote in the autograph's margin. Though the intrusion of Musorgsky's own Promenade theme has brought a kind of reassurance into a world in which all had seemed dehumanized, disorientated and unpredictable, a pervasive frisson remains until, *tranquillo*, a measured melodic fragment is heard four times as the harmony progressively eases the piece towards a quiet, if ambivalent, resolution in B major.

Unusually for consecutive pictures in this set, there is no *attacca* after 'Catacombae', and this points up the separate finale character of the remaining two linked pictures. Yet the explosive introduction to 'The Hut on Hen's Legs (Baba-Yaga)' (No. 9) does wrench the music, as much tonally as expressively, away from the static world of burial chambers before the witch's pendulum begins the frantic ticking that determines the pace of her ride. 'Baba-Yaga walked out onto the yard, whistled—before her appeared a broom, and a pestle and mortar. Baba-Yaga perched herself on the mortar and rode out of the yard, propelling herself with the pestle, covering her tracks with the broom.' Russian mythology visualized Baba-Yaga variously. In Lyadov's orchestral scherzo, to which that description from Afanasyev's *Russian Folk Fairy-tales* was epigraph, she seems diminutive, but Musorgsky clearly chose her alternative incarnation as a cadaverous, grotesque old crone of intimidating size and mien. The chromatically descending tremolando of the central Andante mosso returns a chill to the music, but the twice-heard tritone at the opening of this (and the whole-tone basis of the melody's first phrase) signals that it is demonic enchantment and not earth-bound eerieness (as in 'Catacombae') that is now at work. The hectic ending mirrors that of 'Limoges', but the direction is reversed, for from the supernatural we return to the light and security of the real world. Hartmann's sketch for 'The Bogatyr's Gate (in the ancient capital Kiev)' (No. 10) had included a troika at full gallop as well as casual observers, but Musorgsky invented, as human participation, a choir intoning the traditional chant 'As you are baptized in Christ'. Twice heard, this provides both episodes of a simple rondo structure. The opening theme selfconsciously rekindles the heroic grandeur of the famous 'Slavsya' Chorus which had ended Glinka's *A Life for the Tsar*. Between the second episode and the final grandiose return of the main theme, the bells (Hartmann's Gate had housed three) ring out, incorporating a last recollection of the Promenade (Musorgsky's) theme which had opened the whole set.

'The Bogatyr's Gate' is the most imposing piece of *Pictures*. But more than any other, it raises the question of whether this suite can best be represented on the piano, or whether only an orchestra can do it justice. It is a question reinforced by the numerous orchestrations attempted over the century since a certain Michael Touschmaloff scored it in 1886. Russ has traced eleven scorings, of which Ravel's (1922) is by far the most famed. Yet Musorgsky, who had shown such awareness of the eloquence and force of precise and often highly detailed articulation in the accompaniments of some of his songs, was prepared to forego the range of colour available from the orchestra for the incisive clarity and those abundant inflections of which only a piano was capable. His piano writing may often lack polish, but no orchestra can equal (for instance) the piano's ability to reproduce the boisterous clatter of 'Limoges', match the piano's percussive shock when delivering the convulsions of 'Gnomus' or the chords in 'Catacombae', or convey the myriad of tiny inflections within the infant chatter in the 'Tuileries'. Only 'The Bogatyr's Gate' and, perhaps, 'Il vecchio castello' can really gain from orchestration. In entrusting *Pictures* to the two hands (and feet) of the perceptive pianist Musorgsky knew exactly what he was doing.

The poet Arseny Golenishchev-Kutuzov, with whom Musorgsky became close in 1873, was eleven years younger than he. For Musorgsky it was not simply to be a personal relationship; Kutuzov's verses enraptured him, and in early July he was commending him to Stasov in glowing terms:[12]

> After Pushkin and Lermontov I have not encountered what I have in Kutuzov. He is not an affected poet like Nekrasov, nor does he manifest the birth pangs of Mey (I prefer Mey to Nekrasov). Sincerity leaps from almost everything in Kutuzov, almost everywhere you scent the freshness of a fine warm morning, together with a matchless inborn technique . . . And how he is drawn to the people, to history!

A kindred spirit certainly—but no creative equal, for all Musorgsky's encomium. But this mattered less than the affinity Musorgsky sensed between them. Since Rimsky's marriage he had lived alone, but now

[12] *MLN1,* 149. For fuller biographical information on Kutuzov, and for a spirited defence of his memoirs of Musorgsky, see R. Taruskin, 'Who Speaks for Musorgsky?' *TM,* 3–37.

he had found a new companion, and in due course the two men would at least intermittently share lodgings, an arrangement that would continue until December 1875, when Kutuzov married. His departure struck Musorgsky hard, but the relationship was quickly re-established and lasted until the end of the composer's life, though their creative positions had by then diverged. But before this happened Kutuzov would provide Musorgsky with the verses of his two remaining song cycles, *Sunless* and *Songs and Dances of Death*.

Kutuzov was also the poet of *Forgotten*, composed in May 1874, evidently following on the first song of *Sunless*. His inspiration was a painting by Vasily Vereshchagin, also labelled 'Forgotten', of a Russian soldier left to die on the field of battle. This was exhibited that year until the Tsar ordered it be withdrawn; similarly, Musorgsky's ballad, though engraved for publication, was not released. There is some evidence that the song may have been at first intended as the second item of *Sunless*, but this is implausible; such a grim ballad, with its unsparing description of a hero's solitary corpse picked over by a foraging crow as it lies forgotten on the field of battle while at home his widow rocks her child and assures it of its father's return, was too starkly specific to fit into the shifting, introspective mood-world of the song cycle as we know it.[13] But in quality it would have been worthy, for *Forgotten* is a memorably desolate creation, remarkable not least for its textural economy and brevity, and its ironic juxtaposition of a muffled march with a muted lullaby which briefly seems to echo the Pretender's theme from *Boris*.

But *Sunless* contrasts even more strongly with *Pictures*. This is the more remarkable, considering that work on the two cycles was sandwiched, Musorgsky composing the first four songs between mid-May and mid-June, then occupying himself with *Pictures* and that cycle's preparation for the press until 7 August, after which he returned to *Sunless*, signing the final song 'On the River' on 6 September. Nothing more pointedly demonstrates Musorgsky's versatility—and creative detachment—than that he could shift so readily between the savagely

[13] In fact, it seems that Musorgsky may have at first intended to call the second song of *Sunless* ('You did not know me in the crowd') 'Forgotten', which would have fitted this song well, and that is how the ballad 'Forgotten' was assumed to have been intended for the cycle.

differing demands for vivid, mostly extrovert pictorialism in the piano pieces and intense introversion in the songs.

Before composing 'On the River', Musorgsky had envisaged *Sunless* as the existing five songs in what was to become their published order, but with a sixth, as-yet-unwritten song to open the cycle. However, with 'On the River' finished and placed as the final song, he realized the cycle was complete. The six poems trace a sequence of moods and memories recalled in loneliness. 'Between Four Walls' (No. 1; dated 19 May) sets the scene as the disappointed lover muses alone in the solitude of night. 'You did not know me in the crowd' (No. 2; dated 31 May) recalls a momentary glance exchanged with his past love, an incident ignored by the woman but exciting in the lover sudden memories of former joys and sorrows. That incident had occurred in public, but now again alone after busy turmoil ('The idle, noisy day is ended', No. 3; dated 31 May/1 June) the lover retracks his lost years, and the shade of his long-past love once more rises before him. But in 'Ennui' (No. 4; dated 14 June) the words of love bring only disillusionment; from birth to grave all is tedium—'and God be with you!' 'Elegy' (No. 5; dated 31 August) returns the scene to night—but now come fickle, painful thoughts, a vision of past love, dread of the crowd's mockery and of death's cheerless summons. Daybreak brings no relief. Only 'On the River' (No. 6; dated 6 September) affords escape; the calm, moonlit river offers release beneath its deep waters.

Sunless is the most intimate, least demonstrative of Musorgsky's major works. It is also the least realist, the most lyrical, preoccupied not with his subject's real-world existence but with his inner life; the hero is no rough peasant or urchin type, but a romantic solitary of a familiar genre, enduring the suicidal pains of disappointment in love. It has been called a diary of a Russian man of the seventies. And of all Musorgsky's vocal pieces it is the one in which he concerned himself most with music's own resources to generate and shape the structure. His means of doing this were very much his own, though they often grew from, or were conditioned by, suggestions within the text. There are tonal arch structures, a mirror structure, and rondo-like structures in which the pointed use of theme or key recurrence may amplify or substantiate some element or strand within the text. The cycle also shows him drawn to the song miniature. Russian composers have revealed a particular flair for such songs. Glinka, Borodin, and Cui (for instance) were able to compress the most precise and complete of experiences within morsels that may last barely a minute, sometimes less. Musorgsky, too, had already composed short songs, but none that yielded such dividends from expressive concentration as do the first two of *Sunless*. 'Between Four Walls', one of his most perfect creations, partners the succession of tiny, disconnected fragments from which Kutuzov's poem accumulates with quietly lyrical phrases, between many of which there are close relationships of rhythm, and sometimes contour that increase the sense of confinement, as also does the D pedal which, mostly in the bass but sometimes inside the texture, haunts the entire song, its brief withdrawals rendering each return the more pointed (Ex. 13.3*a*, bars 10–12). Yet equally crucial to the song's effect—and to its structure—is the harmonic course. This always inclines flatwards, and in this regard the first two songs are closely related, for the initial harmonic progression of 'Between Four Walls' is used in reverse to open 'You did not know me' (Ex. 13.3*b*), a tiny encapsulation of the pervasive D major/B flat contrast fundamental to both these songs and which gives them a common colour. In addition, both songs achieve their climactic moments by moving above a pedal D to a chord of A flat, a full tritone removed from their common tonic. But in 'Between Four Walls' this moment (Ex. 13.3*a*, bar 11) strikes yet more strongly, because the D pedal runs through the entire song, its whole structure being spread upon a fitful harmonic journey towards this point of maximum tonal tension and the subsequent return to a last chord of D major. It is a scheme as original as it is effective.

In 'You did not know me' Musorgsky harks back to his earlier style of more pointedly detailed declamation and less consistent accompaniment. It is perhaps a less remarkable song than its predecessor, but it is the dynamic of the feelings exposed here that makes it so effective after the faltering progress of that little masterpiece. Its most arresting moment is at its end, where the opening phrase returns and the bass finally falls, as expected, to D, but now with a chord of B flat a mere crotchet long intruding above and thwarting any resolution. After the earlier abrupt release of feeling, grief has finally silenced the capacity to voice pain.

While the first two songs have been spanned upon an arch whose

Ex. 13.3a

Kom - nat - ka tes - na - ya, ti - kha - ya, mi - la - ya;

[A narrow room, quiet, pleasant;

ten ne - pro - glyad - na - ya, ten bez - ot - vet - na - ya; du - ma glu - bo - ka - ya,

impenetrable shadow, fathomless shadow; a deep thought,

pes - nya u - nï - la - ya; v_byu-shchem-sya serd - tse na - dezh - da za - vet - na - ya,

a melancholy song; in the beating heart a cherished hope,

bï - strïy po - lyot za mgno - ve - nyem mgno - ve - ni - ya; vzor ne - pod - vizh - nïy na

the swift flight of moment upon moment; a motionless gaze upon...]

Ex. 13.3b

[You did not recognise me in the crowd, your glance said nothing. But wonderful and...]

apex was the point of maximum tonal tension, 'The idle, noisy day is ended' anchors itself on a constant return to its tonic mooring, the end of each of its six brief stanzas being targeted on C major, though the intervening passages may voyage far into flat regions. Musically these journeys home foster stability, while material cross-references further tighten the structure: the opening of the song's second half (fourth stanza) distantly echoes its first sounds, while its extension then remembers the piano's crotchet-triplet opening of the third stanza; the recurrence of the magisterially calm F major triad, which had so tellingly set 'Vsyo tikho' ('All's quiet') near the opening, for 'schastya polnoy' ('full of happiness') just before the end can hardly pass unnoticed. All such things are further signs of Musorgsky's concern for musical coherence as well as textual precision. Other writers have observed the similarity between the haunting music that opens the third stanza ('Kak budto vnov') and the beginning of 'Nuages', the first of Debussy's orchestral *Nocturnes*.

After its two predecessors 'The idle, noisy day' may seem a sprawling piece, but it has helped provide solid substance to the cycle's central portion, as well as a more overtly varied experience that will be reinforced in the fifth song, 'Elegy'. Between these comes the more compact, despondent 'Ennui'. The same injunction opens each of Kutuzov's three stanzas: 'Skuchay'—'Be bored/dispirited/lonesome!' (the imperative is untranslatable), each time prompting the same music (Ex. 13.4*a*). Nothing could embody aimlessness and torpidity more instantly than the piano's brief opening phrase, whose tiny burst of quaver energy collapses to an inconclusive discord (★). But though the B♯/C♮ ambivalence of the bass note makes possible a variety of outcomes for each ensuing verse, every new sortie to find a tonal route away from boredom proves to be doomed, and during the third verse ("From the cradle to the grave your journey is predestined: drop by drop you will expend your strength—then you will die—and God be with you!") the music becomes bleaker, a residual disquiet haunting the final cadential benediction (Ex. 13.4c). But then, as though in a final feeble bid, the open-ended discord (★) re-enters unheralded, for an instant the music urges upwards—but in vain, sinking back to find, this time, an unemphatic resolution.

So far explicit pictorialism has had no place in *Sunless*, but in 'Elegy' it finds one in the tintinnabulations from the herds of grazing horses—and, at the dynamic climax of this song (and the cycle), in the cheerless clang of the bell of death. The opening scene-setting provides a measured prologue which will be balanced at the song's end by an epilogue as, with daybreak, awareness of the outside world returns. Between these flanks emotional autobiography resumes with recollections of hopes dashed, with the expected measure of tears and regrets. This Allegro agitato, the most turbulent music of the cycle, is broken by the resurgent image of the beloved rousing old day-dreams and a calmer interlude that provides the centre of the song's mirror structure. But the Andante mosso epilogue does more than simply balance (and partially echo) the opening Andantino mosso, for at its downcast final words (' . . . like my future, mute and impenetrable') the Allegro agitato music is also remembered, though now in slow motion, its passion spent.

The unbroken flow of the final song, 'On the River', brings both stability and, by its end, nemesis. Like the first song of the cycle, all is underpinned with an unbroken pedal (tonic according to Musorgsky's key signature, though sounding far more like a dominant, especially at the inconclusive end). But where the course of the phrases in 'Between Four Walls' had been broken by pauses, here there is a smooth and magisterial flow. Among all Musorgsky's great songs this is the most purely lyrical, with the sumptuous richness of the slowly changing harmony reinforcing the melody's pervasive allure, and unprepared and unresolved seventh chords both colouring and insidiously disorientating

Ex. 13.4a

Andantino comodo assai e poco lamentoso

Sku - chay,—

[Ennui.]

Ex. 13.4b

a tempo
senza espressione

Sku - chay.   S_rozh–

[Ennui.]

Ex. 13.4c

poco rall.

i bog s_to-boy.   i   bog s_to-boy.

[And God be with you.]

the music. Like the first song in the cycle, though more broadly (for this is no miniature), 'On the River' presents something of an arch structure, building mainly by melodic intensification through the increasing prevalence of quavers in the melodic line, which reaches its apogee in the tortuous four-bar piano theme just before the midway break. With this sudden hiatus the melody of the 'unknown voice' enters, luring the lover to escape through death, its insistent recurrences finally banishing all else until it, too, fades into the depths, the final harmony an unresolved dominant seventh.

Sunless is an extraordinary cycle, more remarkable in some ways than *Songs and Dances of Death* still to come. Stasov could give approval only to two or three of its songs and would later describe the whole cycle as 'weak', for its intense subjectivity was a betrayal of that realism which was an absolute in this old dogmatist's aesthetic canon.[14] In fact, in June he had suggested to Musorgsky that he should compose a very different song of a topical and personalized kind—a successor to the lampoon *The Peepshow*, to be called *The Nettle Mountain*. Musorgsky had accepted the idea enthusiastically and entrusted Kutuzov with producing a text to the scheme Stasov had devised. In it the Crab (Herman Laroche, music critic) would convene a meeting of other animals (various of Stasov's and Musorgsky's *bêtes noires*), harangue them on the dreadful state of Russian music, and especially target the Rooster (Musorgsky). Agreeing with the Crab (and undertaking in future to go backwards, like him), all would bellow: 'Anathema to the Rooster!' During August Musorgsky composed a preface to the piece, setting the scene in studiedly sober music (sometimes modifying Kutuzov's words), but then abandoned it because of the demands of other compositions.

Indeed, he seems to have been particularly industrious at this time. Besides work on *Pictures* and *Sunless*, he was (so Stasov reported) occupied not only with *Khovanshchina* but with a new opera, *Sorochintsy Fair*, based on a tale by Gogol. He was still drinking heavily, but this was not affecting his work—so again Stasov asserted. But a blow in his personal life badly unsettled him. On 11 July Nadezhda Opochinina

[14] For an examination of critical reaction to *Sunless* from Stasov and Cui to the late Soviet period, see J. Walker, 'Musorgsky's *Sunless* Cycle in Russian Criticism: Focus of Controversy', *MQ* lxvii, (1981), 382–91.

had died. Nadezhda is a figure as shadowy to us as she was crucial to Musorgsky. Between 1859 and 1867 she had been one of his most favoured dedicatees, receiving five songs and two piano pieces; from September 1868 until June 1871 Musorgsky had lived with her and her brother and after this had continued frequently to dine with them. Eighteen years older than he, she was, by Musorgsky's own confession, at least in part a mother-figure for him, and her death struck him hard:

> When, cast from my native hearth by the death of my beloved mother, and by life's misfortunes of every kind—when broken, angry, exhausted, I timidly, anxiously, like a frightened child, knocked at your saintly soul, sought rescue . . .

There he broke off the text he had prepared for *Epitaph*, and his music for it is also incomplete. It is less a song than a private arioso in three sections. The passionate denunciation of death that constitutes the first (Lento lamentabile) gives way abruptly to a heartbroken eulogy of Nadezhda herself (Con delicatezza). The music of these two sections is some of the most tightly packed with harmonic incident, most astringent, and melodically some of the most tortuous in all Musorgsky's songs; though never sounding Schoenbergian, it has a concentrated intensity that probes towards that dark world of inner communion soon to be explored in the Austrian master's early expressionist masterpiece *Verklärte Nacht*. But there is to be no transcendent consummation here—at least, not in the fragment that Musorgsky left us. Instead, as the words quoted above are reached, the texture thins and the expressive vehemence eases, to pass finally to a clear echo of the music with which Musorgsky had opened the still unfinished *Sunless* and which had also caught so tellingly the desolation of the lover whose beloved is irrevocably lost.

The second half of 1874 was marked by little outer incident in Musorgsky's existence. Work on *Khovanshchina* was proceeding, with Musorgsky at last committing some of the opera to paper. In early July for Stasov he made voice-and-piano arrangements of two lullabies sketched by amateur composers—Alexander Taneyev (a senior civil servant and uncle of the composer Sergey Taneyev) and Nikolay Lodïzhensky (a diplomat who had been for a while within the Balakirev circle). Taneyev's lullaby was intended for publication but never appeared. Productions of *Boris* resumed at the Maryinsky on 21 October, and the preceding rehearsals must have claimed a good deal of time. More than one memoirist that winter recorded Musorgsky's services as accompanist at charity soirées, often organized in support of impecunious students, at which the sometimes likewise indigent Musorgsky played for free. There were also the familiar evenings at the Rimsky-Korsakovs' and Lyudmila Shestakova's; above all, there were regular gatherings at the Stasovs', sometimes in St Petersburg or at Pargolovo and sometimes at Dmitri's dacha at Zamanilovka, during which the latest additions to *Khovanshchina* were aired. The breaks outside Moscow were evidently much relished. Alexandra Molas recalled Musorgsky's visits to Pargolovo. Her view of him is highly sentimental, but there is no reason to doubt its essential truthfulness:[15]

> Musorgsky loved nature passionately. When he came to our dacha at Pargolovo, where Vladimir Stasov also lived, we did everything together as one large company—big outings, some on foot, some in a carriage, and I always on horseback, because I was a great devotee of horseriding. M[odest] P[etrovich] preferred most of all to walk and hunt for mushrooms, which brought back his childhood to him, and he took such naive pleasure in finding a good spot for mushrooms. In particular he loved the sunset, and together we often watched the sun go down. What a wonderfully gentle and poetic soul he possessed! M[odest] P[etrovich] could not bear fish being caught with a rod. 'You should,' he said, 'fish with a net so as not to torture the fish unnecessarily; in general you should always avoid causing pain to any living thing, and not make another suffer either morally or physically.'

But Nikolay Kompaneisky recorded a contrasting side from this period.[16] After performances of *Boris*, when Musorgsky

> was in Elysium, then people, who had nothing in common with him as far as music was concerned, would vie with one another to invite him to their homes, and a flashy set would also gatecrash the guest-night with this fashionable composer. Not noticing at the time how he was demeaning himself, the fashionable composer was carried away by his fame, played and sang to the guests for their diversion, grew tired, expended his nervous energies

[15] *MVS*, 99–100.
[16] *TDM*, 409.

unproductively—and then again had supper with 'poison' [alcohol]—then at 3–4 in the morning was again in the Maly Yaroslavets.

The confident announcement at the beginning of 1875 by the St Petersburg journal *The Musical World* that *Khovanshchina* would be completed by the beginning of the new opera season must have surprised Musorgsky's close associates. Nevertheless, however disturbing the portents in his disordered and disorderly behaviour, Musorgsky was now working systematically on his opera, and the way ahead seemed clear.

CHAPTER 14

Khovanshchina

IT IS SAID THAT IN 1682 THE FUTURE TSAR PETER THE GREAT, on hearing of a challenge to his authority, uttered a single word: 'Khovanshchina!' The word is untranslatable, but in the context in which it was uttered it probably meant: 'The Khovansky plot!' Peter was a mere ten years old, though in physical stature and mental maturity more like sixteen, and a variety of people were struggling for power and control. To become absolute Tsar,[1] he would need to dispose of such challenges. During the years following he did exactly that.

It is this epic struggle and its outcome that is the subject of Musorgsky's *Khovanshchina*.[2] Peter the Great does not appear in it, but he is the giant figure directing events from behind the scenes. The main characters on stage represent three of the elements Peter must crush if he is to drag an almost medieval Russia into the modern age. The first is the old nobility with its entrenched mores and privileges, personified in Prince Ivan Khovansky, commander of the streltsy, (the militia, founded initially by Ivan the Terrible to protect the Kremlin, who became Russia's first professional soldiers). The second is the Old Believ-

---

[1] Peter was initially joint Tsar with his half-brother, the feebleminded Ivan. Ivan would die in 1696, but even before this the power had been increasingly held by Peter.

[2] For a wider summary and some discussion of the historical background to *Khovanshchina*, the opera's relation to historical reality, Musorgsky's purpose in choosing the subject, and the subsequent parts played in the opera's fortunes by Rimsky and Shostakovich, see R. Taruskin, 'The Power of the Black Earth: Notes on *Khovanshchina*', TM, 313–27.

ers, a schismatic group of the Orthodox Church, represented by a congregation led by a dignified and pious monk called Dosifey (a character specially invented for the opera[3]) who sees Peter's proposed reforms as the work of the Antichrist. The third element is the Europeanizing party in Russian society, whose removal is also vital if Peter is to have unconditional control. This is exemplified in Prince Vasily Golitsïn, the lover of the regent, Peter's half-sister Sophia. By the opera's end all have gone. Khovansky has been murdered, Dosifey and the Old Believers have burned themselves alive, and Golitsïn is in exile.

Though Musorgsky was his own librettist in *Khovanshchina*, the initial scenario was Stasov's. Just how far the final plot of the opera related to this is unknown, though radical changes were certainly made along the way, and it is clear from Musorgsky's subsequent correspondence that early on he devised some parts himself, if only to modify or drop them later. When Musorgsky died in 1881 the opera remained incomplete. It consisted of six scenes,[4] of which the first five and the first part of the sixth existed as vocal scores, though beyond this nothing but fragments were extant, and there was no ending. Only two pieces had been scored. After Musorgsky's death Rimsky drastically revised what was complete and constructed the final scene, devising and composing a conclusion. He then orchestrated the whole, and in this form *Khovanshchina* was first produced in 1886, Rimsky's version going on to command the stage for nearly a century. However, in 1958–9 Shostakovich orchestrated Musorgsky's original piano score for a Russian film of the opera, accepting Rimsky's music for the passages Musorgsky did not complete. Since then Rimsky's version has lost favour, and Shos-

---

[3] In the opera Dosifey acquires an historical alias, for in Act 2 he is revealed as having been originally the real-life Prince Mïshetsky.

[4] In the libretto, written out no earlier than 1879, Musorgsky described the opera as in six scenes, but in the final manuscripts of *Khovanshchina*, assembled over a period of some six years, the first two scenes are described as 'acts', the remaining four as 'scenes'. However, in the copy of the Persian dances from the fourth scene, presented to Olga Golenishcheva-Kutuzova in 1876, this scene is described as the 'second scene of the fourth act'. It is possible that a scene in the German settlement in Moscow, projected by Musorgsky but never composed, would have constituted this act's first scene; whatever the case, it indicates that in 1876 Musorgsky envisaged a fourth act consisting of two scenes. In the scenario given here the fourth and fifth scenes are grouped as a single act, as they were by Rimsky in his completion of the opera and by Pavel Lamm in his edition.

takovich's is now becoming standard. A more extended ending including Dosifey as well as the chorus, commissioned by Diaghilev from Stravinsky in 1913 for a Paris production and based on a Russian tune Musorgsky had designated for this, is sometimes substituted in performances of the Shostakovich version.

The scenario of *Khovanshchina* runs as follows (the square brackets at the end indicate the portion left unfinished by Musorgsky and supplied by Rimsky, who established the five-act structure):

Act 1 Dawn breaks over Red Square in Moscow. Kuzka, a drowsy streltsy soldier, is roused by two fellow soldiers who recount the night's brutish activities. As they are leaving, the Scribe enters his booth. A boyar, Shaklovity, enlists his services to write to Peter, denouncing Ivan Khovansky and his son Andrey for plotting to oust the Tsar and replace him by Andrey. Shaklovity leaves, and a crowd, newly arrived in Moscow to seek residence and to pay homage to Ivan Khovansky, enter. They pressure the reluctant Scribe into reading a proclamation by Peter condemning the streltsy for their misdemeanours. All join in a lament for Russia. The streltsy are heard approaching with Ivan Khovansky. He vigorously defends his militia's activities, and they leave with him.

Andrey enters in pursuit of a German girl, Emma. They are observed by Marfa, the former Princess Sitskaya, now an Old Believer but Andrey's one-time mistress, whom he has deserted. She intervenes to rescue Emma, and pulls a dagger when Andrey threatens to kill Emma. Returning with his streltsy, Ivan Khovansky spies the German girl and wants her for himself, but his son defies him, again threatening to kill Emma rather than let his father have her. Dosifey suddenly appears with some of his followers, and restrains Andrey. As Marfa leaves with Emma, Dosifey rebukes the Khovanskys and appeals for allegiance to the true faith. The Khovanskys depart with the streltsy, and Dosifey invokes God's protection. His followers respond.

Act 2 A troubled Golitsïn is in his study reading two letters, one a passionate declaration from his mistress, the regent Sophia, the other from his mother, urging him to remain upright. A Lutheran pastor is admitted to complain of Andrey's behaviour towards Emma, but Golitsïn pleads he cannot intervene in a private Khovansky matter, then deflects a request for permission to build another church in the German settlement. The pastor leaves, and Marfa appears. Gazing into a silver bowl of water, she predicts Golitsïn's future: he will be disgraced and driven into exile, and in suffering and poverty will discover the meaning of truth. On leaving, she hears a panic-stricken Golitsïn order his servant to follow and kill her to prevent her prophecy becoming known.

Ivan Khovansky arrives to complain bitterly that Golitsïn has diminished the boyars' status and privileges. Insults are exchanged and a confrontation ensues. Dosifey enters and steps between them. After some barbed exchanges between the three men, Dosifey turns on Golitsïn and attacks him for his westernizing aims, insisting that Russia's salvation lies in adherence to old traditions and beliefs, and that is what the Russian people want. Khovansky supports him, but Dosifey rounds on him for the abuses committed by his streltsy. He indicates a procession of Old Believers passing outside, and claims that they are the true men of action. This furious war of words is interrupted by Marfa, who rushes in to report an attempt on her life that was thwarted by the arrival of Peter's troops. She accuses Golitsïn. Then Shaklovity bursts in to announce that the Khovanskys have been accused of trying to depose Peter, and that the Tsar has ordered an investigation.

Act 3 Outside the Khovansky house in the streltsy quarter in Moscow. Old Believers pass by, chanting. Marfa sings of her lost love, and prophesies that Andrey will share with her a death in the flames. Susanna, an aged and bigoted Old Believer, berates Marfa for her sinful love. Marfa defends herself, describing the pain of disappointed love as sufficient to earn absolution. Susanna's further denunciation fires the fury of Dosifey, who has emerged from Khovansky's house, and it draws from him an unsparing rebuke. Susanna slinks away. Dosifey comforts Marfa, who repeats her prediction that she and Andrey will die together in the flames. Dosifey leads her out.

Shaklovity, alone, laments the plight of Russia, urging his land not to forget her children, and begging God to send the leader who will deliver her from her misfortunes. Hearing the streltsy approaching, he withdraws. The streltsy intend to carouse, but their womenfolk intend they shall not. To defuse the situation, Kuzka sings a song whose burden is that, in domestic matters, it is better not to listen to gossip. The Scribe rushes in to report that foreign troops, later supported by Peter's, have attacked the streltsy's quarters. The streltsy call upon Ivan Khovansky to tell them the truth, and he appears and warns them that, under Peter, times have changed. They should go home and calmly await their fate. All pray to God for mercy.

Act 4, Scene 1 In the banqueting hall of his estate a morose Ivan Khovansky listens to his peasant women sing at their needlework. Angrily he tells them to give him a more cheerful song. A messenger from Golitsïn warns him he is in danger. Dismissive, Khovansky orders the messenger to be beaten, and his Persian slaves to entertain him. At the energetic climax of their dance Shaklovity arrives abruptly with a message from Sophia that he should attend an emergency meeting of the High Council. At first reluctant, Khovansky is flattered into assent. He calls for his servants to array him and the peasant women to praise him. Their singing is broken off when, as Khovansky is leaving, he is stabbed. Shaklovity stands mockingly over his corpse.

Scene 2 [Some seven years have passed, and Peter has now deposed Sophia as regent.] A crowd of people pour into the square before St Basil's Cathedral in Moscow to watch Golitsïn, in a carriage accompanied by soldiers, passing on his way into exile. With heads bared they follow the procession. Dosifey enters and reflects sombrely on Khovansky's murder and Golitsïn's exile. Marfa brings news that the High Council has ordered the Old Believers to be exterminated. Dosifey tells Marfa the time has come for them to seek a martyr's crown in self-immolation and that she should fortify Andrey to endure the flames. As Dosifey leaves, Andrey rushes in, still seeking Emma. Marfa tells him Emma is now far away, and when he threatens to have Marfa killed she breaks the news of his father's murder. He refuses to believe her and declares he will summon the streltsy. She challenges him to do so. Twice he sounds his horn but, as the cathedral's great bell begins to toll, the streltsy, together with their womenfolk, appear, carrying their own execution blocks. In despair Andrey begs Marfa to save him and she leads him away. The streltsy's women are all for their menfolk being shown no mercy, but trumpeters enter with a herald, followed by Peter's 'poteshny' troops.[5] The herald announces that Peter has pardoned the streltsy. Peter's troops leave to join their leader in the Kremlin.

[5] The 'poteshny' ('toy-soldier') regiment consisted of young men of Peter's own age whom, as boys, he had drilled and trained as soldiers.

Act 5 The Old Believers' retreat in a pine forest on a moonlit night. Dosifey reflects on the past and the crown of glory that soon awaits him. The Old Believers, from offstage, affirm their fidelity to their faith and intent. Marfa begs that her self-sacrifice may attone for Andrey's sin in love. Andrey is heard approaching, still searching for Emma. Marfa attempts to calm him, recalling their former love. As the poteshny trumpet-call is heard from offstage, Dosifey returns and the Old Believers gather. Marfa exhorts a terrified Andrey to accept their fate to die together in the memory of their love, since now there will be no escape from Peter's troops. The offstage trumpets are heard again. Dosifey and the Old Believers pray to God. [Marfa lights their pyre. The Old Believers, together with Andrey, perish as Peter's troops arrive.]

How Musorgsky compiled his libretto for *Khovanshchina* is unknown, though some bits were extracted from historical sources. He did not write it out formally before 1879, when it seems he was simply extracting the words from his completed vocal scores (though omitting passages he may have decided to cut), for the text of the last, incomplete act ends at precisely the point where fully composed music ceases. In contrast to the libretto for *Boris*, that for *Khovanshchina* was set down as prose, though in a letter to Stasov containing a detailed account of the scene between Marfa and Susanna the extracts were laid out as though in verse, this disposition emphasizing that though the language is rarely strictly metred it has a pliability that readily fits it for service in a flow of independent, perhaps balanced, musical phrases. It seems reasonable to believe that words and music were often worked out together, even at times simultaneously.

The subject of *Khovanshchina* had been suggested by Stasov some time in the late spring of 1872 (Peter the Great's bicentenary). The eagerness with which Musorgsky took it up and the zeal with which he delved into the historical background in preparation for tackling this massive assignment have been described in Chapter 12. Exactly when composition started is unknown. As noted earlier, in 1870 Musorgsky had written a divination scene for an abortive opera *Bobïl*, and this was to become Marfa's divination in Act 2 of *Khovanshchina*. But there is no positive sign that anything was added until 1873, and even then

Musorgsky was initially only improvising and memorizing bits.[6] But now action and music seemed to be growing in tandem, his creativity was seething, and his enthusiasm at a peak. 'I am now living in *Khovanshchina* as I lived in *Boris*', he wrote to Polixena Stasova on 4 August 1873. 'The Introduction . . . (dawn over Moscow, matins with cockcrow, the patrol, the taking down of the chains) and the first incursions into the action [up to the Scribe's taking of dictation] are already prepared, but not written down.'[7] He had also planned in some detail much of the opera's final scene, seeking advice from a variety of persons about the Old Believers and the music that might be appropriate to them, and especially reflecting on the relationship of Marfa and Andrei Khovansky, so that he could now claim that 'all this is almost ready though, as happened with *Boris*, it will be written down when the fruit has ripened'.[8]

Even allowing for the incompleteness of what does survive of the final scene, it is clear that much of this earlier planning underwent radical adjustment. In any case, Musorgsky had abruptly shifted his attentions elsewhere, now finding some of his 'fruits' sufficiently ripened to commit to paper, for by 30 August he had finished Marfa's Song in Act 3 and by 17 September could sign the piano score up to Dosifey's entry (indeed, Marfa's Song, based on a folksong communicated to Musorgsky by the actor and writer Ivan Gorbunov, was published by Bessel before the year was out—the only bit of the future *Khovanshchina* to be printed during Musorgsky's lifetime). This significant stretch of a whole act, being now complete, was promptly despatched to Dmitri Stasov so that a trial run could be arranged.

There followed a break of a year before work was resumed. In the meantime *Boris* was produced, and both *Pictures at an Exhibition* and *Sunless* were composed. Then on 4 August 1874, in a letter to the soprano Lyubov Karmalina, Musorgsky suddenly announced that he

---

[6] For Rimsky's recollections of various scenes and incidents not incorporated in *Khovanshchina* but for which Musorgsky prepared (but never wrote down) music, see *RKL*, 110–11 (*Eng. trans.*, 142–3). For Rimsky's account of his own revisions and completion of *Khovanshchina* after Musorgsky's death, see *RKL*, 190–1 (Eng. trans., 259–60).

[7] *MLN1*, 153.

[8] Ibid.

intended to complete a whole comic opera on Gogol's *Sorochintsy Fair* before continuing with *Khovanshchina*. 'This is good as an economy of creative strength', he explained. 'Two heavyweights—*Boris* and *Khovanshchina*—in a row could overburden, and there's something else as well—that is, in comic opera there's the material advantage that the characters and situation are conditioned by a different environment, an historically different way of life, and a national character fresh to me.'[9] But this proved only a fleeting intention; *Sorochintsy Fair* was put on hold for a further year, and by 14 September, a fortnight after finishing *Sunless*, he was back on *Khovanshchina*, at last beginning to write out the Introduction and Act 1.

Though there were the customary unveilings of new bits at the customary gatherings of the customary circles, Musorgsky's progress on this act is only dimly charted, and the demands of his government service taxed him heavily. 'With *Khovanshchina*, the further into the forest, the more brushwood', he observed cryptically to Kutuzov on 10 January 1875.[10] Four days later he dated the end of the exchanges between the Scribe and the Muscovite crowd over the inscriptions. By the end of March he was still stuck on the encounter between Andrey Khovansky, Emma, and Marfa, and it was 11 August before he could sign Act 1.

Straightway he plunged into Act 2. The going was hard and there is little surviving data on progress. It seems perfectly clear that the act, as we have it, is incomplete since the piano score breaks off abruptly,[11] and in August 1876 Musorgsky would tell Stasov that he needed to fill out the historical side of Golitsïn here and that a 'quintet' finale still remained to be written (which it never was), for which he would enlist Rimsky's help ('the technical requirements are tricky: alto, tenor, and three basses', he explained).[12] Nevertheless, in mid-January 1876 he had told both Stasov brothers that all was finished and that he had launched

---

[9] *MLN1*, 180.

[10] *MLN1*, 184.

[11] The final bar heard in any performance is an editorial addition.

[12] *MLN1*, 223. In the end this scene was to remain patently unfinished, though its conclusion corresponded closely to that in an initial scheme set out to Stasov three years earlier, in August 1873.

straight into Act 3,[13] even revealing on 15 January that he hoped to reach its middle that very day (the earlier part, Marfa's Song and the scene with Susanna, was already done). Certainly he had finished the scene between Marfa and Dosifey by 13 February, when he made a presentation copy of Dosifey's final bars for Lyudmila Shestakova.

But then Stasov intervened with characteristic and devastating bluntness. He approved wholeheartedly of Act 1, but Act 2 would not do at all. His letter of 30 May is a catalogue of faults and shortcomings:[14]

> Even your most ardent supporters . . . would begin asking 'Why are *Golitsïn*, *Marfa*, *etc.* in the opera! Throw out the lot of them, and the opera loses nothing—they're purely *inserted* characters, lacking any purpose' . . . As regards music Marfa's witchcraft is excellent but pointless . . . The debate and quarrel between Golitsïn and Khovansky is aimless, it has no subsequent consequences . . . Moreover, Dosifey for a second time 'stops' someone: they'll say perhaps that he's some sort of 'policeman', a lover of order and quiet . . . In Act 3 (the 'streltsy settlement') there are also many things I must object to. There are choruses, there are songs (for both men and women), there is excellent music, but no action or interest. There are also no connections with the rest of the opera . . .

Having set out his criticisms, Stasov proceeded at even greater length to offer his solutions. He completely rethought the scenario to Act 2, and he outlined a new direction for Act 3 beyond the point Musorgsky had reached (vigorously approving, however, of the actual music composed for this). He endorsed what he and Musorgsky had agreed should open Act 4 (that is, Andrey abducting Emma from the German settlement: this idea was later dropped), and drastically rethought what would become Act 4, Scene 1, as we know it, to make it a continuation of the new direction his earlier changes had established. But he fully approved the plan for the final act, though in describing it he revealed that certain things would have been quite different from what seems to be emerging from the fragmentary opening that Musorgsky finally be-

---

[13] The date at the beginning of this act's autograph score, 'Kanun [Eve] 1876', may signify New Year's Eve which, according to the Gregorian calendar, would have been 12 January 1876.

[14] Quoted in *MLN1*, 343–4.

queathed us (Emma, for instance, would have appeared, and Andrey would have attempted to rouse the Old Believers to repel Peter's troops).

Stasov insisted that his proposals were merely suggestions, not prescriptions. They would certainly have produced a more organic scenario, but also a more conventional one. Though most of his criticisms at this stage were of the scenario, the music for much of Act 2 was already written and would now need dismantling, for all Stasov's lavish praise of it.

Writing this letter was perhaps the greatest disservice Stasov ever did Musorgsky. It was some four weeks before Musorgsky replied. But on 27 June, prompted by a second letter from Stasov, he responded as emolliently as he could. Clearly he was still very badly shaken, as his embroidered, sometimes cryptic flow of words characteristically confirms:[15]

My dear généralissime, for the first time you have been pleased to frighten Musoryanin, and been pleased to achieve this by appearing to have become angry. Musoryanin has hardly drawn your wrath, but if I have—then believe, my dear, that Musoryanin will with love accept and bear that wrath. For quite some time Musoryanin has been subject to some doubts, misgivings, speculations, and all those *tutti quanti* of provincial leisure. Musoryanin is working—he needs peace *only for work*. *Khovanshchina* is too large-scale, too unusual a task. You, généralissime, I am sure did not suppose that your observations and proposals would have been received by me other than in a musoryaninish way. *I have halted work—I have become thoughtful*, and now, and yesterday, and *for weeks*, and tomorrow, all is thought—my one thought is to emerge victor, and to speak to people a *new* word of friendship and love—*direct, and with all the breadth of Russian glades*—a true-sounding word of a modest musician, but of a fighter for a true concept of art. And now here's your today's letter;[16] again I have become thoughtful. Your proposal *screams* of something good; the idea must be reflected upon, and already there's a programme regarding Marfa. Incidentally, it's thanks to you that we understood Marfa and are making this Russian woman *pure*. . . . If you're still the same (and for you to change would be a crime) our business

[15] *MLN1*, 219.

[16] This letter has disappeared.

will go forward yet more expeditiously. That's what, after our long separation, I wanted to say to you, my dear You; here's what now is, not what was.

In the end Musorgsky accepted none of Stasov's changes of scenario. But his closest supporter's radical proposals had stopped him in his tracks and precipitated a crisis of confidence. As Musorgsky wrote the same day to Lyudmila Shestakova, who had clearly been wondering what had become of him: 'During this time I have kept myself to myself—it had to be, my very nature ordained it. In my seclusion much thought has been given to *Khovanshchina*, and much has been found that is not as it should be. When we meet I'll explain everything.'[17] The moral support he received from Shestakova at this time proved invaluable. There were encounters and discussions with Stasov, and from mid-August to early October Musorgsky was granted shortened hours or leave which he spent largely at Tsarskoye Selo with Pavel Naumov and the latter's former sister-in-law Mariya Fedorova (*née* Kostryurina), now his common-law wife, during which the peacefulness of the surroundings gave him ideal conditions in which to reflect upon the problems of *Khovanshchina*. Though in mid-August he added a brief and marginal interlude for a Lutheran pastor with Golitsïn at the beginning of Act 2 (an interlude he later dropped, to judge from its omission from his written-out libretto) and did some other work on Act 2, even claiming to Shestakova on 12 September that 'today I shall finish composing the [second] act'[18] and, ten days later, that he had 'successfully cooked up'[19] the streltsy scene in Act 3, virtually all records of actual progress on *Khovanshchina* subsequently vanish from his correspondence until 1880; in August 1878 Shestakova would inform Stasov that Musorgsky had composed a scene for Marfa and Andrey (their final scene before the self-immolation), but that is all. Instead, after pondering Stasov's letter, Musorgsky suddenly resurrected *Sorochintsy Fair*, which a year earlier he had told Karmalina he had abandoned all thought of composing; only three days after replying to Stasov he spent all evening entertaining his critic by playing bits prepared for that opera as well as for *Khovanshchina*.

[17] *MLN1*, 220.

[18] *MLN1*, 224.

[19] *MLN1*, 225.

On 29 July 1876 Stasov confirmed Musorgsky's new strategy in a letter to Rimsky: 'He [Musorgsky] is working *not a little* and, what is more, not only on *Khovanshchina* but also on *Sorochintsy Fair*—two operas at once.'[20] Early in 1877 Borodin wrote to Karmalina that Musorgsky was still so engaged.

This shift of attention sealed the fate of *Khovanshchina*, the failure to complete which was the saddest single event in Musorgsky's creative life. Nothing is more frustrating than the mists which surround the remaining stages of the opera's composition. Although a substantial portion of Act 3 was composed at the beginning of 1876, the only other date recorded is at the end of the autograph score: 10 June 1880. The sole date on Act 4, Scene 1 is also at the end—17 August 1880—though an incomplete piano score of the Persian dances is dated four years earlier; 16 April 1876. Since the folksongs used at the opening were taken from Yury Melgunov's collection printed in 1879, it would seem that this scene (except for the dances) was composed at this later stage. Act 4, Scene 2 lacks any date (a piano-score fragment from Marfa's part is marked 7/8 July 1879). A separate title-page to Act 5 bears the date 14 April 1880. On 17 August 1880 Musorgsky reported to Stasov that only a tiny portion of the self-immolation scene remained to be done, but if this was ever written down, it has disappeared. The opera's libretto, written out no earlier than 1879, omits some portions of text, mostly brief, suggesting that Musorgsky had by this time decided to delete these passages. On 9 December 1879, at a concert conducted by Rimsky, Marfa's Song and 'the awakening and exit' of the streltsy from Act 3 as well as the Persian dances from Act 4 were performed, the dances enjoying great success. The first two pieces had been orchestrated by Musorgsky himself, the dances by Rimsky.

Boris and *Khovanshchina* share three major features. Each chronicles a tranche of Russian history, over each towers the figure of a Tsar, and in each the people appear as commentators on, victims of, as well as to a degree, creators of events, of which the chief casualty is Mother Russia, whose plight is lamented in both operas. But beyond this the two operas are very different. *Boris* had presented a human story, its Tsar a flawed giant, finally destroyed by the canker within. Around him

---

[20] *TDM*, 471.

had circled equally human individuals of all types and qualities, observed with relish in their diverse environments, though some were of only marginal importance to the plot. Only one such character, the Pretender, had really been more than just himself, for he had carried the power, through directing a train of events to their fateful outcome, not simply to dislodge a Tsar but to lay waste his very being.

By contrast, the unseen Tsar in *Khovanshchina* is the conditioner and creator of events, not their victim. And because Peter's preoccupation is the politics of control, the main function of the opera's central characters is to represent movements or groups that challenged that control; the events sifted out are primarily such as exemplify or relate to these challenges and their subsequent rout. In consequence the quotient of human individuality in *Khovanshchina* is less than in the earlier opera, and its plot is more narrowly focussed. All unfolds in or near Moscow; three characters—Ivan Khovansky, Golitsïn, and Dosifey—are central, the opera accumulating largely through their acts, relationships and interactions. To this trio is added Shaklovity, in real life a man of peasant stock (though devoted to Sophia) who would become Khovansky's successor as commander of the streltsy and later secretary to the boyar council—even briefly, perhaps, Sophia's lover. But in the opera we hear none of this; instead Shaklovity ('an archswindler, with a degree of affected importance, a certain grandeur to his bloodthirsty nature,' as Musorgsky put it)[21] remains a stealthy and shadowy figure, a sinister activist yet passionate patriot, whose manipulations help engineer the opera's epic consequences.

Beside these, with one exception, the other participants seem diminished and marginalized. Even Andrey Khovansky is of only secondary importance, present primarily to provide love interest. Musorgsky doubtless wanted to avoid the criticisms of sexual imbalance to which *Boris* had been subject, and Andrey's double affair justified two female roles—Emma, the German girl he is currently pursuing, and Marfa, whom he has loved and left. Yet Marfa is not merely an expedient decoration, but both a formidable figure and an active agent in events. Deeply wounded by Andrey's treachery, she clings to her vision of reunion in a *Liebestod*. In her vulnerability, balanced by resolve

[21] *MLN1*, 156.

and selfless idealism, this stalwart disciple of Dosifey emerges as the finest of Musorgsky's female creations, in stature comparable to any of the formidable male quartet who dominate the opera.

As an opera whose course is conditioned more by the momentous events of the time it chronicles than by the individual fates of the movers, agents, or victims of these events, *Khovanshchina* is more an epic than the tragedy *Boris* had been, and this shift is reflected in its thematic practices, which differ markedly from those of the earlier opera. True, certain characters still have their labels, but these are much reduced in number. One serves Shaklovity (we have Musorgsky's own word for this)—a powerful theme (Ex.14.1*a*) that projects not only the unceremonious mien of this former peasant, disaffected for reasons best known to himself ('cursed from birth, the devil's mediator', as he himself observes cryptically), but also reflecting, by twisting back on itself, the driven singlemindedness of the intriguer. Yet though Shaklovity will reappear three times, his theme never does. In fact, only those associated with Ivan Khovansky and his streltsy recur. The paternity of the latter's (Ex.14.1*c*) is patently to be traced to one of their 'father's' themes (Ex.14.1*b*); the remaining theme (Ex.14.1*d*) is Khovansky's alone. All are rhythmically robust, catching the earthy vigour and rough will of this intimidating representative of a dominant class, and the red-bloodedness of his troops.

Elsewhere, however, there is little that may be tied to a particular person or group; only the very minor Varsonofiev is favoured with a tiny, fidgety morsel that suggests the nervousness of a servant who is accustomed to overbearing treatment at the hands of his master, Golitsïn. Otherwise characters are placed by the kind of music that suggests the social or ideological world that each may represent. The real Golitsïn, the object of Sophia's passion, was a member of the old aristocracy, a highly educated and cultured man who could discourse in Latin, a soldier and experienced politician, and 'perhaps the most civilized man Russia had yet produced',[22] who used his power well until in 1689 he became a casualty of Peter's removal of Sophia as regent and was exiled. But in the opera he is a much diminished figure. If Ivan Khovansky personifies the traditional boyar stereotype (the historical Khovansky has

---

[22] R. K. Massie, *Peter the Great: His Life and World* (London, 1981), 80.

Ex. 14.1a

Andante con moto

Ex. 14.1b

Moderato assai, quasi marziale

f   *cresc.*

Ex. 14.1c

Moderato non troppo lento

sf   *sf*   *sf*

Ex. 14.1d

Moderato assai, non troppo agitato

f

been described as 'a vain, incessantly noisy man whose soaring ambitions were constantly thwarted by his own incompetence'),[23] the Golitsïn of *Khovanshchina* exemplifies little more than the urbanity of the new men driven by a vision of Russia's destiny as part of Europe. The well-mannered theme that introduces Act 2 as he reads his letters seems as related to his cultivated social image as to the man himself: certainly in what follows Sophia's lover seems little more than a manipulator of small moral authority and courage. Not so Marfa. Though on the opposite side of the political divide, she also is of the aristocracy, and the gracious theme that announces her to Golitsïn in Act 2 is conditioned by the culture that had nurtured them both, as is the theme that will precede her song in Act 3. But because Marfa has all the depths Golitsïn

[23] Op. cit., 41.

lacks, Musorgsky can exploit her responses to her bitter experiences in love, as well as the demands made on her courage in her new vocation, to give her music a diversity and expressive range that build a palpable image of this vulnerable yet resolute woman.

But what of the hidden figure dominating events? Here one intriguing thematic relationship does remain. The Prelude to *Khovanshchina*, as perfect an instrumental piece as Musorgsky ever shaped, establishes a process that is one factor in fostering the opera's special character, for the tranquil initial theme (Ex.14.2*a*) opens out into new forms (*b* and *c*) as dawn breaks over the cupolas of Moscow and the bells call the faithful to matins; it exemplifies a process of thematic evolution that is to be observed not infrequently in the opera that follows. Yet in the form it has attained by Ex.14.2*c* it will return just once within the opera itself: at the conclusion of Act 2, when Marfa recounts her rescue from Golitsïn's assassin by the soldiers of Tsar Peter himself. Could it be that this opening music does not merely set the scene, but also represents the colossus who presides over it?

When in January 1873, as he prepared to set about *Khovanshchina*, Musorgsky had presented the score of *The Marriage* to Stasov, he wrote in the accompanying letter: 'I am giving you, irrevocably, myself.' It would be too ingeniously cynical to attribute a double import to the adverb, but ironically, what resulted in *Khovanshchina* could have pointed to a very different significance in this gift; Musorgsky might have been, symbolically and 'irrevocably', throwing out the doctrinaire lumber of that earlier experiment in realism. Time and again in *Kho-*

Ex. 14.2a,b,c

vanshchina the music would seem to proclaim a total negation of those values so implacably paraded in *The Marriage*. For Musorgsky was too much a musician to be long imprisoned in dogma—and, to judge from his enthusiasm for the music of the new opera, Stasov too perceptive a critic not to realize the worth of what was now being created. In January 1877 Musorgsky himself openly described to Stasov the objective behind his new treatment of speech; without reneging on his fundamental principle of creating a melodic line that truthfully carried the content of the words, he aimed at a new synthesis—and his talk is all of *melody*, of melody that was '*true to life*, not classical', he disclosed:[24]

> I'm working on human speech—I've arrived at a melody created by that speech, I have arrived at an embodiment of recitative in melody . . . I should like to call this justified/meaningful melody. And this work gratifies me; suddenly, unexpectedly, ineffably, will be sung something inimical to classical melody (so favoured), and immediately understood by each and everyone. If I achieve this, I shall consider it an artistic gain, and it must be achieved . . . There are already some earnests of this in *Khovanshchina* (Marfa's grief before Dosifey) [see Ex.14.4*b* below].

But it is not just that such music is far removed from the more extreme manifestations of realism; every musical device, even the once unthinkable (*even* italianate cabaletta!) that can have its use, is incorporated. Yet for all the abundance of lyrical melody of every variety in *Khovanshchina*, Musorgsky always retained a special alertness for the words themselves. The opening exchanges of Act 1 between a drowsy Kuzka and his two fellow-streltsy are still conditioned by those principles of mitigated realism from which the Inn Scene in *Boris* had been fashioned. Much is barely harmonized, the music as basic as the chatter it companions; only with the fidgety theme that marks the Scribe's entry does it seem that truly autonomous musical material is beginning to form itself. Shaklovity's abrupt entry, backed by his own theme (see Ex.14.1*a*), unceremoniously kicks the action forward; this has been a splendidly controlled opening, and the subsequent engagement between Scribe and client now sets the plot rolling purposefully. Clearly terrified of his customer, the former, as seems to be his wont in such strained

[24] *MLN*1, 227.

circumstance, briefly inclines to a churchy idiom; later a frenetically repeated agitato figure mirrors his hasty writing, and a plunging theme reflects his terror when he realizes the full import of Shaklovity's letter.[25] The latter's melodic manner in dictation is plain but strong, confirming him as closer to the people than the court. Musorgsky's introduction of the newly arrived crowd, passing offstage as background to the Scribe reading back what he has so far written, is deftly placed. The opera gains dramatic momentum as its participants are progressively revealed— for shortly afterwards a second offstage chorus, this time of massed streltsy, will be briefly heard flaunting their master-related melodic badge (see Ex.14.1c).

All the participants (both single and collective) so far seen, or only heard, have been of one clan: unreconstructed sons of the old Russia. Whatever their social positions, and however divergent their postures in the current political struggle, their musical worlds easily interchange. Shaklovity's parting shot to the Scribe had begun almost as a folksong (he was, after all, of peasant stock), the offstage chorus of new arrivals could have been singing another. Mindful of one purpose that has brought them to Moscow, they now enter to an echo of the streltsy's chorus theme; already they are tuning themselves for their intended, self-interested homage to the streltsy's master, Ivan Khovansky. They debate quietly what the written proclamations may be, then show their native canniness by intermingling their intimidation of the Scribe with a modicum of mock deference, twice mirrored in a gracious folky theme ingratiatingly harmonized—an invention as alluringly beautiful as it is tactically calculated. And if in all this the crowd have been determined manipulators, their mood changes as they learn what has been written. There is no doubting the truthfulness of their ensuing outburst of pain and grief. Absolutely right for the dramatic stage which the opera has now reached, this virtually unaccompanied chorus crystallizes in the simplest, most poignant terms the true tragedy that lies beneath the surface:

> O Mother Russia, there is no peace for you, no way forward, with your breast you have shielded us, but you are the one, O Mother, that is op-

---

[25] As Musorgsky explained to Stasov, Shaklovity, though now literate, dictated his letter for fear Khovansky would recognize his handwriting.

pressed. And what oppresses you is not an evil fiend—evil, alien, unin-
vited—but your very own, bold children . . .

By this stage it has become obvious how different *Khovanshchina* is to
be from *Boris*. The peasants lamenting their plight at the opening of
Boris had done so in terms of their own predicament; the Muscovites
of *Khovanshchina* bewail the plight of Russia herself—and the difference
is reflected in the musical method. At the opening of *Boris*, the present
reality had been embodied as realistically as music's resources would
allow through a collage of personal utterances and exchanges mingled
with more sustained corporate pleadings. With all of this the accompaniment had been totally complicit, both in its imagery and in its
readiness to dislocate, or even dispense with, its natural mechanisms of
musical propulsion (especially orthodox, triad-based harmonic structures that would have imposed their own kind of regular thrust), so
that priority might be given to placing each onstage detail as informally
as possible in a semblance of real time. By contrast, the peasants in
Khovanshchina lament the broader tragedy of Russia itself through the
universal medium of corporate song, formalized in phrases whose momentum a triadic harmonic structure will effortlessly reinforce. Grief
has been ritualized, elevated from the (multi-) personal to the collective,
and made, if not so poignant, the more weighty.

But it is not just in directing its spotlight away from the personal
plights of its players to the corporate issues and predicaments into which
they are caught that *Khovanshchina* contrasts with *Boris*; in dramatic
structure it is also different. In the earlier opera two massive stage pictures had flanked the whole,[26] and in both the chorus had provided a
continuing background against which substantial interventions contributed extra information or added human interest (in the Prologue
Shchelkalov's and Boris's monologues and the pilgrims' choir; in the
Kromy Forest Scene the appearance of the Simpleton and his final
monologue, as well as the lynching of the Jesuits and the Pretender's
appearance). By contrast, Act I of *Khovanshchina* is compiled from eight
distinct if inter-related incidents, with shifting personnel, and various
engagements between individuals and groups. Through these by the

[26] The decision to run the two scenes of the Prologue together at the première confirms
that this is really a single entity.

end of the act a clear view of the issues and tensions that will generate the plot has been compiled. The result is a masterly coherence and sense of purpose. At the same time Musorgsky has been constantly concerned with structural cohesion. Frequently he has introduced sounds of the scene to come into the last stages of its predecessor to mask the hiatus between what are sometimes quite separate events, while (as will be observed) the urge to give individual scenes, or even scenes-within-scenes, a clear musical shape by musical repetitions is sometimes strongly evident.

In all so far Musorgsky has not put a foot wrong. And even as the people have been lamenting, offstage trumpets have forewarned of the grandiose appearance of Ivan Khovansky, heralded by the streltsy with their women and children. A vain and self-confident man, accustomed to ostentatious displays of devotion and unquestioning obedience, he is stung by accusations of treachery, which he proposes to rebut by an exemplary sweep of Moscow with his streltsy. The vigour of his denial is underscored by his thematic singlemindedness and the orchestra show their collective support by merely doubling his line, to which his followers respond matchingly; while his orations rotate round his more laconic emblem (Ex.14.1d), their lightning rejoinders are dutifully underpinned by his other, more active agent (Ex.14.1b), for his followers are merely echoing his sentiments, not voicing their own. Having ordered his troops, and commanded the people to sing his praises, the 'white swan' (as his 'children' call him) leaves. His appearance has been brief, its impact great. The scale of one challenge facing Tsar Peter is manifest.

This taut incident affords a central landmark for the whole act. It is also a point of stylistic division. Emma's thrice-heard outburst (Ex.14.3, bars 1–4) in her ensuing scene with Andrey—and, later, Marfa—stands out the more strongly for being designed like a studiedly Germanic cadential phrase (a twice-heard chromatic tonic-to-dominant descent in the bass, with a central perfect cadence) that points to Emma's racial origin. But, more pervasively, there is a pronounced shift towards lyrical melody and repetitions, often unobtrusive, for dramatic or expressive emphasis and for structural tightness. One series of structural reference points is provided by the numerous recurrences of Emma's 'terror' music, but more significant is the rounding of the first part of this brief scene by the same dozen bars that had opened it. The Coronation Scene

Ex. 14.3

in *Boris* had also been a ternary structure, but that had been determined naturally by the dramatic situation itself. Such preconditioning hardly applies here. Even more integrated is what follows when Marfa intervenes. It is not merely that her opening bars (see Ex.14.4*a*) will also be rerun to conclude this scene: the parts for Emma and Andrey that had been added to the immediate repetition of these bars at the opening are also paraphrased in this concluding restatement. Such an ensemble, in which three individuals each pursue simultaneously an independent line of thought in a texture where only snippets of each text would be audible, was a surrender to an ensemble practice that Musorgsky would once have scorned.

Andrey Khovansky is a very different creature from his father. A wilful brat (of, one suspects, small courage), ready to force himself upon

Ex. 14.4a

[Thus, then, Prince, you have remained faithful to me!]

It is clear, my dear, you have quickly become tired of me.]

Ex. 14.4b

the passion of the heart worn out by suffering;]

Emma, then kill her rather than let another have her, he is a further figure characterized not by a theme but by the prevailing style of his music: strongly contoured, athletic, passionate melody, purposefully driven by its harmony when he is at his most rampant (see Ex.14.3, bars 5–8). This produces some patches of fevered love music in which his obsessiveness in pursuit of his objective led Musorgsky sometimes to build each successive phrase around its predecessor after the fashion exemplified in the opera's prelude (see Ex.14.2).

Emma is little more than the necessary third side of the triangle, the catalyst who creates the state of affairs that gives Marfa her personal mission. The dark-toned melody with which Marfa confronts Andrey (Ex.14.4*a*) is some of the quietest and most instantly character-defining in any opera. It, or similar music, is unique to Marfa. Always in deep flat keys until the opera's final act, chromatically inflected and rich in seventh chords, it can reflect both the pain of her love and the prospect of its consummation in a hallowed death. The genes of this aching music lie in Marfa's Act 2 divination,[27] the first portion of the opera to be written, and especially in the E flat minor passage of her invocation. But its sibling is Ex.14.4*b* from Act 3 where, first to the bigot Susanna, Marfa recalls bitterly the bliss of a love now lost and, later to Dosifey, laments the conflict between love and conscience.[28] Finally, in quiet ecstasy, she will repeat it to Andrey himself just before their self-immolation: 'Your hour of death has come, my dear, I shall embrace you for the last time. Alleluia! Alleluia! . . .'

The concluding stages of Act 1 are dominated by Dosifey. The fraught father—son confrontation over possession of Emma creates a background against which the Old Believer's dignified authority is the more instantly apparent. Even Ivan Khovansky is brought up sharp by the intervention of Dosifey, whose rebuke and call to faith, delivered with imposing dignity and endorsed by its plain, measured, and firmly directed harmony, impresses even the streltsy. But it does more than simply serve the dramatic moment; it brings stability as the act approaches its end, and after Ivan Khovansky has made a lordly but expeditious withdrawal, it is left to the Old Believers to enter the Kremlin, intoning a simple hymn of worldly renunciation against the tolling of the cathedral bell.

As a piece of drama, varied but coherent, well paced, and set to music of wide-ranging but consistent quality, Act 1 of *Khovanschina* is as fine as any Musorgsky composed. Ivan Khovansky's return had restored the act's earlier style after the Emma/Marfa/Andrey Khovansky scene, and the incorporation of an Orthodox church idiom had led us finally into a world even more audibly Russian—at least, to outside ears. All but one of the main characters have been presented in a well-paced succession that has given each time to display the essentials of

[27] Such music for Marfa, composed in the earlier part of 1875, had also been foreshadowed very briefly but even more clearly in 'On the River', the final song of *Sunless* (in the four bars preceding the central fermata), which was composed the previous year.

[28] In a portion of this present scene, evidently cut by Musorgsky, Marfa had sung Ex.14.4*b* when demanding of Andrey whether he had forgotten his oath not to subscribe to the Lutheran creed. It had been created for the scene with Susanna in Act 3, where Musorgsky had described it to Stasov as a 'sensual theme of a clear folk character' (*MLN1*, 167).

his/her personality and dramatic stance. Only Golitsïn remains hidden, and producing him is the urgent business of Act 2, the first sounds of which provide as sharp a stylistic contrast with what has gone before as any in the opera. The orchestral preamble is a conspectus of Golitsïn's opening soliloquy: the refined, spacious opening, with its suave melody and yearning harmony, reflects the amorous pining of his mistress's letter which he is reading aloud; the minor-key octaves portray his resolve not to be trapped within a past love; the return to his mistress's tone of address points the irony with which he will weigh her trustworthiness. This opening scene introduces the remaining factor in the opera's power equation, and the interview with the Lutheran pastor protesting over Emma's abduction was clearly designed to fill out the character of the opera's sole representative of a Europeanized aristocracy. Very different from the real-life model, Musorgsky's *parvenu* Golitsïn was a man who 'knew little of the "high court", and had not been received by the Tsaritsa Natalya [Peter's mother]', as Musorgsky himself put it.[29] He displays both bluster and insecurity, and Musorgsky furnished him with two contrasting themes to reflect these two sides—one a vaunting martial tune (see Ex.14.6a) parading his forceful drives and responses,[30] the other (Ex.14.5) a twisting line much at odds with its harmony, exposing his apprehensions, even his terror.

The latter theme recurs, with ample cause, after Marfa's dire predictions for Golitsïn's future. The divination transfers well from the context for which it had been composed in 1870. Its solemnly expressive melody is strong, sometimes tortuous, and the spacious theme to which the prophecy itself is delivered is one of Musorgsky's noblest, the whole scene reaffirming Marfa's stature and authority, though hardly absolving its composer from the charge of failing to give some account later in the opera of the events that engineered the prophecy's fulfilment.

With the one-to-one encounter of Ivan Khovansky and Golitsïn a scene develops that invites direct comparison with one in *Boris*—the even more tense confrontation of the guilt-ridden Tsar and Shuisky in

---

[29] *MLN1*, 165.

[30] However, in the scene with the pastor Golitsïn softens into an ingratiating cantilena when he suggests, for fear of embroiling the Khovanskys, that his visitor should seek some alternative favour.

Ex. 14.5

[By what is my destiny threatened?]

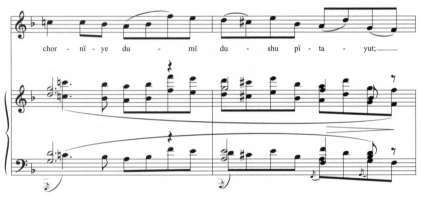

Black thoughts torment my soul;]

the Tsar's Palace Scene. It confirms that the dramatic shift represented by the macro-structure of the first act of *Khovanshchina* may be matched within the micro-structure of an individual scene, though the nature of the shift is different. It is evident in both the stylistic and structural parameters. When he composed the Boris/Shuisky scene, Musorgsky's pursuit of musical realism had been at its most intense in terms of the earlier opera: the vocal lines engaged with the speech rhythms, and the harmony, at its most emancipated, facilitated a stream of often stunning musical imagery, with recurrences of musical materials determined by their significance in the wider drama, not by their function in helping to give musical shape to the scene. Already in *Khovanshchina* the greater store set by fully formed melody has been clearly evident, as has the trend towards balanced and integrated musical forms through cross-references and repetitions: the examples noted in Act 1 by no means exhaust such instances there. So, too, harmonic boldness has been curbed and the employment of vivid, sometimes highly original musical imagery drastically reduced. The result is a different musical world, plainer and less exciting maybe, but, taken on its own terms, no less impressive.

All this emerges as Golitsïn and Khovansky join battle. The campaign's course, set out diagrammatically in Ex.14.6, is worth examining more closely as an instance of how things have changed. At the centre of its 127 bars is Golitsïn's heaviest attack: his studied goading of Khovansky at the weakening of his power-base under Peter's rule. This takes up one quarter of the scene and contains barely an echo of material found elsewhere. But the remainder is filled with repetitions, all exact (including retention of key), except for such minor modifications as are required by differing texts. There are four pieces of such material. Two are for Golitsïn: a vaunting tune (Ex.14.6*a*), and a following emollient theme (Ex.14.6*b*), twice heard as he reins himself in. Two are for Khovansky, the first (Ex.14.6*c*) seeming to relate to his dignity, whether affronted or asserted, the second (Ex.14.6*d*) to his status as boyar. All recur elsewhere in Act 2. Of the 94 bars remaining after account has been taken of Golitsïn's Khovansky-baiting, one third is occupied by chunks of repeated material.

Musorgsky defines firmly each of his combatants, even when they are simultaneously required to project the cut-and-thrust of heated debate. Khovansky, a plain man, expresses himself bluntly, often without aid of harmonic support; Golitsïn never foregoes the dash of refinement insinuated by a fluent, well-mannered harmonic structure or, when he is not rattled, by the civilized cachet of a firm, smoothly contoured phrase. But Khovansky is wily too, astute enough to realize self-control can be imperative, as when, having been taunted almost beyond endurance, his music abruptly borrows an almost Golitsïnian smoothness of line and harmony as he smothers his rage before returning to that ruggedness, bare of harmonic decoration, that is more typical of this formidable warrior.

Uncompromising firmness more than forcefulness marks Dosifey's

Ex. 14.6

Bars

1	10	20	30	40	50	60	70	80	90	100	110	120	128
Khov. (see Ex. 14.1d)	Khov. dig.	DIALOGUE	Khov. dig.	KHOVANSKY GOADING	Gol. vaunt.	Khov. stat.	GOLITSÏN GOADING			Khov. self-control			CLIMAX OF QUARREL
	c		c		a	d				Khov. stat.			
					Gol. emol.	Gol. emol.				d			
					b	b							
						Gol. vaunt.							
				D I A L O G U E		a							

(a) Golitsïn vaunting

[etc.]

(b) Golitsïn emollient

(c) Khovansky's dignity
[in octaves]

(d) Khovansky's status

Ex. 14.7

[Princes! Has not Almighty God sent you counsel and wisdom?]

music. Ex.14.7 epitomizes his vocal style at its most authoritative, as he doggedly seeks to focus the three men's predictably futile discussion on the crucial issue by clamping his own line around a single note, which is underpinned with the special three-chord progression whose reiterations will reinforce his implacable message: that Russia's salvation lies in submission to the will of God and the authority of holy books, after which the people themselves will point the way. But while the stimulus to the preceding Khovansky/Golitsïn confrontation had come not from the argument but from the shifting passions it had aroused, dialectic can cool inspiration. Certainly the discussion that follows Dosifey's appearance was hardly the stuff to fire the imagination, and Musorgsky's treatment is mostly pretty featureless—until, that is, the irreconcilable positions of Dosifey and Golitsïn meet head on, and in fury the former turns on his adversary, fortifying his point with a martial tune which Golitsïn promptly takes up for his riposte and which Dosifey instantly re-uses. Had both singers joined in the final statement, it could have been a cabaletta adapted from an Italian opera.

The opportune passing of an offstage chorus of Old Believers, their two lines, tenor and bass, floating in and out of unison and bringing the result close to a kind of folk heterophony, provides Dosifey with a useful audio-aid to drive home his message: they are doers, not talkers. But an act that had started so well is now about to run out of steam. Marfa's breathless entry and narration is adequately handled and Shaklovity's equally unceremonious appearance gives promise that the dramatic level might be restored. But within a dozen bars Musorgsky had abruptly broken off composition, and anything further he may have composed for this scene remains untraced.

With this brusque curtailment, the unbroken impetus that has marked *Khovanshchina* ceases equally abruptly. Act 3 is really three discrete scenes, the central one a monologue for Shaklovity who then vanishes except for the most momentary of appearances to engineer the end of Act 4, Scene 1, the main function of which was to excuse a dose of dancing; apart from its sudden final twist, it has nothing to do with the action. The concluding three scenes see the departure in turn of the remaining characters: Khovansky in Act 4, Scene 1, Golitsïn in Act 4, Scene 2, and Dosifey, together with Marfa and Andrey Khovansky, in Act 5.

In Act 3 epic matters are laid aside for a while, once the Old Believers have again sung their chorus. Marfa's sadly tender song (founded on a folksong whose repetitions are given the familiar Russian changing-background treatment) and the ensuing scene with Susanna were the first parts of *Khovanshchina* to be written out. Musorgsky was mightily pleased with this encounter, in which he had set 'a wholehearted, strong, and loving woman' against 'an aged spinster, who places her whole life's delight in malice, in searching out and pursuing adulterous sin',[31] as he put it to Stasov on 18 September 1873 in a lively commentary on the whole scene, which he had finished only the previous day. Dosifey enters. Having attempted unsuccessfully to reason with Susanna, he denounces her blisteringly. This accomplished, the stern priestly figure, who had been the unbending adversary of the ironhanded Ivan Khovansky and the self-serving Golitsïn, now reveals the depth of his Christian compassion, first in his kindly counsel to Marfa, then in his gently reassuring dismissal that drew from Musorgsky some of the tenderest music in the whole opera.

What follows exposes the very heart of *Khovanshchina*. While the Muscovites' lament in Act 1 had briefly wrenched attention from personal matters to their country's plight, Shaklovity now sets this issue squarely centre-stage in a monologue that contains some of the most

---

[31] *MLN1*, 166. The 1873 manuscript has survived, and shows that Musorgsky later made significant cuts and also transposed Marfa's Song a tone higher, from F to G major (the transposition was made during bar 3 of Susanna's Allegretto mosso); when the song was published by Bessel in 1873 the original key was reinstated.

deeply moving music of the whole opera—and some of the most in-delibly national in character. Absolutely fundamental to Musorgsky's melodic invention in *Khovanshchina* is Russian folksong. Sometimes his own themes might be folksongs; far more often, however, it is some pervasive affinity with the native product that can be detected. The opening phrase of this aria could never have been composed as it was if Musorgsky had not absorbed totally the spirit of melismatic folksong. And not only the spirit; just as so many of these folksongs unfold as constant variations against a melodic protoshape, so each successive new phrase of this aria's first section is some sort of variation on its prede-cessor. Expressively the piece mines that 'heroic' vein first fully revealed by Glinka in the hero's great second-act aria in *Ruslan and Lyudmila*. But while Ruslan had gone from despair to resolve, there is no such passage in this austere boyar's reflections, only a seemingly ineradicable grief. Within the main section of this ternary structure, as on occasions earlier in the opera when a single dramatic or emotional issue has been at stake, the process of thematic evolution from phrase to phrase both drives home and amplifies an all-absorbing point, and the aria's con-cluding line, which twists tortuously upwards through nearly two oc-taves, catches perhaps more than any other single moment the opera's prevailing emotion: agony at Russia's seemingly inescapable fate.

There is nothing of the special crowd realism of *Boris*—or of pivot pitches—in the very contrasting but equally splendid choral scene that follows. Indeed, it is another mark of how radically Musorgsky's ideals and procedures had changed since *Boris* that there is no trace of pivot pitches anywhere in *Khovanshchina*.[32] In fact, the streltsy's revelry and their womenfolk's equally spirited interventions could well be dance movements; even their lively exchanges are framed in neatly balancing phrases that might have come from folksongs. With Kuzka's infectious song this choral scene makes an excellent interlude, to be broken by the Scribe's entry, characteristically fidgety, with ominous news.

But it is the act's end that impresses most. A recontoured version of

---

[32] The G which had run loosely through the first part of Marfa's Act 2 incantation had simply been Musorgsky following the traditional Russian method for signalling the presence of the supernatural: sustain a single pitch to suggest an unbreakable grip and, by confining the harmonic choice to the limited range of chords that contain this pitch, guarantee a measure of tonal disorientation that will mirror the destabilizing effect of magic.

the streltsy theme (its rhythm identifies it) had erupted in the orchestra as the import of the Scribe's news sank in; now, following great cries of woe, this recontoured version itself shapes the opening of the streltsy's so-contrasting appeal to their leader, aggression now gone and only desperate supplication remaining. Khovansky's entry music, set in six flats like Golitsïn's 'exile' music and Shaklovity's aria, and audibly related to both, prefaces the most unaffected and touching of greetings and responses. Tyrant this man may be, brutal on occasion, but there is a deep two-way bond between this father and his children. Of all the major players in *Khovanshchina*, Ivan Khovansky most invites comparison with Boris, though the former's are the rough mores and customs of a tribal chieftain, not the mitigated usages of a Tsar. It is a subdued version of his first theme that accompanies the master's disconsolate recollection of their past exploits; it carries echoes from his manner of address when he had coveted Emma in the first scene, but now all is heavy-hearted and increasingly laced with tiny but lacerating dissonances as the pain bites—for the world has changed, their time has passed, and nothing remains but to return home and await their fate. Now leaderless, the crowd invoke God's protection.

As a moment of muted but grievous solemnity, perfectly judged and realized, this final stage of Act 3 is unsurpassed in any opera. If the date at the end—10 June 1880—records its completion, it provides the clearest proof that even at this late stage Musorgsky could still match anything he had composed in less disordered days. But it was precisely here that Rimsky was to find a fundamental objection; from the moment the Scribe had entered all had centred on one key, E flat minor, and in his butchered version Musorgsky's reviser-cum-improver transposed the final scene into D minor. Elsewhere in Musorgsky's music, however, he found the fault was the contrary: Musorgsky was 'unrestrained and undisciplined in his modulations'.[33] In fact, *Khovanshchina* reaffirms (especially in Act 1) something of the general principle established in *Boris* of a sharp/flat apportionment according to a positive/negative situation in the drama. Moments or passages of cheerful, untroubled feelings or situations drew sharp keys, while cheerless, troubled ones inclined the music flatwards. The Prelude is entirely in sharp keys; significantly, per-

[33] *RKL*, 191.

haps, the passage that will later recur, perhaps with direct associations with Peter, is in F sharp major, the most sharpwards music in the whole opera. Act 1 opens in A major, and though the Scribe prefers A minor, it is when Shaklovity gets down to business that the music lurches flatwards. The offstage Muscovites chorus in G major, and even the offstage streltsy are heard in a neutral A minor. Only as the Scribe prepares to read the dire proclamations does the music move abruptly back into flat keys and remain there until the Muscovites have sung their lament. Addressing his own people Ivan Khovansky, for all his roughness of manner, maintains a sternly benign B minor/F sharp minor tone—but when he prepares to lead his streltsy, his agents of oppressive control, on a sweep of Moscow, he suddenly plunges flatwards. Andrey Khovansky's oscillation between supplication and despair conducts him erratically through a series of keys, but Emma constantly reasserts G minor and Marfa pours out her heartache and bitterness in an insistent D flat. If the tonal indicators become less consistent in what follows, they are firmly restored in the pure white-key music through which the Old Believers invoke God's support in what they will face.

Such significant tonal calibration runs through the opera, but is less consistent. In Act 2, for instance, Khovansky appears to Golitsïn in his familiar B minor/F sharp minor, and the two men maintain a sharp-key self-discipline until Khovansky's control begins to crack; thereafter they quarrel in flats. In Act 3 there is initially a clear sharp/flat distinction between Marfa and the malevolent Susanna; before turning to console Marfa in a clear C major, an enraged Dosifey had sent Susanna packing in A flat minor, the darkest of flat keys. In fact, deep flat keys do have particular significance. Marfa's disappointments in love are voiced above all in D flat, and E flat minor is the key of disaster. In it Dosifey has already predicted the dark days that lie before him and his followers in the struggle for their faith, in it we see Golitsïn's fate being fulfilled (Marfa had predicted that fate yet one flat deeper, in A flat minor); it is the key in which Shaklovity will agonize over Russia's misfortunes, in which the streltsy will learn that their days are numbered, and in which Ivan Khovansky will recognize that his power has gone. And it is the key in which, it would seem, the opera was to end.

Act 4, Scene 1 is little more than a digression. The Persian dances were the first part to be composed (some at least were done by 1876), but the remainder of the scene is much later: the manuscript of the scene is dated 17 August 1880. The arrangements of two folksongs with which Khovansky's women serfs open proceedings (in five sharps) in an attempt to prop up his spirits have great charm,[34] while Khovansky's obsessive reiteration of the theme to which he had bade 'his children' farewell underlines the depression into which he has fallen. He responds contemptuously to the warning from Golitsïn of personal danger, dismissing it with this same music; whatever Khovansky's current problems and preoccupations, it is *that* earlier moment which haunts him. The lengthy oriental-style dances do everything that one may reasonably expect of such purely decorative music, and a beautiful arrangement of a third folksong [35] is sung as Khovansky is arrayed for attendance at the Grand Council. The act's end has brutal abruptness, and Shaklovity's echoing of the women's last words, 'Praise to the White Swan!' carries the same bitter irony as Iago's parallel action over the Moor's prostrate body would have when Verdi came to write Act 3 of *Otello* a few years later.

As just noted, to open Act 4, Scene 2 a mute Golitsïn is conveyed into exile to an extended version of Marfa's foretelling of this outcome, Dosifey then maintaining the dark six-flat aura as he sombrely reflects on the fulfilment of all fate had ordained—on Golitsïn's disgrace, and Khovansky's destruction through his own pride. Significantly Dosifey had shed his six-flat mood when his thoughts had fastened on the fallen boyar, and his tone had lightened; after all, Khovansky had been of his own persuasion in the broader struggle between the old and new, and he was a man whose forthrightness could be respected, however much his pride and harshness were to be deplored. With Marfa's entry Musorgsky does little more than repeat the compassionate music from the scene where Dosifey had calmed and comforted her after Susanna's assault, though now it is less apposite, accompanying as it does an exchange on current events: the ominous moves being taken against

---

[34] The first, curiously, could have provided the suggestion for Khovansky's own first thematic label—except that Musorgsky had composed this before becoming acquainted with the folksong.

[35] Communicated to Musorgsky by Makar Shishko, head of lighting at the Maryinsky Theatre.

the Old Believers by decision of the High Council. Again Dosifey ends with the music of benediction to which he had dismissed Marfa on that earlier occasion. To an exultant phrase she responds, foreglimpsing the crown of glory her passage through the flames will win her.[36] Not seen since Act 1, Andrey clearly indicates, by raging through the kind of music with which he had then pursued Emma, that his objective remains unchanged. It was not unreasonable for Musorgsky to re-use something from Marfa's incantation to depict Andrey's accusation that his former mistress had invoked supernatural means to ruin his life, but fastening his choice on Golitsïn's exile music produced a confusing musical metaphor. Nevertheless, this aside, all works well until the final stages; the appearance of the manacled streltsy with their womenfolk is accompanied by the last resonance from that family of thematic labels that had run through the opera, and the herald's proclamation (in a bright E major) of the streltsy's pardon will do—just. But the swift conclusion, with a blank silence from those who have been spared, sounds perfunctory, and the rerun of the Poteshny March inadequate. The signs of Musorgsky's intermittent haste seem all too evident.

One excellent stretch remains. Though the final act had been one of Musorgsky's earliest preoccupations when scheming *Khovanshchina*, we still have no knowledge of when he committed any of it to paper; but there is no reason to think that the opening, as he had first envisaged it, was not the basis of what actually resulted. 'Prelude to the retreat—woodland sounds on a moonlit night, now growing stronger, now dying away—like breakers; against this background Dosifey will begin his confession: . . . my brain is now in a ferment about this', Musorgsky had written to Stasov on 14 August 1873.[37] The quiet flow of even orchestral quavers with which Act 5 opens confirms convincingly that Musorgsky held to his pictorial intention. Dosifey is a different person when musing to himself. The kind of rhetorical declaration hurled at Khovansky, Golitsïn, or his own followers is displaced by the more flexible, informal delivery of a man whispering his thoughts privately

---

[36] Roland John Wiley has argued the case for a relationship between this phrase of Marfa's and one of Gilda's in Act 3 of Verdi's *Rigoletto*. See R. J. Wiley, 'The Tribulations of Nationalist Composers: a Speculation concerning Borrowed Material in *Khovanshchina*' *MIM*, 163–77.

[37] *MLN1*, 162.

as they arise. It is an impressive monologue, and Dosifey's manner changes instantly he turns in the direction of his followers and signals the beginning of their final, awesome ritual, Musorgsky now stripping his music to its barest bones so that nothing shall distract from its stark solemnity. Only when Dosifey shifts from spiritual exhortation to a brief instruction concerning the conduct of the ritual does he for a moment break his hieratic manner; to the end Musorgsky remains dramatically alive to the needs of detail. Intoning a solemn chorus deriving from the white-key hymn with which they had ended the opera's first act, the Old Believers begin their procession.

Thus breaks off Musorgsky's vocal score of *Khovanshchina*. Some further fragments remain, notably vocal parts from a scene between Andrey and Marfa, and two Old Believers' choruses intersected by an exhortation from Dosifey (the second was founded on a melismatic Old Believers' theme communicated to Musorgsky by his singer-friend Lyubov Karmalina). Otherwise we have had to depend on the inventiveness (or, at least, good intentions) of other composers to fill the gaps and supply an ending. But while we cannot know the details of what would have followed, one thing is clear; like the ending of *Boris*, that of *Khovanshchina* would have been deeply pessimistic, for where, in the earlier opera, a single innocent had predicted the most desolate of futures for a whole nation, the present work's only representatives of virtue (as Taruskin put it, 'the only characters in the drama who have displayed any redeeming humane characteristics whatever')[38] are driven to self-destruction because the present could have no place for them.

---

[38] *TM*, 322.

CHAPTER 15

Songs and Dances of Death: Last Songs

SONG COMPOSITION IS THE ONE THREAD THAT RUNS THROUGH Musorgsky's entire creative life. Though as 1875 opened he was at last systematically working on *Khovanshchina*, he remained prepared to be deflected by other projects, and at the beginning of March he completed a new and substantial song, 'Trepak', which became the third of his four *Songs and Dances of Death*. This cycle was to be Musorgsky's other major collaboration with Kutuzov. It was prompted by Stasov, who proposed at least seven situations where an individual is confronted by death.[1] Whether Musorgsky might have tackled more of these if the claims of *Khovanshchina* had permitted cannot be said. As it was, he composed the opening three songs during the earlier part of 1875. In the first (as published), 'Lullaby' (dated 28 April), Death lulls a dying child from its distraught mother, in the second, 'Serenade' (dated 23 May), he woos a young girl in the guise of a lover, while in the third, 'Trepak' (dated 1 March), he dances with a drunken peasant lost in a blizzard, urging him to rest and seek refuge in sleep. At this stage Musorgsky considered calling the cycle *She* (here signifying '*Death*': the

---

[1] The three unused subjects envisaged by Stasov were: a stern, fanatical monk dying in his cell to the distant tolling of a bell, a political exile returning home but perishing beneath the waves within sight of his homeland, and the death of a young woman while recalling her love and final ball. In July 1876, according to Stasov, Musorgsky made a beginning on setting two of these. Kutuzov provided an even longer list of other candidates for songs, none of which was pursued further.

word in Russian is feminine), but two years later he added a fourth and final song, 'The Field Marshal' (dated 17 June 1877), in which Death appears after battle as a commander ordering his troops (the slain) to parade before him. The first three songs were dedicated to the great trio of survivors from the Glinka era, the first to Anna Vorobyova, who had created Vanya in Glinka's first opera, and the third to her husband Osip Petrov, who had created the leading male roles in both Glinka's operas as well as Varlaam in Musorgsky's own *Boris*; the second was inscribed to Lyudmila Shestakova, Glinka's sister. The final song was allotted to the poet himself, Kutuzov.

Whereas in *Sunless* Musorgsky had found his stimulus in trawling through the tearful inner world of a conventional incompetent in love, and (like Schubert in *Winterreise*) sublimating the plight of personal inadequacy into affecting romantic tragedy, in *Songs and Dances of Death* he ranged through a world of harsh reality to present instances of nameless humanity confronted in pitiful or barbaric circumstances with the ultimate destiny of us all. All four songs are species of drama. The first becomes an explicit duologue, the second and third are largely monologues targeted on a present, though unheard, recipient. But the final song has more of the epic about it, culminating in a triumphal oration. There could be no greater contrast than between the epic grandeur of this concluding tableau and the pathetic intimacy of the opening song. In 'Lullaby', the unobtrusive exploitation of tonal resource is fundamental, both as a quiet agent in the drama and as a stabilizer in a taut duologue whose course is disjointed. The initial drifting line of quavers, which sets the desolate, candle-lit scene of the mother rocking her dying child, may seem unanchored, but the tonal mists clear and F sharp minor becomes clearer. Yet it is A, both as a key[2] and as a pitch, that is crucial to the duologue that follows; in everything that Death utters this pitch is omnipresent, as a pedal underpinning his substantial opening address, which is prefaced by the first bar of the phrase that will become his solitary but irresistible weapon (see Ex.15.1). The mother's contributions—desperate, breathless, and tonally insecure—show Musorgsky at his most maturely realist, each textual detail scrupulously observed.

---

[2] Whether A major is ever *really* established in this song is a matter for debate. There is ambivalence elsewhere also, for B is sometimes sharpened in the F sharp minor contexts.

Ex. 15.1

[he has fallen asleep to my quiet singing. Bayushki, bayu, bayu.]

Death answers with measured and implacable singlemindedness—first a chord of F sharp minor, then a shift towards A, with a further promise of resolution on to an A major triad, each time denied by the intervention of the minor third (C natural) in the last, clipped chord. Four times this is heard, providing structural stanchions as well as a dramatic refrain. But whereas after its first three occurrences a response from the mother had swiftly ensued, there is no such intervention after its fourth, the very brevity of the final sound seeming to draw the ensuing void into the song itself (Ex.15.1). Thus the final sound is silence itself—for the child is no more.

'Lullaby' proved to be Musorgsky's last truly realist song, and its presentation of the drama through naked textual projection makes it the most harrowing of the present four. In the remaining three the emphasis shifts towards lyrical melody—and especially (and rightly) so in 'Serenade', with death now cast as seductive lover, his lilting serenade here, together with the explicit trepak in the following song, constituting the dance element in this cycle. It would be easy, but mistaken, to place 'Serenade' below its companions because of its unassuming melodic manner and repetitiveness, for once the languor of the introduction has set the atmosphere, the concise melodic components of the serenade itself are soon reshuffled to afford a quietly bemusing unpredictability, reinforced by asymmetries and variations in phrase lengths. And if the constant melodic re-emphasis is an integral tactic in luring his young, vulnerable victim, so also is the reassuring tonal stability—

E flat minor (mostly) throughout, except for a central shift to its relative major, G flat, to climax death's most blandishing words. There is a deft touch here too, for after the piano has returned formally to the serenade's opening, the singer has, within three bars, tugged back to this central section in a further bid to ensure his quarry is netted; only then is he confident of possessing her. Something of the harmonic allure of the G flat section resurges in the pedal-supported final stages in which Death consummates his seduction.

If thematic reordering is an element in 'Lullaby', melodic evolution is fundamental to 'Trepak'. The source theme is uncovered in the four-note bass motif in the piano's introduction (Ex.15.2a), which suffices memorably to set the desolate, snow-covered forest scene, for though semiquaver rumbles from this *Dies irae* fragment haunt the bass for a further few bars, it is the theme emerging above, built against contours from the more extensive *Dies irae* melody (x and y in Ex.15.2b), that is to be the foundation of most of what follows; as this theme grows clearer, its progressive conversion into a dance is spiced with pungent harmony. The trepak itself begins (Ex.15.2c), and Death sets about his business. What follows is a series of variations, both of background and theme; even the lulling melody that ushers in the song's final section reflects a contour from the *Dies irae* (z in Ex.15.2d). There were precedents in plenty for the changing background treatment, but few, if any, for the abundant twists and extensions to the main tune that Musorgsky's protean inventiveness presents. Their significance is ambivalent. They may fairly be seen as mimicking the totterings of the drunken peasant; equally they may be heard as reflecting that disorientating instability which is part of Death's weaponry. Thus the repeated first two bars of Ex.15.2c are unbalanced by two six-beat bars, each repeated; on its second statement (bars 5–6) the theme's second bar is expanded to six beats, now answered by the opening bar (transposed), which this time grows (with, perhaps, some brief conditioning from bar 4) into a three-bar phrase that twists back to the second bar of the dance's first phrase. Nor is this three-bar phrase repeated, as had happened with all previous phrases; instead it is balanced by a variant of itself. And (moving beyond the end of Ex.15.2c) the following, third statement of the trepak theme now amplifies the *first* bar to six beats.

There are few songs which, having opted to be so thematically (and

Ex. 15.2a

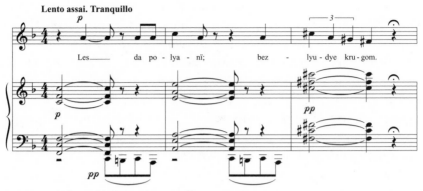

Les—— da po - lya - nǐ; bez - lyu - dye kru - gom.

[A forest and clearings, no person around]

Ex. 15.2b

Ex. 15.2c

Ex. 15.2d

tonally) confined, go on to achieve such flexibility. The dividend is an intensely focussed but never cramped reflection of a psychological process. The tempest in the torrential semiquavers at the song's centre impresses less than the dichotomy of the closing pages, where the sweetness of Death's intermittent lullaby contrasts with the faltering trepak of the doomed peasant. To end, Musorgsky returns to his opening three chords (though without the wisp of the *Dies irae*), but the third chord is now stripped of its sharps. Instead of the tonal wrench which at the opening had warned of something to follow, the last chord now provides the baldest and most conclusive of resolutions.

The fourth song has little of pathos about it, only a monumental irony, for Death is now imaged as commander presiding over a victory review. Forty-one years earlier Glinka had treated the same subject in perhaps the most remarkable of all his songs, *The Midnight Review*. But where Glinka's creation impresses by its sinister bleakness, Musorgsky's strikes through its vivid and intimidating immediacy. Unlike its three predecessors, in which the introduction does little more than set the scene, a good half of 'The Field Marshal' is a narrative, conjuring the clatter of the battle, subsiding abruptly as nightfall brings a silence broken only by the groans of the dying, then signalling (to a muted funeral march) the solemn entry of the mounted figure of Death ('gleaming with the whiteness of bones'), who slowly circles the field (already the piano ghosts the theme of his oration), mounts a hill, surveys the scene, smiles, then begins his address: 'The battle's done! I have conquered all!. . . . ' It has been a narrative as compact as it is powerful, in its range and aptness of detail displaying in miniature a mastery matching that demanded by the equally shifting situations and sentiments in the final Kromy Forest Scene of *Boris*.

The graphic strengths of this section are instantly self-revealing; less so, perhaps, is the admirably pointed variety in the accompaniments to the five statements of the four-phrase Polish hymn 'Z dymen pozarow', which form the musical basis for Death's address. Variety is not confined to the accompaniments, however. Musorgsky varies the tune (the final phrase in statement 2), truncates it (statements 3 and 4 present its first two phrases only), and finally dismantles it (statement 5 uses only phrases 1 and 3, while lengthening each phrase by a single bar) to break out of its four-square symmetry; by this expansion he could absorb three instead of two of Kutuzov's last four lines, thus permitting the final line to be highlighted with its own, new phrase. As for the accompaniments, they confirm how far Musorgsky had travelled in the fourteen years since composing *King Saul*, the song with which 'The Field Marshal' obviously invites comparison. The earlier song has nothing of the textural variety and varied inventiveness of the later one, for, despite the determination of events by repetitions of the Polish tune and an appropriate readiness at times to use a very full-textured piano support, Musorgsky now has the insight to launch Death's oration with the most skeletal of chordal textures (Ex.15.3*a*); the bonus will come later when he fills this out both texturally and rhythmically. But in this whole section such sonorous passages are mingled with others of very contrasting style and texture, marked by finer brush-strokes and, with this, by more refined detail. *King Saul* has nothing that can match Musorgsky's quietly acerbic variant (Ex.15.3*b*) on the harmony of Ex.15.3*a*, with its open texture in which every chromatic point and tiny dissonance will tell.

Musorgsky's musical memory seems to have been remarkable. Back in 1863, after hearing a couple of performances of Serov's new opera *Judith*, he had been able to give Balakirev a highly detailed account of the piece, even writing out extracts; now, having attended the première of Rubinstein's *The Demon* on 25 January 1875, he took himself off to the veteran singer Osip Petrov, and played 'all the high spots from it, caricaturing them' (or so reported Nikolay Kompaneisky).[3] Nor did he find the *Danse macabre* of Saint-Saëns, who was currently visiting Russia to participate in concerts, any more to his taste when he encountered it later in the year ('tiny little ideas in rich orchestral colours'), or have any confidence in what the Frenchman's new opera *Samson et Delila* would turn out to be. 'We don't need only music and words', he would reiterate to Stasov on 5 December. ' . . . Offer living thoughts, conduct living conversation with people, whatever the *subject* you may have chosen to converse with us on.'[4] It was no doubt this communicative

---

[3] *MVS*, 130. In fact, Musorgsky had heard the piece in September 1871, when Rubinstein himself had played it through privately to a group that included members of the Balakirev circle. There is no reason, however, to believe Musorgsky had encountered any part of the opera in the intervening years.

[4] *MLN1*, 207.

Ex. 15.3a

[The battle's done! I have conquered all! You have all abased yourselves before me, warriors!]

Ex. 15.3b

[Year upon year passes unnoticed; the memory of you will likewise vanish from peoples' minds.]

integrity that earlier in the year had led him to a very different verdict on another French composer. 'I saw [Anna] Judic in Offenbach's *Madame l'archiduc*', he had written to Kutuzov on 30 March. 'Within his little world he [Offenbach] is a sympathetic and well-bred artist. I saw no superfluous gestures, I heard no mindless forcing of the voice, observed no indecent twitching or grimaces, . . . the cancan was completely absent. I went to see it a second time with old grandad Petrov, and he approved.'[5] Yet it is Musorgsky's open, if not unqualified accolade for Verdi's radicalism that is the more significant. That Musorgsky

[5] *MLN1*, 187.

had been unable to resist his influence during the 1860s is suggested by the contexts in *Boris* that appear to benefit from Verdian precedents. But now, five days after *Aida* had been heard for the first time in St Petersburg, he set him beside Saint-Saëns. 'How different is maestro-senatore Verdi!' he continued his letter to Stasov. 'See how grandly he *steams ahead*; this innovator has no inhibitions. All his *Aida* = 'aida' [colloquial Russian for 'let's go!']—beyond everything, beyond everyone—and beyond himself. He's flattened *Trovatore*, Mendelssohn, Wagner—and almost Amerigo Vespucci. It's wonderful spectacle . . . ' —though Verdi had failed in projecting the 'teeth-grinding' African temperament. But some other areas of Western music remained totally unacceptable; as Borodin noted to Karmalina in April: 'I have sketched a string quartet—to the horror of Stasov and Modest.'[6]

Information on Musorgsky's more personal existence during 1875 is sparse. March saw further promotion for him in the Forestry Department, but in December he confided mysteriously to Shestakova that he had been the target of some 'miserable little intrigue' and that he had 'been got at'—though he affected to brush the matter aside.[7] There were also troubles in his domestic arrangements: in early June, because he had been thrown out of his lodgings, he asked Shestakova to allow him to leave with her books Nikolsky had lent him. Within days he had begun sharing a furnished flat with Kutuzov, but in early August, when the latter left for one of his periodic extended absences, Musorgsky appeared at five o'clock the next morning at the apartment of his friends Pavel Naumov and Mariya, seeking refuge. Musorgsky later told Stasov this was because Kutuzov had taken their apartment's key with him and he could not get access to it, though to Kutuzov himself he explained his precipitate migration as a consequence of his fear of being left alone. Naumov's niece recalled the incident very differently; the rent had not been paid and Musorgsky had returned home to discover his suitcase on the doorstep.

Yet the worst blow would come from Kutuzov himself at the year's end. Despite a serious attack of bronchitis, Musorgsky's interlude with Naumov and Mariya was thoroughly congenial. There were also the

[6] *TDM*, 431.
[7] *MLN1*, 209.

usual musical gatherings, Musorgsky finding much to approve in Borodin's latest additions to *Prince Igor*, the most recent including the Po-
lovtsian Dances. All of which compensated handsomely for Kutuzov's
delay in returning to St Petersburg. But then, in mid-November, Musorgsky scribbled a hasty, anxious letter to his friend, for the latter had
arrived, evidently by arrangement, at the Naumovs' while Musorgsky
was out, but had then precipitately departed and had now become
incommunicado. Finally the truth emerged, and on 4–5 January 1876
('at night, "Sunless" '—as he pointedly noted on his letter), a distraught
Musorgsky poured out to Kutuzov his bitterness at the betrayal represented by the latter's forthcoming marriage to a fifteen-year-old girl,
Olga Gulevicha. Sentimental Musorgsky's letter may be, but the gen-
uineness of his pain is unmistakeable, even if its meaning is at times
veiled in cryptic terms:[8]

> My friend Arseny, it is quiet in my warm, cosy room at the writing desk—
> only the fire splutters. Sleep, the great miracle-worker for all who have
> tasted earthly sorrow, prevails—powerful, noiseless, loving. In this quiet, in
> the peace of all minds, of all consciences and all wishes—I, worshipping
> you, alone threaten you. My threat is gentle; it is still as is a nightmare-less
> sleep. I would stand before you neither as goblin nor ghost: I would wish
> to be your simple, artless, hapless friend. You have chosen your course—
> go! You disdained everything: the empty allusion, the light-hearted sorrow
> of friendship, confidence in you and in your thoughts—*in your creations* you
> disdained the cry of the heart—you still disdain it! It is not for me to judge:
> I am not an augur, not a prophet. But when at leisure from the cares that
> are in prospect *for you alone*, do not forget
> > 'The narrow room, quiet, peaceful,'
> > > and curse me not,
> > > > my friend

To Stasov a week later Musorgsky was more explicit, confessing he had
been unsparing in what he had said to Kutuzov and that he had refused
to meet his future wife. It cannot be said whether Musorgsky's aversion
to this girl who had so disrupted his personal life had sharpened his

---

[8] *MLN1*, 210. Musorgsky's letter contains a pointed echo of the opening of Kutuzov's own
text for his recent *Sunless* cycle.

awareness of the debt he owed the woman who now daily catered for his needs—but on 2 January (that is, 21 December, old style) he dedicated to Mariya Fedorova a brief song, *The Sphinx*, by way of Christmas present. Nor can it be said whether there is significance in the new song's three-fold ghosting of the opening of 'Ennui', the fourth song of the *Sunless* cycle. But the text Musorgsky himself wrote is a furious rebuff to those who pointed the finger at Mariya in her irregular relationship:

> Quiet and taciturn, her silence frightens you, you savages of the omniverous throng! She is unassuming, ironical, perhaps? Very likely! But what of it? You don't mean she is too proud? And you wretched, sly beings, you dare to rise and hurl accusations! Be silent! I have said: be silent, as she is silent, and heed the hammer blow upon your own fossilized conscience!

The Sphinx is as quietly but effectively pointed a song as any Musorgsky wrote. But if 1876 had started badly for him, matters improved rapidly. Reconciliation with Kutuzov was swiftly effected, for the latter composed a poetic encomium on his friendship with Musorgsky and on the debt he owed the composer, while Stasov, anxious to meet the new wife, stated his intention of inviting the pair to his home where, presumably, Musorgsky would have encountered her. Certainly the past was swiftly set aside—for, having completed the Persian Dances for *Khovanshchina*, on 16 April Musorgsky copied and despatched an extract to 'our shining friend, Countess Olga Andreyevna',[9] on the occasion of her sixteenth birthday.

There was also cheer to be found in performances of his own music. On 28 March *The Destruction of Sennacherib* reached Moscow, and a week later at an FMS concert in St Petersburg Alexandra Molas, accompanied by Musorgsky, sang *The Orphan* to such effect that it was encored. Later in the year, on 1 November, *Boris* would be revived (though with such heavy cuts, including the entire Kromy Forest Scene, that Stasov sent an enraged letter to *New Time*); three further performances followed over the next three months. On 6 May Musorgsky had enthusiastically attended the golden jubilee celebrations of Osip Petrov's debut as a singer. And though three weeks later Stasov's letter proposing draconian

[9] *MLN1*, 216.

revisions to *Khovanshchina* arrived, disrupting Musorgsky's creative momentum and prompting him to make *Sorochintsy Fair* an equal competitor for his creative attentions, his productivity remained impressive at least until early October, when he was forced to settle again in St Petersburg after his two months with Naumov and Mariya in Tsarskoye Selo. But little evidence survives from the ensuing winter of what progress was made on the operas, though on 31 January 1877 Borodin reported to Lyubov Karmalina that Musorgsky was 'working very doggedly' on both.[10] Nor is there any hard evidence why he should suddenly, between 16 March and 2 April, have composed five romances on texts by Alexey Tolstoy.

We may hazard two reasons for his decision. First, his chosen texts. Kutuzov's verses for *Sunless* had traced a personal, introverted narrative of disappointed love; Tolstoy's (with one exception) reflected broadly on the misery of the human condition and the imprisonment of the spirit. Since October Musorgsky had for five months been tied to the treadmill of his civil service duties, and though there is a break in his correspondence during almost the whole first half of 1877, even without such evidence as this might have yielded there can be no doubt that he was in a mood to respond powerfully to Tolstoy's verse. Indeed, *Is spinning man's work?* (dated 1 April) is a precise metaphor of Musorgsky's own predicament: is it right that 'the psaltery-singer should sit in an office, blackening the ceiling with [tobacco] smoke? Give him a horse, a sonorous gusli; to the meadow with him . . . into the darkened garden, where the nightingale sings the whole night through in the bird-cherry tree'. And though one song, *Pride* (dated 27–8 March), is a satirical portrait, the remaining three present dismal views of existence: the first, *Not like thunder* (dated 16–17 March), bewails the insidious power of misfortune, the second, *Softly the spirit flew up to heaven* (dated 21 March), contrasts the misery of earth with the bliss of heaven, and the fifth, *It scatters and breaks* (dated 2 April), enjoins the young man to search out the moment of gaiety before, once again, he lays down his 'ill-starred, hapless head'. Whether the five songs were intended as a set remains unknown, but their single poet and their swift and systematic creation suggest they were, and they make a convincing group

[10] *TDM*, 488.

when sung in their order of composition. Three have dedications: *Not like thunder* is given to Fyodor Vanlyarsky, once a fellow-cadet, who had introduced Musorgsky to Dargomïzhsky some twenty years earlier, *Pride* is inscribed to Anatoly Palchikov, the editor of a collection *Peasant Songs*, and *It scatters and breaks* to Olga Golenishcheva-Kutuzova.

Yet the second reason why Musorgsky may have created these songs is perhaps the more important. Too often this set has been heard as no more than the product of a creativity enfeebled by personal decline. In fact, it seems to represent a new experiment in vocal composition, one for which Tolstoy's texts afforded an ideal basis. The bulk of Musorgsky's mature, post-*Savishna* songs had been in varying ways dramatic, all enabling him to respond to the act or feeling of each moment. But Tolstoy's verses being for the most part broad reflections on mankind's lot—that is, laden with feeling, but depersonalized—the pressure of the moment was removed, leaving the melodic line free to evolve at will and requiring a sharp shift in Musorgsky's song style, though one in line with trends already evident in *Khovanshchina*. Taruskin has suggested that the pointer to this new approach is Musorgsky's disclosure to Stasov only two months before he set about these songs that he had been working on human speech and had 'arrived at a melody created by that speech, . . . at an embodiment of recitative in melody', and that he wished to put this melody to the test in some 'pictures'.[11] Taruskin speculated that among these five songs are Musorgsky's 'pictures', observing how 'Musorgsky sets—or rather transcribes—the poem "as read" . . . The voice has been generalized; the singer/speaker has become anonymous, transparent . . . He is no longer "preventing the phrases of his recitative from being a theme." '[12] As an example, Taruskin points especially to *Softly the spirit*, since Musorgsky here specifically directed the singer to perform his part 'quasi recitando, ma cantando'. But similar features also mark *Not like thunder*, *It scatters and breaks* (though rather less so), and the first half of *Is spinning man's work?* The single most obvious shift is towards a steady crotchet movement and, in consequence (in three of the songs), some variations in bar length conditioned by the syllabic structure of Tolstoy's lines (especially

[11] *MLN*1, 227.
[12] *TM*, 360–1.

in the first half of *Is spinning man's work?*, which has as many changes of time signature as bars). And with the removal of the impulse to italicize a trail of emotional or dramatic 'points' and the resulting increased opportunities for a more consistent melodic flow, there comes a matching shift in the harmonic language. Gone are the abundant rhetorical, at times empirical dissonances and progressions and the often fitful harmonic progress. In their place is a vocabulary almost exclusively of plain triads innocent of dissonance (even seventh chords are a rarity) in a syntax that may be plainly diatonic and firmly directed (as at the opening of *Not like thunder* (No. 1; Ex.15.4*a*)) or unfold a quietly chromatic course (as in the opening of *Softly the spirit flew up to heaven* (No. 2; Ex.15.4*b*)). But *Not like thunder* later uses the chromatic juxtaposition between bars 3 and 4 less gently, exploiting this insistently as an harmonic wrench which, aided by inbalances of phrasing, adds a bracing tension to the song's second half where the opening music returns; this then constantly turns back upon itself, now seeming as inescapable as the misfortune that is Tolstoy's subject. Musorgsky's refashioned style in *Not like thunder* makes for a modestly epic but sober idiom appropriate for this increasingly despondent reflection on pervasive adversity.

Softly the spirit flew up to heaven (No. 2) offers some hope of respite, for here a heavenly being, touched by the plight of those on earth, voices its longing to return thither and bring some comfort. The bright-registered tremolando of the opening (see Ex.15.4*b*) conventionally reflects disembodied numinosity, and the vocal line, by reassembling elements of the previous song's opening (see Ex.15.4*a*), seems to confirm that Musorgsky did hear these songs as a set. This song's structure is noteworthy. The lyric divides neatly in the middle, the first half probing the grounds for the spirit's depression, the second recording her compassionate response in a loose self-contained ternary structure, though it is the song's opening music (Ex.15.4*b*) that here provides the centre. But returning to this opening also brings something of an ABA structure to the whole song, thus creating an overall scheme of two interlinked ternary structures as set out in Fig. 15.1. The result is an unusual and tightly organized design.

Sorrow can yield to reason, so seek the unrevealed gaiety—but sorrow has returned anew, and you can only submit: such is the burden of the last song, *It scatters and breaks* (No. 5). There is here a pronounced

Ex. 15.4a

[Grief did not strike through God's thunder, did not fall like a heavy crag.]

Ex. 15.4b

[Softly the spirit flew up to heaven]

bias towards a more overtly tuneful manner, with change of metre confined to the whole central section, where the fleeting hope of a happier lot (Espressivo) brings also a firm shift to the major and release from the piano's predominantly in-crotchet progress. The opening (Ex.15.5) has an appropriate ambivalence; there is confidence in the firm tread and strong contour of its first two vocal bars, but pulses of pain in the inverted pedal in the two that follow (a phrase which, with its brief echo in the final cadences to the first and third verses, provides the only dissonance in the whole song except for a single seventh chord). But whereas in *Not like thunder* Musorgsky had finally reworked further the opening music to underline misfortune's power, here he is content

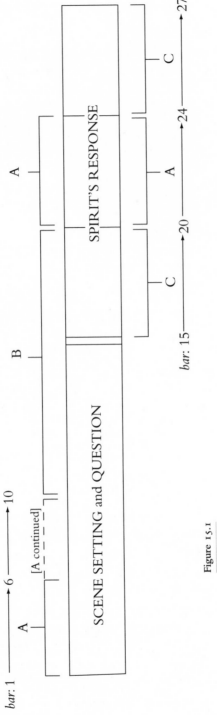

Figure 15.1

to end with a repetition of the whole opening section, charging the singer with establishing the contrast between the confidence underlying its initial delivery (Andante, ma non troppo. Energico) and the despondency explicit in its conclusion (Andante lamentoso).

The central section has provided a well judged contrast in a quietly dignified song that is all the more effective for following on the rippling ending of *Is spinning man's work?* (No. 4). As already noted, even more than in the set's first two songs there is here an abundance of metrical shifts in the first half while the scene is being set. But with the dream of escape celebrated in spread piano chords that dutifully mimic a gusli, these disappear and the song proceeds to an end that seems musically premature but is perhaps intended to underline the brevity of this glimpse of happiness. *Pride* (No. 3) is more noteworthy. For Musorgsky it represented something of a stylistic retreat, for, as in *Pictures*, an image is projected by capturing into music its demeanour and movements. Borodin would also set this text some seven years later, though Mu-

Ex. 15.5

[Melancholy is dispersed, gives way to powerful thoughts,]

sorgsky excised a portion of the text that Borodin would use, perhaps to keep his setting within the scale of its companion songs. Nor could the two composers' subjects be confused; where Borodin's music (Allegro moderato, marciale) catches the flamboyance of a lightly swaggering fop, Musorgsky's (Marziale. Pomposo) suggests the self-importance of a lumbering, more elderly figure.

Nevertheless, for all the care that must have gone into evolving the new style of these songs, they cannot compare with the best of their predecessors. They would have but three successors, and only the last of these is of substantial interest. The first, *The Vision* (dated 18 April 1877), followed hard upon the last Tolstoy song. The verse was Kutuzov's, the dedicatee the poet's sister-in-law, Elizaveta Gulevicha. Ostensibly the verse is a panegyric to the night seen as a maiden—an adoration expressed in extravagant terms such as a lover *in extremis* might have unleashed to win his beloved; Olga Golenishcheva-Kutuzova may have needed very secure trust in her husband and sister not to be uneasy. The song itself is unimportant, stylistically a companion of its immediate predecessors but with little of their substance. *The Wanderer* sets a translation by Pleshcheyev from Friedrich Rückert, and the year of composition remains uncertain, though it is thought to be 1878. Its natural stylistic companion is *Evening Song*, which had been composed in 1871 and dedicated to Sofiya Serbina, possibly as a farewell offering on her departure from St Petersburg. *The Wanderer* could also be such a gift, its final lines pointing to the traveller's predicament: 'Those close to me, dear to my heart, are not with me, and now I would embrace them so closely.' Whatever the case, *The Wanderer* is a slighter piece even than *Evening Song*.

It may seem ironic that only with his very last song did Musorgsky create one that would achieve world-wide popularity, bringing his name to people who otherwise would never have heard of him. His *Autobiographical Note* records that *Mephistopheles' Song of the Flea* was composed during the three-month concert tour of southern Russia that he embarked on with the singer Darya Leonova early in August 1879, and the text was clearly chosen because Musorgsky reckoned he could make from it an audience-rouser, though there is no record of it being performed during the tour. But subsequently Leonova certainly sang it, and later still Fyodor Shalyapin would make it a staple item in his con-cert programmes, thus perpetuating its popularity into the twentieth century—a popularity that has sometimes ill-served its reputation in more recent years as awareness has grown of Musorgsky's full range as a song composer. The ballad, based on Strugovshchikov's translation of the satire with which Mephistopheles entertained the customers in Auerbach's wine cellar in Part 1 of Goethe's *Faust*, is neither Musorg-sky's most characteristic song nor his subtlest, but its music has an aplomb and flair that never falter, and the song is a paragon of a 'pop-ular' piece of true merit—excellently scaled and structured, admirably characterized, cleanly composed as regards both material and texture, and relishing Goethe's satire on royal favouritism to its last siphonap-teric bite. *Mephistofeles' Song of the Flea* is the clearest of evidence that, however disordered Musorgsky's personal life may have become by the second half of 1879, his innate capacity to conceive clearheadedly, in-vent appropriately, and craft a piece impeccably, remained undiminished.

Yet it remains true that not even this satirical ballad, and certainly none of the seven songs that immediately preceded it, could really match what Musorgsky had achieved in the best of those already com-posed, even in some of the earliest—*King Saul*, *Night*, *Kalistratushka*, the Ostrovsky *Cradle Song*, for instance—and certainly not in the most vivid of the 'realist' songs—*Savishna*, *Gathering Mushrooms*, *The Raga-muffin*, *The He-goat*, above all *The Orphan* and *Eremushka's Lullaby*—or in the songs of the three cycles (this list is by no means exhaustive). As a composer of piano music Musorgsky is of minor importance, for all the imaginative brilliance of his single large-scale work, *Pictures at an Exhibition*. As an opera composer he is obviously in a very different league. *Boris* is not merely one of the peaks of nineteenth-century opera but one of the greatest tragic operas ever composed. But *Khovanshchina*, which might have proved the equal of *Boris*, was never finished, and *Sorochintsy Fair* was left in too fragmentary a state to assess properly the scale of his gift for operatic comedy. Even if we discount the disparity between the sheer heft of the operatic oeuvres of Verdi and Wagner and the smaller and often fragmentary bulk of what Musorgsky left us, the gifts of the latter still cannot be incontrovertibly advanced as matching theirs in breadth. But the songs are, surely, a different matter. Their number is impressive, their individual qualities, their variety and their technical competence even more so. Taken together they are sufficient certainly to warrant Musorgsky a place not only among the most original of all songwriters, but among the greatest.

C H A P T E R   1 6

Sorochintsy Fair

FOR MOST OUTSIDERS NIKOLAY GOGOL IS THE MOST RUSSIAN OF
Russian writers. Born in 1809 at Sorochintsy, near Poltava, in
1831–2 he published a collection of eight tales, *Evenings on a Farm near
Dikanka*, which brought him instant fame. Rooted in Ukrainian folk-
lore (and with a leaven from German romance), with language that
could be colourful, teeming with vivid imagery, and brimful with atmosphere, the stories told of communities peopled by simple souls (or
supernaturals) caught up in situations or events that might be comic,
pathetic, touchingly human, fantastic, creepy—but almost all, in their
own ways, fun. True, they owed much to the stock characters of the
Ukrainian puppet theatre, and some literary critics have scoffed at what
they see as no more than juvenile tales of conventional cartoon characters and emotions, set within picturesque cardboard environments.
But that mattered not to a composer endowed with a flair for wide-
ranging, kaleidoscopic colour, for conjuring a wide variety of simple
moods and feelings, and for gentle but precise characterization or caricature that could be exploited in the scenarios that might readily be
devised from some of Gogol's stories, with their element of 'somewhat
youthfully operatic' romance.[1] Tchaikovsky would compose his most
heart-warming opera, *Vakula the Smith on Christmas Eve*. Rimsky would
turn to *May Night* and later, after Tchaikovsky's death, come up with

[1] D. S. Mirsky, *A History of Russian Literature* (London, 1968), 150.

his own version of *Christmas Eve*. And for Musorgsky it would be *Sorochintsy Fair*.

Gogol's tale is structured as thirteen mini-chapters. The peasant Cherevik travels to Sorochintsy (I) for the fair, taking his eighteen-year-old daughter Parasya and his second wife, the shrewish Khivrya, whom a handsome young Ukrainian peasant (or Parubok) called Gritsko infuriates when he hurls a well-aimed handful of mud in retaliation for an ill-tempered verbal exchange. The party settles in the cottage of Tsibulya, a friend of Cherevik. At the fair (II) Parasya is excited by the ribbons and baubles on offer, and instantly develops a mutual attraction with Gritsko. Cherevik overhears (III) talk of the 'Red Jacket' (the devil's uniform, subsequently used synonymously for the devil himself) and of the old barn from which a pig's snout has been seen protruding, but is then distracted on seeing his daughter in Gritsko's embrace; he is mollified on hearing the peasant is the son of an old friend, and he immediately agrees to their marriage. But Khivrya (IV), remembering the mud missile, will have none of it, and Cherevik capitulates helplessly.

Gritsko is musing (V) over his dashed hopes when he is approached by a strange Gypsy who asks whether he would take twenty roubles for his bullocks if the Gypsy will get Parasya for him. A love-sick Gritsko tells him he can have them for fifteen if he delivers on his promise. Meanwhile at Tsibulya's empty cottage (VI) Khivrya is cooking in preparation for entertaining her lover, the priest's son Afanasy Ivanovich. He arrives and eats greedily, and unashamedly sues for more intimate pleasures. Suddenly Cherevik, Tsibulya, and friends are heard returning, a panic-stricken lover is told to hide above the rafters, and Khivrya, very ill-at-ease, greets the crowd. Rumours have been circulating (VII) of supernatural happenings in Sorochintsy. Everyone is very edgy and, on request, Tsibulya tells the story of the Red Jacket—how a devil had been turned out of hell, had settled in the old barn at Sorochintsy and had run up a debt for liquor at the local tavern. Finally he had had to pawn his red jacket to a Jew, promising he would return in a year to redeem it. But the Jew had sold the jacket, and denied all knowledge of it when the devil reappeared. That night pigs' snouts had appeared at every window of the Jew's house; then the pigs had entered and plagued him. By now the jacket had passed through several owners, all suffering misfortune in consequence. Attempts to destroy it had failed; finally it had been cut up, and the devil came back every year to try and find the pieces. As Tsibulya ends his narration, a pig's snout appears at the window. Everyone is petrified (VIII). In terror Tsibulya jumps up, hits the rafters, and the priest's son crashes to the floor. Cherevik runs into the street in terror, pursued by Khivrya. Finally he collapses and she falls on top of him—to the great amusement of a crowd of villagers (IX).

Next morning (X) Cherevik and Khivrya awake in Tsibulya's barn. Khivrya orders her husband to take their mare and sell it. On the way to market he is accosted by the Gypsy. Suddenly he finds himself holding only the bridle; the mare has disappeared—and attached to the bridle is the sleeve of a red jacket. Again terrified he runs off, is pursued by a group of young men (XI), and finds himself accused of stealing the mare. Tsibulya likewise has discovered a piece of red jacket in his pocket, has fled in terror, and has been apprehended by another group of young lads. Both men are tied up. In this sad state they are found (XII) by Gritsko, who has Cherevik freed—on condition he can marry Parasya; he reports that the mare has been found and Cherevik will find buyers for her and his wheat. The Gypsy claims his bullocks from Gritsko.

In Tsibulya's cottage (XIII) Parasya muses on what has happened, admires herself in the mirror, her spirits rise, and she begins to dance. Cherevik enters and joins in, then summons her to her instant wedding—while Khivrya is still at the market. The latter returns enraged at what she finds, but—for once—Cherevik puts his foot down.

The process through which *Sorochintsy Fair* came into existence remains heavily clouded, especially during its earlier stages. It is possible it was the Gogol tale that Alexandra Purgold suggested to Musorgsky as an opera subject in January 1872 but which he rejected as not suiting his current purposes. If that was so, by July 1874, in changed circumstances, he had come to view it very differently. As he explained to Karmalina, he needed to 'draw in the reins' on *Khovanshchina*, and working on a comic opera would afford some creative relief. *Sorochintsy Fair* would fit the bill perfectly, he had decided, though according to Stasov Musorgsky's true motivation was a wish to create a comic role for Osip Petrov. Yet less than a year later, on 2 May 1875, Musorgsky told Karmalina that he 'had given up on the Ukrainian opera. The reason for this renunciation,' he continued[2]

> is the impossibility for a Russian to pretend to be a Ukrainian and, in consequence, the impossibility of mastering a Ukrainian recitative—that is, with all the nuances and peculiarities in the musical contour of Ukrainian speech. I prefer to lie rather less and speak the truth rather more. In an opera of everyday life you must treat recitative even more strictly than in an historical one, for in the former there is no weighty historical happening which will, like a screen, mask any false step or slovenliness. And so masters who have an inadequate command of recitative avoid everyday scenes in historical opera.

Gerald Abraham admirably identified Musorgsky's problem: the libretto would have to be 'a tolerable compromise between standard Russian and a dialect that differs from it considerably more than broad Scots differs from standard English, a dialect moreover that Musorgsky is said to have known only slightly'.[3] Yet though another one-year gap followed before further news emerged of *Sorochintsy*, Musorgsky overcame his reservations about his inadequacy in this regard. Stasov was positively enthusiastic. 'He [Musorgsky] is working *not a little* and, what is more, not only on *Khovanshchina* but also on *Sorochintsy Fair*—two operas at once', he informed Rimsky on 29 July 1876. 'And here, there, and everywhere he has produced such wonderful things as will certainly excite you.'[4] A week later Shestakova disclosed that *Sorochintsy Fair* had acquired 'a girls' chorus' (possibly the one after Parasya's first solo in Act 1). On 31 January 1877 Borodin reported to Karmalina that Musorgsky was working tenaciously on both operas.

Yet what, and how much, had been composed so far remains unknown. And it was not until 31 May 1877 that Musorgsky, while visiting the Petrovs, had at last set down a clear scenario—though the alternative names by which Cherevik is designated (Chumak, Chevrik, Chivrik) seem curious, and raise the possibility that some of the scenario

[2] *MLN1*, 189.

[3] *CAM*, 156.

[4] *TDM*, 471.

Sorochintsy Fair · 313

had been devised earlier and that this was merely the date of its completion. In the opera Tsibulya has become Kum:[5]

Orchestral Prelude
'A Hot Day in the Ukraine'

ACT 1

1 The Fair (chorus).
2 Entrance of the Parubok [that is, Gritsko] with his companions (allusion to Parasya and Khivrya).
3 Chumak and Parasya (individualities—the wheat—beads).
4 Little choral scene of the merchants about the Red Jacket—the fourth scene must issue from this: Kum and Chumak, Parasya and the Parubok.
5 A little later Chevrik intervenes in the affair between Parasya and the Parubok. Scene in recitative of the Parubok's and Chevrik's recognition [of each other] (the tavern). NB. The Gypsy a witness to the scene from the other side.
6 Khivrya's entry—scene with Chivrik (the Parubok witnesses the scene). Khivrya takes her husband off.
7 The Parubok's grief. Appearance of the Gypsy (the agreement about the bullocks apropos Parasya).
8 A little gopak.

NB! Intermezzo.

ACT 2 (Kum's cottage)

1 Cherevik is asleep. Khivrya wakes him (conversation about housekeeping, but mostly about getting her husband out of the house).
2 Khivrya's recitatives—*cooking*—appearance of Afanasy Ivanovich. Duettino.
3 The entry of everyone from the fair. Tale of the Red Jacket. Grande scène comique.

ACT 3

1 Night. The rumpus (a. Praeludium and a tzigane. b. The Gypsy) after the flight from the Red Jacket. Kum and Cherevik collapse helplessly. Shouts about the theft of the horse and bullocks. Arrest of both. Comic conversation of the detainees. The Parubok saves them.

---

[5] *MLN2*, 153–4

2 The Parubok's dumka.

3 It is just light. Parasya goes into the front garden. A dumka. Thought about Khivrya—independence—triumph and hopping around.

4 Cherevik and Parasya—dance.

5 Kum. The Parubok with his laughter—the marriage is arranged. (Talk of Khivrya's greed.)

6 Finale.

Musorgsky also wrote out a separate scenario for the Parubok's dream (adapted from 'Yaromir's Dream' in the *Mlada* music, which was itself remodelled from the orchestral *St John's Night*), which must have been the Intermezzo placed between Acts 1 and 2:[6]

THE PARUBOK'S DREAM

The Parubok sleeps at the foot of a hillock, far, far from the cottage in which he should find himself. *In his dream there appear to him:*

1 Subterranean rumble of non-human voices, uttering non-human words.

2 The subterranean kingdom of darkness comes into its own—it mocks the sleeping Parubok.

3 Foreshadowing of Chernobog's (Satan's) appearance.

4 The Parubok is left by the spirits of darkness. Chernobog's appearance.

5 Glorification of Chernobog, and Black Mass.

6 *The Sabbath.*

7 At the very height of *the Sabbath* a bell stroke from a Christian church. Chernobog vanishes instantly.

8 The devils' sufferings.

9 Voices of the church's clergy.

10 Disappearance of the devils, and the Parubok's waking.

As noted earlier (see p. 210), it is now believed that the manuscript of the 'Parubok's Dream' is also the 'lost' manuscript of 'Yaromir's Dream' from the unperformed *Mlada* music of 1872, with the necessary adjustments now incorporated. There is no real justification for its inclusion in *Sorochintsy Fair*—except that Musorgsky could not resist the chance of using a piece that had had two previous incarnations, neither of which had reached performance. That said, this *St John's Night* music

[6] *MLN2*, 154.

provides a sustained splash of vivid colour which extends very accept-
ably the relatively narrow range of that directly drawn from Musorgsky
by Gogol's tale.

How and if work on *Khovanshchina* and *Sorochintsy Fair* interleaved
during the next three years is virtually unknown; apart from a scene
for Marfa and Andrey, there is no record of anything being added to
the historical opera in this period. But now, in the summer of 1877,
creation of the comic opera seems suddenly to have begun in earnest.
On 27 August Musorgsky wrote to Kutuzov, giving the first clear indication of how work had been and was progressing:[7]

> I, dear friend, have immersed myself sufficiently in *Sorochintsy* so that, if the
> Lord helps me to carry it forward in the present circumstances, then I should
> think it would be possible to decide between us in the season after next
> whether *Sorochintsy Fair* is a good or bad opera. I set at once not about the
> first act which, in its scenic organization, will demand more concentration
> and freedom (I am not yet on leave), but about the second—that is, the
> core of the whole opera. This act (the second), as you'll remember, follows
> immediately upon the Intermezzo (the *Sabbath on the Bare Mountain*—it will
> be called "The Parubok's Dream"). I have already written Khivrya's scene
> with Cherevik, the scene of that same Khivrya with the priest's son [a copy
> of the song Khivrya sings as she awaits her lover's arrival is dated 22 July
> 1877], and have even managed to bring in Kum and Cherevik with the
> guests—all this is written; now I'm setting about the core: the story of the
> Red Jacket. The task is inordinately difficult.

Indeed it was, and Musorgsky left only the opening few bars of this
narration. And what follows in his letter clearly touches on what he
saw as the fundamental challenge of this subject:[8]

> You know, friend, that your modest Modest simply has to track down in
> an author—makes bold to reproduce musically—something which, per-
> haps, eludes the feeling and attention of another, less modest musician. It
> is not my first acquaintance with Gogol (*The Marriage*), and in conse-
> quence his capricious prose now does not scare me so much; but *The
> Marriage* was an exercise within the capabilities of a musician—or, more

[7] *MLN1*, 231.
[8] *MLN1*, 232.

correctly, of a non-musician who wanted to learn and grasp the inflections of human speech in its unmediated, true delivery as reproduced by
the genius of Gogol. *The Marriage* was a trial study for chamber performance; [but] with a large stage it is necessary that the speeches of those
participating (of each according to his distinctive nature, habits and 'dramatic inevitability') should be projected in relief to the audience: it is
necessary to arrange it so that the audience will lightly sense all the artless
peripeteia of urgent human affairs—and that, along with this, these are
artistically interesting. Imagine, my dear friend, that what you read in the
speeches of Gogol's *characters* my *characters* must, from the stage, pass on to
us in musical speech *without violation* of Gogol. There will be many trials,
much feeling of weariness from the thirst to take by storm a stronghold
which frightens, it seems, all musicians; but afterwards, when you have
succeeded in conquering but a tiny lunette of this impregnable stronghold—somehow you will take wing and your soul will rejoice: you see,
you want much, very much, to communicate truth to people—even if
it's only a tiny scrap of that truth you succeed in communicating! And
how great Gogol is! My delight when setting out my musical account of
Pushkin (in *Boris*) is born again in setting out my musical account of Gogol (in *Sorochintsy*).

This is the old, adventurous Musorgsky, his brain boiling with ideas,
with irrepressible urges to venture into the unknown, to seek 'new
shores', and he was now clear about the overall structure:[9]

> I will add further, that in *Sorochintsy* the tale of the Red Jacket is the finale
> of the second act; this means that in a short time, with God's help, one act
> of *Sorochintsy* will be already done—and the whole scenario is ready (this is
> important—and in the highest degree important) with the kindest of help
> from that genius, Anna Vorobyova.

It would have been reasonable to suppose that in this mood progress
would be purposeful, the more so since from 13 September Musorgsky
had been granted six weeks' leave. It is in fact quite possible that the
finale to Act 2 was written but then withdrawn, and again a suspicion
arises that Stasov was largely responsible for this. 'During the summer

[9] *MLN1*, 233.

he [Musorgsky] wrote a lot of *rubbish in Sorochintsy Fair*', Stasov reported to Kutuzov on 9 November, 'but now, after our universal attacks (especially mine), he has decided to throw all this out, and only what is good will be left. But now, during these last weeks, he has composed two superlative gypsy choruses (for it), one of which, for women "with stamping and whistling", is simply a masterpiece.'[10]

However, on 22 November Kutuzov received Musorgsky's own reaction to what had happened. There can be little doubt as to the cause of Musorgsky's depressive ailment:[11]

I have been absolutely exhausted by a nervous fever, for about twenty days I have not closed my eyes, and I have been so gloomy that it would have been a sin to write to you . . . At the first airing of Act 2 of *Sorochintsy* I became convinced of the fundamental lack of understanding of Ukrainian comedy on the part of the musical gurus of the disintegrated kuchka; such a hard frost began to blow from their opinions and demands that 'the heart was frozen', as the Archpriest Avvakum says. All the same, I have stopped, become pensive, and more than once have tested myself. Having rested from this heavy labour regarding myself, I am again picking up *Sorochintsy*. It cannot be that I am entirely wrong in my aims, it cannot be. But it is sad that you have to talk with the musical gurus of the disintegrated kuchka across the *barrier* behind which they remain. Nevertheless, Ukrainians beg me fervently to get *Sorochintsy* staged quickly; I am almost sure that my novelty is much to their liking. However that may be, I haven't been nodding, and already I've prepared some decent materials; and it seems in fact that I should just go on working and writing. If you'd like an example of one of the many pronouncements of the aforementioned musical gurus, here it is: 'The text is the most commonplace, everyday prose, ludicrously trivial, but in the music all these people are very serious, infusing their speeches with a sort of pretentiousness'. Is it not curious? Gogol's humour consists in this—that the most trivial (for us) interests of the Ukrainian carters and country tradesmen embody totally sincere truth. *Sorochintsy* is not slapstick but a genuine comic opera grounded in Russian music and, moreover, chronologically the first. How well these musical gurus understand what constitutes comedy! It wasn't so

[10] *TDM*, 501.
[11] *MLN1*, 234–5.

long ago that they were laughing at *Savishna* and *The Seminarist* until someone explained to the musical gurus that the leaven of both pictures was tragic. Varlaam and Missail (in *Boris*) provoked laughter until they appeared in the 'tramps' scene [the Kromy Forest Scene], then they saw what dangerous wild beasts these apparently funny people were. You, my friend, I am sure see praise in the 'kuchkist' pronouncement I've quoted but, believe me, my friend, it was uttered as a bleak observation on the opera's fundamental shortcomings.

The next and, by now, most critical blow fell the following spring. On 12 March 1878 Osip Petrov, whom Musorgsky had always had in mind for the part of Cherevik, died. The result, Shestakova remembered, was that Musorgsky 'felt himself alone and languishing'.[12] And with Petrov's death, the course of the creation of *Sorochintsy* disappears into a black hole—except that on 9 August Balakirev, who was now reasserting himself in the creative enterprises of others, wrote to Stasov reporting favourably on Musorgsky's new-found deference and willingness to listen, adding that he 'has taken from me his score of *The Witches' Sabbath* to recast and compose anew'.[13] Yet it seems odd that Musorgsky, who a year earlier had mapped out so detailed a new programme to turn this piece into 'The Parubok's Dream', should even have felt the need of, let alone submitted to, Balakirev's prescriptions. As it is, the vocal score is dated nearly a year later, 22 May 1880, presumably the day of its completion (though a letter to Stasov of 3 September suggests that Musorgsky was still not completely done with it even then). A manuscript of 'Parasya's Dumka' (her solo that opens Act 3, Scene 2) is dated 15 July 1879, and some weeks later, after performing bits from the opera during the extended concert tour of southern Russia undertaken with the singer Darya Leonova, Musorgsky received moral encouragement to proceed with the piece; as he wrote to Stasov on 22 September: 'everywhere in the Ukraine *Sorochintsy* has elicited the greatest sympathy; the Ukrainians, man and woman, recognized the character of the music of *Sorochintsy* as thoroughly national, and I am myself convinced of this, having now tested myself in Ukrainian

[12] *TDM*, 509.

[13] A. S. Lyapunova and E. E. Yazovitskaya, eds., *Mily Alekseyevich Balakirev: letopis zhizni i tvorchestva* [Balakirev: Chronicle of his life and works] (Leningrad, 1967), 219.

lands'.[14] Yet there is no evidence that this boost to his creative confidence had any positive consequences for his productivity.

From the beginning of 1880 Musorgsky was jobless, his personal and material conditions were pitiable, and Stasov tried to drum up help. Accordingly, on 15 January he wrote to Balakirev, who suggested a benefit concert. But meanwhile Stasov himself and four others had come up with a more viable plan, proposing between them to fund Musorgsky 100 roubles a month if he would complete *Khovanshchina*. On 28 January Musorgsky gratefully acknowledged this help, but within weeks Stasov discovered that another group was paying the composer 80 roubles a month to finish *Sorochintsy Fair*. By May Rimsky was revealing to Stasov how pressures on Musorgsky to publish excerpts from *Sorochintsy Fair*, coupled with incompetence on the part of the publisher himself, meant that *Khovanshchina* could not possibly be finished until 1881. Stasov was abroad, but on returning to Russia in mid-August, he wrote to Musorgsky, evidently expressing himself forcefully about the latter's double dealing. Musorgsky attempted to be reassuring: 'I'll write to you in detail about *Sorochintsy Fair*, much has been done and Chernobog [the Parubok's dream] is all done'[15]—though, as noted earlier, a fortnight later he was admitting to Stasov only that it 'is coming out well'.[16] It was the last that was heard of the opera's progress.

Unlike Puccini's incomplete *Turandot* or the (formerly) truncated *Lulu* of Alban Berg, both of which could run their course in a finished form until close to their endings, thus allowing some sort of plausible performance, the fragmentary and higgledy-piggledy musical legacy finally bequeathed us by Musorgsky makes *Sorochintsy Fair* unstageable without the intervention of a second composer. A number of performing versions of the opera have been made, the first staged in Moscow in 1913, when dialogue extracted from Gogol's tale linked musical numbers edited and orchestrated by Lyadov and Karatïgin, supplemented by Rimsky's revision of *St John's Night*. But the version of the opera that has now firmly established itself is that of Vissarion Shebalin, based on Pavel Lamm's edition and first performed in Moscow on 12 January

[14] *MLN1*, 254.

[15] *MLN1*, 260.

[16] *MLN1*, 261.

1932. When Musorgsky came to compose his opera he himself significantly modified his own 1877 scenario, and Shebalin made further revisions (notably the replacement of the Parubok's Dumka in Act 3 by the 'Intermezzo' following Act 1 ('The Parubok's Dream', i.e., *St John's Night*); the displaced Dumka now afforded 'The Parubok's Sorrow' towards the end of Act 1). The following summary of the plot is as completed by this distinguished Soviet composer whose contributions, of both words and music, are shown in italics.

Act 1 The crowded, lively market at Sorochintsy: a hot summer's day (by the end of the scene it is evening). Into the colourful bustle come the young Parasya who is excited by the ribbons on sale, and her father, Cherevik, who is more preoccupied with selling his wheat. Everyone is brought up sharp by the entry of the Gypsy, who warns they are holding the fair on unwholesome ground: as night falls pigs' snouts will appear and the Red Jacket will be seen. Cherevik is appalled. But the young peasant Gritsko has already spotted Parasya, and she him, and their mutual interest is aroused. Seeing them embracing, Cherevik intervenes, but on discovering that Gritsko is the son of an old Cossack friend, he immediately agrees to their marriage. They go off to drink to this and the general hubbub resumes; then all disperse as evening closes in.

Cherevik and his friend, Kum, enter tipsily. The former is already apprehensive how his wife, Khivrya, will take the news of her stepdaughter's betrothal. *As they part, Khivrya enters, Cherevik breaks the news to her, and she berates him for agreeing to the wedding. He attempts to defend his choice of bridegroom, but Khivrya will have none of it, and finally leads him out. Having observed the last part of this scene,* Gritsko reflects despondently upon his dashed hopes. *His lament is broken by the entry of the Gypsy, who undertakes to make Cherevik give Parasya to Gritsko if the latter will sell him his bullocks for twenty roubles. Gritsko is so eager that the Gypsy can have them for fifteen. A bargain is struck.*

Act 2 In Kum's cottage. While Cherevik is asleep Khivrya is cooking. She grumbles to herself about her husband, then reflects amorously upon her lover. On waking, Cherevik is unable to remember whether he has sold the mare, but he had told a nice young man that he had wheat and the mare for sale and, on being asked his mare's name, had said it was Khivrya. His wife is furious, and a lengthy exchange ensues, Khivrya enraged, Cherevik plaintive. The former finally appeals to the audience's sympathy for having a husband who never listens to her and gives himself airs, and Cherevik tries to calm her by declaring that 'Cherevik understands his Khivrya better than Khivrya'—then asks—hopefully—for whom she is cooking. She blusters and orders him off to guard the wheat and the mare, and to sleep under the wagon. Despite his fear of the Red Jacket she banishes him.

Alone, Khivrya returns to her cooking, smartens herself up, and rehearses her courtesies for the priest's son. Still hearing Cherevik's voice outside, she watches from the window as he disappears, then waits anxiously for her tardy lover. To cheer herself she sings a folksong. Suddenly someone is heard approaching. Thinking it is Cherevik returning, she prepares to pour a bucket of water over his head, but quickly replaces her weapon when it turns out to be the priests' son, who falls into a bed of nettles. She brings him in and an awkward conversation ensues, including details of what his father has received by way of Lenten offerings. Her lover sets voraciously about Khivrya's food, though his greater interest is in Khivrya herself. But as finally he kisses her Cherevik and Kum are heard knocking at the gate. A terrified lover is told to hide above the ceiling boards. The two men enter with guests, and Kum notices how Khivrya is trembling. Indeed, they are all very nervous, for while they were drinking some old women had frightened them with tales of gruntings and the Red Jacket. But now, after more drink has restored Kum's courage, he claims that, if the devil himself were to appear now, he would hold a gun to his snout—but then his nerve gives way. All join in a rowdy folksong to fortify their courage—until a tin vessel falls from where the priest's son is hiding. Khivrya tries to distract attention from this, but more movement is heard, and panic rises. Cherevik begs mercy from the Red Jacket itself, to everyone's horror. To clarify the situation Cherevik asks Kum to tell the tale of the Red Jacket.

Kum begins: A devil was once driven from hell, *but he found it so boring, he started drinking out of grief. However, an innkeeper in Sorochintsy stopped giving him credit and made him deposit his red jacket with him for a third of its value. The devil told him to guard it well, for in exactly a year he would return to redeem it. But meanwhile the innkeeper sold it to a gentleman. The devil duly returned, and the innkeeper disclaimed all knowledge of the red jacket. So the devil left without it, but that night, as the innkeeper went to bed, he heard a noise, and saw pigs' snouts at every window. The innkeeper fainted, but in a moment the pigs slid in through the windows and revived him. The innkeeper confessed all, and since then the devil each year searches the fair for his jacket. Suddenly through the window a pig's snout appears, everyone is terrified, and in the confusion the priest's son is dislodged from his hideaway.*

Act 3, Scene 1. Evening in a street in Sorochintsy. Cherevik (with a pot on his head) and Kum rush in, pursued by a crowd of young men led by the Gypsy. The two men collapse on each other and the Gypsy tells the others to tie them up, accusing them of stealing a mare. Cherevik protests that the mare belongs to him, and Kum explains that they were running away from the Red Jacket. The Gypsy says he does not believe them and goes off, leaving some of the young men as guards. He returns with Gritsko, whom Cherevik recognizes as the young man who, by downing a whole jugful of drink without turning a hair, had provided the best possible recommendation of himself as a worthy son-in-law. Now Cherevik admits he has wronged Gritsko by breaking his promise. The latter offers to have the two men freed—and tomorrow there will be a wedding! Cherevik agrees. Cherevik learns that if he returns home he will find he has buyers for both his wheat and mare. Alone with Gritsko, the Gypsy claims his bullocks, then leaves.

Alone, an exhausted Gritsko lies down under a tree, falls asleep, and dreams. In a wild mountain place is heard a subterranean choir of devils. Gritsko is now seen to be sleeping at the foot of a mountain, surrounded by witches and devils. Fiery serpents appear on the mountain; Chernobog and attendants rise from the earth, and the worship of Chernobog follows, concluding with a wild dance that is interrupted by sounds of the mattin bell. Clouds envelop the scene: dawn breaks, and the sounds of the hellish crowd fade as a male church chorus is heard from backstage. Gritsko awakes and looks wildly around him; the clouds disperse as the sun rises.

Act 3, Scene 2. The street in front of Kum's cottage. Parasya comes out into the porch, pining for Gritsko. But she is far from truly despondent, and soon breaks into a lively dance. *Suddenly Kum brings in Gritsko, Parasya greets her beloved and the two join in a joyful duet, more young men and girls appearing and joining in. Cherevik enters to report that Khivrya is pleased the mare has been sold, and has gone off to do some shopping—so everything can now be got through before she returns. But his hopes are dashed; Khivrya suddenly arrives, determined to prevent the wedding. Nevertheless, the Gypsy appears equally suddenly, grabs her, and instructs the young men to restrain her. Cherevik thereupon regains his confidence: 'What's done is done: I don't like changing my mind', he declares importantly. A still protesting Khivrya is carried off, and the Gypsy exhorts all to not to spare their legs in dancing a gopak.*

As a prose story, Gogol's *Sorochintsy Fair* offered only a limited amount of direct speech and Musorgsky had to invent much of the dialogue himself, though using Gogol's own text, with minimum adjustment, where he could. In what survives of Act 1 only Gritsko's disclosure to Cherevik of his love for Parasya, plus Cherevik's response, is taken or adapted from Gogol, and in Act 3 no more than the first verse of 'her favourite song' that Parasya incorporates into her dumka. Musorgsky himself devised the entire opening scene of Act 2 between Khivrya and Cherevik, including the hilarious exchange that follows Cherevik's revelation that the name he has given the mare is also Khivrya (potent evidence of Musorgsky's humorous inventiveness), as well as Khivrya's monologue; the one truly substantial slab drawn directly from Gogol is the scene that follows (from when Khivrya leads in Afanasy Ivanovich up to the return of her husband, Kum, and the guests).

It was predictable that, in setting a subject so indelibly regional, Musorgsky should have drawn abundantly on folksongs. At least nine have been identified, and some are used intensively. They are heard above all from Cherevik, a peasant of peasants. It is to a Ukrainian folktune that he makes his first impact on the action (when he challenges the Parubok embracing his daughter), and he sings another in his brief, tipsy appearance with Kum later in the act (the latter song will recur twice in Act 2—first drowsily near the opening as Cherevik awakens, then later from offstage after Khivrya has ejected him); a third folksong ('Ru-du-du, ru-du-du') provides their exit music, and also resurges in Act 2 when Cherevik and company bellow it to banish superstitious fears. Earlier Cherevik had used two folksongs in tandem as he had continued his attempts to pacify his furious wife, then enquired for whom her cooking was intended. With Cherevik's exit the trail of folksongs is blazed further by Khivrya. Her first is interrupted by the retreating offstage sounds of her banished husband; she sings a second more extensively as she watches from the window for her lover, then launches into a full-scale performance of a third, just before her lover arrives. The gopak that Shebalin transferred to the opera's end is also folksong-based.

Adapting a plot, devising his own libretto, and incorporating folksongs were operations well practised by Musorgsky. But when in August 1877 he had set out his aspirations, he specified the new challenge that faced him. As he had continued to Kutuzov: 'Pushkin wrote *Boris* in dramatic form [but] not for the stage; Gogol wrote *Sorochintsy Fair* as a tale—emphatically, of course, not for the stage. Yet both giants with their creative powers planned the contours of the scenic action so finely that it only requires colours to be provided'. Nevertheless, this could prove a very exacting process:[17]

> You know me, my friend, through your artistic creations which you submitted to the labour of your modest Modest; your modest friend remains the same in his relation to Gogol. Once the artist's *real, sensitive* nature has created in words, the musician is faced with relating 'very courteously' to what has been created, with searching out the very heart, the very essence of what the musician intends to embody in a musical form. *What is genuine, truly artistic* cannot be other than capricious because *as itself* it cannot be lightly embodied in another artistic form because *as itself* it demands profound study with sacred love. But when an artistic kinship between operators in different spheres of art does work out—the journey's good!

This revealed a radical rethinking of the attitude with which Musorgsky had set about *The Marriage* nine years before. Earlier in this same letter he had described his approach then as that of a 'non-musician' who had suppressed musical values in his search for a doctrinaire truth. Now, in *Sorochintsy Fair*, while retaining the dramatic ideal of his earlier treatment of Gogol, he would strike a balance between, on the one hand, the vivid presentation of the drama as projected in the words Gogol had put into the mouths of his characters or of the text Musorgsky himself would devise where such words were lacking, and, on the other hand, the potential of music to search out on its own terms the full range of human feelings and experience implicit within that text. The Alexey Tolstoy songs provide the clearest pointers towards Musorgsky's solution: simple but eloquent vocal phrases moulded on the words but not straitjacketed by their tonic accents or intonation—phrases that may, where required, readily assemble into broader melodic entities. Put in

[17] *MLN1*, 232.

the most basic terms: recitative could also be melody, which could be underpinned by clean-textured, clear harmonic structures in which the potential of tonality, chromatic incident or variation of harmonic pace may be exploited. Certainly there is not a moment in *Sorochintsy* where, as in *The Marriage*, the listener might mutter: 'this is not music'.[18]

As in *Khovanshchina*, the prelude to *Sorochintsy Fair* sets the scene and mood, but it also foretells things to come. It is the loveliest of beginnings: first a benign opening phrase, its repetitions borne upon a succession of chromatically related major triads, theme and harmony conjuring an instant pastel projection of a hot Ukrainian day; then a preliminary airing of Parasya's first song; finally the sounds of the market that is in full spate when the curtain rises. This boisterous opening chorus takes its departure from Musorgsky's market scene for the abortive *Mlada*, but it is more compact, less wide-ranging, and far more practical, its realism heightened by the division of the singers into various groups (stallholders, gypsies, Cossacks, Jews, and so on). The driving vitality is matched in the pace of events, Parasya adding the personal touch to music already familiar, the chorus likewise picking up on music from the prelude.

The Gypsy who now steps forward is an enigma. Is he more than he seems—the one character in this tale who is rather more than merely representative of a type, the one character with some real character? Musorgsky's description of him in one source as 'in charge of the comedy. Quasi deus ex machina' confirms his special potency. In *Christmas Eve*, another of the *Dikanka* tales, Gogol had placed a real devil in the village, indistinguishable from the mortals except for tiny horns and a concealed tail. That devil was prey to human emotions and could be outwitted—but woe betide any who allowed themselves into his clutches. Gogol's description of the Gypsy of Sorochintsy is ambivalent; there was, in his dark-complexioned features

> something malicious, sarcastic, base and at the same time haughty: a person casting a glance at him would readily have been aware that substantial qualities seethed in this strange soul—though such as whose only reward on

---

[18] For an examination of the historical and cultural context in which Musorgsky's opera was created, and for an investigation of Musorgsky's 'rationally justified melody' in *Sorochintsy Fair*, see R. Taruskin, '*Sorochintsï Fair* Revisited', *TM*, 328–94.

earth would be the gallows. His mouth, completely sunken between his nose and pointed chin and forever darkened by a malicious smile, his small but fire-bright eyes, and his face's continually changing lightning flashes of schemes and designs—all this demanded just such a peculiar, strange costume as he was wearing . . .

But Gogol uncovered no demonic excrescences this time, and while the Gypsy is certainly a risky acquaintance, any satanic affiliations are concealed. In the opera he introduces himself with a genial insouciance; there is little menace apparent in his admonitions concerning things supernatural, and his concluding warning about the resident devil (which introduces the Red Jacket motif of a descending minor ninth: (Ex. 16.1)) oozes relish rather than malice. If this is the devil himself, he takes mischievous rather than malign delight in what he relates, and his penchant seems not for eternal damnation but simply for stirring up earthly fear and for discomforting pranks—and even, when he is so disposed, for doing a good turn.

The little trio that follows runs on two levels; while the Gypsy continues his narration, Parasya and Gritsko sing of their love. And if in this ensemble's continuous texture only the words of the uppermost voice have much chance of being clearly heard, the progressive entwining of the lovers' lines signals audibly their ever-growing intimacy. Cherevik responds with vigour and a folksong, three further statements in different keys providing the bass for the first part of his dialogue with Gritsko. The Parubok substantiates his feelings by returning to the lover's music of the trio; he is accepted, the marriage bargain is struck,

Ex. 16.1

[The Red Jacket!]

and the chorus rounds off the first part of the act, returning initially to its opening music before retreating as the dusk gathers.

Though there have already been some departures from the original scenario, the essential outlines have remained. The brief scene Musorgsky composed for Cherevik and Kum, in which the former views apprehensively Khivrya's reaction to the agreed marriage, has no place in the scenario but, though an afterthought, was clearly a preliminary to Khivrya's entry and can follow quite naturally on the market scene. It does little more than reinforce the two men's peasant stock by setting their parts almost entirely to folksongs (for surely Kum's first bleary utterance is also of peasant origin). Beyond this point no more music survives for Act 1, but Shebalin chose to draft 'The Parubok's Dumka' from Act 3 to make it serve as 'The Parubok's Sorrow'. Set to a recitative-and-aria pattern, Musorgsky's stylistic model is the melismatic folksong, but the melodic invention is entirely his own in this unharmonized but most eloquent of dialogues with a high solo bassoon, which each time lays out the despairing peasant's feelings before he himself sets them forth in words. The aria that follows is Musorgsky at his most plangent, its high quota of painful dissonance and tense chromatic harmony resounding all the more powerfully for occurring in a work otherwise little concerned with such things.

That Musorgsky has not lost his flair for pantomimic suggestion is evident in the first bars of Act 2; the heavy breathing of a sleeping Cherevik is deftly caught in a ponderously heaving phrase (Ex. 16.2*a*, bars 3–6). Nor could anything uncover more touchingly the clement side of his normally turbulent wife than the sweet-tempered melody (Ex. 16.2*b*) that shadows her thoughts of the tryst in prospect with her lover; this will be heard some ten times in what follows. Such multiple recurrences do much to focus the musical expression and tighten the structure of this act: challenged by his wife, Cherevik will also display much thematic singlemindedness, and portions of Khivrya's private rehearsal for her lover and her ensuing reflections will return after her lover has arrived. Though a sibling of the opening theme of the opera's prelude and evidently an original melody, Khivrya's theme has marks of folksong on it, beginning like Cherevik's when he upbraided Gritsko for excessive familiarity with his daughter—then, as do many Russian folk melodies, turning back on itself.

Ex. 16.2a

Ex. 16.2b

Ex. 16.2c

Cherevik:
pod-kho-dil pa-nich,   yu - nets,——   da spro-sil:——   'shto—— pro - da-yosh?'

[A young chap came up and asked: "What are you selling?"]

Waking (to a folksong) and then facing hostile interrogation from his consort, Cherevik responds with what could be yet another folksong (Ex. 16.2c), proceeding doggedly to cling to it as his only anchorage in the torrent of castigation that billows over him. Cherevik's theme, and his use of it, is just one tiny pointer to a fundamental difference between *Sorochintsy Fair* and *Boris*. In the latter, peopled by individuals whose often complex personalities and feelings had to be projected with the utmost precision of which music was capable, Musorgsky had fitted out their individual phrases, even their words, with custom-designed music that served that purpose to the ultimate degree. Folksong, as the collective product of a peasant society, cannot define individual personality, but since in *Sorochintsy* there were no substantial personalities to project, this scarcely mattered. But folksong (and folksong idioms) can suggest that society and its members, and Cherevik's (presumably) pastiche phrase fixes clearly his environment and class, though telling us nothing about the peasant himself except that he is a simple soul. As for free melody in *Sorochintsy*, though direct resonances from folksong may be absent in much of it, its general style remains compatible. And Cherevik's dogged repetitions of his new invention serve a second function: to provide a musical focus to an evolving scene. The suggestion may have come from Glinka, who had used the device in Act 3 of *A Life for the Tsar* when Susanin had reflected with his daughter Antonida on her forthcoming wedding before being interrupted by a detachment of Polish troops. Less extensively Musorgsky had, of course, already done much the same when Cherevik and Gritsko had met for the first time in Act 1.

In the last stage of this marital confrontation the Red Jacket motif, the one thematic element to travel between acts, had resurged, now joined by the chords particularly associated with it (see Ex. 16.1, orchestral part). In dealing with a recalcitrant husband, Khivrya had retaliated by sticking increasingly to her own thematic guns before being finally rid of him. But now the delights—and uncertainties—in prospect when her lover appears liberate her amorous feelings in a flow of flexible arioso, by turns tender and yearning, explosively indignant when recalling her husband's fecklessness, apprehensive in regard of her lover. This is a peasant past her best, no longer confident of her charms, who finally attempts to cheer her long wait with a full-scale solitary

Ex. 16.2d

Ex. 16.2e

song-and-dance act. Opening heavy-heartedly, with Khivrya musing to one Ukrainian folksong, it passes to a five-fold rendition of a second against varying backgrounds. This last stretch was to be published separately as 'Khivrya's Song', perhaps even during the composer's lifetime, and certainly by 1886, the year in which 'Parasya's Dumka' from Act 3 was also issued.

Khivrya's scene with Afanasy Ivanovich is delicious. Now she can repeat, though in reverse order, her carefully rehearsed invitation to her lover to partake of her cuisine, as well as re-run the music to which she had privately voiced her fears that he had deserted her for another. Afanasy Ivanovich himself has clearly caught something of the pomposity of his parental environment—indeed (as Vladimir Morosan has observed),[19] he borrows from the Obikhod itself (for instance, a fragment from the litany is echoed in bars 7–10 of Ex. 16.3a) as he prepares his attempt on Khivrya's virtue. This priest's son is disposed to grandiloquence, with a readiness to inflate his phrase-ends portentously for greater effect, as with his flowery affectation when recalling a ponderous

[19] See V. Morosan, 'Musorgsky's choral style', *MIM*, 128–30.

Ex. 16.3a

[Concerning this I will tell you, if only regarding myself,

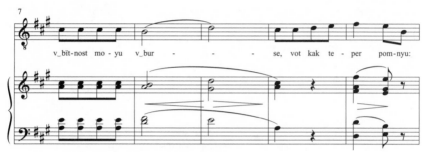

in my existance in the seminary, as I now remember it:]

attempt at striking imagery once made by his father's predecessor; the self-conscious harmonic 'sophistication' of this moment (Ex. 16.3*b*) serves to highlight the lack of affectation in Musorgsky's music elsewhere in this scene.

Despite its confined, domestic world, what follows has much of the turmoil of the opening stretch of the Kromy Forest Scene that had concluded *Boris*. But where that had proceeded as a chain of musically separate episodes, this is almost symphonic in its growth around a tightly-knit fund of musical materials. The quasi-gopak orchestral interlude that follows Afanasy Ivanovich's panic-stricken pleas for divine mercy and his retreat to the rafters provides two elements (Ex. 16.2*d* and *e*; the latter turns out to be Kum's thematic badge); a third is provided by the Red Jacket motif (see Ex. 16.1), which exposes the preoccupation of Kum, Cherevik, and company as they burst in; Cherevik still clings to his quasi-folksong (see Ex. 16.2*c*); and Khivrya's now familiar theme (see Ex. 16.2*b*) finds its place too. Even the 'Ru-du-du' folksong returns, once again to bolster courage. The result is a very taut scene.

Even before the dish dislodged by Afanasy Ivanovich has unnerved the moral fibre stiffened by the chanting of 'Ru-du-du', the chords of Ex. 16.1 have intimated the presence of the Red Jacket. It is Cherevik who now utters the dread name, supplying the drooping ninth and prompting a mood of petrified terror. Cherevik invents a new phrase to which he characteristically clings for security, and finally Kum begins his tale of the Red Jacket. The angularity and uncertain tonality of his opening phrase (Ex. 16.4) promise some spine-chilling moments in store. But, as noted earlier, Musorgsky recognized that setting this would prove 'inordinately difficult', and harsh criticism from friends,

Ex. 16.3b

Afanasy: Vï-klyu-cha-ya tol-ko u - yaz - vle-ni-ya so sto-ro-nï kra-pi - vï, "se-

[Except only being wounded on the part of the nettles,

vo___ zmi - ye - no - dob - no - vo zla - ka,"

"that serpent-like weed"]

Ex. 16.4

[Once, for some fault—honest, I don't know for what—

a devil was turned out of hell...]

led by Stasov, evidently caused him to destroy whatever he may have composed of it.

Thus nothing more survives of Act 2. Faced with what Musorgsky did complete, it is difficult to forgive Stasov for his intervention. Only 'Parasya's Dumka' and the 'Parubok's Dumka' (re-sited by Shebalin in Act 1) survive of what would have been the final act.[20] The six flat signature of 'Parasya's Dumka'[21] forewarns of sadness in store, and the beginning catches the pain of a girl facing her first disappointment in love. But then, her mirror having confirmed her good looks, she launches into a gopak, and youthful optimism dispels gloom. And the

[20] The incomplete 'Gopak of Merry Peasant Lads', a choral dance (Musorgsky wrote out the text but never added the vocal parts) based on a Ukrainian folksong and presumably intended to round off Act 1, was used by Shebalin to end the opera.

[21] Musorgsky orchestrated the first section (Andantino) of this.

dumka has one unique characteristic that points to the prevailing brightness and buoyancy of so much of the rest of the opera, whatever the
passing pains of love and however much turbulent wives may tyrannize
and supernatural forces thrill and chill—it is still virtually the only piece
in the opera that Musorgsky set in a flat key.

CHAPTER 17

Final Years

THE FALTERING, THEN FAILING, HISTORY OF *SOROCHINTSY Fair* is paralleled in the everyday course of Musorgsky's own last years, his life now unfolding fitfully, mostly chaotically; there is, for us, a final terrible sense of what might have been that is as total and dispiriting as with the opera itself. His creative course during this last period (the composition of *Khovanshchina*, *Sorochintsy Fair*, and the last songs) has been charted in preceding chapters, though there were to be a few minor additions. On 14 July 1877 he signed the vocal score of a choral-orchestral piece, variously known in English as *Joshua* or *Jesus* (or *Iisus*) *Navin*, based on a text that Musorgsky himself devised from the Old Testament on Joshua's defeat of the Amorites; the first part was a call to action from Joshua, the second the women of Canaan's lament (first from a soloist, then the chorus), finally a shout of praise to Joshua, then Jehovah. In fact, Musorgsky had sketched *Jesus Navin* in 1874–5, reworking material from *Salammbô*, the nearly identical outer choruses being drawn from the opening and closing sections of the Libyan War Song in Act 1, the central solo from Mâtho's lament in Act 4. Stasov stated that the bases of the piece were 'original Jewish themes, which Musorgsky once heard from a window during prayer in the courtyard of his Jewish neighbours',[1] and this is supported by Musorgsky's note on his score: 'founded upon Israeli national songs'. It may seem puzzling

---

[1] *SMPM* (in *SSM3*, 109).

that Jewish tunes should first have found their way into *Salammbô*, but Gerald Abraham suggested tentatively that 'Musorgsky may have argued that the Carthaginians were a Semitic people—though as it happens both themes are sung in the opera by Libyans.'[2] Musorgsky revealed his own approach to Kutuzov some six weeks later: 'I forgot to inform you, my friend, that I have written a biblical picture, *Jesus Navin*, strictly following the Bible—and I have even followed the route of Navin's triumphant processions through Canaan. This morsel is composed on themes you already know.'[3] Boris Schwarz has identified the Jewish theme sung in the opening and closing choruses as a 'Hasidic *niggun* [tune] attributed to Rabbi Abraham ha-Mal'akh (1741–81)', adding that Hasidism was 'a religious movement which originated among the Jews of Poland in the 18th century'.[4] Despite Musorgsky's mention of 'tunes', this is the only Hebrew melody to have been identified in the piece. Though Musorgsky would play the piece as a piano solo during his tour of southern Russia with Leonova in 1879, *Jesus Navin* was never orchestrated or otherwise performed during his lifetime.

In fact 1877 was a good year for Musorgsky as regards his civil service employment. In early April he had received a 200-rouble bonus, on 13 May he was promoted, and on 13 December he reached the rank of collegiate counsellor. Nine months later he was moved, through the intervention of a senior civil servant and close friend of Balakirev, to another department ('very glad' was the terse personal observation of the director of the Forestry Department), where his erratic behaviour seems to have been treated with extraordinary indulgence until his final dismissal on 13 January 1880. During the winter of 1877–8 he continued to participate as pianist in charity concerts, and for one he orchestrated a trio, *To the East*, by Dargomïzhsky. But the death of Petrov in March 1878 shattered him. At Petrov's requiem he wept uncontrollably, and for several weeks was inconsolable. The great singer's passing also signalled the end of the special evenings at Shestakova's. 'Sometimes we got together, but already it wasn't the same!' Glinka's sister remembered:[5]

[2] *CAM*, 182.

[3] *MLN1*, 233.

[4] See B. Schwarz, 'Musorgsky's Interest in Judaica; *MIM*, 90.

[5] *TDM*, 509.

Musorgsky, deprived of Petrov whom he loved and revered so much, felt isolated and dispirited. Rimsky-Korsakov had a family, was terribly busy, and kept more and more away. True, sometimes Borodin and Musorgsky were both there, and they had a sincere regard for each other . . . Through her friendship for me Alexandra Molas came along: she performed so well all the Russian pieces of the new school! But the one who was ever true to the circle was Vladimir Stasov.

From 1878 Musorgsky was to a degree compensated by a renewed intimacy with Balakirev which had followed on their meeting at Shestakova's on 22 July. It was some seven years since the two men's previous close relationship had lapsed, and the evening was a great success, the more so since Musorgsky seemed to have re-gained control of himself after Petrov's death. Balakirev was now again in circulation, and his return was greeted enthusiastically by his old associates. Subsequently Balakirev invited Musorgsky to his own home where they reminisced about the old days—and where the old autocrat tried to resume instant control over his former disciple. Musorgsky appeared outwardly compliant, even saying that he had nothing against Balakirev's advice to take harmony lessons from Rimsky and, as noted earlier, bearing away with him his score of *St John's Night* for revision by the autumn. But the private pleasure that Stasov and Balakirev took in Musorgsky's orderly mien was soon to be shattered. In early August Musorgsky had re-ported to Shestakova that he was racked by a 'nervous fever' (one of the euphemisms he employed for a bout of dipsomania); now, daily for the best part of several days, he had appeared at Shesta-kova's 'looking frightful, and had stayed a long time. Seeing that everything was getting more violent, I decided to do something to save him and protect myself. I wrote him a letter in which I begged him not to call on me when in his mood of nervous irri-tation (as he calls it). In my letter I set out everything, but of course put it as gently as I could.' But only the previous evening, Shestakova continued in her letter of 21 August to Stasov, Musorg-sky had appeared 'in *complete* order, and gave me his word that he would never again distress me . . . It is a pity about Musorgsky, he is such a wonderful person! If there were some possibility of tear-ing him away from Naumov, I think it would be possible finally to save him.'[6] In reply Stasov begged Shestakova to increase her invitations to Musorgsky, since she and Balakirev were now his only hopes of salvation—if that was still possible.

Stasov's hopes were not to be fulfilled. In late October Balakirev reported that Musorgsky had not kept an appointment, and over the next few weeks he and Stasov made determined efforts to draw Musorgsky out, but with only limited success; 'he's doing absolutely nothing and, it seems, is unable to do anything', Stasov told his brother Dmitri.[7] In December Musorgsky did appear at a belated celebration of Shestakova's sixty-second birthday, but then his ailments returned with a vengeance, leading the doctor to predict (so Musorgsky claimed) that he only had two more hours to live. His condition dragged on through the month, though he recovered enough to score the piano part of his early song *King Saul* for a charity concert in the Maryinsky Theatre on 7 January 1879. Three weeks later, at an FMS concert, Rimsky conducted the first ever performance of the Cell Scene from *Boris*. At the rehearsal—so Rimsky remembered—Musorgsky 'behaved eccentrically'. Whether under the influence of wine or because of his penchant for showing off, he showed most delight in the performance of individual instruments:[8]

> often during the most ordinary and prosaic musical phrases now bowing his head thoughtfully, now lifting it proudly and shaking his hair, now raising his hand in a theatrical gesture, which had been an old habit of his. When at the scene's end the tamtam was struck pianissimo in imitation of the monastery bell, Musorgsky accorded it a deep and respectful bow, his arms crossed on his breast.

Yet two days later he was again in a condition to accompany Alexandra Molas in a programme of songs by Balakirev, Borodin, Rimsky, and himself, as well as extracts from Dargomïzhsky's *Stone Guest*.

Two further public appearances as accompanist followed in early March and three more in April; at the last Dostoyevsky, no less, read a

[6] *TDM*, 513–14.

[7] *TDM*, 516.

[8] *RKL*, 158.

portion of *The Brothers Karamazov*, which he was in the process of publishing in instalments. Unsurprisingly, perhaps, the writer drew the greater interest and applause. But Musorgsky's most significant participation had been at a choral-orchestral concert conducted by Rimsky on 25 March, in which Darya Leonova had sung Musorgsky's *Gopak* (with Musorgsky as pianist), and 'Marfa's Song' from Act 3 of *Khovanshchina*. Musorgsky had known Leonova as long ago as 1868, when she had given the first public performance of *Gopak*, and in February 1873 she had taken the part of the Hostess in the presentation of three scenes from *Boris* at the Maryinsky Theatre, the first occasion on which any part of Musorgsky's masterpiece had been heard. He seems to have had no further contact with her until 1878 when, in April, he had accompanied her in performances of an aria from Meyerbeer's opera *Le prophète* and of his own song *Gopak*, for which she clearly retained a partiality. Then from the middle of June he had been Leonova's guest at her dacha at Peterhof. He seems to have spent the better part of three months switching between St Petersburg and Peterhof, and the time he passed at the latter with Leonova has led to speculation about their relationship. But Stasov was emphatic that there never was any liaison between them.

The musical association with Leonova was to prove the most important performing relationship of Musorgsky's life, for on 2 August 1879 the pair left St Petersburg on an extended concert tour of southern Russia. Musorgsky seems to have been conducting himself in a very orderly fashion in the weeks leading up to this, and he spent the three weeks before their departure at Peterhof in preparations, evidently composing 'Parasya's Dumka' for Act 3 of *Sorochintsy Fair* with a view to including it in their repertoire. He was enthusiastic about the enterprise, reckoning it could net him some 1000 roubles. Stasov, who only got wind of the project at the last moment, was apprehensive at the prospect of Musorgsky among people of whom none would know his failings, and Balakirev even more vehemently begged Shestakova to intervene 'to wreck this shameful excursion with Leonova'.[9] It was too late; within days the couple, accompanied by Leonova's common-law husband Fyodor Gridnin, were in Poltava giving their first concert.

[9] *TDM*, 532.

Musorgsky's surviving letters from 1878 had been few and far between, and only two are extant from the first half of 1879. But the geographical distance that now separated the composer from his friends—and, above all, the excitement of the tour, with its public appearances and personal successes and the new sights, sensations and acquaintances it afforded—produced a number of often very long letters that offer vivid insight into what for Musorgsky was (during its opening stages, at least) one of the most exciting and patently successful episodes of his whole life. Their first concert in Poltava, given immediately after their arrival, must have been a success, for only days later they gave a second. The programme for this has survived. There were twelve items, including songs by Schubert and Glinka, excerpts from operas by Dargomïzhsky and Serov, and four pieces by Musorgsky himself: *The Orphan*, two piano transcriptions (a portion of the Coronation Scene from *Boris* and *The Destruction of Sennacherib*), and the piano piece *The Seamstress*. 'The takings were good, but less than expected', Musorgsky informed the Naumov ménage, 'but the artistic triumph we managed was *absolute* . . . Darya Mikhailovna was, is, and always will be incomparable. What an extraordinary person! Her energy, power, her fundamental depth of feeling, everything, irresistibly captivating and riveting. And there was an abundance of tears, not to mention rapture—we were covered with flowers—and with what flowers!'[10] On the estate on which they were staying he saw a peasant hut which he decided could have been Parasya's, and this prompted the dedication of 'Parasya's Dumka' to their hostess, Elizaveta Miloradovicha. The scenery, the sky, the panorama, the stillness, and the softness of the air enraptured Musorgsky, and the character and inhabitants of Little Russia charmed him.

Their second concert had been on 10 August; three days later they were in Elizavetgrad, where Petrov had been born. Musorgsky visited his birthplace and was deeply moved by the sense of closeness to 'grandpa Petrov',[11] as he had become accustomed to call him. Their concert on 14 August was a triumph not only for Leonova but for Musorgsky, who received a personal ovation for his performance in Schubert's *Erlkönig*—'something unheard of even in St Petersburg', he

[10] *MLN1*, 244.
[11] *MLN1*, 246.

observed to Stasov.[12] After the concert a deputation appeared urging them to perform a second time, but their schedule would not permit; they headed straight for the train, and the next day were in Nikolayev, where they remained ten days. Here was a naval base, and the two visitors were welcomed by the fleet commander and other senior officers. They were taken to the Observatory to view the city's panorama and the planets Jupiter and Saturn, visited the home of the editor of the *Nikolayev Herald*, Andrey Yurkovsky, where Leonova persuaded Musorgsky to introduce the Yurkovsky children to *The Nursery* and then accompany her in the *Erlkönig*. Also included among their excursions was a guided tour of a capital ship, the 'Popovka', followed by an evening reception held for them by a 'delightful, splendid, and most sympathetic gentleman', Admiral Bazhenov.[13]

On 19 August they gave their first concert. Their repertoire was constantly evolving. Already *Après le bal*, a composition by Leonova herself, had been incorporated (though there is more than a suspicion that only the tune was hers, the words and accompaniment being Musorgsky's); now she was adding Liszt's *Es war ein König in Thule*, Borodin's *The Sea*, and *My spoiled darling* by Chopin, an aria from Meyerbeer's *Le prophète*, Balakirev's song *Come to me*, Musorgsky's *Gopak*, and Marfa's song before the self-immolation (presumably her D-dorian address to Andrey Khovansky in Act 4). Their audience was not large, Musorgsky attributing this to the poor quality of so many performers touring the provinces, but was 'very representative', and they had a great success. At a second concert on 22 August they further expanded their repertoire to include, amongst other items, Rimsky's song *Southern Night*, four more songs by Glinka, and Musorgsky's *Jesus Navin* performed as a piano solo, as also were two entr'actes from Glinka's incidental music for Nestor Kukolnik's play *Prince Kholmsky*. A third concert, (24 August), this time with the participation of a ship's orchestra and including Leonova in a whole scene from Glinka's *A Life for the Tsar*, drew a good audience. The programme contained Musorgsky's song *Forgotten!*

Kherson came next, with a concert on 27 August. Musorgsky's ex-

[12] *MLN1*, 253.
[13] Ibid.

cellent mood and relish for all things beautiful and evocative is reflected in the letter he wrote earlier that day to the Naumovs:[14]

> How magical is the entry into Kherson along the Dnieper! Enchantment upon enchantment! In this watery avenue of historic rushes (in places two or three times a man's height), whence dashing Zaporozhian Cossacks in hollowed out oaken boats fell upon the Turks, where in the mirror-like smooth surface of the blue Dnieper great trees gaze upon themselves reflected almost to their full height—and this is to be seen not only from the bank but across the broadest, most luxurious stretch of the river, all lit by the lavender-pink sunset, by the moon and Jupiter. . . .

The impression created by this mighty river would remain with him after the tour was over and prompt him to revisit and revise his song of thirteen years before *On the Dnieper*, now adding a subtitle: 'My Journey through Russia'.

Again Musorgsky found some musically sympathetic souls in the town, his *Nursery* enjoying the same success with the younger members of a family Boshnyakov in Kherson as it had with the Yurkovsky children in Nikolayev. His personal triumph as pianist in Schubert's *Erlkönig* was repeated at the first concert, while in their second he included for the first time items from both *Khovanshchina* and *Sorochintsy Fair* (the Preobrazhensky March from the former, the Gopak from the latter). Like Leonova, Musorgsky continued to expand his repertoire as the tour proceeded, in later concerts including the overture to Glinka's *Ruslan*, two of his own piano pieces, *Ein Kinderscherz* and the early *Intermezzo in modo classico* (now picturesquely entitled *By a Difficult Road through Snowdrifts*), the Polonaise from *Boris*, and three more extracts from *Khovanshchina* (Golitsïn's departure into exile; 'The cavalry assault on the Streltsy settlement', presumably drawn from the Scribe's narration in Act 3; and a portion of the Persian dances).

Odessa might have been expected to prove musically the most sophisticated city of their tour. It was Russia's third city, and with its large Jewish community, its long established support of opera and its familiarity with visiting international celebrities, it is no surprise that their impending visit aroused considerable notice from the local press. Yet

[14] *MLN1*, 249–50.

the concert was not the hoped-for success. Writing to Stasov on 22 September, Musorgsky offered his own rather curious explanation for this: 'Russian cities, in particular those visited by performers and artists (Odessa, Nikolayev, Sevastopol), are not only not musical, but in general do not defer to art; on the other hand, Russian cities rarely, or else never visited by performers and artists, are very musical and in general rejoice in art (Elizavetgrad, Kherson, Poltava).'[15] But perhaps it was not the musical indifference of the former cities but, as already suspected by Musorgsky, their lower expectations when it came to native performers that accounted for the disappointingly small audience for their concert on 9 September, though press reaction was complimentary. Musorgsky was bitter: 'Odessa! O "Beauty of the South"! She has no truck with art; all her interest is in wheat and roubles', he castigated her to Stasov.[16] He discovered more delight from attending services in two synagogues. 'I was in raptures. I remember clearly two Israeli themes: one of the kantor's, the other of the clergy's choir—the latter in unison. I shall never forget them', he told Stasov.[17] He also encountered an old acquaintance, the painter Grigor Myasoyedov, who was in the city in connection with the seventh Touring Exhibition of the *peredvizhniki*, an association of artists that Myasoyedov had founded on his return from Italy in 1869 and which was not only populist in creative intention but in its resolve to take its members' art to the people— hence their peripatetic exhibitions. Musorgsky had a natural empathy with such aims, and he visited the exhibition, then went round Odessa's museums of history and antiquity with the Myasoyedovs, noting how little patronized they were by the local populace. Here he was pleasantly struck by Ukrainian portrait painting which was new to him, signed the visitors' book, and bore away a catalogue.

The journey from Odessa to Sevastopol was by sea, and while others were succumbing to sea-sickness Musorgsky was taking down Greek and Jewish songs from the singing of some women fellow-travellers. At this point the exact chronology of events becomes clouded; so, increasingly, did Musorgsky's morale. As already noted, their success had begun

[15] *MLN1*, 253.
[16] *MLN1*, 254
[17] Ibid.

to falter. In Sevastopol there were two concerts. The city itself still showed painful scars of the year-long siege it had endured twenty-five years earlier during the Crimean War, and in artistic matters Musorgsky rated its population no more interested than that of Odessa. By 19 September he and Leonova were in Yalta, a modest-sized health and holiday resort with few other local facilities and services. Mid-September was also near the height of the tourist season, no accommodation had been booked for him and Leonova, and the only lodging they could find was in 'a kind of mud hut with centipedes that bite, beetles with pincers that similarly bite, and with other insects that based their earthly existence on the ideal of making life unpleasant for people'.[18] At their concert the next evening the audience was poor, and during the interval Stasov's daughter, Sofiya Fortunato (formerly Serbina), who was currently living in Yalta, remembered finding Musorgsky slumped in an armchair 'like a wounded bird'.[19] Next day she had them transferred to the excellent Grand Hôtel de Russie, and for the remainder of their visit her home became their main haven. She and her husband took their guests on visits to various sights and scenes around Yalta, Sofiya remembering that Musorgsky 'usually climbed onto the footboard [which was at the back] of those comfortable basket-carriages in which one travelled in the Crimea at that time. He did this so that he would not have to converse and spoil his mood.'[20] In return for these pleasures there were private performances of various of Musorgsky's songs and excerpts from his operas. Their second concert was a very different matter; Sofiya personally canvassed their fellow-guests in the hotel, and the result was, so she recalled, a triumph.

If it was, it would seem to have been about the last of their tour. In fact, Sofiya's recollections passed over the negative side of Musorgsky's passage through Yalta, to judge from the reply her father sent to her private account of Musorgsky's stay in the town. 'There was just one thing it was very distressing to learn from your letter', Stasov would write on 31 October:[21]

---

[18] *MLN1*, 252.

[19] *MVS*, 179.

[20] *MVS*, 181–2.

[21] *TDM*, 557.

namely, that all the time he continues to carry on outrageously, as he does here. Earlier we had been unable to discover this from anybody—and it is just this that particularly interested us. We had all been hoping that maybe a change of place and persons, and the unexpected novelty of the journey, would produce in him something in the nature of a revolution and would put him right. A vain hope—everything remains as before.

The first of their two engagements in Rostov-on-Don, their next stop, had already been fixed for 4 October. Whether it was just that they had time on their hands and could not drag themselves away from the Crimea, or whether Musorgsky needed time to recover from a bout of dipsomania, is unknown: whatever the case, it appears that on 24 September they left Yalta, arriving in Rostov a week later, having taken in Feodosiya and Kerch, as well as Taganrog, en route. Their appearance at Rostov's Winter Theatre was as the second part of an evening which had begun with a two-act operetta, *Feminine Curiosity*, by an unnamed composer. Leonova opened her share of the event by singing, with the orchestra, a Ukrainian folksong, *I do not want to sleep*, and Spiridonovna's song from Serov's *The Power of the Fiend*; for the remainder Musorgsky accompanied and played solo. Two days later there followed their second performance in a similarly designed programme.

Inevitably with appearances such as these (and a whole trail of such occasions now faced them), with a shared billing and with audiences of which a proportion had come for the dramatic rather than the musical content of the evening, the zest was going out of the tour. From Rostov Musorgsky wrote to the *maître d'hotel* at the Maly Yaroslavets in St Petersburg, painting the best picture he could of their enterprise and its positive sides, but pleading that expenditure had soaked up income and that he still could not clear his debts. The letter offers a revealing insight not only into the disappointment of an undertaking from which he had hoped to profit handsomely, but also into the financial disorder of his St Petersburg existence—and with this cheerless plea his flow of letters dries up completely. All this can have done nothing to counter the behaviour that Stasov had so desperately deplored in his letter to his daughter. Yet even at this stage their plan was to proceed to Tsaritsïn and return thence to St Petersburg by a grand trip up the Volga. Within days a more modest itinerary had been decided on.

There is little point in detailing the rest of their tour. In Novocher-kassk they gave a single concert. Then on to Voronezh, where, on 15 October, occurred the first of no less than four appearances in the Winter Theatre. Such a number might seem to be flattering, but again they were only part of each evening. The first began with a play, *A Female Othello*, by a local dramatist, there followed Leonova's and Mu-sorgsky's joint contribution, and then a second play, *In the Dust*, by another Voronezh luminary. The marathon concluded with Act 3, Scene 1 of Dargomïzhsky's *Rusalka*, with Leonova as the Princess (the part she had created at the opera's première twenty-three years before), presented with orchestra, 'complete with scenery and in costume as in the St Petersburg Imperial Theatres'.

Clearly Leonova was now getting a far greater proportion of the attention, and Musorgsky's role had been correspondingly diminished. Nevertheless, by now he had gained at least one enthusiastic, if con-fused, admirer—an unnamed correspondent of the Voronezh newspaper *The Don*, who set out to show that he could recognize a composer of unusual gifts when he heard one, despite all his difficulties in making out what his music was all about:[22]

> Beneath its sounds each person involuntarily senses all his own sins, he falls prostrate, he suffers, he is tortured—but the menacing orator will suddenly become quietly melancholy: it is his grief at the errors that people commit at every step. True, you do not understand Mr Musorgsky's music imme-diately, but when you listen to it attentively, you cannot tear yourself away from it: and at one and the same time you suffer, yet delight in it.

The critic had turned to a fellow-Voronezhian for a second opinion. 'Mr Musorgsky converses with his listener in a lofty, allegorical lan-guage', this 'born musician' had replied:

> That is why you bow before him: you see, lofty thought is always combined with lofty speech—and that is why the majority do not understand him. You need to have a spirit that has still not completely mouldered if you are to understand this fresh, true music—but nerves accustomed to narcotic

---

[22] *TDM*, 554–5.

polkas, waltzes and operettas will remain passive, for there is no longer any life in them . . .

Sadly, these well-intentioned but absurd encomia no doubt reflected the less extravagant but equally benign incomprehension with which many in the audiences on this provincial tour must have heard Musorgsky's music.

Two concerts were given in Tambov, the second most notable for Musorgsky playing a portion of Gritsko's dream (that is, *St John's Night*) from *Sorochintsy Fair*, billed as 'The Worship of Chernobog and the Witches' Sabbath on the Bare Mountain'. Tver, where they arrived on 28 October, was their final engagement. This time only one concert was presented, but it seems this made a considerable impression, for the two performers were to return to the town the following May for two further concerts. At the beginning of November, they slipped back into St Petersburg. A three-month enterprise that had started with such hope and excitement ended mutedly, for all that Musorgsky would claim in his *Autobiographical Note* of 1880 that it had been 'a veritable triumphal procession for two major Russian artists'.[23]

The same *Autobiographical Note* also records three or four creative by-products of the tour, though these receive no mention in Musorgsky's letters surviving from 1879. 'As an impression of his journey through the Crimea Musorgsky has already published two capriccios for piano: *Baydary* and *Gurzuf*', he would write in this personal record. These pieces, each prompted by a place visited, were printed in 1880 as supplements to issues 2 and 6 of *Nouvelliste*. Though the manuscript of *Baydary* (usually known as *On the Southern Shore of the Crimea*) has no date, that of *Gurzuf* (usually known as *Near the Southern Shore of the Crimea*) is signed January 1880. Both are no more than neatly turned ternary pieces. A third piano piece, 'a large musical picture, *Storm on the Black Sea*' was 'composed and performed by the composer himself in several concerts', but no trace of this exists, and it was obviously an improvisation never committed to paper, though still dredged up from memory on occasions after Musorgsky's return from tour. By far the most significant of these pieces is the fourth, of which account has

[23] *MLN1*, 269.

already been taken. 'While en route, the composer conceived the idea of reproducing in music a composition of the great Goethe, never before given musical treatment by anyone: "Mephistofeles' song in Auerbach's cellar about a flea".'[24] Musorgsky's statement that his was the first musical treatment of this song from Goethe's *Faust* was mistaken, Beethoven having already set the lyric in 1809. The song was dedicated to Leonova, and though there is no record of her singing it during the tour, she introduced *The Song of the Flea* (as it is customarily known in English) to the St Petersburg public in a concert on 20 April 1880.[25]

Musorgsky's physical condition when he returned from his tour was bad, and for some three weeks nothing is heard of him. Then, towards the end of November, stimulated by the impending publication of Kutuzov's play *Tsar Vasily Shuisky*, with its dedication to Musorgsky himself, the latter urged his friend to write a new drama on the 'Life-Campaigners', a grenadier company formed in 1741 by Catherine the Great from the life-guards of the Preobrazhensky Regiment and who had been instrumental in the defeat of the Pugachev rebellion; when Kutuzov had completed it, Musorgsky would compose an opera on it. In 1877 he had already weighed the possibility of an opera, *Pugachevshchina* ('The Pugachev Affair'), as the follow-up to *Khovanshchina*, even noting down folk material that he could use. At that stage—so Stasov claimed—Musorgsky had intended basing it on Pushkin's novel *The Captain's Daughter*, which was set against the background of the Pugachev rebellion. But in 1879 this old idea faded as quickly as it had arisen. In any case within a fortnight, at an FMS concert, excerpts from *Khovanshchina* would at last be heard, and Musorgsky was required to give immediate attention to scoring two excerpts from Act 3: Marfa's Song and the initial Chorus of the Streltsy. With this event in prospect he seems (according to Stasov) to have pulled himself together, though

[24] Ibid.

[25] Though both the source of the lyric and its musical character might suggest that *The Song of the Flea* is a man's song, and the two known manuscripts of the song notate the singer's part for a bass, neither is Musorgsky's original manuscript, which is lost. One copy was made by Stasov, the other by an unknown hand (though certified by the composer), and it is possible that they present a version transposed for a man's voice.

then (according to Rimsky) he lost momentum. Certainly the instrumentation of Marfa's Song was finished only two days before the concert, and the Persian dances, which were also to be included, had to be scored by Rimsky himself, who used the opportunity to rectify what he saw as faults in Musorgsky's harmony and part-writing—changes which, Rimsky alleged, did nothing to reduce Musorgsky's expressions of gratitude after the performance.

Rimsky conducted the concert on 9 December, and Leonova sang Marfa's Song. It seems to have been a notable success, both singer and composer receiving numerous recalls. But then in January 1880 came the devastating blow of dismissal from government service. As recorded earlier, two separate groups of friends endeavoured to repair the total void in his finances by subsidies that would allow completion of *Khovanshchina* and *Sorochintsy Fair*. On 28 January Musorgsky expressed his gratitude to Stasov for the first of these:[26]

A heartfelt thank you, généralissime, for your good news. Despite minor misfortunes, I have not given way to faintheartedness, nor shall I give way. My motto, known to you, remains unaltered: 'Be bold! Forward to new shores!' If fate provides the opportunity to broaden my well-trodden path to the vital aims of art, I shall be delighted and shall exult; the demands of art upon the contemporary activist are so immense that they can swallow up the whole man. The time of writing *at leisure* is passed; give all of yourself to the people—that is what is now needed in art.

Yet again I thank you, généralissime.

The intentions are faultless, the recourse to old ideals impeccable, but the airy dismissal of 'minor misfortunes' was unreassuring, and experience had taught Stasov to attend results. He had not long to wait; a month later he was telling Balakirev that 'yet another company is giving Musorgsky assistance at the rate of eighty roubles a month, but with the single condition that in a year or thereabouts he should finish his opera *Sorochintsy Fair*. That's why he is now resisting so diligently composing *Khovanshchina*.[27]

[26] *MLN1*, 259.
[27] *TDM*, 576.

One other small task briefly, but fairly, distracted Musorgsky's attention from weightier matters. Early in 1880 a number of Russian composers, including Borodin, Rimsky, Tchaikovsky and Musorgsky, were commissioned to provide music for a series of *tableaux vivants* as part of the festivities for the silver jubilee of Alexander II's accession. As his contribution Musorgsky composed a march, *The Capture of Kars*, to celebrate the taking of this eastern Turkish town in 1877 during the Russo-Turkish war. But having no intention of creating afresh when viable but unused material was to hand, he recycled his march for the princes and priests from the abortive *Mlada* of 1872. The march's outer sections conveniently contained a Russian folksong, and to increase the piece's organic connection with its new context Musorgsky replaced the central section, completing the piece on 15 February and retitling it 'March with a *trio alla turca*'. The proposed festivities were cancelled, however, and the piece was first heard on 30 October at a concert of the RMS, conducted by Eduard Nápravník. Clearly moved by the patriotic resonances of the composition, the audience gave Musorgsky an ovation.

During March and April it seems Musorgsky was working on *Sorochintsy Fair*, for the publisher Nikolay Bernard planned to issue extracts from the opera in piano reductions. In early April Musorgsky also scored 'the concluding scene of Marfa, the Old Believer, from the final scene' of *Khovanshchina* (the score of this has vanished), which Leonova sang in a concert conducted by Rimsky on 20 April. In the same concert Musorgsky accompanied in the first official performance of *The Song of the Flea*, which was encored. Also played were the Persian dances from *Khovanshchina*. Two concerts in Tver took Leonova and Musorgsky away from the capital for the earlier part of May. In the first, on 9 May, Leonova included *The Song of the Flea* and an untitled 'ballad' (presumably *Forgotten*) by Musorgsky, while the latter played his *Storm on the Black Sea* and the prelude to *Khovanshchina*, all four pieces enjoying such success that they were repeated by public demand in the second concert three days later. Here Musorgsky received an ovation as much for his songs as for his solos.

Back in St Petersburg on 13 May Musorgsky urged Bernard to hasten publication of the extracts from *Sorochintsy Fair*. But here there had been a disaster. Rimsky's letter of 23 May to Stasov is a mine of information about what had been happening, and about the fate of the *Sorochintsy Fair* extracts:[28]

He [Musorgsky] is *terribly busy*, wearied by continuous *writing of music*, wearied by two concerts which he gave with Leonova (the Japanese)[29] in Tver. He has written, it seems, the fifth (I think [in fact, fourth]) scene of *Khovanshchina* where Golitsïn is taken into exile. He says also that he has almost finished the Interlude (the scene on the Bare Mountain, or the Parubok's dream) in *Sorochintsy* up to the pedal on C sharp (the bell); however, when I asked to see the music, it turned out that all this was old, left over from *Mlada*, and, except for two or three pages, not even copied out afresh. He is thinking of spending the summer in the Japanese's home at Oranienbaum, but the Japanese is going off elsewhere. He has published *The Seamstress* through Bernard. I learned from him that Bernard had lost the manuscripts of two or three numbers from *Sorochintsy Fair* that he had taken for publication, so that Musorgsky has had to write them out again. He [Bernard] is also printing the Fair from *Sorochintsy* for piano. I think that Vanlyasky and Co., who are paying Musorgsky for *Sorochintsy*, are acting misguidedly in forcing him to publish separate numbers through Bernard, for he has to prepare them for the press; meanwhile Bernard loses them, and Musorgsky is distracted from finishing an opera which, nevertheless, he says he is *obliged* to complete by November. He is putting off the completion of *Khovanshchina* to next year. I strongly urged him to come to our dacha in the summer as our guest. At first he declined, afterwards began to give way. Perhaps we'll manage to entice him. He has promised to orchestrate the Interlude from *Sorochintsy* for the FMS concerts; that would be good. . . . I called on him in the morning, at noon. He was still in bed, and throwing up nearly every minute; but it seems he was little embarrassed by this, just as though it was the most commonplace of events, and assured me that this got rid of his bile and that this, he says, was very good.

At the beginning of June, despite Rimsky's persuasions, it was into Leonova's dacha at Oranienbaum that Musorgsky settled, and there he

---

[28] A. S. Lyapunova ed., *N. Rimsky-Korsakov: Literaturnïye proizvedeniya i perepiska* [Literary works and correspondence], v, (Moscow, 1963), 370.

[29] A nickname the singer had acquired through having once included Japan in a concert tour.

remained for most of the summer. Initially this move produced some good results; on 10 June he dated the manuscript of Act 3 of *Khovanshchina*, and further work was done on that opera during the ensuing weeks: on 17 August the vocal score of Act 4, Scene 1 was signed. The same day to Stasov, who had been in Paris fretting that he had received no letter from Musorgsky, the dilatory correspondent was blandly reassuring about the near-completed state of *Khovanshchina*: 'only a tiny fragment of the self-immolation scene remains to be written, and then it's all ready. I'll write to you in detail about *Sorochintsy Fair*. Much has been done of this, and Chernobog is completely ready.'[30] This was simply not true—yet, with so much remaining to be done, he could still claim he had had time to think of his next project, dreaming up an orchestral suite (with harps and piano) on motifs he had collected from 'various good wanderers of this world: its programme is from the Bulgarian shores, across the Black Sea, the Caucasus, the Caspian, [the province of] Fergana, to Burma'.[31]

This was fantasy, of course—as was the notice in the St Petersburg press that during the coming season *Sorochintsy Fair* would be in the Opera's repertoire. There was no reassurance about his personal condition to be found in such accounts as emerged from independent witnesses during this summer interlude. The historian Sergey Rozhdestvensky, later a professor of history at St Petersburg University but in 1880 only eleven years old, recollected (as recorded by Ivan Lapshin) seeing Musorgsky daily at this time. 'His exterior vividly recalled Repin's celebrated portrait [painted only days before the composer's death]. His clothes were always somewhat dowdy, and Mr Drury later told me that he had occasion more than once to acquire clothing for the unfortunate musician.' Contrary to her earlier intentions, Leonova had remained in residence and had mounted a weekly musical soirée with supper. 'From the back room', continued Rozhdestvensky,[32]

> the sound of plates and uncorking of bottles was to be heard. Each time Musorgsky emerged, he was becoming ever more 'tight'. After supper the concert began, where Musorgsky would appear (already completely 'plas-

[30] *MLN1*, 260.
[31] *MLN1*, 261.
[32] *KYM*, 151.

tered') as accompanist and solo performer. He played his own compositions with amazing perfection, making 'a stunning impression' upon his listeners ... At this time Musorgsky was suffering from frightening hallucinations (often to be observed in alcoholics). Leonova reported on this in her recollections.'

On returning to St Petersburg in the autumn Musorgsky continued his association with Leonova on a new footing. Now into her fifties, the contralto's professional singing career was effectively over, and she turned to teaching, with Musorgsky as her pianist—an attractive role for him since it provided some modest income. Rimsky commented on the new enterprise in his memoirs. Far better an actress than vocalist, Leonova had a fine voice but little training, and could not really teach singing technique. But she was an impressive performer, Rimsky continued, and her strength lay in coaching songs and arias. For his part, Musorgsky could ensure pieces were properly learned, and he could accompany classes. According to Rimsky he taught some elementary theory, even 'composing some trios and quartets with dreadful part-writing as exercises for Leonova's pupils'.[33]

Two short piano pieces appear also to belong to 1880. *Une larme* is one of Musorgsky's feeblest pieces, nor can *Impromptu: In the Country* rate much higher, though the folksong on which the first section is based provides some borrowed character, and the series of short dances that comprise the second half are at least engaging. A third, also rather characterless, piece, *Méditation (Feuillet d'album)*, was composed in the early autumn, to be published by Bernard as the supplement to No. 11 of *Nouvelliste* for 1880.

On 30 October Musorgsky's march *The Capture of Kars* was rapturously premièred. Far less successful—though, tragically, far more significant—was a performance four days later at a gathering in the home of Terty Filippov, head of the department in which Musorgsky's civil service career had come to an abrupt end, but also a friend, musical enthusiast, and one of the composer's four financial supporters in the cause of completing *Khovanshchina*. At this soirée Musorgsky introduced his new opera to a group of 'like-minded' persons, including members of the kuchka. There seems to be no direct record from any of those

[33] *RKM*, 168.

present of how the evening proceeded, but the librettist and composer
Ilya Tyumenev later recalled the oral account of Mikhail Berman, a
choral conductor connected with the FMS. It seems to have gone much
as in the kuchka's old days: a lot of criticism, only more insistent, it
seems (especially from Cui), and less constructive in spirit. Curiously,
the one whose censure was most restrained was Balakirev. And all this
in public, before other listeners. Musorgsky, as was his habit in such
predicaments, outwardly bowed to the criticism, though the event can
have done nothing to encourage him to proceed with the opera, and
it seems that not another note was ever added to *Khovanshchina*. Nor
would there have been much time for this; he had little more than four
months to live.

For the biographer nothing is more demoralizing than to trace the decline of a once great creative artist, to see such scattered facts of personal
biography as may emerge become little more than pathetic trivia evi-
dencing personal degradation, and to see the material quality and expressive richness of his creative output progressively falter because the
capacity for sustained application has gone and, worst of all, the creative
mind seems no longer to command the clarity, sharpness, alertness—
or, one suspects, the dynamic—to search out, seize, then embody its
profoundest insights in forms and materials that may enchant, move,
even stun, the listener. This is the condition towards which the personal
and creative biographies of Musorgsky had for some years been sinking.
To note only the consequences for the operas: *Khovanshchina*, though
no more than a torso, must rate in its potential among the greater operas
of the nineteenth century, yet there is little sign in the sometimes very
sketchy fragments extant from its later stages that these, fully realized,
would have made a conclusion worthy of the opera's opening stretches.
But even if they had had that potential, *Khovanshchina* (and, even less,
Sorochintsy Fair) could still never have equalled the stupendous achievement of *Boris Godunov*, so grandly conceived and so prodigiously inventive—above all, perhaps, so blindingly illuminating in its dramatic
insights. Any list of the dozen greatest operas of Musorgsky's century
would surely have to include this colossus. In fact, he had composed
only a handful of isolated pieces of any significance since 1877, the year
of the five Alexey Tolstoy songs, and it is yet more depressing, after

such reflections, to return to the pitiful course of Musorgsky's personal biography. There is little point in lingering over it. A tiny note to Rimsky is not only all that remains of Musorgsky's correspondence from the rest of 1880, but it is also his last surviving letter. For further information we have to go to the recollections of others.

The memoirs of the composer and conductor, Mikhail Ippolitov-Ivanov, at that time a student of Rimsky's at the St Petersburg Conservatoire and later a friend of Tchaikovsky, usefully bring some perspective to the tempo of Musorgsky's decline.[34]

> I became acquainted with Modest Petrovich at the end of 1878 when he as yet gave no impression of going downhill, was neatly, though not fashionably dressed, and walked with his head held proudly which, with his characteristic hairstyle, gave him a lively appearance. After this he quickly started to let himself go, appeared not always in good order, and talked mostly about himself, attacking us—the young ones. 'You *young ones*', he said to me once during a walk, 'sitting in the conservatoire, do you want to know nothing beyond your *cantus firmus*, do you think that the Zaremba formula, "the minor is original sin, but the major is redemption", or "rest, movement, and again rest", settles everything? No, my friend, in my view, transgress, go ahead and transgress; if there's movement, then there's no going back to rest—but onwards, smashing up everything'. During this he proudly shook his head. The last time I saw him before his illness was in the Maly Yaroslavets restaurant, where I, Laroche, and Glazunov had looked in to see him. We found him totally unstable. He promptly fell upon Rubinstein, Balakirev, Rimsky-Korsakov for their erudition and, having repeated several times: 'You must create, create', he fell silent. Then raising his bleary eyes towards me, he unexpectedly asked: 'How do you get a spot out of a morning coat?'
>
> 'I try not to get one in, Modest Petrovich', I replied.
>
> 'But I, you know, get it out very well with green soap', he said.
>
> With that our conversation ended.

It is impossible to fix the period of Ivanov's second meeting with Musorgsky, but the first encounter between the latter and the soprano Alexandra Demidova dates from late 1880, when she had called to seek

---

[34] *MVS*, 187–8.

lessons from him and Leonova. The latter 'had loudly summoned Modest Petrovich, and a middle-aged man of medium height, not handsome in appearance, with wavy hair, emerged in a shabby frock-coat and rather sternly asked me over to the piano'. Demidova was instantly impressed by Musorgsky's vivid playing of a Schubert song accompaniment. But when lessons began, she recalled how 'there usually stood alongside on the table his sustenance, a plate of mushrooms and a wine glass. Darya Mikhailovna (Leonova) lamented that he often resorted to it and had visibly let himself go.'[35]

Little information on Musorgsky's day-to-day activities survives from the first weeks of 1881. On 15 February, at a concert of the FMS conducted by Rimsky, *The Destruction of Sennacherib* and the song *Forgotten* were performed, Musorgsky presumably acting as pianist in the latter. The following day there was a literary soirée in memory of Dostoyevsky, who had died a week earlier, and as the great writer's portrait was carried in 'Musorgsky sat at the piano and improvised a funeral knell like that which rings out in the final scene of *Boris*', the historian and archaeologist, Vasily Druzhinin recalled (or so Ivan Lapshin remembered). 'This was Musorgsky's penultimate public appearance, and his musical improvisation was his final "farewell" not only to the departed singer of "the insulted and injured", but to all living beings.'[36]

This was not quite true; Musorgsky's own 'final farewell' came only five days later at a charity concert for impoverished students. Two more days, and the final crisis was reached. It is clear that Leonova had long assumed, as far as she could, an almost maternal role in Musorgsky's life, and it was to her that he now turned. On the morning of 23 February, as Leonova later recorded:[37]

> He came to me in the most nervous, distraught state and said that he had nowhere to go, he would have to walk the streets, that he had no resources, and that there was no way out of his situation. What could I do? I began comforting him, saying that though I hadn't much, I would share with him what I had. This calmed him a little. That evening I had to go with him

---

[35] *TDM*, 589, 591.

[36] *KYM*, 151. Druzhinin's memories were recorded by the philosopher and writer on music, Ivan Lapshin

[37] *MVS*, 183–4.

to General Sokhansky, whose daughter was our pupil and who had, at her home, to sing for the first time to a large company. She sang very well, which probably had its effect upon Musorgsky . . . After the singing there began dancing, and it was suggested that I should play cards. Suddenly Sokhansky's son ran up to me, and asked whether Musorgsky had fits. I replied that in all the time I had known him I had never heard of this. It appeared he had had a stroke. A doctor who was present attended him, and when it was time to leave, Musorgsky was already completely recovered and on his feet. We rode away together. On arriving at my apartment, he began pressing me to let him stay, pleading some sort of nervous, fear-ridden condition. I agreed to this with pleasure, knowing that if something happened to him again in his one-man flat, then he could be without any help. I gave him the little study and ordered the maid to watch over him all night, instructing her, if he should be taken ill, to wake me immediately. He slept the whole night sitting up. In the morning when I went into the dining room for tea, he also came in, very cheerful. I asked how he was feeling. He thanked me and replied that he felt well. With these words he turned to the right and suddenly fell headlong. My misgivings had not been unfounded—if he had been alone he would certainly have suffocated, but here we turned him over, gave him immediate help, and sent for the doctor. By evening there had been two more such attacks. Towards evening I summoned all his friends who had displayed concern for him, primarily Vladimir Stasov, Terty Filippov, and others who loved him. The general consensus was: in view of the supposedly complex treatment and the need of constant nursing, to propose to him that he should go into hospital, explaining why this was important and advantageous to him. He was promised that a separate and first-class room would be arranged for him in the hospital. For a long while he would not agree, absolutely insisting he wanted to stay with me. In the end they persuaded him. The next day he was taken by carriage to the hospital.

Musorgsky was installed in the Nikolayevsky Military Hospital. Cui's wife, Malvina, arranged this with the help of Lev Bertenson, a doctor who twelve years later would be the central figure in attending Tchaikovsky on his deathbed. The hospital had many good points: 'completely free, sisters of mercy, and—most important—total removal from wine', Stasov informed Balakirev. ' . . . Sometimes he remembers things (when *I* was with him yesterday, and then *Filippov*), but another time he is beside himself, as though delirious.'[38] Borodin and Rimsky visited, a small procession of friends and well-wishers followed over the next fortnight, and soon notices of his illness were appearing in the press. The early stages of epilepsy were diagnosed, his ramblings suggested touches of insanity, and the doctors pronounced his state terminal, predicting he might live a year—or a day. The baritone Ivan Melnikov proposed to give a charity concert for his benefit, but was prevented by the assassination of Alexander II, which had plunged the whole nation into obligatory mourning. Repin visited during one of Musorgsky's better phases, and in four sittings produced the most famous of all images of the composer. When the art patron Pavel Tretyakov paid Repin for his portrait, the latter asked Stasov to divert his fee tactfully to Musorgsky. But Stasov declined, despite Repin's protests: the painter had a wife and family, and in any case those who had funded Musorgsky for his unfinished operas' sakes would continue their support. Repin could join in at that stage, if he wished (subsequently he sent his fee of four hundred roubles to Stasov who allocated it to the fund for a memorial over Musorgsky's grave). Even Filaret, the brother with whom Musorgsky seems to have had little or no contact for five years, appeared with money. For some ten or more days there was a visible improvement that led some to hope. But then came the fatal act. In his craving for alcohol, which had been totally forbidden him, Musorgsky bribed one of the orderlies to bring in a bottle of wine or cognac. The result was catastrophic: 'suddenly an unexpected change occurred in him', Stasov recorded, 'terrible new symptoms set in, paralysis struck his arms and legs'.[39] His breathing became difficult. Now that the end was imminent, it was decided he must settle his affairs, and he assigned all his royalty and publishing rights, both present and future, to Filippov, assessing them at 2000 roubles. In all other regards, Musorgsky died a pauper. It was Stasov who later discharged his debts at the Maly Yaroslavets.

Musorgsky died at 5 a.m. on 28 March, a week after his forty-second birthday. Stasov described his end: 'almost to the last moment he was

---

[38] *TDM*, 601–2.

[39] Obituary of Musorgsky, printed in *The Voice*, 29 March 1881 (in *SSM3*, 45).

fully conscious and lucid. He expired without pain, without suffering: the agony lasted in all a few seconds.'[40] This was anodyne, and Ippolitov-Ivanov's obituary was less sparing, his open admission of Musorgsky's alcoholism earning him a public rebuke from Stasov at the funeral: 'No one was with him except two medical attendants. They tell how once or twice he had cried out loudly, and within a quarter-hour all was finished.'[41] The following day two requiems were conducted in the hospital's chapel. Some 200 persons attended the first, including Stasov, the Rimsky-Korsakovs and Borodin, while at the second a wreath appeared from the conservatoire, Rimsky, presumably, being responsible for this. No doubt Musorgsky himself would have fully agreed with Ippolitov-Ivanov's comment: 'how ironic this wreath seemed, coming from an institution that had never recognized him'.[42] An exhibition of the *peredvizhniki* was running in St Petersburg, and Stasov ensured instant public display of Repin's portrait.

The following day Musorgsky's remains were taken for burial. An account, evidently written by Stasov, was printed in *The Voice* the following day and presented as dignified an impression as possible of the occasion. But the record confided by Ivan Tyumenev to his private diary on the day of the funeral itself has the greater ring of truth. Fewer gathered in the hospital chapel than had attended the requiems, but Balakirev was there, together with the Rimsky-Korsakovs, Borodins, and Cuis, Lyadov, Nápravník, Leonova, and the Stasov brothers. Because the officiating deacon was late the procession was delayed, and only about 100 people joined it. The arrangements left much to be desired; those responsible seemed to have no clear idea of how best to reach the cemetery, and Balakirev grabbed a cab to go ahead and check that a cross was ready for the grave. It had been hoped the choirs of the conservatoire and FMS would have provided singing on the way, but none appeared, and when the cortège entered the cemetery, the mourners did their best to supply this deficiency. The service in the Dukhovskaya Church was far better arranged, a good number of people were waiting, including Karl Davïdov, director of the conservatoire,

---

[40] Ibid.

[41] Obituary of Musorgsky, printed in *New Time*, 29 March 1881 (in *TDM*, 611).

[42] *KYM*, 150.

plus a number of soloists from the Imperial Opera, and the building was nearly full. The Nevsky Choir was in place, and the archimandrite Iosif officiated, all giving their services. Even the grave in the Tikhvinsky cemetery was allotted at no charge. An unidentified lady attached to the wreaths surrounding the coffin the two ribbons which had been presented to Musorgsky after the première of *Boris* in 1874. One read: 'To new shores!', the other 'Glory to you for *Boris*, glory!' As the interment concluded Melnikov read a poem by Grigory Lishin. There were none of the expected speeches—except that is, from Rimsky, who 'in an intentionally loud voice (probably by prior agreement)' announced to Stasov that he would scrutinize what Musorgsky had left unfinished, and would edit, complete, and publish it, beginning with *Khovanshchina*. 'For musicians such an announcement was more precious than many, many speeches', Ilya Tyumenev noted in his diary.[43] And at the end of this purely private, personal record of the day's event, Tyumenev added his own intimate tribute and benediction: 'Peace, peace thrice-over to your ashes, you good sympathetic man, mild gentle heart, and talent so passionately serving your beloved, great, native land.'[44]

[43] *TDM*, 618.
[44] *TDM*, 619.

Postlude: The Century Since

RIMSKY WAS AS GOOD AS HIS WORD. YET HE WOULD FINALLY receive small thanks for his labours, especially when, a half-century after Musorgsky's death, publication of Pavel Lamm's complete edition brought into the public domain nearly all that composer's original texts. After this it became fashionable to censure Musorgsky's colleague for what was now seen as, at best, a patronizing service to his friend's work, at worst a self-interested decking out of another composer's creations in more glamorous and fashionable clothing that might advertise their couturier's superiority in taste and workmanship. No accusation could have been more unjustified. When Musorgsky died Rimsky was already a composer with a personal reputation large enough and an output successful enough for him to need no reflected glory. In fact, he expended on his self-imposed task a vast amount of time, care, and effort at the expense of his own interests. One may wonder what made him set about the task in the first place, considering how blistering was his judgment on Musorgsky's shortcomings: 'absurd, incoherent harmony, ugly part-writing, sometimes staggeringly illogical modulations, sometimes a dispiriting absence of such, inept instrumentation in the orchestral pieces, in general a certain, irreverent, self-admiring dilettantism, at times moments of technical dexterity, but more often utter technical feebleness'. But to set against all this Rimsky found most of Musorgsky's compositions were 'so full of talent, so original, presented so much that was new and alive, that their publication was an imperative'.[1] His missionary devotion being partnered by moral outrage, he felt no scruples about rewriting what he heard as clumsy and illiterate, nor did he hesitate to cut and reorder where he felt this would be beneficial, but only because he believed such interventions would put his friend's work into a condition that would give it a better chance of winning public recognition. And he recognized that, if the public later wanted to hear Musorgsky's originals, they were still there for the having. As it is, without Rimsky's selfless service, the early reception history of Musorgsky's music would have turned out very differently.

While in hospital during his last illness Musorgsky had made Filippov his executor, and the latter agreed with the publisher Bessel that he should handle Musorgsky's works in return for a promise that they would be issued as soon as possible. In 1882 the first results of this agreement appeared: twelve songs, all edited by Rimsky, including the *Songs and Dances of Death* and the five Alexey Tolstoy songs. Four more songs, the orchestral score of the piano *Intermezzo in modo classico*, the B flat Scherzo for orchestra, *Jesus Navin*, and the chorus for *Oedipus in Athens* followed in 1883, and also—most important of all—both full and vocal scores of *Khovanshchina* as edited ruthlessly by Rimsky, who had also composed an ending and orchestrated the entire opera. In this version *Khovanshchina* was first performed in St. Petersburg on 21 February 1886. Also in that year both *Pictures at an Exhibition* and *St John's Night* were issued, the latter especially heavily edited.

The most famous—some would say notorious—of Rimsky's revisions was still to come. His first incursion into *Boris Godunov* was made in 1888, when he orchestrated the polonaise from the Polish Act. Four years later he tackled the Coronation Scene, and between 1892 and 1896 he reworked the whole vocal score, rewriting, cutting, and rearranging freely, then orchestrating and publishing the result. Rimsky himself conducted a concert performance of this in St Petersburg in 1896, and in 1898 it was staged in Moscow. But in 1906 he reworked it a second time, a year later substantially expanding the choruses in the Coronation Scene with newly composed music. This version, with Shalyapin singing the title role with which this great Russian bass would be inextricably associated for the next thirty years, was mounted in Paris

---

[1] *RKM*, 184.

on 19 May 1908, and was to hold the stage for the next half-century until the movement to reinstate Musorgsky's original began to gather strength.

With Rimsky's death in 1908 the task of preparing Musorgsky's few remaining works for publication passed to others. The one major piece still left was the third opera, *Sorochintsy Fair*. The posthumous history of this is complex, and the details need not concern us here. From 1886 various bits appeared in vocal score. A patched-up version, with Musorgsky's completed numbers orchestrated by Lyadov and Vyacheslav Karatïgin, plus Rimsky's revision of *St John's Night* and some new music by Yury Sakhnovsky—all glued together with spoken dialogue from Gogol's original—was given in Moscow in 1913. Yet the first entirely musical production was of Cui's edition (1915–16), in which Musorgsky's old colleague (and sometimes scourge) composed new music to plug the gaps, then orchestrated the whole; this was heard in St Petersburg on 26 October 1917. A completion and orchestration by Nikolay Tcherepnin was produced in 1923, but the text that has become standard, and seems likely to remain so, is Vissarion Shebalin's, prepared in 1930 and based on Lamm's edition. Shebalin scrupulously used everything he could of what Musorgsky had composed, though he reordered some numbers, then supplied extra music, relating this wherever possible to that which Musorgsky had composed. This was given in its final version in Moscow on 12 January 1932.

What now remained was for Musorgsky's other two operas to be reclaimed for their composer. *Khovanshchina* would, of course, always require the participation of a second musician, and this came from Shostakovich who, in 1959, completed a revision and orchestration based on Lamm's edition of Musorgsky's vocal score but retaining Rimsky's music (though not his scoring) for the opera's ending. Originally prepared for a film, this version was staged in Leningrad on 25 November 1960. Though it has now become the standard version, Shostakovich's readiness to amend Musorgsky's musical text denies it final authoritative status. Twenty years earlier, in 1939–40, Shostakovich had given the same treatment to *Boris*, a service as unnecessary as it was undesirable, in view of Lamm's publication in 1928 of Musorgsky's full score (on 16 February 1928 this had been staged in Leningrad). During the 1930s there were occasional productions based on Lamm's edition (the UK première was at Sadler's Wells, London, on 30 September 1935). But in 1975 David Lloyd-Jones published the opera's full score in both its initial and final versions, all based on Musorgsky's autographs, together with a full critical commentary. This edition, despite all the debates about exactly what Musorgsky may have cut or adjusted, has rightly become the basis for most productions, and is likely to remain so.

And so, finally, Musorgsky's music (or almost all) has been returned to its composer.

Calendar

Year	Age	Life	Contemporary Musicians/ Events
1839		Modest Musorgsky born, 21 March, at Karevo, near Toropets, son of Pyotr Musorgsky, a landowner, and Yuliya Chirikova.	Alyabyev aged 52; Balakirev 2; Berlioz 36; Bizet 1; Borodin 6; Brahms 6; Bruckner 15; Cherubini 79; Chopin 29; Dargomïzhsky 26; Donizetti 42; Glinka 35; Gounod 21; Liszt 28; Mendelssohn 30; Meyerbeer 48; Moniuszko 20; Offenbach 20; Rossini 47; Rubinstein 10; Saint-Saëns 4; Schumann 29; Serov 19; Smetana 15; Verdi 26; Wagner 26.
1840	1		Tchaikovsky born, 7 May.
1841	2		Chabrier born, 18 Jan.; Dvořák born, 8 Sept.
1842	3		Boito born, 24 Feb.; Cherubini dies, 15 Mar.; Massenet born, 12 May; Sullivan born, 13 May. Glinka's *Ruslan and Lyudmila* given, St Petersburg. Gogol's *The Marriage* and *Dead Souls*.
1843	4		Grieg born, 15 June.
1844	5		Rimsky-Korsakov born, 18 Mar.

1845	6		Fauré born, 12 May.
1846	7		
1847	8		Mendelssohn dies, 4 Nov. Dargomïzhsky's *Esmeralda* given, Moscow.
1848	9		Donizetti dies, 8 Apr. Glinka's *Kamarinskaya*.
1849	10	Family moves to St Petersburg to begin M.'s formal schooling.	Chopin dies, 17 Oct.
1850	11		Rubinstein's first piano concerto.
1851	12	Plays the piano in charity concert. Enters School for Guards' Cadets.	Spontini dies, 24 Jan.; Alyabyev dies, 6 Mar.; d'Indy born, 27 Mar. Rubinstein's Ocean Symphony.
1852	13	*Porte-enseigne polka* composed and published.	Gogol dies, 4 Mar.; Stanford born, 30 Sept.
1853	14		
1854	15		Janáček born, 3 July. Britain and France declare war on Russia (Crimean War).
1855	16		Chausson born, 21 Jan.; Lyadov born, 11 May.
1856	17	Leaves School for Guards' Cadets and joins Preobrazhensky Guards. Meets Borodin.	Schumann dies, 29 July; Taneyev born, 25 Nov. Dargomïzhsky's *Rusalka* given, St Petersburg.
1857	18	Meets Dargomïzhsky, Cui, Balakirev (who begins to teach M.), and Vladimir Stasov.	Glinka dies, 15 Feb.; Elgar born, 2 June.
1858	19	Leaves the army. Continues work with Balakirev. Nervous disorder. Scherzo in B flat composed.	Leoncavallo born, 8 Mar. Balakirev's Overture on 3 Russian Themes.
1859	20	Visits Moscow and is deeply impressed. Composes a chorus for Vladisláv Ozerov's *Oedipus in Athens*.	Spohr dies, 22 Oct.; Ippolitov-Ivanov born, 19 Nov. Gounod's *Faust* given, Paris. Russian Musical Society (RMS) founded.
1860	21	Scherzo in B flat performed at RMS concert, conducted by Rubinstein. Suffers second nervous disorder.	Wolf born, 13 Mar.; Mahler born, 7 July.
1861	22	*Oedipus* chorus performed. Liberation of the serfs to which M. is sympathetic in principle though, as landowner, he suffers financially. Meets Rimsky-Korsakov.	Arensky born, 11 Apr.; Marschner dies, 14 Dec.; MacDowell born, 18 Dec.

1862	23	*Intermezzo in modo classico* for piano composed. Financial constraints force M. to live with his brother Filaret.	Delius born, 29 Jan.; Debussy born, 22 Aug.; Verstovsky dies, 17 Nov. St Petersburg Conservatoire grows out of RMS classes, with Tchaikovsky in its first intake. Balakirev and Lomakin found the Free Music School (FMS) to counter 'westernizing' conservatoire. Verdi's *La forza del destino* given, St Petersburg.
1863	24	First major song, *King Saul*, composed. Enters civil service, and joins a 'commune' with other young men. Opera *Salammbô* begun.	Mascagni born, 7 Dec. Serov's *Judith* given, St Petersburg.
1864	25	Composes *Kalistratushka*, his first thoroughly characteristic song. *Salammbô* continued.	Meyerbeer dies, 2 May; Richard Strauss born, 11 June.
1865	26	M.'s mother dies. A bout of dipsomania and serious illness follows. Is persuaded to leave the commune and resume living with Filaret.	Nielsen born, 9 June; Glazunov born, 10 Aug.; Dukas born, 1 Oct.; Sibelius born, 8 Dec. Serov's *Rogneda* given, St Petersburg. Dargomïzhsky begins opera *The Stone Guest*.
1866	27	Meets Glinka's sister, Lyudmila Shestakova. *Darling Savishna* proves to be the first of a series of wholeheartedly 'realist' songs. Work on *Salammbô* peters out. *St John's Night on the Bare Mountain* conceived.	Kalinnikov born, 13 Jan.; Busoni born, 1 Apr. Liszt's *Totentanz* first heard in Russia, and makes a great impression on M.
1867	28	In May loses his civil service post. *St John's Night* completed. More songs, including *The Magpie, Gathering Mushrooms,* and *The Ragamuffin*.	Granados born, 27 July. Borodin completes his first symphony.
1868	29	*With Nurse*, the first of the *Nursery* cycle, composed. 'Realist' opera on Gogol's *The Marriage* begun (June), then abandoned in favour of one on Pushkin's *Boris Godunov*. In September begins a three-year residence with the Opochinins.	Rossini dies, 13 Nov. Cui completes opera *William Ratcliff*.

1869	30	Reappointed to civil service in Forestry Department. Full score of *Boris* (first version) completed.	Roussel born, 5 Apr.; Dargomïzhsky dies, 17 Jan.; Berlioz dies, 8 Mar. Balakirev composes *Islamey*. Borodin begins second symphony and *Prince Igor*.
1870	31	*Boris* submitted to the Imperal Theatres. Lampoon *The Peepshow* composed and *The Nursery* completed.	Lvov dies, 28 Dec.
1871	32	*Boris* rejected for performance; M. begins a revision. Vocal score completed, 12 March. From September shares accommodation with Rimsky-Korsakov.	Serov dies, 1 Feb.; Auber dies, 12 May. Serov's *Hostile Power* given, St Petersburg.
1872	33	*Boris* (revised version) submitted. Coronation Scene and opera's Polonaise given in concerts. Collaborates on music for an opera-ballet, *Mlada* (incorporating a revision of *St John's Night*), and projects a new opera, *Khovanshchina*.	Skryabin born, 6 Jan.; Vaughan Williams born, 12 Oct. Dargomïzhsky's *The Stone Guest* given, St Petersburg.
1873	34	Three scenes from *Boris* successfully given in St Petersburg, February. Planned visit to Liszt cancelled, but is heartened by Liszt's reported praise of *The Nursery*. New bout of dipsomania. Meets the young poet Arseny Golenishchev-Kutuzov, with whom he will intermittently share an apartment. Death of his artist-friend Viktor Hartmann. Work on *Khovanshchina* proceeds.	Reger born, 19 Mar.; Rakhmaninov born, 1 Apr. Rimsky-Korsakov's *The Maid of Pskov* given, St Petersburg.
1874	35	*Boris* given complete, 8 February, except for the Cell Scene. More dipsomania, but work on *Khovanshchina* resumes after a break. Composes song cycle, *Sunless*, and *Pictures at an Exhibition*, for piano. Nadezhda Opochinina dies. Envisages an opera on Gogol's *Sorochintsy Fair*.	Suk born, 4 Jan.; Schoenberg born, 3 Sept.; Holst born, 21 Sept. Tchaikovsky's *The Oprichnik* given, St Petersburg.

1875	36	First three songs of *Songs and Dances of Death* composed. Act 1 of *Khovanshchina* and opening of Act 2 completed. Further promotion in the Forestry Department. When evicted, he moves in with Pavel Naumov and Mariya Fedorova.	Glier born, 11 Jan.; Ravel born, 7 Mar.; Bizet dies, 3 June. Rubinstein's *The Demon* and Verdi's *Aïda* given, St Petersburg.
1876	37	Thoughtless intervention by Stasov leads to dislocation of work on *Khovanshchina* and increased attention to *Sorochintsy Fair*.	Wolf-Ferrari born, 12 Jan.; Falla born, 23 Nov. Cui's *Angelo* given, St Petersburg.
1877	38	Last of *Songs and Dances of Death* and the five Alexey Tolstoy songs composed. Work on *Sorochintsy Fair* begins in earnest. But tactless criticism (especially from Stasov) depresses M. and causes disruption of work. Briefly envisages an opera, *Pugachevshchina*, as a sequel to *Khovanshchina*.	Dohnányi born, 27 July.
1878	39	Death of the veteran singer Osip Petrov, whom M. had envisaged as the lead in *Sorochintsy Fair*, seals that opera's fate. M.'s dipsomania becoming worse, despite his friends' moral support. Erratic behaviour (and inside influence) prompts his removal to another civil service department. Association with the singer Darya Leonova begins.	
1879	40	First performance (in concert) of the Cell Scene from *Boris*. Concert tour of southern Russia with Leonova (August–November). M.'s condition on his return is bad. Excerpts from *Khovanshchina* given concert performance.	Frank Bridge born, 26 Feb.; Respighi born, 9 July. Tchaikovsky's *Eugene Onegin* given, Moscow.
1880	41	M. loses his civil service post. Two groups of friends independently subsidize him to complete (respectively) *Khovanshchina* and *Sorochintsy Fair*. His condition allows only minimal work on	Medtner born, 5 Jan.; Bloch born, 24 July; Pizzetti born, 20 Sept.; Offenbach dies, 4 Oct. Rimsky-Korsakov's *May Night* given, St Petersburg.

either opera. In the autumn
joins Leonova in a teaching enterprise as pianist and teacher of
elementary theory. Plays *Khov-*
anshchina to a group of friends,
but criticism, especially from
Cui, further demoralizes him.

1881	42	Performs at a literary soirée in memory of Dostoyevsky, who had died a week earlier. On 23 February appears at Leonova's in a distraught condition. Collapses and on 24 is taken into hospital. Repin paints his portrait. On 28 March M. dies.	Dostoyevsky dies, 9 Feb.; Bartók born, 25 Mar.; Myaskovsky born, 20 Apr.; Vieuxtemps dies, 6 June.

List of Works

The prime source for this list is the detailed description of Musorgsky's musical autographs in Valentin Antipov, 'Proizvedeniya Musorgskovo po autografam i drugim pervoistochnikam: annotirovannïy ukazatel' [Musorgsky's works according to the autographs and other primary sources: an annotated guide], published in E. Levasheva, ed., *Naslediye M. P. Musorgskovo: sbornik materialov. K vïpusku polnovo akademicheskovo sobraniya sochineny M. P. Musorgskovo v tridtsati dvukh tomax* [Musorgsky's legacy: a collection of materials. Towards the issue of a scholarly edition of Musorgsky's compositions in 32 volumes] (Moscow, 1989). In all cases dates are adjusted to the Western calendar. Publication dates are given, in parentheses, for works published during Musorgsky's lifetime.

Stage

Han d'Islande (opera: after Hugo), projected 1856

Oedipus in Athens (incidental music to Vladisláv Ozerov's tragedy), 1858–61, incl. some
 pieces recycled in *Salammbô* and *Mlada*

Salammbô (opera: after Flaubert), 1863–6, incomplete

Zhenitba [The Marriage] (comic opera: Gogol), 1868, Act 1 only

Boris Godunov (opera: Musorgsky, after Pushkin and Karamzin)
 (i) First version, 7 scenes in 4 parts, 1868–9
 (ii) Second version, prologue and 4 acts, 1871–2 (vocal score, 1874); première St
 Petersburg, 8 Feb. 1874

Bobïl [The landless peasant] (opera: after Spielhagen, *Hans und Grete*), projected 1870

Mlada [with Cui, Borodin, Rimsky-Korsakov] (opera-ballet: V. A. Krïlov), 1872,
 incomplete

Khovanshchina [The Khovansky plot] (opera, 6 scenes: Musorgsky), 1872–80,
 incomplete
 completed (in 5 acts) and orchestrated Rimsky-Korsakov; première St Petersburg,
 21 Feb. 1886

Sorochinskaya yarmarka [Sorochintsy Fair] (comic opera, 3 acts: after Gogol), 1874–80,
  incomplete
  completed and orchestrated Lyadov, Karatïgin, and others; première, Moscow, 21
  Oct. 1913
Pugachevshchina [The Pugachev plot], projected 1877

Choral

Marsh Shamilya [Shamil's march], T., B., chorus, pf, 1859
Porazheniye Sennakheriba [The Destruction of Sennacherib], chorus, orch., 1866–7
  (vocal score, 1871), rev. 1874
Iisus Navin [Jesus Navin (or Joshua)], A., B., chorus, pf, 1874–5, rev. 1877
3 vocalises for 3 female vv., 1880
5 Russ. folksongs, arr. 4 male vv., 1880:
  1 Skazhi, devitsa milaya
  2 Tï vzoydi, solntse krasnoye
  3 U vorot, vorot batyushkinïkh
  4 Uzh tï, volya, moya volya (with 2 T. soloists)
  5 Plïvet, vosplïvayet zelenïy dubok

Songs

Songs existing also in a revised version are indicated by an asterisk
*Where art thou, little star? (Grekov) [1857 in one autograph, though probably later],
  1858, orch. 1858
Meines Herzens Sehnsucht (anon. German text, trans. D. Usov), 1858
*Tell me why (anon.), 1858 (1867)
*Hour of Jollity (Koltsov), 1858
Sadly rustled the leaves (after Pleshcheyev), 1859
*What are words of love to you? (Ammosov), 1860
I have many palaces and gardens (Koltsov), 1863
Old Man's Song (Goethe, trans. ?Musorgsky), 1863
*King Saul (Byron, trans. Kozlov), 1863 (1871), orch. 1879 [lost]
But if I could meet thee again (Kurochkin), 1863
The wild winds blow (Koltsov), 1864
*Kalistratushka (Nekrasov), 1864
*Night (after Pushkin), 1864, orch. 1868, (1871)
Prayer (Lermontov), 1865
The Outcast: essay in recitative (Holz-Miller), 1865
*Cradle Song (Ostrovsky, from *The Voyevoda*), 1865 (1871)
*Why are thine eyes sometimes so cold? [also known as 'Malyutka', 'Little One']
  (Pleshcheyev), 1866.
*The Wish (Heine, trans. Mey), 1866
From my tears (Heine, trans. Mikhaylov), 1866
*Darling Savishna (Musorgsky), 1866 (1867)
You drunken sot! (Musorgsky), 1866
*Gopak (Shevchenko, trans. Mey), 1866 (1867), rev. for orch. 1868
*The Seminarist (Musorgsky), 1866 (1870)
Yarema's Song, 'On the Dnieper' (Shevchenko), 1867 [lost]; surviving version, 1879

⋆Hebrew Song (Mey), 1867 (1868)

⋆The Magpie (Pushkin), 1867 (1871)

Gathering Mushrooms (Mey), 1867 (1868)

The Feast (Koltsov), 1867 (1868)

⋆The Ragamuffin (Musorgsky), 1867 (1871)

The Garden by the Don (Koltsov), 1867/8

The He-goat: a worldly story (Musorgsky), 1868 (1868)

⋆The Classicist (Musorgsky), 1868 (1870)

⋆The Orphan (Musorgsky), 1868 (1871)

⋆Eremushka's Lullaby (Nekrasov), 1868 (1871)

⋆Child's Song (Mey), 1868 (1871)

The Nursery (Musorgsky) (after 1872)

   ⋆1. With Nurse, 1868

    2. In the Corner, 1870

   ⋆3. The Beetle, 1870

    4. With the Doll, 1870

    5. Going to Sleep, 1870

⋆The Peepshow (Musorgsky), 1870 (1871)

Evening Song (Pleshcheyev), 1871

At the Dacha (Musorgsky) [now often incorporated as nos. 6 and 7 of The Nursery]:

    1. The Cat Sailor, 1872

   ⋆2. On the Hobby Horse, 1872

Sunless (Golenishchev-Kutuzov), 1874 (1874):

    1. Between Four Walls

    2. You did not know me in the crowd

    3. The idle, noisy day is ended

    4. Ennui

    5. Elegy

    6. On the River

Forgotten (Golenishchev-Kutuzov), 1874 (1874)

Epitaph (Musorgsky), 1874, incomplete

The Nettle Mountain (Musorgsky), 1874, incomplete

Songs and Dances of Death (Golenishchev-Kutuzov):

    1. Lullaby, 1875

    2. Serenade, 1875

   ⋆3. Trepak, 1875

   ⋆4. The Field Marshal, 1877

⋆The Sphinx (Musorgsky), 1876

Not like thunder (A. K. Tolstoy), 1877

⋆Softly the spirit flew up to heaven (A. K. Tolstoy), 1877

Pride (A. K. Tolstoy), 1877

⋆Is spinning man's work? (A. K. Tolstoy), 1877

It scatter and breaks (A. K. Tolstoy), 1877

The Vision (Golenishchev-Kutuzov), 1877

The Wanderer (Rückert, trans. Pleshcheyev), ?1878

Mephistopheles' Song of the Flea (Goethe, trans. Strugovshchikov), 1879

Orchestral

Scherzo, B flat, 1858 [?orig. for pf]
Alla marcia notturna, 1861
Symphony in D, projected 1861
St John's Night on the Bare Mountain, 1867, rev. 1872, ?1880
Intermezzo in modo classico, 1867, orig. (1862) for pf, ?with added trio (1863)
Poděbrad the Czech (symphonic poem), projected 1867
The Capture of Kars (march), 1880

Piano

Porte-enseigne polka, 1852 (1852)
Souvenir d'enfance, 1857
2 sonatas, E flat, F sharp minor, 1858, both lost
Scherzo, C sharp minor, 1858
?Scherzo, B flat, 1858 [lost: perhaps the original form of Scherzo, B flat, orch., 1858]
Impromptu passionné, 1859
In the Corner (scherzo), 1859, rev. as Ein Kinderscherz, 1860 (1873)
Allegro and Scherzo [transcribed from Scherzo, C sharp minor, 1858] for a Sonata in
  C, pf duet, 1860
Intermezzo in modo classico, 1862, rev. ?1863 (1873), orch. 1867, retranscribed for pf
  1867
From Memories of Childhood [Souvenirs d'enfance], 1865:
  1. Nurse and I
  2. First Punishment: Nurse shuts me in a dark room, incomplete
Rêverie, on a theme of Vyacheslav Loginov, 1865
La capricieuse, on a theme of Login Heyden, 1865
The Seamstress (scherzino), 1871 (1872)
Pictures at an Exhibition, 1874
Storm on the Black Sea, 1879, lost
On the Southern Shore of the Crimea [or Gurzuf], 1879 (1880)
Near the Southern Shore of the Crimea [or Baydary or Capriccio], 1880 (1880)
Méditation (Feuillet d'album), 1880 (1880)
Une larme, ?1880
In the Country, impromptu, ?1880

Arrangements

Gordigiani: 'Ogni sabato avrete il lume acceso' (Tuscan popular song), arr. as vocal
  duet (A., B.), pf, 1860
Leonova: 'Après le bal' (melody), words and pf accompaniment by Musorgsky, 1879
  (1879)
Lodïzhensky: 'Oriental Cradle Song', pf accompaniment by Musorgsky, 1874
A. S. Taneyev: 'Cradle Song', pf accompaniment by Musorgsky, 1874

Transcriptions

Balakirev: Overture and entr'actes to *King Lear*, arr. pf duet, 1859–60
Balakirev: 'Georgian Song', voice and orch., orch. part transcribed pf, 1862 (1862)

Beethoven: String Quartets, transcribed pf solo or 2 pf, 4 hands:
1. Op. 59, No. 3: movement 2, 1859 (solo)
2. Op. 130: movements 1, 2, 4, 5, and 6 (incomplete), 1862 (2 pf)
3. Op. 59, No. 2: movement 3, 1867 (solo)
4. Op. 131: movement 5, 1867 (solo)
5. Op. 135: movements 2 and 3, 1867 (solo)

Glinka: Persian Chorus from *Ruslan and Lyudmila*, 1858 (pf duet)

Glinka: *Recollections of a Summer Night in Madrid*, 1858 (pf duet)

Personalia

Albrecht, Konstantin [Karl] (1836–93). Teacher and administrator. He worked
for many years at the Moscow Conservatoire, where he was a colleague
of Tchaikovsky, who became a lifelong friend. He was also a cellist and
a highly respected choral conductor, and wrote a textbook on choral
singing.

Alyabyev, Alexander (1787–1851). Composer. He served in the army until
1823, but two years after leaving was imprisoned after a man had died,
allegedly from having been struck by Alyabyev in a card game; he was
then exiled to western Siberia, where he continued to compose. Though
he wrote operas and much incidental music, he is usually remembered
for his 170 songs.

Antokolsky, Mark (1843–1902). Sculptor. A member of the *peredvizhniki*
('wanderers') and very popular in his own time.

Balakirev, Mily (1837–1910). Composer and musical catalyst. Entrusted by
Glinka to continue his pioneering work, Balakirev collected a group of
equally untrained composers—notably Borodin, Cui, Rimsky-Korsakov,
and Musorgsky (collectively dubbed the 'moguchaya kuchka', or
'mightly handful')—whom he coached (and cajoled) with remarkable
creative results. In 1862 he founded (with Gavriil Lomakin) the Free
Music School (FMS) in opposition to the new St Petersburg Conservatoire. The 1860s was Balakirev's period of greatest influence.

Bessel, Vasily (1843–1907). Viola player, later music publisher. From the 1870s
he was perhaps the most important music publisher in Russia, his lists
including works by most of the prominent Russian composers of the
later nineteenth century. He was also an occasional writer on music.

Borodin, Alexander (1833–87). Chemist and composer. One of the most distinguished of Russian scientists, he could compose only in his increas-

ingly limited free time. Nevertheless he completed two symphonies, two string quartets, the orchestral *In the Steppes of Central Asia*, and a handful of remarkable songs. A third symphony and the epic opera *Prince Igor* remained unfinished.

Chernïshevsky, Nikolay (1828–89). Radical writer and journalist. He was a believer in the necessity of science for progress and in the potential of the peasantry as the foundation for Russia's economic and social future. During a term of imprisonment (1862–4) for his political activities he wrote his novel *What is to be done?*, which set out a model for ideal living and which was briefly very influential. He lived the rest of his life mostly in exile.

Cui, César (1835–1918). Fortifications expert and composer. He wrote over a dozen operas (including four for children) but was at his best as a miniaturist. He is remembered primarily for his critical writings, which could be very barbed, even when assessing his musical colleagues (Musorgsky was particularly distressed by Cui's review of *Boris Godunov*).

Dargomïzhsky, Alexander (1813–69). Composer. He was Glinka's junior partner in establishing the nineteenth-century Russian musical tradition. Especially noted as a song writer, his final unfinished opera, *The Stone Guest*, a verbatim setting of one of Pushkin's 'little tragedies', was highly influential on Musorgsky, who was a regular attender at Dargomïzhsky's musical soirées.

Famintsïn, Alexander (1841–96). Music critic, editor, composer, and professor of music history and aesthetics at the St Petersburg Conservatoire. He wrote several books on subjects relating to Russian musical folk culture, but was intensely hostile to the Balakirev circle. For this he was lampooned by Musorgsky in his songs *The Classicist* and *The Peepshow*.

Filippov, Terty (1826–99). Senior civil servant, amateur singer, and collector of folksongs. He was Musorgsky's chief in his final civil service department and, after Musorgsky's dismissal, one of the group who subsidized him to complete *Khovanshchina*. Musorgsky appointed him his musical executor.

Flaubert, Gustave (1821–80). French novelist, a pioneer of the realist school. He was most famed for *Madame Bovary*, a story of adultery that led to his being tried for immorality. Both this and his historical novel *Salammbô* were used as a subject by a number of composers.

Glinka, Mikhail (1804–57). Composer, the 'Father of Russian music'. Though he had little formal musical training, his two operas *A Life for the Tsar* and *Ruslan and Lyudmila* and his three most significant orchestral pieces, the two Spanish Overtures and (especially) *Kamarinskaya*, laid the foundations of the nineteenth-century Russian musical tradition, offering an abundance of styles, idioms, and structural suggestions, which composers of the next generation eagerly made their own.

Gogol, Nikolay (1809–52). Novelist and dramatist. His early *Evenings on a Farm near Dikanka* provided popular operatic subjects for his compatriots, while his novel *Dead Souls* and short story *The Overcoat* are held to be the sources of nineteenth-century Russian literary realism. For Musorgsky, Gogol was the greatest of Russian writers.

Golenishchev-Kutuzov, Arseny (1848–1913). Poet and playwright. He was a minor figure and for a while a close friend of Musorgsky (it was even said they were distantly related), who set some of his early poetry and even contemplated collaboration on an opera. The reliability of his memoirs of Musorgsky has been the subject of sharp disagreements. Golenishchev-Kutuzov's later work aimed at a revival of a more classical style.

Hartmann, Viktor (1834–73). Artist and architect. During 1864–8 he travelled in Europe, sketching and painting. Through his acquaintance with Vladimir Stasov he was introduced to Musorgsky, and they became close friends. Musorgsky was deeply distressed by Hartmann's sudden death; his *Pictures at an Exhibition* was prompted by a posthumous exhibition of Hartmann's work.

Herke, Anton (1812–70). Pianist and teacher, from 1862 a professor of piano at the St Petersburg Conservatoire. He taught Musorgsky.

Ippolitov-Ivanov, Mikhail (1859–1935). Composer, teacher, and conductor. He worked in Tbilisi, Georgia, and from 1893 in Moscow, where he taught at the conservatoire until his death. He had contact with Musorgsky in the latter's last years, and his memoirs are a very valuable source.

Karamzin, Nikolay (1766–1826). Russian historian. Though a creative writer in his earlier years, he is chiefly remembered for his twelve-volume *History of the Russian State*, which (via Pushkin) was the subject source of Musorgsky's *Boris Godunov*.

Karmalina, Lyubov (1836–1903). Singer, a pupil of Glinka and Dargomïzhsky. She had associations with the Balakirev circle in the 1860s and with Lyudmila Shestakova's soirées in the 1870s. She provided Musorgsky with Old Believers' melodies for *Khovanshchina*.

Koltsov, Alexey (1809–42). Poet. He was most noted for his Russian songs, quasi-imitations of folk poetry, and has been described as the Russian Burns.

Kutuzov. See **Golenishchev-Kutuzov.**

Laroche, Herman (1845–1904). Music critic. He was a fellow-student and lifelong friend of Tchaikovsky and taught for a while at both the Moscow and St Petersburg Conservatoires. Laroche was probably the finest Russian music critic of his generation, though he had blind spots, which included the Balakirev circle in general.

Leonova, Darya (1829–96). Singer. She had singing lessons from Glinka and there is some suspicion that she became his mistress. At the Imperial Opera she created the parts of the Princess in Dargomïzhsky's *Rusalka*, the title role in Serov's *Rogneda*, and the Hostess in Musorgsky's *Boris Godunov*. In 1879 she toured southern Russia and the Crimea with Musorgsky as her pianist, and did much for his welfare in his last months.

Lyadov, Anatol (1855–1914). Composer and teacher. A composer of almost compulsive indolence, his inability to apply himself purposefully accounts only in part for the absence of any large-scale piece among his compositions, for he was a natural miniaturist. He was also severely self-critical. In 1878 Lyadov became a teacher at the St Petersburg Conservatoire. Musorgsky had recognized Lyadov's outstanding gifts as early as 1873 when he began to appear at some of the former kuchka's soirées.

Mey, Lev (1822–62). Poet, translator, and verse dramatist. His lyrics were popular with Russian composers; Rimsky-Korsakov based four operas (including *The Maid of Pskov* and *The Tsar's Bride*) on his dramas.

Nápravník, Eduard (1839–1916). Composer and conductor of Czech extraction. He was chief conductor at the Maryinsky Theatre in St Petersburg from 1869 until his death. He conducted most of the major operatic premières given there during these forty-seven years. Noted for urging cuts, he was nevertheless from the beginning a supporter of Musorgsky's *Boris Godunov*, of which he prepared and conducted the first performance.

Naumov, Pavel (mid-1830s–later 1880s). Naval officer. He evidently had a reputation for pleasure and married well, subsequently living with his sister-in-law, Mariya Fedorova, for whom Musorgsky had a great respect on account of her kindness to him. During 1875–8 Musorgsky lodged with them, and Naumov's influence caused considerable anxiety to some of Musorgsky's friends.

Nekrasov, Nikolay (1821–78). Poet and journalist. He had a special concern for the plight of the Russian peasantry. From 1846 until his death he was (successively) editor of the highly influential journals *The Contemporary* and *Notes from the Fatherland*. Early works of both Turgenev and Tolstoy were published in the former.

Nikolsky, Vladimir (1836–83). Scholar of Russian literature and history, inspector at the Alexandrovsky Lycée, a professor at the St Petersburg Ecclesiastical Academy, and a Pushkin specialist. An intimate of Musorgsky (who invented the nicknames 'Pakhomïch' and 'dyainka' (little uncle) for him within the broader Balakirev circle), he was especially crucial to the inception and history of *Boris Godunov's* creation.

Opochinin, Alexander (1805–87). Civil servant and an amateur bass singer, he had studied with Tamburini and Lablache. He was a good friend to Musorgsky. He and his sister Nadezhda cared for Musorgsky during his first year in St Petersburg (1849–50) and between 1868 and 1871, when he was resident with them.

Opochinina, Nadezhda (1821–74). Sister of Alexander. Clearly something of a mother-figure to Musorgsky, she was the dedicatee of a total of seven songs and piano pieces. Musorgsky was greatly distressed by her death, composing in her memory *'Epitaph'*, a song (unfinished) on a specially written text of his own.

Ostrovsky, Alexander (1823–86). Dramatist, generally held to be the greatest of Russian realist playwrights. Originally a legal clerk, he began writing plays in the 1840s. A number became the bases of operas, for example Rimsky-Korsakov's *Snow Maiden*, Janácek's *Kát'a Kabanová*, Tchaikovsky's *The Voyevoda*, and Serov's *Hostile Power.*

Petrov, Osip (1806–78). Bass. He created the leading bass parts in Glinka's two operas (Susanin in *A Life for the Tsar*, Ruslan in *Ruslan and Lyudmila*) and a host of other leading roles in the premières of later Russian operas (including Varlaam in Musorgsky's *Boris Godunov*). He gave great moral support to Musorgsky, and his death was a severe blow to the composer.

Platonova, Yuliya (1841–92). Soprano. She created the part of Marina in *Boris Godunov*, claiming (perhaps exaggeratedly) that it was at her insistence that the opera was given its first complete performance. She also sang in the premières of Cui's *William Ratcliff*, Dargomïzhsky's *The Stone Guest*, and Rimsky-Korsakov's *The Maid of Pskov.*

Purgold (later **Molas**), Alexandra (1844–1929). Singer, sister of Nadezhda Purgold. One of the most frequent (and respected) performers in meetings of the Dargomïzhsky and Balakirev circles. After her marriage her home became a centre for trials of compositions by Musorgsky and his fellow-composers. Before her marriage she was romantically attracted to Musorgsky.

Purgold (later **Rimskaya-Korsakova**), Nadezhda (1848–1919). Pianist, sister of Alexandra Purgold; in 1872 she married Rimsky-Korsakov. Like her sister, one of the principal performers in meetings of the Dargomïzhsky and Balakirev circles (for her role as accompanist Musorgsky sometimes gave her the nickname 'Orchestra'). Subsequently she gave great help and support to her composer-husband; this included making piano transcriptions of his music.

Pushkin, Alexander (1799–1837). Russian writer, held to be Russia's greatest poet, and accorded in his homeland the kind of status enjoyed by Shakespeare in England. Pushkin's poetry provided the texts for countless songs, and his fictional writing was freely raided by composers for operatic subjects. He was killed in a duel, aged only 37.

Repin, Ilya (1844–1930). Painter. His own creative ideals made him a natural admirer and friend of Musorgsky. Repin earned his reputation mainly for his paintings of populist subjects and his depictions of episodes from

Russian history. His most famous work outside Russia is his harrowing portrait of Musorgsky, painted only days before the composer's death.

Rimsky-Korsakov, Nikolay (1844–1908). Naval officer, then composer and teacher. As a composer he started under Balakirev's tutelage but subsequently inclined to more traditional ways (becoming a professor at the St Petersburg Conservatoire), though retaining his individuality and his active relationships with his old associates in Balakirev's group. He was a prolific composer, especially of operas.

Rubinstein, Anton (1829–94). Pianist and composer. He was the driving force behind the early years of the Russian Musical Society (RMS: founded 1859) and the St Petersburg Conservatoire (founded 1862), of which he was the first principal. A prolific composer, he was initially seen by the Balakirev circle as the epitome of the 'westernizing' musician, but later there was a quiet rapprochement, and at one stage he even composed national-style pieces.

Serov, Alexander (1820–71). Opera composer and critic. At first employed in the civil service, in 1851 he resigned and scraped a living through writing very readable, but often pungent, musical criticism. He had been a fellow-student and friend of Vladimir Stasov, but they later quarrelled violently over their differing musical views. He achieved real public success in 1863 with his third opera, *Judith* (which had some palpable influence on Musorgsky); its successor, *Rogneda* (1865), was an even greater triumph. He died before completing his next opera, *Hostile Power.*

Shestakova, Lyudmila (1816–1906). Sister of Glinka and, for the Balakirev group, the living emblem of the predecessor to whom they owed so much. She was the most active of supporters of these composers, and of none more so than Musorgsky. Her soirées, where their latest works could be tried out, were of enormous importance to them.

Shevchenko, Taras (1814–61). Ukrainian poet and nationalist, exiled for ten years from 1847 for his activities. His verses were set by both Musorgsky and Tchaikovsky.

Shilovskaya (later **Begicheva**), Mariya (1830–79). Amateur singer. Her husband's estate at Glebovo became something of a musical centre (Tchaikovsky composed part of *Swan Lake* and most of *Eugene Onegin* there). It is possible Musorgsky was briefly attracted to Mariya; in 1860 he dedicated two songs to her.

Stasov, Dmitri (1828–1918). Lawyer, brother of Vladimir Stasov. In 1859 he was one of the founders of the Russian Musical Society (RMS) and, in 1862, of the St Petersburg Conservatoire. Though this might seem to have placed him squarely in the 'westernizing' camp to which the Balakirev group was generally so hostile, he was very open-minded and had excellent relations with that circle.

Stasov, Vladimir (1824–1906). Art and music critic, brother of Dmitri Stasov;

head of the art department in the St Petersburg Public Library. A polymath and passionate devotee of all things Russian, as well as a prolific writer (his works include biographies of Musorgsky and Borodin), he was a fierce supporter of Balakirev and his circle. He was also a fertile provider of subjects and programmes for composers to use (not only *Khovanshchina* for Musorgsky but, for instance, *Prince Igor* for Borodin, and *The Tempest* and (indirectly) *Manfred* for Tchaikovsky). Stasov was Musorgsky's most consistent, if sometimes uncomfortable, ally.

Tolstoy, Alexey (1817–75). Writer; a second cousin to Lev Tolstoy. Alexey was a dramatist and novelist, but is now mostly remembered for his poetry, which proved very popular material with song composers. Among others, Cui, Rimsky-Korsakov, and Tchaikovsky set him repeatedly. Musorgsky's last group of five songs also use texts by Tolstoy.

Tolstoy, Feofil (pseudonym: **Rostislav**) (1810–81). Music critic and composer. He was a famously reactionary critic with a partiality for Italian music and a general hostility to the newer Russian music. Musorgsky lampooned him as 'Fif' in *The Peepshow*, devising a text in praise of Adelina Patti which he set to a trivial mock-Italianate waltz tune with a coloratura cadenza.

Vereshchagin, Vasily (1842–1904). Painter. An ardent 'realist', he travelled to scenes of conflict, including India, the Balkans, and the Pacific (he was killed on a battleship during the Russo-Japanese war). He produced over 100 pictures from the war between Russia and the Emirate of Bokhara in 1867; these made a great impression when exhibited in St Petersburg in 1874.

Zaremba, Nikolay (1821–79). Teacher and composer. German-trained, he was one of the first teachers of harmony and composition at the newly opened St Petersburg Conservatoire (he was Tchaikovsky's teacher). He had the reputation of a pedant, especially with the Balakirev group. He was a subject for satire in Musorgsky's *The Peepshow*.

Zhukovsky, Vasily (1783–1852). Poet and translator of the pre-Pushkin generation, who believed poetry should be concerned more with feeling than with reason. He was responsible for Glinka's choice of subject for his first opera, *A Life for the Tsar*, writing part of the libretto.

Select Bibliography

This is purely a working bibliography. Readers requiring a more detailed bibliography should consult the entries on Musorgsky in *The New Grove Dictionary of Music and Musicians* (1980, 2nd ed. 2001) and especially in *The New Grove Dictionary of Opera* (1992). The only Russian-language sources cited here are the principal ones used in writing this study. The selection of English-language titles is broader, though articles have been included only when they contain material or comment of some substance. Selected chapters of particular interest in symposia are given individual entries.

Abbreviations used in the main text as references to particular volumes are given in square brackets at the end of the relevant entry.

Editions

M. P. Musorgsky: Polnoye sobraniye sochineny [Complete works], ed. P. Lamm, with B. V. Asafyev (Moscow, 1928–34, 1939; repr. 1969)
Boris Godunov
(i) Vocal score, ed. P. Lamm, Eng. trans. by D. Lloyd-Jones (London, 1968) [incorporates the 'definitive' (1872) and 'initial' (1868–9) versions]
(ii) Full score [both versions], ed., with Eng. trans. and critical commentary, D. Lloyd-Jones, 2 vols. (London, 1975)
Romansï i pesni [Romances and songs], ed. A. N. Dmitriyev (Leningrad, 1960)

Russian-Language Titles

Catalogue, documentary sources (letters and memoirs), studies

E. Durandina, *Vokalnoye tvorchestvo Musorgskovo* [Musorgsky's vocal works] (Moscow, 1985)
E. Fried, ed., *M. P. Musorgsky: kartinki s vïstavki* [Pictures at an exhibition]. Facsimile (Moscow, 1975)
E. Gordeyeva, ed., *M. P. Musorgsky: pisma* [Letters] (Moscow, 1981)
——, *M. P. Musorgsky v vospominaniyakh sovremennikov* [Musorgsky in the recollections of contemporaries] (Moscow, 1989) [*MVS*]
Y. Keldïsh and V. Yakovlev, eds., *M. P. Musorgsky k pyatidesyatoletiyu so dnya smerti: stati i*

materiali [Musorgsky on the fiftieth anniversary of his death: articles and materials] (Moscow, 1932) [*KYM*]

E. Levasheva, ed., *Naslediye M. P. Musorgskovo: sbornik materialov* [Musorgsky's legacy: collection of materials] (Moscow, 1989) [contains a detailed inventory of the manuscript sources of Musorgsky's music, and Eng. and Ger. translations, mostly abridged, of 4 articles]

A. Ogolovets, *Vokalnaya dramaturgiya Musorgskovo* [Musorgsky's vocal dramaturgy] (Moscow, 1966)

A. Orlova, ed., *Trudï i dni M. P. Musorgskovo* [Musorgsky's works and days] (Moscow, 1963) [*TDM*] [see also **English-Language Titles** below]

A. Orlova and M. Pekelis, eds., *M. P. Musorgsky: literaturnoye naslediye* [Literary legacy], 2 vols. (Moscow, 1971–2) [*MLN1/2*]

A. N. Rimsky-Korsakov, ed., *M. P. Musorgsky: pisma i dokumentï* [Letters and documents] (Moscow and Leningrad, 1932) [*RKM*]

N. Rimsky-Korsakov, *Letopis moyei muzïkalnoy zhizni* [Chronicle of my musical life] (St Petersburg, 1909, 9th ed. 1982) [*RKL*] [see also **English-Language Titles** below]

R. Shirinyan, *Opernaya dramaturgiya Musorgskovo* [Musorgsky's operatic dramaturgy] (Moscow, 1981)

N. Simakova and V. Protopopov, eds., *V. V. Stasov: stati o muzike: vïpusk trety, 1880–1886* [Articles on music: part 3, 1880–86] (Moscow, 1977) [*SSM3*]

V. Stasov, *M. P. Musorgsky: biografichesky ocherk* [A biographical study], printed in *Vestnik Yevropï* (1881); repr. in Simakova and Protopopov (above) [*SMPM*]

English-Language Titles

G. Abraham, 'Musorgsky', in M. D. Calvocoressi and G. Abraham, eds., *Masters of Russian Music* (London, 1936), 178–248

———, 'Musorgsky', in D. Brown and others, *Russian Masters 1* (London, 1986), 109–42; repr. from S. Sadie, ed., *The New Grove Dictionary of Music and Musicians* (London, 1980)

———, 'Mussorgsky's "Boris" and Pushkin's', *Slavonic and Romantic Music* (London, 1968), 178–87

———, 'Russia', in D. Stevens, ed., *A History of Song* (London, 1960), 338–75; repr. in G. Abraham, *Essays on Russian and East European Music* (Oxford, 1985), 1–39

———, 'The Artist of *Pictures at an Exhibition*', *MIM*, 229–36

———, 'The Collective Mlada', *On Russian Music* (London, 1939), 91–112

———, '*The Fair of Sorochintsy* and Cherepnin's Completion of it', *On Russian Music* (London, 1939), 216–24

———, 'The Mediterranean Element in *Boris Godunov*', *Slavonic and Romantic Music* (London, 1968), 188–94

———, 'Tolstoy and Musorgsky', *Studies in Russian Music* (London, 1935), 87–101

K. Agawu, 'Pitch Organisational Procedures in Musorgsky's *Nursery*', *Indiana Theory Review*, v/1 (1981), 23–59

N. Basmajian, 'The Romances', *MIM*, 29–56

M. H. Brown, ed., *Musorgsky in memoriam, 1881–1891* (Ann Arbor, 1982) [*MIM*]

M. D. Calvocoressi, *Modest Mussorgsky: His Life and Works* (London, 1956) [*CM*]

———, *Mussorgsky: The Russian Musical Nationalist* (London, 1919) [Eng. trans. by A. Eaglefield Hull of the Fr. edition (Paris, 1908, rev. 1911)]

M. D. Calvocoressi [and G. Abraham], *Mussorgsky* (London, 1946; rev. 1974) [*CAM*]

C. Emerson, *The Life of Musorgsky* (Cambridge, 1999)

C. Emerson and R. Oldani, *Modest Musorgsky and 'Boris Godunov': Myths, Realities, Reconsiderations* (Cambridge, 1994) [*MBG*]

A. Frankenstein, 'Victor Hartmann and Modest Musorgsky', *MQ*, xxv (1939), 268–91

E. Garden, 'Balakirev's Influence on Musorgsky', *MIM*, 11–27

———, 'Russian Folksong and Balakirev's 1866 Collection', *Soundings*, xi (1984), 52–9

———, 'Three Nights on a Bare Mountain', *MT*, cxxix (1988), 333–5

N. John, ed., *Boris Godunov: Modest Mussorgsky* (London, 1982)

J. Leyda and S. Bertensson, eds., *The Musorgsky Reader: A Life of Modeste Petrovich Musorgsky in Letters and Documents* (New York, 1947) [*MR*]

H. Lindenberger, 'Opera as Historical Drama: *La Clemenza di Tito, Khovanshchina, Moses und Aron*', *Idee, Gestalt, Geschichte: Festschrift für Klaus von See*, ed. G. W. Weber (Odense, 1988), 605–26

G. McQuere, 'Analyzing Musorgsky's *Gnome*', *Indiana Theory Review*, xiii/1 (1992), 21–40

V. Morosan, 'Folk and Chant Elements in Musorgsky's Choral Writing', *MIM*, 95–133

'A Musorgsky Symposium', *Music Analysis*, ix/1 (March, 1990) [contains: A. Forte, 'Musorgsky as Modernist: the Phantasmic Episode in *Boris Godunov*', 3–45, M. Russ, 'The Mysterious Thread in Musorgsky's *Nursery*', 47–65; D. Puffett, 'A Graphic Analysis of Musorgsky's 'Catacombs', 67–77]

G. Norris, 'An Opera Restored: Rimsky-Korsakov, Shostakovich and the Khovansky Business', *MT*, cxxiii (1982), 672–4

A. Orlova, *Musorgsky's Works and Days: a Biography in Documents* (Bloomington and Indianapolis, 1983) [trans. of *Trudï i dni M. P. Musorgskovo*: see **Russian-Language Titles** above]

A. Orlova, ed., *Musorgsky Remembered* (Bloomington and Indianapolis, 1991)

A. Orlova and M. Shneerson, 'After Pushkin and Karamzin: Researching the Sources for the Libretto of *Boris Godunov*', *MIM*, 249–70

M. Papp, 'Liszt and Musorgsky: the Genuine and False Documents of the Relationship between the Two Composers', *Studia musicologica*, xxix (1987), 267–84

E. Reilly, 'The First Extant Version of *Night on Bare Mountain*', *MIM*, 135–62

E. Reilly, *The Music of Musorgsky: A Guide to the Editions* (New York, 1980)

N. Rimsky-Korsakov, *My Musical Life*, (3rd ed. New York, 1942) [originally published 1923; trans. of *Letopis moyei muzïkalnoy zhizni*: see **Russian-Language Titles** above]

M. Russ, *Musorgsky: Pictures at an Exhibition* (Cambridge, 1992)

B. Schwarz, 'Musorgsky's Interest in Judaica', *MIM*, 85–94

V. I. Seroff, *Modest Musorgsky* (New York, 1968)

R. Taruskin, *Musorgsky: Eight Essays and an Epilogue* (Princeton, NJ, 1993) [*TM*]

———, *Opera and Drama as Preached and Practiced in the 1860s* (Ann Arbor, 1981)

R. Threlfall, 'The Stravinsky Version of *Khovanshchina*', *Studies in Music* [Australia], no. 15 (1981), 106–15

J. Turner, 'Musorgsky', *Music Review*, no. 47 (1986), 153–75

J. Walker, 'Musorgsky's *Sunless* Cycle in Russian Criticism: Focus of Controversy', *MQ*, lxvii (1981), 382–91

Index